Social Work Practice with Children and Adolescents

Steven R. Rose
Louisiana State University

Marian F. Fatout
Louisiana State University, Emerita

Boston New York San Francisco
Mexico City Montreal Toronto London Madrid Munich Paris
Hong Kong Singapore Tokyo Cape Town Sydney

Series Editor: *Patricia M. Quinlin*
Editorial Assistant: *Annemarie Kennedy*
Marketing Manager: *Taryn Wahlquist*
Composition and Prepress Buyer: *Linda Cox*
Manufacturing Buyer: *Andrew Turso*
Cover Administrator: *Kristina Mose-Libon*
Editorial-Production Service: *Omegatype Typography, Inc.*
Electronic Composition: *Omegatype Typography, Inc.*

For related titles and support material, visit our online catalog at www.ablongman.com.

Between the time Website information is gathered and then published, it is not unusual for some sites to have closed. Also, the transcription of URLs can result in typographical errors. The publisher would appreciate notification where these errors occur so that they may be corrected in subsequent editions.

Library of Congress Cataloging-in-Publication Data

Rose, Steven R.
    Social work practice with children and adolescents / Steven R. Rose, Marian F. Fatout.—1st ed.
        p.   cm.
    Includes bibliographical references (p.) and index.
    ISBN 0-205-30938-0
    1. Social work with children—United States.   2. Social work with teenagers—United
States.   I. Fatout, Marian.   II. Title.

HV741 .R653 2003
362.7'0973—dc21

                                                                                        2002075797

Printed in the United States of America

10 9 8 7 6 5 4 3 2 1   07 06 05 04 03 02

CONTENTS

PREFACE

In recent years emphasis on social work with children and adolescents as a client population has been renewed because many social problems are being manifested at younger ages. Increasing public and professional awareness and concern about maltreatment and mental disorders of children and adolescents are in evidence. Furthermore, working with children and adolescents, as an attempt to stem the likelihood of them developing more serious difficulties later in life, is gaining credibility as the research evidence mounts in favor of this approach.

Pragmatic concerns underlie this book. Many children and adolescents with severe difficulties do not have a parent available who could come to a social worker for assistance. Often, working parents are unable or unwilling to become directly involved in forms of treatment that require their ongoing, direct, active participation. Consequently, many children and adolescents do not receive help. Therefore, direct work with the youngster is often the most realistic and prudent choice for providing needed services.

This book is intended to provide material that will be useful to practitioners who work directly with children and adolescents. In this book the child is viewed as the center of attention and is the focus for determining methods of giving help. This book is focused on children and adolescents as individuals in need of direct services. As such, this book is designed to fill a major gap in the extant literature and will be useful for courses on social work practice with children and adolescents.

The book uses a broad approach to conceptualizing social work processes and practices with children and adolescents, and demonstrates its applicability to major fields of social work practice with young people. The book focuses on significant social problems of children and adolescents that practitioners address, explicating the processes of providing social services to this client group. Research knowledge and practice examples related to social work in schools, agencies, and communities are examined. The issues, purposes, methods, procedures, techniques, and dynamics of working directly with children and adolescents are described and illustrated. This book provides a contemporary view of direct practice with children that emphasizes the process and interaction that takes place between the practitioner and the client. Furthermore, it describes the expectations and actions of the social worker in formulating and implementing a treatment plan. The examination of social work processes is usable by child-care professionals of diverse backgrounds and theoretical interests.

This book consists of three parts. The first part, "The Context of Practice with Children and Adolescents," contains three chapters. Chapter 1, which considers selected aspects of history and social policy, examines prior attempts at providing direct services to children and adolescents that have contributed to current methods of social service delivery. The chapter begins with a consideration of the historical development of public and private services for children and adolescents. The origins of the professional interest in the process of social work practice with children and adolescents are described.

Chapter 2 examines the broader context of children's contemporary lives and considers interpersonal, cultural, and social factors that underlie the development of today's child and adolescent. The chapter is based on the assumption that practitioners helping children are often confronted with human diversity. Values, religions, spirituality, and languages are key aspects of attaining an overall understanding of children and adolescents. The contemporary acculturation, socialization, and competencies of children are also examined. Within a community context, the impact of the family on the helping situation is reviewed.

Chapter 3 examines current social issues that affect children and youth in changing families. The nature of the stressors experienced by changing families that affect children and adolescents, including marital separation and divorce, and the formation of single-parent and blended families are considered, as are intervention methods.

The second part of the book presents the helping processes of direct social work practice with children and adolescents. Chapter 4 describes the essential features of the process of helping children and adolescents. The stages of helping children and adolescents are described and include referral; assessment; goal orientation, setting, and attainment; and ending. The chapter traces the practitioner's development of a plan for helping, and considers the setting and materials of helping.

Chapter 5 examines the assessment of children and adolescents as a primary role of the direct service practitioner. Assessments of competent and problematic interaction are conceptualized to form a balanced and bilateral view. The social and emotional, moral and ethical, cognitive and language, and physical and perceptual-motor developmental domains of assessment are considered in regard to normal development and lags in development.

Chapter 6 examines multiple theoretical aspects of social work with children and adolescents. In particular, cognitive theory, crisis intervention, task-centered practice, behavior theory, client-centered play therapy, communication theory, problem solving, existential social work, and role theory are examined.

Chapter 7 proceeds from the reality that social work with young people tends to occur within organizational systems. Social agencies are analyzed as settings in which social work practice is useful for helping children. The types of resources underlying service provision, interorganizational environment, processes of referral, conflict and crisis, organizational structure, leadership, accountability and expectations, scope of direct and indirect services, and practice settings are all considered.

The third part of the book is an examination of applications of social work with children and adolescents to three major fields of practice. Chapter 8 examines social work in school systems, including school-based and school-linked services. The social context of schooling, mobility and diversity, attendance, students with disabilities, community factors, nature and goals of schools, academic performance, education, types and conditions of schools, violence, school-based health clinics, school-linked services, school social work roles, and the future of school social work are examined.

Chapter 9 emphasizes, yet is not restricted to, working with children and adolescents who have been identified with mental health difficulties. The importance of child mental health and the role of developmental psychopathology, particularly in regard to prevention, are delineated. The emotional problems of young people are also described. The chapter addresses stress and anxiety; the spectrum of depressive disorders and suicidal behavior;

aggression and conduct disorder; attention deficits and hyperactivity, which are increasingly prevalent and notable problems of children; cognitive deficits and head injuries; eating disorders; severe mental disorders, such as schizophrenia and autism; and substance abuse. Mental health services for youngsters, in the areas of school, family, and community mental health as well as sexual abuse are also presented.

Chapter 10 indicates how the social worker helps maltreated children and adolescents. This chapter on child welfare issues considers risk assessments; decision making; working with involuntary clients; and the impact of processes of attachment, separation, loss, and mourning on the developing child. The relationship of such processes to maltreatment are considered. Finding replacements or substitutes to take the parental role of caring for children is examined in regard to foster home placements and adoptions.

Acknowledgments

This book has benefitted from the helpful input of many people. In particular, we gratefully acknowledge the assistance of Deana Evers-Ward, Erica Morgan, and Anne Stuckey, and the support of Mark Emmert, Daniel Fogel, Howard Karger, Catherine Lemieux, Kenneth Millar, and Alan York. Many heartfelt thanks are due to Patricia Quinlin, Annemarie Kennedy, Taryn Wahlquist, Judy Fifer, Karen Hanson, Judy Fiske, Alyssa Pratt, Jackie Aaron, and Donna Simons at Allyn and Bacon, as well as Mary Young and Dona Biederman at Omegatype Typography, and our indexer Judy Davis.

We also thank the reviewers of the manuscript: Jerrold R. Brandell, Wayne State University; Carla Edwards, Northwest Missouri State University; Sharon Eisen, Mott Community College; Charles Garvin, University of Michigan; John M. Herrick, Michigan State University; Carol Massat, University of Illinois at Chicago; and Mary Rodwell, Virginia Commonwealth University.

We appreciate the support of family and friends in the development of this book. As authors, we share jointly in the writing of this book. We dedicate it to Betty Stewart, who was devoted to helping children seek a brighter future.

S. R. R.
M. F. F.

1

History and Social Policies Shaping Practice with Children and Adolescents

The focus of this chapter is major social policies and their historical development. The first areas for clarification are the development of the periods of life finally identified as childhood and adolescence and the identification of need for special services. The historical context, the need for services, and the policies that developed are traced from the twentieth century to the present time. Child labor laws, compulsory school attendance, the Social Security Act and the needs that it met, poverty, public education, health, adoptions, and the development of juvenile courts are included in this chapter.

Societies need rules and policies to function in an organized way. Social policy in child welfare is concerned with child and family life as it is developed by government through its executive, legislative, and judicial branches. Social policies include both official decisions made about social issues and broad principles concerning the operation of the social welfare system.

Three broad areas have been the focus of concern in recent years. One is the policy and administrative practice in social services that include health and safety, Social Security, education, employment, community care, and housing management. Social problems such as crime, disability, mental health, learning disabilities, unemployment, and aging have also been points of focus. The third area is concerned with issues relating to social disadvantages, including poverty, race, and gender.

As society and lifestyles change, new problems and issues emerge. Consequently, new approaches need to be developed to meet these particular situations. Evidence of changes in society that require addressing and deliberation appears in the mass media. The public is greatly concerned about accounts of child abuse, homelessness experienced by families, truancy, school violence, and runaway adolescents. Why are unfortunate things happening to children and adolescents?

Public consternation causes communities and government agencies to attempt to alleviate these types of dilemmas. A primary method of dealing with issues is to develop social policies. Policies define the nature of services or aid to be given, who shall receive services, standards of practice, and specific criteria and procedures for services (Costin, Bell, & Downs, 1991). As we focus on children, the family ultimately must be the center of concern. Steiner (1981) identifies the purpose of family policy as follows:

Family policy has to do with mechanisms for identifying family dysfunction, and with the organization of responsibility in public support systems; decisions about when public programs will take up the slack and the conditions under which they will do so. (p. 9)

Social services for children are based on an assumption about the triadic relationship among parents, children, and society. Child welfare services are predicated on the conclusion that at certain times the well-being of the child is insufficiently attended to because of a conflict in roles and rights. Other reasons for services are inadequacies of the system or when pressing demands are made on any part of the triad (Coll, 1970; Golden, 1997). Policies result in family-related programs and services such as child protection, adoptions, aid to families with dependent children, and family preservation (Zimmerman, 1995).

In the historical development of social policies for children, it was necessary to recognize childhood as a particular period of life, one that differed greatly from the life of adults. Early on these differences were neither widely recognized nor well understood.

The Recognition of Childhood and the Needs of Children

In early history childhood was perceived in terms of adulthood. Later, in the seventeenth century, a few people began to think of childhood as a distinctive phase of life. Artists, authors, and scientists began to produce materials that recognized children's needs, abilities, and development as differing from adults (Levine & Sallee, 1999). During the eighteenth century and first half of the nineteenth century, few advances were made in the understanding of childhood. It was only in the last half of the nineteenth century that knowledge of the childhood period was extended. Biographies of children were written and more focus on both physical and mental attributes of children became evident. In 1893, at the Chicago World's Fair, G. Stanley Hall, later known as "the father of the child study movement," organized the National Association for the Study of Children. This was the first study group on children in the United States (Hurlock, 1942). Other study groups of this kind spread rapidly.

In England, the Elizabethan Poor Laws of 1601 promoted the recognition of children as a separate group. Poor, orphaned, and trouble children were placed in almshouses, where generally few services were provided. Children were often mistreated, and suffered and lived in terrible conditions in these homes.

Gaining knowledge and an understanding of childhood and adolescence is promoted by taking a historical perspective. The concept of a child, and later an adolescent, evolved over a long period of time. By understanding this evolution, one is better able to understand social policies that developed and changed our perceptions of children today.

In very early times, children were seen as the property of their family. Infanticide, the killing of infants and young children, was a common practice for a variety of reasons in most cultures. The Roman practice of infanticide permitted the father to expose to death any deformed or female child. Eight days after birth, the child formally became a member of the Roman family by means of a solemn ceremony. Even then the father continued to have power of life and death, including selling the child into slavery. Abandonment was a widespread practice (Hewett & Forness, 1984). The purpose may have been to rid a society of disabled and female children to maintain a strong race without overpopulation. Other reasons for these practices were to regulate the population so that the resources could be used for the stronger and more valued members of that society, for families to limit their size to maintain financial security, to attempt to prevent the shame of unwed mothers, and sometimes as a sacrifice to God (Crosson-Tower, 1998; Levine & Sallee, 1999).

In the Middle Ages children often died, so parents were hesitant to commit themselves to them. Many children contracted infectious diseases, and many were born with significant deformities. Not only were children dependent on their families for their existence but also for their ongoing survival. The feudal system in England established the idea of ownership with rights and privileges. Children were on the bottom and poor children in an even worse position. The fate of children who were not poor was dependent on their families.

Children were regarded as chattel who were expected to help their parents. When the child no longer wore swaddling clothes, they were dressed as adults and treated as such. From a very early age they were expected to help their parents in the fields or to help in whatever endeavor that was required (Popple & Leighninger, 1996).

In America, colonists followed the pattern set by the English Poor Laws of 1601. One implicit assumption underlying these Poor Laws was that the individual's primary responsibility was to provide for themselves, their families, and their near relatives. The government was responsible for supplementing insufficient efforts. Finally, the government adapted its activities to the needs of that person. If families were unable to support themselves and their children, they were sent to poorhouses.

Until the mid–nineteenth century, provision for the welfare of orphaned or abandoned children took the form of institutional custodial care (Lindsey, 1994). A general law was passed authorizing the arrest of vagrant and truant children, on the complaint of any citizen before a magistrate. With regard these children the state was expected to assume the position and responsibility of parents of educating, "securing their usefulness, and promoting the well being of society" (Pumphrey & Pumphrey, 1961, p. 108). Orphaned and abandoned children were placed in poorhouses with aid provided. The subsistence in poorhouses was meager and many children did not survive. As early as 1851 the Association for Improving the Conditions of the Poor (AICP), a voluntary charity, established the Juvenile Asylum to take care of homeless and neglected children. Dorothea Dix made some state legislators and county governments aware of the deplorable conditions in some institutions in which children were living (Costin, Bell, & Downs, 1991; Haynes & Holmes, 1994).

Able-bodied people were sent to work, and on occasion women and children were provided food and clothing at home. Education was not seen as a right or privilege for children (Popple & Leighninger, 1996). By the age of seven or eight, children were often apprenticed to other families, living away from their own family for the rest of their childhood. For some children the arrangement was satisfactory, for others, it meant that they were beaten and neglected because of their lack of skill or ability to do what was required.

Gradually, children were no longer perceived as miniature adults (Kadushin, 1980). Childhood came to be seen as a unique period during which physical, educational, and psychological needs were to be met. Placement in almshouses was generally more destructive than helpful in aiding children. By the 1800s, institutions were constructed for orphans and a variety of disabled children.

Within the next 50 years, an industrial revolution occurred in the United States. Massive immigration from Europe, Asia, and other countries had begun. In addition, shifts of large populations from rural to urban areas within the United States were producing more chaos. This resulted in major social changes. Migration and shifting populations brought poverty, family disorganization, and slums. Many urban areas were overwhelmed with these new citizens. They were often called the tenement class. This population was primarily composed of immigrants who lived in desperate poverty. Many families lived in one-bedroom basement apartments. Often the father abandoned the family because he was unable to support them. Ragged children sold papers, shined shoes, and peddled flowers to survive. The children worked and played in the streets. The colonists considered the child a sinner who could be saved if born again into obedience, discipline, and respect for the authority of religion, parents, and the state (Golden, 1997). Reformers for children were impelled by both compassion and fear of the exploding immigrant class.

Concern for children grew out of the upheaval accompanying these great social and economic changes. Women and children were beginning to join the work force. Child labor laws had not yet been passed, and children were often required to work 15 to 18 hours a day to contribute to their families. Little recognition had been given to children's needs, such as the need of protection, education, caring, and guidance by responsible adults.

Early Social Services for Children and Adolescents

In the mid–eighteenth century, social services for children and youth were often religiously based and provided by voluntary organizations. These agencies received authorization from a group of citizens and undertook responsibility for a defined and limited part of a community's social services for children (Axinn & Levin, 1992).

The second half of the nineteenth century was the era of child-saving activities. Attempts were made to save children from crime, vice, and poverty (Coll, 1970). The Society for the Prevention of Cruelty to Animals was founded, and later the Society for the Prevention of Cruelty to Children was established in the 1870s. This was a project of the wealthiest of men, such as Cornelius Vanderbilt, Peter Cooper, and August Belmont. It originated in New York and soon spread worldwide. Policies of this organization were not the same for all cities and communities. The emphasis for Boston and Chicago was on family rehabilitation. These Puritans had laws that defined the child, parent, and the state's relationship known as *parens patriae*. American law considered children as the property of the parents; however, the children could bring their grievances to the authorities. This law was concerned more with the poor and less with criminal youth. It was believed that children are savable.

The Children's Aid Society was founded by Charles Loring Brace, who recognized that immigrants' increasing misery was forcing society to pay attention to the human consequences of urbanization and industrialization. Living in New York, he wrote about working with the "dangerous classes." The early approaches for working with these children were either punitive or paternalistic. Some of these attempts at relieving the strained situation, in addition to almshouses and foundling homes, were setting up industrial schools and night schools.

The homeless children who wandered the streets of New York and who were increasingly involved in crime and poverty were a primary concern for Charles Loring Brace. He described the Children's Aid Society as a moral and physical disinfectant. Brace was interested in "draining" New York of destitute children. His solution was to take the homeless or needy children from the city to rural localities to work in the homes and fields of farmers and tradespeople of the area. Laborers were needed on the frontier, and thousands of children could be "rescued" from urban slums in this manner. The motto of the day was "Go west young man." Orphan trains of vagrant, abused, neglected, delinquent, and runaway children of the immigrant working class were sent from New York City to rural communities in the Midwest. This may have alleviated some problems in New York, but overall was not a successful solution. Some children found suitable situations in which they could live and work, but many others did not. By the early 1900s, dependent youth became more of a problem because the market for apprentices was declining as the colony moved into a factory system. In 1920, still more than 750,000 orphaned children lived in the United States.

Clearly, during this time, conflicts in policies regarding child welfare were evident. Was the solution to support or control the children? A history of channeling public tax monies to voluntary agencies had existed since the early 1800s. One early advocacy agency was the New York Society for the Prevention of Cruelty to Children. Later settlement houses, such as Hull House in Chicago and Lillian Wald's Henry Street Settlement, took on the role of advocacy.

Another area of conflicting interests was that of education and the early child labor movement. The industrial revolution had made possible the widespread exploitation of young children in work situations. Many children less than 10 years of age worked in seasonal agriculture, street trades, and sweatshops, often in the garment and tobacco industries. Money for survival for the child and family seemed much more important than an education.

From this historical background, a need for public notice and the solutions to many interrelated issues were evident. Policies regarding child labor, schooling, children with disabilities, health and mental health, and child welfare continued to be the focus over a long period of time.

Twentieth-Century Progress

The twentieth century was sometimes called the century of the child. More serious studies of the child occurred during this time. Many agencies concerned with providing social services to children and their families were established around the turn of the century. Organizations such as the Family Service Association, 1911; U.S. Children's Bureau, 1912; National Committee for Mental Hygiene, 1909; Young Women's Christian Association, 1906; Boy Scouts, 1910; Visiting Teachers Movement, 1906, and many others were established at this time (Kanner, 1962b; Key, 1909). Until the early twentieth century, policies regarding children and families were in the domain of the local government and private charities. Most modern professional community-based services for children were established between 1890 and the beginning of World War I.

In 1906 a beginning attempt was made to limit the use of child labor through federal legislation. One bill prohibited the employment of children in factories and mines. Another bill was proposed to prohibit the employment of children in the manufacture or production of articles intended for interstate commerce. However, these bills did not make it out of committee (Costin, Bell, & Downs, 1991).

The first significant involvement of the federal government was the White House Conference of 1909, during the Roosevelt administration. The importance of the family was confirmed. It was believed that children should not be deprived of their family except for urgent and compelling reasons. Poverty was not a reason to remove children from their families. The preferred method for providing help was a voluntary charity. It must, however, be noted that removal of children continued for some time.

In 1911, Illinois was the first state to enact a mother's aid law. Conflict about who was to implement this law followed. Should a public or voluntary agency provide these services? For many, distinguishing between public aid to needy mothers and charity or outdoor relief was very important. To help further distinguish these two programs, it was important that administration of these two programs be placed in different settings. Ways of administering these differing programs by the states varied.

Another contribution of the 1909 conference was a recommendation that a federally funded children's bureau be established. In 1912, Julia Lathrop was appointed as the first chief of the U.S. Children's Bureau. Because of conflicts in child welfare policies, the purpose of organizing this bureau was to legitimate its dual mission of supporting distressed families and enforcing compliance with their standards (Golden, 1997). This bureau played a major role in discovering and augmenting needs of children so that they could be addressed.

As social issues and problems emerged, social policies were formulated. A variety of policies and programs related to addressing the needs of children emerged during the twentieth century.

Policies and Implementations Affecting Children

Child Labor Laws

The Protestant ethic of the colonies was deeply ingrained in the American people. The importance and dignity of work was generally recognized and agreed on. However, a wide difference of public opinion existed about the employment of children.

The industrial revolution made possible the widespread exploitation of children. Jobs were available and children worked in factories, mines, and in agricultural industries because they were willing to take the lower wages. An additional factor was that in colonial days, parents and citizens in the community felt an obligation to prevent idleness of adults and children. A primary goal during the colonial period was community survival. This meant that the poor and indigent were expected to work: having a trade was considered necessary for full participation in the community. Children needed to be taught work habits at an early age to prevent their "natural slothful inclination" and to prepare them for a hard life

(Costin, Bell, & Downs, 1991). It was seen as a public duty to provide training of children so that the towns and colonies would be more profitable as these children reached adulthood. A widely held belief was that children's labor was important and that claims to profits were essential for families and the community.

Reformers were especially concerned about children employed in cotton, wool, and silk mills in the clothing industry. Youngsters were also working in mines, quarries, and iron and steel operations. Many children worked in seasonal agriculture, sweatshops, street trades, and tobacco industries. President Teddy Roosevelt exposed these industries and called them muckrakers.

As industry expanded, even more children were employed. Some were as young as 7 years old. The hours were long, and accidents were common. Few if any safety protection practices were in place. The children were tired, immature, and in poor health. Jane Addams (1903), at a national conference, described the condition of the children. She said:

> The boys and girls have a peculiar hue, a color so distinctive that anyone meeting them on the street even on Sunday in their best clothes and mixed up with other children who go to school and play out of doors, can distinguish almost in an instant the children who work in a factory. (p. 279)

Corporal punishment was frequently used if children were lax or misbehaved. Discipline in factories was maintained by kicks and blows. Because of accidents, some children were deformed and some were even killed (Durant & Durant, 1965). The children's meager earnings were given to their parents.

During the latter part of the nineteenth century, federal and state authorities investigated child labor. In 1919 the U.S. Children's Bureau investigated the conditions in the shrimp and oyster canneries. One 4-year-old child and one 5-year-old child were found working in this industry. Another exploitative practice was that manufacturers sent work to tenement homes that served as an extension of the factory. As a result, children were often kept out of school to work. Again the pay was inadequate.

In the early twentieth century some states enacted legislation as a way of protecting children against exploitation. The first federal legislation was proposed in 1906 but was stopped in committee. A child labor law was passed in 1917 but was finally declared to be unconstitutional. By this time however, many states had enacted their own child labor laws. Finally, in 1924 the federal law was adopted, but by 1931 only six states had ratified it.

With the Depression in 1930, unemployment spread like wildfire, but children could still be hired at the lowest wages. This caused a regression in the progress of protecting children in work settings. In 1933 the National Recovery Act (N. R. A.) was passed. This law brought various industries under control but soon was declared to be unconstitutional. Finally in 1938, the Fair Labor Standards Act was passed with provisions related to child labor (Meltzer, 1967). Two examples of these protections for children were that any child under 6 years of age could not be employed in any occupation and that no children less than 18 years of age could be employed in certain occupations, especially hazardous occupations.

Over time, exceptions to these laws were sometimes made. Often departures from these policies were made in cases of a child employed by a parent, actors or performers, children on farms, and newspaper carriers. Costin, Bell, and Downs (1991) note that even today widespread violations of child labor laws continue. These infractions occur often in garment factories, fast-food restaurants, supermarkets, and in the case of migrant children farm workers. Today, public concern over child labor is global. Such practices, which still exist in a few industries, need to be addressed.

An important issue related to labor laws was the child's need for an education. Many believed that education was essential to the American way of life (Lindsey, 1994; Smith & Merkel-Holguin, 1996).

Compulsory Attendance in Schools

A difference of public opinions existed regarding the importance of work as opposed to education. Many families needed the wages of the children to help support the family. Others believed that education was necessary for citizens in a democracy. An ongoing conflict existed between the family's need for money and the need for education. An example of an attempt to recognize both positions was a principle of the Benevolent Society: children cannot be sent out to beg during the hours that school is in session.

From 1850 to 1900, social class differences existed among parents concerning the usefulness of formalized learning (Costin, Bell, & Downs, 1991; Lassonde, 1996). Work was viewed as important because it was a process that moved the child toward adulthood. Still another opinion of working-class parents was that schooling was a kind of idleness. Educators had grave doubts about the commitment of working-class parents to their children's schooling. Also, they were concerned about their ability to attract children of the middle class to the public schools.

As early as the 1850s, some states established a public school system. New Haven had created a citywide public school system. By 1872 the system had developed into a statewide public education system and was compulsory by law. This law of the Connecticut General Assembly required that children between the ages of 8 and 14 years of age attend school for 3 months of the year. Of this period, 6 weeks had to be consecutive (Lassonde, 1996). Laws passed in other states were very similar to the one passed in Connecticut.

Social expectations of girls and boys differed regarding school attendance. Girls in the city often did not attend school. They worked in stores and did light work in shops, or they were kept at home to help in the work of the family. Little attention was given to what was happening to the young women. Boys seemed to present a vague social nuisance. They fit into either of the expectations, school or work. Boys when unoccupied or unregistered were regarded as naturally given to roam in the street (Lassonde, 1996).

Gradually, most cities demanded that children be trained and prepared for adulthood rather than work in tenement houses, factories, mills, or mines. Compulsory education laws were passed by 28 states in the late nineteenth century. Still, enforcement of these laws was a problem. Not all parents understood and accepted the importance of education. This problem of school attendance was further aggravated by the lack of school accommodations. Many schools began to use waiting lists for admitting children into schools.

How was public education to be funded? Many taxpayers did not want to be compelled to bear the burden of supporting the system unless they actually directly shared in its benefits by having children who received instruction (Abbott & Breckinridge, 1917).

Another major obstacle were those citizens who questioned the state's power to interfere with parental rights to make a determination about their children.

The pre–Civil War generation had largely won the fight for free public schools and universal education. Over time, differences in intelligence among children were recognized and a need for individualized instruction was proposed. John Dewey stressed that children learn through self-discovery and urged that educational curriculum allow for such activities. As early as 1896, special classes began as disciplinary units. Their major intent was not to meet educational needs but to control behavior. Consequently, special classes and schools were often designated in an attempt to cope with specific problems of children in the school system.

From the 1830s a rise in juvenile delinquency occurred. Reform schools were turned into dumping grounds for adolescent felons and troublemakers. Truant schools provided a way of dealing with youths who had unoccupied time, which might eventually land them in trouble. Furthermore, many states enacted legislation to promote education for individuals with mental retardation and other disabilities. By the 1920s visiting teacher programs had been developed by 34 states. The purpose of these programs was to attempt to secure cooperation between schools and families (Kanner, 1962a).

While progress was made in educating children, landmark legislation was passed for their protection and other needed services. The federal government was beginning to take responsibility for the well-being of children.

The Social Security Act

In the late 1920s and early 1930s the United States was greatly affected by a major economic depression. A series of social programs stemmed from this chaos and were included in the Social Security Act of 1935. Over the years, policy making fluctuated between the states and the federal government with private voluntary organizations playing a major role in providing social services. Passage of the Social Security Act was clearly an indication of the federal government's willingness to assume responsibility for social services and other programs supportive to children and their families.

Laws made and enforced at the state level were often extended and included in the Social Security Act. Mothers' Pension administered by private charities became a public entitlement. Child Protection Services, such as committing children to almshouses and dispensing services through the Society for the Prevention of Cruelty to Children, became a part of the developing protective services to be administered under the Social Security Act (Levine & Levine, 1992). The federal government legislated programs and mandated states and localities to provide services.

Two types of programs, direct cash assistance and "in kind" services, resulted from the Social Security Act. Cash assistance programs were designed to provide families with a minimum allotment to purchase the necessities of life. Aid to Families with Dependent Children (AFDC) was the largest and best-known service provided under this act. Federal grants are made to the states, which are to distribute the funds as needed within that state. A major principle of this form of administration is that of local responsibility. Another program that is especially significant for the care of children is Dependents' Benefit. This benefit provides for the support of the family after the breadwinner is disabled or dies and is only available to those who would otherwise fall into poverty. "In kind" services provide assistance and resources such as health care, employment training, and housing.

Funding for social services for families and children is provided by federal, state, and local appropriations. Today these programs are channeled through the Department of Health and Human Services. Many services provided for children and adolescents today are based on needs that were well recognized in the twentieth century, yet only piecemeal solutions were developed and used until the Depression created a crisis. The Social Security Act centralized concerns and refined programs for meeting the needs of children and their families.

The historical perspective illuminates current social concerns and policies. Some special concerns are health and mental health care for children, social services, education, and services for children with disabilities. However, the influence of poverty on the lives of children is overwhelming.

Contemporary Concerns in the Lives of Children

The Social Security Act was very helpful in ensuring that families and children receive required services. As the country developed and lifestyles changed, it became necessary to reassess the needs of children and families. As a result, many new policies have been legislated to ameliorate some of these new developing conditions. A primary underlying condition of concern is poverty, which has been a major concern since the United States was settled and continues to be to the present. Sometimes poverty becomes an explicit focus of concern, then, as other problems arise and receive more attention, it again fades into the background. Poverty is so related to many other social problems for children that being aware of its existence is especially important.

Poverty

Although many strategies have been used over the years to attempt to alleviate it, poverty persists. Major changes occurred during the time of the Industrial Revolution. Levine and Levine (1992) noted that the rise of an industrial society in the United States after the Civil War was accompanied by a lower standard of living for the laborer.

Poverty continues to be one of the greatest social problems affecting children today. Even with a sound economy in the late twentieth century, the number of children living in poverty in the United States was 14.7 million or nearly 21 percent (Annie E. Casey Foundation, 1999). In recent years it has been recognized that there has been a "juvenilization of poverty." Historically, state laws have established the responsibility of the noncustodial parent to provide child support. Federal laws in 1975, 1984, and 1988 ordered child support to be provided. With this legislation a standardized formula was used. If judges deviate from this standard, they must provide a reason for doing so. The enforcement of this system is difficult to control. Some noncustodial parents do not pay for various reasons, and others are difficult to find. An increase in poverty of children has occurred as a result of the rise in the number of women living in poverty and female-headed households. Thirty-nine percent of divorced women with custody of children live in poverty (Behrman & Quinn, 1994). Such poverty begins immediately after divorce. Child abuse, mental health, alcohol, drug abuse, and suicide are all positively correlated with poverty.

The risk of acquiring developmental problems is greater for children who live in poverty. Furthermore, poverty contributes to unmanageable stress levels for vulnerable family systems. A lack of geographic stability and other critical resources adds to the deprivation. Children who are born and grow up in poverty suffer from inadequate nutrition, housing, and health care (Allen-Meares, 1995; Garbarino, 1992; Levine & Sallee, 1999).

Homelessness, health problems, and disabilities are also common among poor children and adolescents. Long-term poverty increases the youngster's chances of performing poorly, becoming pregnant, abusing drugs, and being involved in crime and the juvenile justice system (Lindsey & Henly, 1997). Often, educational opportunities are unavailable to poor children, thereby increasing the likelihood that they will remain in poverty throughout their lives.

Moreover, high poverty inner-city neighborhoods are increasingly remote and removed from centers of metropolitan job growth. When poverty is concentrated in secluded neighborhoods, few positive adult role models exist for adolescents. Unfortunately, potential role models are often involved in the sale and use of drugs. This has led to an increased vulnerability of the families to drug abuse and dependency (Annie E. Casey Foundation, 1999). Thousands of homeless children and adolescents live as runaways or as "throwaways." This is often an invisible group, which has received relatively little publicity. These youth may never really become a functioning part of society.

Poverty wastes human potential (Allen-Meares, 1995). Education is often viewed as one way to overcome poverty, but schools have not always been seen as desirable and often have not been available to the public. The development of the public school system will be described in the next section.

Public Education

From a historical perspective, to generalize about the educational system in the colonial period is difficult because it is not always clear what constituted a school (Katz, 1976). Enormous diversity in the existing type of schooling arrangements from one colony to another could easily be perceived. The first compulsory educational law in American history was passed on June 14, 1642. The Puritan elders were fearful that too many parents and masters were neglecting their child-rearing responsibilities so this law was passed to "transform a moral obligation into a legal one" (Katz, 1976, p. 11). Even to this time, supported mass education is evidently very related to compulsory attendance. Katz (1976, p. 5) noted that "Universal education opportunities could be provided but these would not assure mass education without the means of assuring attendance." It also must be recognized that compulsory education and its success depend on law to regulate the labor of poor children. In 1917 Abbott and Breckinridge suggested that a good compulsory education law, well enforced, may prevent child labor. Over the next several years, compulsory schooling laws became reasonably effective.

Changes and expansion of compulsory schooling have been made since the beginning of the twentieth century. Initially compulsory education was a relatively simple statute requiring a fixed period of school attendance but later became a complex network of legal rules. The attendance office was established, the school census became institutionalized, and the professional qualifications of truant officers gradually were upgraded.

At first, school counselors largely took the role of educational/vocational advisers. By 1950 the role of the counselor had expanded and by 1960 counselors were trained and placed in elementary schools. The child guidance movement, which had been weakened by the Depression, was renewed in part within the school.

Challenges to compulsory schooling rules continued. In 1925 and 1972, suits were filed questioning who should exercise the most control over the content and manner of the child's formal education. The issue was infringement on parental control of their own children. Currently, social services for children and adolescents depend on the availability of resources and on legislation authorizing specific programs. Schools have a major influence on children's lives. It is especially important that communities and schools work together to address concerns about violence and improving education in the United States.

Each year many children fail or drop out of school as an outcome of poverty (Allen-Meares, Washington, & Welsh, 1986). The quality of learning is compromised due to inadequate housing, health care, nutrition, and lack of availability of early childhood education programs. Other factors contributing to school failure are the lack of successful role models, insufficient social support, emotional and psychological problems, and the need for employment.

Concerns of the public and of school personnel are reflected in a variety of new methods and special programs, which are being tested. Charter schools are a current example of experimental programs that are being used to try out different educational methods and environments for learning. As positive outcomes are determined, such methods are expected to be tried out in regular public schools.

It was quickly discovered that not all children are capable of participating in public education as it had developed. Due to various disabilities, some children and adolescents need special teaching methods, a curriculum plan to fit their needs, a physical setting conducive to their learning, transportation, and many other special accommodations.

Special Services for Educating Children

Some of the earliest federal efforts to provide special services for children in need occurred in the early and mid-1800s. Such efforts were in the form of government grants to states for asylums for the "deaf and dumb" (Martin, Martin, & Terman, 1996). However, these funds were very limited. By 1920 many states had enacted legislation to promote education of children with mental retardation. A visiting teacher program, whose primary purpose was to secure school and family cooperation in children's education, was initiated by 34 states.

The federal government's next major involvement in the educational system was in the 1950s. The Soviet Union had launched Sputnik, a satellite that orbited the earth, which was seen as a challenge to the American educational system. Under President Dwight Eisenhower, Congress passed the National Defense Educational Act (NDEA) in 1958. NDEA provided a grant to improve science and math education and opened the door for federal involvement in elementary and secondary education.

The first major federal effort to subsidize direct services to selected populations in public schools was the Elementary and Secondary Education Act (ESEA) of 1965. Initially, ESEA did not provide for direct grants for children with disabilities. In the second year, Congress passed Public Law 89-313, which provided children in state-supported schools for the disabled to be counted for entitlement purposes (Martin, Martin, & Terman, 1996).

A year later, Congress mandated a Bureau for the Education of the Handicapped (BEH), which expanded and improved programs for youngsters with disabilities. In the 1960s and early 1970s, no state served all its children with disabilities. Early efforts to serve these children were often piecemeal. Sometimes children of normal intelligence with physical disabilities were placed in classes designed for children with mental retardation. Though many states had already passed a law for education of children with disabilities, a proper educational program was still unavailable. Consequently, many children with disabilities languished at home. Some states attempted to provide help by maintaining residential schools for children who encountered deafness, blindness, and mental retardation.

Through most of their history, public schools in the United States provided minimal services to children with disabilities and such services tended to be provided at the discretion of local school districts. The BEH recommended that many existing federal programs be codified into a more comprehensive Education of the Handicapped Act (EHA), which was passed in 1970. However, the EHA still did not resolve the problems. Until the mid-1970s, laws allowed school districts to refuse to enroll any student they considered "uneducable," a term that was defined by the local schools. As a result, litigation determined the rights to education from 1971 to 1973. In 1972, Title IX of the federal Education Amendments was passed. Gender could no longer be the basis for excluding some children from participating in selected educational programs. An amendment to the Social Security Act consolidated social service titles into a new Title XX. Funding for these services grew to 3.3 billion dollars by 1980.

The next important piece of federal legislation was the Education for All Handicapped Children Act of 1975, which provided for quality education for all children in the "least restrictive environment." Consequently, youngsters with disabilities were integrated or mainstreamed into regular educational programs to the maximum extent. All states participate in grant programs for children with disabilities ages 3 through 21 years of age. States developed strategies for finding these children so that services could be dispensed. This Act also provided for preschool children with disabilities, and deaf and blind children and youth. An individual education program (IEP) is required for all children who participate. Parents are guaranteed the right to participate actively in the formulation of educational programs and their signature is required on the individualized learning plan (Terman, Larner, Stevenson, & Behrman, 1996). Services were to be provided by social workers, psychologists, guidance counselors, and other qualified persons (Newton-Logstron & Armstrong, 1993). The act also made provisions for related research and demonstration programs.

In 1978, children with developmental disabilities were added to the populations for whom services were to be provided. The Rehabilitation, Comprehensive Service, and Developmental Disabilities Act (P.L. 95-602) was to be extended to developmentally disabled children. These disabilities were to have occurred before the age of 22 years and were to have hindered the individual's development. Developmental disabilities include mental retardation, which is the largest single category, as well as fetal exposure to drugs, autism, cerebral palsy, epilepsy, and various other conditions. Presumably poor children have higher rates of mental retardation than other children.

In 1990, Congress passed the Americans with Disabilities Act (ADA), which expanded the rights of people with disabilities by outlawing discriminatory practices in employment, public accommodations, transportation, and telecommunications. In that same year the Handicapped Children Act of 1975 was amended to be the Individuals with Disabilities Education Act (IDEA). Under IDEA, schools are required to provide access to classrooms, assistive technology, extended school years, and extended day school. The courts have required that programs be designed so that school-age children with severe disabilities do not regress over the summer. Basically, IDEA lays out broad mandates for services to a broad age range of children and adolescents from the first grader with a speech impediment to a college-bound high school student in a wheelchair (Martin, Martin, & Terman, 1996).

Many lawsuits have been filed to decide the exact services needed for a particular child or youth. Lack of understanding and agreement about the boundaries of the term *disability* is evident. Finally, it was determined that students are to be designated as disabled because of real, persistent, and substantial individual differences and educational needs that regular education has been unable to accommodate. Individual differences vary from medical conditions such as cerebral palsy to chronic maladaptive patterns of behavior (Terman, Larner, Stevenson, & Behrman, 1996).

One in 10 schoolchildren has been evaluated and found to have a disability using this definition. Classification of disabilities occurs following a comprehensive evaluation by a team of specialists. The areas assessed are academic achievement, learning characteristics, social and physical development, and management of needs. A code of Federal Regulations was developed in 1993. Identified conditions covered by these regulations include autism, emotional disturbance, multiple disabilities, orthopedic impairment, speech impairment, traumatic brain injury, and other health impairments.

The Improving America's Schools Act (P.L. 103-382), which was passed in 1994, called for more involvement of pupil personnel services in helping disadvantaged children. The Individuals with Disabilities Education Act (IDEA) (P.L. 101-476), which was amended in 1997, emphasized the importance of a family-centered approach in the intervention process (Atkins-Burnett & Allen-Meares, 2000). Family goals and needs are gathered as a part of the assessment process and family service plans are developed.

Many youngsters who are disadvantaged have mental retardation and other developmental disabilities. It became recognized that legislation that was applicable to other persons with disabilities could be applied to children and adolescents. There has been a continual evolution of federal legislation in this area. In addition, making many special accommodations for children with disabilities was important.

Children with Developmental Disabilities

With the enactment of the IDEA legislation in 1975, social services for children with developmental disabilities became a component of legislated services for all children with disabilities. At first mental retardation was little understood and thus was viewed as a unique disability.

The first American institution for persons with mental retardation was the Perkins Institute of Boston, which was established in 1848. Its original goal was curing mental retardation (Davies & Ecob, 1959). Nineteenth-century European attitudes about "mental defectives" influenced practice. It was believed that treatment occurred with the use of cruelties such as whippings. By 1870 the goal of the Perkins Institute changed to one of protecting people with mental retardation.

With the development of public education it was recognized that exceptional learners did not easily fit into the schools. By 1890 care for the retarded became a responsibility of the state and private agencies that emerged to supplement services. Educators were beginning to be concerned with the child's total personality, which led them to focus on the importance of individualized instruction.

Many persons continued to be concerned about the causation of mental retardation. The American Breeders Association, which was organized in 1903, appointed a committee on eugenics. This group was convinced that the cause of mental retardation was a defect in the nervous system that was transmitted intergenerationally. The way to stop propagation of this condition was thought to be segregation and sterilization. Some advocated that persons with mental retardation should not be allowed to move freely in society.

The approach to the situation in the early twentieth century was to warehouse persons with mental retardation, as inexpensively as possible, and to continue the sterilization program. They were often placed in colonies, on parole, or in foster homes. Institutions were built in rural areas to remove them further from the mainstream (DeWeaver, 1983). Over the next decade, persons with mental retardation were found to be neither immoral nor a threat to others. By 1911 public school classes had been developed for them in 99 U.S. cities (Hewett & Forness, 1984).

By 1920, investigations were being conducted to determine the relationship between brain injuries at birth and mental retardation. It was found that Down syndrome and endocrine disorders were related to mental retardation. The Great Depression and World War II temporarily delayed progress in this research. Soon, demanding parents and enthusiastic professionals became involved and began to use federal, state, and private funding to continue with the investigation.

Until the civil rights movement of the 1950s, education was viewed as a privilege. Through a celebrated court decision, *Brown v. Board of Education,* education for persons with mental retardation became a right. P.L. 94-142 guaranteed free education for all handicapped persons.

Persons with profound levels of mental retardation were considered to be in need of lifetime custodial care whereas those with less severe levels were seen as candidates for some level of gainful employment. Indeed, such ends were encouraged by a new organization named the National Association of Retarded Children, later changed to the National

Association of Retarded Citizens. As a result, the focus moved from devaluing mentally retarded persons to maximizing their potential and engaging in community planning (Doll, 1962).

This change in attitude was further enhanced by President John F. Kennedy, who had a sister who had mental retardation. He called for and set in motion research and reform for this condition. A President's Panel on Mental Retardation recommended a national plan of action. In 1963 the Mental Retardation Facilities and Community Mental Health Centers Construction Act was passed. A major contribution of this Act was the development of a mental retardation branch of Child Health and Development and funding to build university affiliated facilities. An outgrowth of the President's Panel was the Maternal and Child Health and Mental Retardation Planning Amendment, which authorized funding for a preventive program.

Those who wished to stress the functional needs of people with mental retardation and other conditions developed the concept of developmental disabilities. Until the 1960s, most persons with severe and profound levels of mental retardation had been institutionalized. In the early 1970s there was a movement to deinstitutionalize persons with mental retardation. Planning, administration, case management services, and direct services had been developed to allow persons with mental retardation to leave the institutions and be served in the community (DeWeaver, 1983).

The Developmental Disabilities Assistance and Bill of Rights Act of 1990 (P.L. 101-496) further amended previous legislation. The term *developmental disability* was clarified to mean a severe, chronic disability of a person 5 years of age or older with the following characteristics:

Attributable to mental or physical impairments

Manifested before the age of 22

Likely to continue indefinitely

Substantial functional limitations in three or more of the areas of major life activities, self-care, receptive and expressive language, learning, mobility, self-direction, capacity for independent living, and economic self-sufficiency

The Act added infants and children, from birth to 5 years of age, who have substantial developmental delays or specific congenital or acquired conditions, with a high probability of resulting in developmental disabilities if not addressed (DeWeaver & Kropf, 1992). Conditions that fit into this evolving definition are mental retardation caused by biological damage to the brain, chromosomal abnormalities, or psychosocial causes, such as poverty.

Half of the school populations with disabilities also have learning disabilities. The common characteristics for children with disabilities are that they required greater consistency and intensity of instruction and greater individualization than other children. According to Terman, Larner, Stevenson, and Behrman (1996), six disability categories are included under IDEA:

1. Learning disabilities (51 percent of students served; 5 percent of all students in public schools)
2. Speech and language disorders (22 percent of students eligible for IDEA)

3. Mental retardation (11 percent of students eligible; because of poverty and racial discrimination, African Americans were more than twice as likely to be found to be eligible)
4. Serious emotional disturbance (SED) (9 percent of students eligible for IDEA; defined as inability to build relationships, inappropriate behavior or feelings)
5. Physical or sensory disabilities (7 percent of IDEA; includes multiple disabilities)
6. Attention deficit hyperactivity disorder (ADHD) (the number of children has increased dramatically)

Given the improved preventive services and the increases in technology in the social services, it is surprising that more children and youth continue to be identified as eligible for various disability categories. Terman, Larner, Stevenson, and Behrman (1996) suggest that one reason this is occurring is that funding incentives in most states encourage school districts to label students as having disabilities. Another reason for the increase is that the ongoing pressure to raise academic standards causes some children to fall behind. A final suggested reason is that parents and schools recognize the important long-term impact of less apparent disabilities. Emotional disturbance is one of those disabilities. The Comprehensive Community Mental Health Services Program for Children with Serious Emotional Disturbances (P.L. 102-322) was enacted to provide grant funds to states. This law is meant to establish systems of care for children and adolescents with serious emotional problems.

A major ongoing concern is how children and adolescents with disabilities need to be educated to prepare for life. A study by Wagner and Blackorby (1996) examined the transition of high school students with disabilities from school to the community. They found that a majority of the students planned to enter the work force upon leaving school. More than half of these young people had a goal of finding competitive employment, 10 percent had a goal of supported employment, and 2 percent sought sheltered work after leaving high school.

An important issue is whether these students need more academic courses or vocational courses. In a study by Wagner and Blackorby (1996), it was discovered that no one panacea offers a benefit for all students' differing disabilities. Generally, a focus on traditional schoolwork has been the pattern with little explicit help with the mental health needs of the student and family. It was determined that postschool transitional planning was needed to develop a model of cooperation among services to assist with employment.

The Individuals with Disabilities Education Act (IDEA) was revised in 1998. It requires that the school district complete a functional assessment of each child's performance. Today, special education for students with disabilities is the largest categorical program in public schools. Other disadvantaged children are also part of the school system and need special help to reach their potential. Sometimes programs developed for children with disabilities also include other types of children with special needs. Children affected by poverty and language difficulties have needs and require services to overcome their disadvantages.

Language Differences and Poor Children

In addition to disabilities, poverty and language differences have made it difficult for many children to achieve in school. Poverty was recognized as a condition that affects children as they enter school. The War on Poverty and passage of the Economic Opportunity Act of 1964 were attempts to prepare children for entry into school systems.

The Head Start program, which stemmed from this Act, provides comprehensive health, educational, nutritional, and social services for economically disadvantaged preschool children. The Department of Health and Human Services administers this program. A major eligibility requirement is that the family must be living below the poverty line. This program reaches only a small portion of children needing these services.

Other laws that have been passed provide services to improve the education of children. The federal Bilingual Education Act of 1965 and 1973 provides financing for instruction (Costin, Bell, & Downs, 1991). Chapter I of the Education Consolidation and Improvement Act provides compensatory education for educationally disadvantaged children. These services include both basic and remedial services, such as remedial instruction, guidance, transportation, and health services. It is administered by U.S. Department of Education and state and local educational agencies. Services are provided for children who are disabled, migrant, neglected, delinquent, and the most educationally disadvantaged.

Language has always been a problem for some children who enter school systems. Situations arose in which attempts were made to keep migrant children out of schools. For example, in the past, Texas authorized the withholding of state funds to local school districts for education of children who were not legally admitted into the United States. In *Plyer et al. v. R. Doe et al.* (1982), the U.S. Supreme Court ruled that this action violated the equal protection clause of the Fourteenth Amendment.

Children who speak a non-English language at home are particularly challenged in relating to mainstream society in the United States. They often require special programs in preschool and school because they are less able to rely on family for help. Children who live in "linguistically isolated" households in which no member of the household, age 14 and older, speaks English, at least "not well," are especially challenged (Lewit & Baker, 1994).

A related controversy is the acceptability of the use of Ebonics in the public schools. Because some African Americans use it as a language in their community and homes, it has been argued that schools should use, integrate, and teach it. Not providing these services is seen as creating a disadvantage for a segment of society. Adopting the use of Ebonics would require special funding for preparation of teachers and other school personnel.

Barriers for children's development and survival have taken many forms. Specific potential issues have included ethnic/cultural, physical disabilities, learning disabilities, and mental retardation. Health and mental health can also be an impediment to the functioning of children. It has required many years to learn and understand the problems that exist and to begin to understand the possible causes, dynamics, and treatment of these conditions.

Health

Prior to the nineteenth century the causes of most medical problems were unknown. Often even minor injuries and illnesses were fatal because of the limited state of medical knowledge. Usually, people only went to hospitals to die. In the second half of the nineteenth century, germs, viruses, and genetic and functional causes of illness were discovered and medicine became scientific (Lindsey, 1994). Since then knowledge of public health has increased. The role of nutrition in health has become more widely understood.

Today, food stamps, an in kind program to help people become and remain healthy and to prevent malnutrition and starvation, provide food and nutrition to low-income persons. The legislation was enacted in 1964. It is administered by the Food and Nutrition Service of the U.S. Department of Agriculture. This program originally was a federal program to distribute surplus food. Now, coupons are issued to those that meet the criteria for these services. Food stamps can then be redeemed for food. This program is administered by the state but is entirely funded by the federal government. Eligibility is determined by state and local welfare agencies.

Other programs were enacted to meet the health needs of both children and adults. In 1965, Medicaid, which is both a cash assistance and a medical program, was adopted as Title XIX of the Social Security Act. States administer the program and contribute funds for its operation. The providers of the medical services are directly reimbursed by the state.

Another government program to address early nutritional needs of infants is the Supplemental Food Program for Women, Infants, and Children (WIC), which is administered by the U.S. Department of Agriculture. State health departments operate the program, which is funded entirely with federal money. Eligible recipients include pregnant, postpartum, or breast-feeding women; infants; and children less than 5 years of age. They receive supplemental foods, such as eggs and milk, either directly or through vouchers (Allen-Meares, 1995).

Title V of the Social Security Act provides block grants for Maternal and Child Health Services. The purpose of these grants is to provide services that help to reduce infant mortality and preventable diseases among children. The primary recipients of this service are mothers and children with low incomes. Services are made more available to this population. Part of the funding for this program is set aside to facilitate the development of special programs and research projects. Title V is administered at the state level and funded by the state and federal government.

The use of health care services for children varies among differing populations. Despite a higher burden of illness in low-income families, these children use fewer services (McLanahan & Booth, 1989). A contributing factor is the high rate of divorce and births to unmarried mothers, which leads to the growing proportion of female-headed families. Angel and Angel (1993) found that children in single-parent families use fewer health care services than those in two-parent families even though single mothers are more likely to report their children to be in poor health. It is unlikely that the *need* for health services is any higher for children of two-parent families than for those of single-parent families.

Poor children in mother-headed families were also found to be less likely to use preventive care than children from higher-income families regardless of their health care coverage. Being poor, lacking transportation, and the unavailability of health care providers in poor and low-income residential areas were seen as possible reasons for these differences. A study by Newacheck (1992) revealed that even with universal health coverage, children in mother-headed families would still be less likely to use ambulatory care, either for preventive or illness-related purposes. Need is only one motivating aspect in the use of health care services. Other factors, especially economics, play a substantial role in lower health care use by children. Out-of-pocket costs for health care are a significant obstacle to accessing and using services for poor and low-income families.

Children in mother-present (father-absent) families also have greater emotional and behavioral problems (Cunningham & Hahn, 1994). The findings indicate that even if all children had private or public health care coverage there would still be a difference in use among family types. Cunningham and Hahn (1994) suggest that service delivery and outreach should be major concerns. Neighborhood or community health centers could serve as a primary source of health care, health promotion, and education for parents and children.

Adolescents have generally been regarded as healthy and in little need of health care. However, research has found that one out of five adolescents has a minimum of one serious health problem. Common health problems of adolescents that are behavioral or unintended include pregnancy, sexually transmitted diseases, motor vehicle accidents, gun-related homicide, drug abuse, eating disorders, depression, and suicide. Such difficulties are found in all ethnic groups.

Urgent challenges accompanying the growing ethnic diversity of the U.S. population encompass the delivery of appropriate health care, child care, education, and social services to immigrant and native-born children (Lewit & Baker, 1994). Not only are health problems a concern for children and adolescents, but in this stressful society many also are in need of mental health services.

Mental Health Services

During the sixteenth and seventeenth centuries, persons with mental illness wandered the countryside, seeking shelter in stables and pigsties. They were mocked and beaten and, if apprehended, placed in chains along with murderers. Some of them were never set free (Hewett & Forness, 1984). Colonial America saw them simply as one group among many needy people.

Kanner (1962b) wrote that no allusion to emotional disorders of children in the eighteenth century are found in the professional literature. Children with mental illness often did not live to adulthood. The Stubborn Child Act of 1654 permitted parents to put "stubborn" children to death for noncompliance (Donohue, Hersen, & Ammerman, 1995). If they did live, and the family was poor or there was no family, the public authorities provided other alternatives. Children were boarded out, and placed in cellars, attics, almshouses, and jails (Donohue, et al., 1995; Popple & Leighninger, 1999). In affluent families children with mental illness were often cared for at home.

Mental illness in children was usually referred to as disordered child behavior and was thought to be caused by them being inherently evil (Kanner, 1962b; Mash, Dozois, & Barkley, 1996). Mental illness in the 1800s was described as irreversible, and was explained by heredity, degeneracy, parasites, masturbation, or overwork.

Credit is given to several people for the beginning of services offered to children with mental illness in the United States. Lightner Witmer opened the first psychological clinic in the United States at the University of Pennsylvania in 1896. He was concerned about giving service to exceptional children, especially those with mental retardation.

Less attention was given to the study of psychopathology in children than in adults. The first American psychiatrist, Benjamin Rush, suggested that children were less likely to suffer from mental illness than adults because of the immaturity of their brains. This condition was expected to prevent them from retaining the mental events that caused mental illness (Donohue, Hersen, & Ammerman, 1995). William Healy is credited with having started the first "real" psychiatric clinic for children in 1909, as a part of the juvenile court in Chicago.

The child guidance movement owes its existence to Clifford Beers, a former patient himself (Lassonde, 1996). In 1896 a psychiatric institute, the Child Guidance Clinic, was founded in New York City with the purpose of counseling children. Child guidance clinics continued to take shape in the decade following World War I. The clinics continued to expand so that almost every community in the United States had one. The focus in these clinics was working with parents to help their children.

Since the middle of the nineteenth century, there has been interest in the causes of mental illness and the classification of childhood disorders. Efforts were made to separate emotional disturbances and mental retardation. About the beginning of the twentieth century, a variety of publications replete with anecdotes began to make the world aware that children could display psychosis. "Insanity of Early Life" was the title of a chapter in a book by Maudsley titled *Physiology of Pathology of the Mind.* He tried to correlate symptomatology with the developmental status at the time of onset and suggested a classification of infantile psychosis. Lassonde (1996) identified three main directions of childhood disorders present in the early nineteenth century as systematic theories of child development, emergence of special treatment facilities for children, and application of principles of child behavior to education.

Sigmund Freud in Austria and Adolph Meyer in the United States became interested in the psychodynamics of mental illness. They studied the relationship between early childhood events and the adult's current functioning (Morris & Kratochwill, 1998). This psychodynamic view of children was formally realized in the literature in 1909. With the publication of Freud's detailed case of Little Hans, others became aware of this orientation to the treatment of children. Even in the case of Little Hans, the father, with the support of Freud, did the treatment.

Almost 2 decades later, Freudian psychoanalytic child therapy came into existence. Anna Freud developed a theory of child therapy that veered from the strict analytic stance used in working with adults. Melanie Klein pointed out that infants feel a range of emotions from anger to joy and mothers become the primary object of support and hostility. According to Klein, children's subjective perception of reality causes emotional disturbances. Melanie Klein and Anna Freud developed techniques especially useful in working with children. Play activities were used for free association, and drawing and dream interpretation were used to understand children's problems more completely.

At the beginning of the twentieth century, the term *children's emotional conditions* was used as a generality. Later on, progress began to be made in regard to conceptual or terminological boundaries and distinctions among the variety of psychotic reaction types. By the 1930s consistent attempts were made to study children with severe emotional disturbances from the viewpoint of diagnosis, etiology, therapy, and prognosis, particularly in regard to childhood schizophrenia.

Behavior modification, which developed from the experimental psychology laboratory rather than from direct interaction with patients, emerged as a major therapeutic approach for children. Behavior therapy is based on the assumption that all behavior occurs in response to internal and external stimulation. Techniques developed to work with children included reinforcement, aversive techniques, extinction, and later token economies.

In practice, the variety of techniques available for working with children included play therapy, behavioral approaches, and medical approaches. Much of the therapy took place in child guidance clinics, which finally were subsumed into the community mental health centers. During this period, services were described as inconsistent and unorganized (Lassonde, 1996). Early clinics for children worked closely with schools. By 1960 it was common for clinics to have little or no contact with schools. The interest in therapy for children was renewed with the rediscovery of child abuse and neglect in the late 1960s and 1970s.

Today it is more widely understood that children and adolescents commonly experience a variety of mental, emotional, and behavioral problems. Brandenberg, Friedman, and Silver (1990) estimate that 14 to 22 percent of all children are affected by psychopathology, and fewer than 20 percent receive appropriate treatment. Anxiety disorders, such as phobias and posttraumatic stress related to physical and sexual abuse, are the most common mental disorders (Popple & Leighninger, 1999). Approximately 5 percent of children have attention deficit hyperactivity disorder. Major depression among children and adolescents is becoming more prevalent.

Whereas it was once widely believed that children outgrow mental health problems, it is noted that significant numbers of children do not outgrow them. The ways in which these problems are expressed is likely to change as children develop and mature. Furthermore, recent changes in families and society place children at increasing risk for the development of severe mental disorders. Research has demonstrated the impact of parental psychopathology, and child abuse and neglect. A significant number of children are subjected to maltreatment, and chronic maltreatment and psychopathology in children are highly associated (Wekerle & Wolfe, 1996). The lifelong consequences associated with child psychopathology are exceedingly costly in economic terms and in regard to their toll on human suffering.

Lassonde (1996) identified limitations to and concerns about contemporary mental health systems. The systems operate on a medical model, primarily treating voluntary clients, and waiting lists for services are typically long. Currently, clinics have little invested in community agencies, consultation, or community schools.

A study by the Center for Research on Child and Adolescent Mental Health Services reported that children in foster care exhibit significantly more developmental and mental health problems than do other children. Minority status plays a role in both entering the foster care system and receiving mental health services. Maltreated children receive services at a higher rate than neglected children. Maltreatment was found not to predict need but rather the services given. Those children who were given continuous treatment showed the greatest gain.

The preliminary results showed that children who experience neglect do not fare well. There is a need for systematically linking children with appropriate services and using more flexibility and creativity in treatment choices, particularly for children in foster care. Foster care was found to be the gateway to mental health services for many children.

Child Welfare Services

Throughout the nineteenth century and the first decades of the twentieth century, large numbers of children lost their parents very early in their lives. Consequently, many children were made wards of the state. In 1920 there were more than 750,000 orphaned children in the United States (Lindsey, 1994).

The Social Security Act was the first federal child welfare legislation that formalized funds for economic assistance through Aid to Dependent Children (ADC) to *deserving women,* such as abandoned or widowed women. The philosophy was that children of the poor should be allowed to remain in their own homes (Vasey, 1958). There was also some recognition of abused and neglected children and the need for foster care and adoption. The Children's Bureau was given the responsibility for oversight of these state programs. Through knowledge-generating research and factual reports, the Children's Bureau powerfully influenced the development of child welfare programs.

Following the Social Security Act, child welfare services remained spotty and poorly funded (Popple & Leighninger, 1996). When children were removed from their homes and placed in new homes, generally the case was closed and there was no follow-up on the child. The Great Depression and World War II diverted attention from these programs. The modern child welfare system emerged as a major public institution during the 1950s. Professional state agencies provided foster care, adoptions, and other services. The original purposes of the programs were *supportive* (counseling to the parents), *supplementary* (giving income assistance [AFDC]), and *substitutive* (a temporary placement in a home away from the biological parent) (Lindsey, 1994).

As a result of the rediscovery of child maltreatment in the late 1950s and early 1960s, foster care became a major component of public child welfare services. Title XX of the Social Security Act, which was implemented in 1972, provided millions of dollars for children's services through the states. The Act provides numerous state programs such as child protection, child day care, family planning, and referral and counseling services (Allen-Meares, 1995).

The Federal Child Abuse Prevention and Treatment Act of 1974 required mandatory reporting of abuse by professionals and citizens. As the years passed and during difficult economic times, foster care and its accompaniment, crisis intervention, became a major focus of child welfare services. Services such as counseling and parent training were frequently the first to be cut to allow for the new emphasis on managing crises. The separation of investigation from the service function suggested a return to orphanages. The child welfare system is involved, almost exclusively, in seeking change at the individual and family level. Foster care emerged as a major tool for child protection. Such changes resulted in a lack of services for children and families until they found themselves in dire circumstances. Unfortunately, by that time the child may be so damaged that child welfare services can do little either for the child or for the parents.

A recurrent issue in child welfare practice is whether the family or the child should be the focus of services. With the passage of the Adoption Opportunity Act (P.L. 96-266) in

1978, the family clearly became the unit of concern. The Act allowed the federal government to monitor the delivery and financing of foster care services. An additional requirement for state child welfare agencies was to make "reasonable efforts" to reunite the family.

An increase in home placements, mostly in foster care, was reported across the United States. It was recognized that more children were "adrift." Individual case planning for children was lacking. Often, children moved from one foster home to another until they reached their age of majority. Little emphasis was placed on helping children and parents stay in contact during this time. Concern developed over such conditions and the overall importance of children's "well-being" became a focus.

As a result, the Adoption Assistance and Child Welfare Act (P.L. 92-272) was passed in 1980. The Act was an attempt to ensure permanency for abused and neglected children through three avenues, namely returning them to their biological parents, placing them for adoption, or planning for them to remain in permanent long-term foster homes. To implement the Act, funds were provided for case management and training for children and families (Levine & Sallee, 1999).

With an increase in child abuse reports, an increased need for foster homes was created. Furthermore, child welfare agencies were changing from emphasizing foster home care to providing protective services. Also, research suggests that the amount of clinical services that were provided to children after they were removed from their biological parents tended to decrease (Lindsey, 1994).

The child welfare program has been subject to extensive criticism. One, it has been stated that the program dissolved families and disallowed due process. Two, the program is seen as treading on the rights of parents accused of abuse or neglect. Three, foster care is seen as a child rescue approach to the problem. Four, some have noted that genuine developmental needs of children often get neglected in the crisis of placement (Mental Health Needs of Children, 1996). Five, those who are distressed about children's emotional condition believe that the services primarily focus on changing the parents' behavior and children's environment, with correspondingly less actual treatment and little focus on the child's emotional and social development or education.

In addressing the needs of neglected children, scholars and policymakers have questioned whether to focus attention on the behavior of parents or on the broader ecological factors of stress, including poverty. Some believe that the problem of neglecting families must involve attention to large-scale social problems of inadequate housing, drug abuse, and community violence. At the same time, it is necessary to intervene in family systems through family therapy, parent education, placements, and therapeutic day care (Wattenberg, 1994).

Two sets of responses to child neglect tend to run counter to key aspects of U.S. values and ideologies: namely, coercive intrusion into the family's privacy, autonomy, and life, and expending public resources to alleviate the condition. Many persons in the United States believe that families should be left alone and that each family should take care of their children without governmental support or intervention. It is suggested that we have permitted the well-being of children to be overshadowed by our zeal to reform and to reduce the cost of the foster care system.

The Family Preservation Act (P.L. 103-66) of 1993 represents an attempt to improve social services for abused and neglected children. Family preservation services evolved out of the child welfare and mental health arena. It is funded through Title IV-A and Title IV-E of the Social Security Act and Medicaid. This is an attempt to work with abused and neglected children within their own families and to avoid placement (Hooper-Briar, Broussard, Ronnau, & Sallee, 1995). The hallmarks of this service are that it is family centered, home based, crisis oriented, family empowered, community oriented, and uses case management approaches (Schuerman, Rzepnicki, & Littell, 1994). The approach to the problem is to provide intensive casework services to families during a crisis.

Placing abused and neglected children with extended family members during crisis situations is another reemphasized contemporary practice (Hegar & Scannapieco, 1999). Extended families had been used for such assistance in the past, but because of the focus on nuclear families today, their strengths and value had been overlooked. Also, subsidized foster homes are given special allowances to support the extra care and equipment required for children with special needs.

The Adoption and Safe Families Act (P.L. 105-89) of 1997 expanded provisions for termination of the parental rights of biological parents (Hollingsworth, 2000). The number of children in foster care had reached 500,000; many children could not be returned home because their parents could not care for them. State statutes did not lend themselves to grounds for termination of parental rights. A growing number of child fatalities and serious injuries had been reported. Again the pendulum swung from family-centered to child-centered policy and practices with child safety and permanence as the predominant goals. The Act clarified *reasonable effort* and directed states to develop *concurrent planning* in each case, which means that a plan is made to reunify the family at the same time that a plan for termination of parental rights is in place if ordered by the judge.

Concern is now being expressed about consequences of the Act on society (Hollingsworth, 2000). Reasonable efforts requirements often produce a conflicting attempt to determine reunification or adoption. Adoption incentives are provided to states to increase adoptions with no similar incentive for professionals to support and strengthen the biological family.

Adoptions

Adoption is an important means of providing permanent placements for children. A knowledge and understanding of the history of adoptions is useful in understanding current processes and procedures.

In seventeenth-century England a variety of customs such as "putting out," indenturing, and apprenticing were convenient means of solving the problem of dependent children (Hollinger, 1991). Inheritance was determined solely by blood lineage. These practices were brought to the New World by the Puritans and continued to be used throughout the seventeenth and eighteenth century. Hollinger (1991) states that adoption is "purely a creature of the statutes which have been enacted in this country since the mid-nineteenth century" (p. 1). Another practice brought from England was the informal transfer of children. During periods of harvest, plantation owners took many children to work. This practice continued into the nineteenth century on an individual basis.

Foundling homes were used in the United States for infants and young children. However, pediatricians began to report striking developmental delays they observed among children in foundling homes. The reports indicated that these problems were insurmountable and that mortality rates were high. The pediatricians attributed the problems to institutionalization, and it was recommended that these institutions be closed. At first, many of these children were placed with wet nurses. However, not enough placements were available for these infants, and states began to enact some form of adoption laws.

At the beginning of the nineteenth century, the means of caring for dependent children were inadequate to meet their needs. During this century, adoption laws, which were developed to give legal status to children who were not living in their own homes, encouraged more available and better care for dependent children (Sokoloff, 1993). Many adoptive parents wanted to ensure that their "adopted" children would share in their estate and sought legal sanction. England had an absence of laws related to adoption apparently because no need was recognized for this practice. In the United States the first adoption statute was passed in Massachusetts in 1851. For the first time, the interest of the child was emphasized, and adoption had to be approved by a judge (Hollinger, 1991). The following provisions applied to this law:

- Written consent from the parents or guardian
- Consent of children over 14 years of age
- Adoptive parent had to join in the petition for adoption
- Judge had to be satisfied that the petitioners had the ability to bring up the child
- Once the adoption was approved, the child would become the legal child of the petitioner
- Natural parents would be deprived of all legal rights and obligations regarding the adopted child

By 1926 all states had enacted some form of adoption legislation. Standard adoption practice supported secrecy, anonymity, and sealing records. At first all persons were barred from inspecting files and records of adoption. This was not intended to preserve anonymity between biological parents and adopters; it was to shield the proceedings. "This movement toward secrecy is said to have been urged by social workers in child placing agencies with the goal of removing the stigma of illegitimacy from children born out of wedlock" (Sokoloff, 1993, p. 22). These new laws were accompanied by a dramatic demand for adoption. Prior to 1920 there were concerns about "bad blood," the high death rates because of the difficulty in feeding infants without an adequate supply of breast milk. World War I and the influenza epidemic that followed created a sharp drop in birth weight and an increased interest in infant adoption.

The passage of the Social Security Act in 1935 inaugurated a change in child welfare policy; federal grants were awarded to the states. A resurgence of interest in the adoption of healthy infants accompanied the end of World War II. This period experienced an equal number of babies and applicants. Children with known pathology in their background were considered to be unadoptable (Cole & Donley, 1990).

By 1950 the demand for adoptable infants exceeded the supply, and social agencies began to develop criteria for selecting potential adoptive parents. Some adoptions were conducted by private agencies and their professional intermediaries such as doctors and lawyers. They tried to find adoptable children for childless couples. As birth control, abortions, and single parenthood became more feasible and acceptable, the number of infants surrendered for adoption decreased even further. An additional factor was the increase in infertility of married couples. All these conditions created the beginnings of a movement to consider "special needs" children for possible adoptions. Despite the official rhetoric about the integrity and the importance of preserving the family, in fact, child welfare funding and resources were skewed to saving children from their parents (McKinzie, 1993).

Most states had expanded their adoption efforts by 1970. It became clear that age, race, and disability were not insurmountable barriers to adopting children. However, conflict arose concerning matching adoptive families with children to be adopted by race. The National Association of Black Social Workers took a stand opposing the practice of adoption of African American children by white families. Some associations, such as the Homes for Black Children in Detroit, organized to provide foster homes that were ethnically and racially compatible for the children who were to be placed. Another example of such conflict was the placement of Native American children with white families without the approval of the chief of the tribe, a situation that was resolved with the passage of the Indian Child Welfare Act in 1978.

By 1980, children with special needs, including older children; children of color; children with physical, mental, and emotional problems; and children who are part of a sibling group, became seen as desirable candidates for adoption (McKinzie, 1993). They tended no longer to be perceived in terms of special needs. The shortage in supply of available children contributed to the increasing acceptability of transracial and international adoptions of infants and children.

In the 1950s a significant rediscovery of the battered child syndrome took place. A number of reformers, including medical professionals, psychiatrists, pediatricians, and radiologists codified an unrecognized social problem as child abuse. This concern had been first recognized by the Society for the Prevention of Cruelty to Children but was no longer actively pursued. The rediscovery of child abuse led to the removal of maltreated children from their families for placement in foster care. Some of these children will never be able to be reunited with their parents. In such cases the rights of the parents are terminated and the child becomes, or continues to be, a ward of the court and is freed for adoption. Many of these children have experienced significant early trauma contributing to developmental delays. Other issues of concern in working with these children are attachment difficulties and an inability to trust others. They will be seen as special needs children available for adoption.

State adoption laws vary and have been inconsistently applied by the courts, lawyers, and child welfare agencies (Rycus & Hughes, 1998). Attempts have been made to achieve uniformity in adoption laws. So far, fewer than 20 states have enacted the Uniform Parentage Act. Attempts still are being made to accomplish uniformity (Hollinger, 1991).

Shifts in values and practice are occurring across the United States related to the importance of "the best interest" of the child versus the focus on family preservation. Other incompletely resolved adoption issues include the desirability of disclosure and access to medical records of adoptees, search for birth parents by adoptees, and "open adoptions," which allow adoptees to know the identity of and have some degree of contact with their birth parents. Adoptions also are sometimes disrupted, and children must be removed from their adoptive homes and new decisions made about their best interest.

Health conditions that are new challenges in this field of practice include prenatal exposure to alcohol (fetal alcohol syndrome), children with substance abuse disorders, and children and adolescents with HIV and AIDS. Another major factor, as reported by the American Public Welfare Association in 1990, is a 28 percent increase in the number of children in foster care, which requires an increase in the availability of adoptive homes. Important positive steps in adoptions over time include the preparation of adoptive parents and the increased emphasis on providing postadoption services.

The establishment of the juvenile court system was essential to foster care as a part of child welfare. Socially sanctioned decisions had to be made about the care and well-being of children. The court provides a means of legal intervention in the lives of children that could support families. In relation to child welfare, courts are essential for the removal of children from their families, approval of treatment plans, timely review of progress, the return of children to their families (when possible), and for termination of parental rights.

Juvenile Courts and Delinquency

The New York House of Refuge, the first reformatory for juvenile delinquents, was founded in 1825 (Bremner, 1970). As reformatories were developed, educators joined in by developing special instructional facilities for juveniles with auditory, visual, and intellectual disabilities (Kanner, 1962).

Early courts were structured to establish guilt and to punish the guilty. In the beginning, delinquent behavior or dependency often resulted in imprisonment or being placed in an institution. In 1899 juvenile courts were established in Chicago and Denver. By 1917, 25 states had enacted legislation to establish juvenile courts, whose purpose was to identify children's problems and to plan and ensure compliance with remedial interventions.

Major policies and laws were influenced by decisions of the U.S. Supreme Court. State policies that had been developed were overturned as federal policies were created. Two significant cases, *Kent v. U.S.* in 1966 and *re Gault* in 1967, established constitutional rights for juveniles. Some of the rights established were due process to hearings on the matter of a waiver to a criminal court, entitlement to counsel, written notice of a scheduled hearing to children and their parents or guardians, the right to confront and cross-examine witnesses, and the privilege against self-incrimination (Mather & Lager, 2000).

After World War II, delinquency became a major concern (Wattenberg, 1994). The Juvenile Justice and Delinquency Act, which was passed in 1974, stressed prevention and treatment of juvenile delinquents. It provided for state grants to develop programs to strengthen the family, to serve delinquent youths, to provide alternatives to incarceration, and to support special education programs. Diversion and probation became a method of legal intervention. In 1992 the Act was amended to provide additional funds for more preventive programs for juveniles. The Runaway Youth Program made federal funds available for temporary residential care for runaway and homeless children. Funds were allocated according to the population under 18 years of age in a state. The funds are used for providing shelter, general operating costs, counseling, and staff training.

Violence is now a part of life for many youths in the United States. In 1990, 16.3 percent of the total number of arrests in the United States were youths 17 years of age or less. Of this number 5.5 percent were for violent crimes (Earls, 1994). More than 95,000 youths are incarcerated in the United States, an increase of more than 20 percent in less than a decade. Of these, 25 percent are crimes against persons. Earls (1994) found that violent incidents are increasing at a higher rate than nonviolent incidents for all racial/ethnic and socioeconomic groups. The proportion of adolescent murder victims killed with a gun increased from 66.5 percent to 72 percent. Weiner (1989) noted that most violent crimes are committed by persons 17 through 25 years of age, and that these acts are usually a culmination of long histories of nonviolent offenses.

Many studies have indicated that incarceration cuts crime. The Violent Crime and Incarceration Act, which was passed by the House in 1995, provided an incentive for states to keep incarcerated violent felons behind bars for a longer time. However, this approach considers violent and chronic offenders in the same category as persons who commit petty drug crimes (Dilulio, 1996).

Much of the underlying problem related to juvenile delinquency is beyond the control of the criminal justice system. A National Academy of Science study concluded that adults in poor neighborhoods differ in important ways from those in more affluent areas. A lack of good role models for adolescents and a far higher percentage of adults involved in illegal markets are significant neighborhood factors (National Research Council, as cited in Garfinkel, Hochschild, & McLanahan, 1996).

Homicide is the leading cause of death for youth 11 to 17 years of age in the United States. Earls (1994) reports that 40 percent of crime is committed in neighborhoods of extreme poverty. Not all poor neighborhoods are full of crime. Protective factors encompass resiliency, and, in comparison to nonresilient children, resilient children have easy temperaments, higher measured intelligence, are more autonomous, have a good relationship with at least one adult, and are more successful and involved in school (U.S. Congress, Office of Technology Assessment, 1991).

Social problems related to substance abuse, lack of affordable housing, homelessness, and environmental hazards pose difficulties for children now and in the future. In the search for ways of reducing violence, two controversial strategies considered are gun control and reducing the amount of violence that appears in the mass media. One concern of the public, to be decided in the courts, is whether children who murder should be tried and treated as adults or as juveniles.

The adequacy of conditions and services in juvenile facilities are of particular concern. The existence of deteriorating, overcrowded, and sometimes abusive conditions in such facilities in the United States has been a matter of grave concern (Becker, 1999). The U.S. Justice Department filed suit against the state of Louisiana for failing to provide adequate care in the state's juvenile correction facilities. Youth were alleged to be at substantial risk of harm from staff abuse as well as from other juveniles, and the state allegedly failed to provide incarcerated youth with adequate medical, mental health, educational, and rehabilitation services. Similar charges, which had been made in the past against Kentucky, Georgia, and Puerto Rico, have been resolved.

A federal district court in Connecticut ruled that, under the provisions of the Individuals with Disabilities Education Act, youth in juvenile detention facilities must be provided with a broad array of services. However, the court refused to specify which services must be provided. The decision must be made in regard to the needs of each child. This decision has national ramifications because the services to be provided are broadly defined (Becker, 1999).

Are juveniles best served by public facilities or should juvenile correction facilities be administered and managed by private companies? Are children's rights better protected in one type of facility than in another? In many states the questions remain unanswered. Although the origins of such facilities are in the public sector, in recent years some have been transferred to the private sector, with uneven results.

Conclusion

In reviewing social services for children and adolescents, clearly policies are fragmented and complex, and differing services may undermine each other, which makes it possible for youngsters to be denied care or receive inadequate care. Conflicts exist about the beliefs and values, and existence, causes, and interventions to be used in helping children. Social service provision becomes comprehensible within the context of history and major social policies. Furthermore, the application of policies must take into consideration cultures, communities, and families.

CHAPTER

2 Cultures, Communities, and Families

Social work practice with children and adolescents is characterized by diversity. Diversity adds to the richness of human experience and presents a challenge in regard to the understanding and tolerance of individual and group differences. Young clients, while similar to each other in characteristics such as age and age-related experience, may vary in regard to other sociodemographic characteristics, such as ethnic background.

The purpose of this chapter is to explicate how human diversity impacts social work practice with children and adolescents. Understanding by all concerned, practitioners and clients, is the key to humane, ethical, and effective practice. In this chapter, the importance of attaining an overall understanding of values, as related to the moral and character development of children, are emphasized. Religion and spirituality are described as factors in the development of children. The contemporary languages, acculturation, socialization, and competencies of children are also examined. Within a community context, the impact of family composition, structure, and interaction on the assessment and helping situation is reviewed.

Minority Children and Adolescents

For many young children home is a culturally homogeneous setting. However, some young children have culturally diverse families. Moreover, by participating in social systems and settings within society at large, that is, outside of the home environment, including day care and education, older children and adolescents often face the challenge of relating to persons whose cultural heritage and background differ from their own. Older children and adolescents may possess attitudinal barriers to social interaction with persons from diverse backgrounds. Such differences are often stimulating and enrich social interaction. Young children and adolescents may be curious about persons who differ from them in appearance or behavior.

Majority or minority background influences youngsters' participation in and perception of family members, practitioners, peers, and teachers, as well as their risk for social problems. A research study indicated that African American and Puerto Rican adolescents are primarily at risk for adolescent delinquency and secondarily at risk for substance abuse (Brook, Whiteman, Balka, & Cohen, 1997).

Social interaction varies according to the neighborhoods and communities in which children live. That is, some youngsters grow up in diverse and cosmopolitan urban environments in which minority and immigrant populations are large, whereas others develop in rural areas and small towns in which minority and immigrant populations may be small. Where children grow up influences their abilities as well as their attitudes toward persons of differing majority or minority backgrounds. A research study showed that children living in urban areas in Bangladesh had higher levels of basic competencies than did rural children (Mohsin, Nath, & Chowdhury, 1996).

The life experiences of majority and minority children tend to differ. Social workers consider the impact of race and ethnicity on youngsters. Whereas majority status usually provides a sense of self-esteem to children, minority status is usually a stressor, given its association with being the subject of hostility and prejudice (Tharp, 1991). A research study of adolescents who recently emigrated from China to the United States indicated that they were at a low level of acculturation and had a moderately high level of self-esteem (Yu & Berryman, 1996). Differential treatment tends to be accorded to children in conjunction with their majority or minority status. During crises, majority children are more likely to receive effective support than minority children (Moritsugu & Sue, 1983).

Majority and minority status is related to coping styles. Minority youngsters are at risk for developing ineffective cognitive coping styles. Therefore, there appear to be more challenges to treating minority children and youth effectively, particularly during times of crisis. Minority children experience the stress of being different from majority children. However, minority children may differ in ethnicity among themselves as well as from majority children. Minority children may experience stress and support from three sources: minority children of the same ethnicity, minority children of different ethnicity, and majority children.

Majority children are those youngsters whose ethnicity matches that of the dominant power in the country at the national level. As a consequence of demographic changes, the ethnicity of the dominant power will be in the numerical minority in the United States in the future. Moreover, regional variations exist. In some geographical regions, the ethnicity of the dominant power is the same as at the national level whereas in other regions it differs. Youngsters may experience such subtleties and complexities by feeling some mix of being a part of the majority and the minority.

Minorities are distinguished on the basis of history and settlement, which has implications for the education, achievement, motivation, and adjustment of children, particularly in school settings (Gibson & Ogbu, 1991). Children of more recent minority groups, who are likely to see that education leads to prosperity, tend to be involved and striving in school, often at the insistence of their parents, who may have a strong belief in the value of education and, in the United States, the American dream. Children of minority groups that have been in the country for a longer period of time tend not to be as motivated as children of minority groups which have more recently arrived. Children of less recently arrived minority groups, who may have had a longer period of experience being downtrodden or functioning as part of the underclass within the country, are less likely to see that education leads to prosperity, and tend to be withdrawn and hostile in school.

Furthermore, less recently arrived minority groups, namely indigenous minorities, have characteristic child and adolescent difficulties. For instance, due to much death and displacement, Crow Indian children tend to suffer chronic mourning and depression (Long, 1983). Moreover, as a consequence of many political, historical, societal, economic, interpersonal, and intrapsychic factors, African American male adolescents are at high risk for acting out and being depressed, poor, and alienated (Paster, 1985). However, African American families can buffer adolescents from the risks that are associated with growing up poor (Jarrett, 1995).

Immigration consists of processes of acculturation, which involves the child's adoption of new language and cultural patterns, and assimilation, which involves the extent to which the youngster is accepted into the host culture without prejudice or discrimination (Patel, Power, & Bhavnagri, 1996). Acculturation may be associated with well-being (Curtis, 1990). However, children who are visible immigrants, namely youngsters of color originating from Asia, Africa, and South America, may have difficulty in assimilating in Western countries (Sam, 1992).

Immigrant children are subject to many stressors. In the process of adjusting to new communities, social customs, and schools, they are prone to experience feelings of loss, depression, and alienation (Congress & Lynn, 1994). Their families may have been forced to migrate, due to ethnic conflicts, political turmoil, and civil wars in their country of origin. Following the inevitable difficulties faced in the new country to which they have immigrated, which relate to unmet expectations and difficulties in language, culture, socialization, and employment, to the surprise of many, some of those families migrate back to their country of origin.

The changes accompanying emigration challenge the adaptive capacity of families. Whereas parents are likely to maintain the norms and values of their country of origin, their children are quick to adopt the new mores. Such discrepancies in norms and values tend to engender parent–child conflict, which is actually an intrafamilial cultural conflict that is exacerbated by developmental factors. Roizblatt and Pilowsky (1996) recount, "When a Chilean father living in the United States told his 14-year-old daughter that 'we' do not let 'our children' date at that age, she simply replied, 'Now we live in a different country' " (pp. 517–518).

Social workers conduct formal assessments, including diagnoses of mental disorders, of children and adolescents of various cultural backgrounds. Limitations exist in generalizing the use of diagnostic instruments to other cultures. Given that the Diagnostic and Statistical Manual of the American Psychiatric Association (2000) appears to have more validity for American children than for children of other cultures, it poses a challenge for social workers to assess and diagnose youngsters from other cultures in the United States, as well as to diagnose non-American children who live in countries other than the United States (Krener & Sabin, 1985).

Child-rearing practices vary across cultures and normative practices in one culture have the potential to be misconstrued as psychopathology in another culture. Furthermore, certain approaches to practice tend to be more applicable in some cultures than in others. Patterns of traditional family structure and interaction, modes of child rearing, beliefs about childhood problems, and attitudes about the roles of doctors vary cross culturally. A study by Lieh-Mak, Lee, and Luk (1984) showed a culturally based reluctance of Hong Kong Chinese parents to be mediators of a behaviorally oriented therapy approach. Indeed, it has been recognized that practitioners who want to use behavior therapy approaches in parent training, which has been an effective means of intervening with children who have externalizing problems such as aggression, must begin to take into account the effect of the cultural context and values on parenting (Forehand & Kotchick, 1996).

Values, Morality, Character, and Religion

Social interaction between practitioners and young clients is influenced by many factors, including their cultural background, ethnicity, gender, age, education, and social class. Hans and Rowena were practitioner and client, respectively. They both were middle-class Mennonites. Hans's values were relatively stable and Rowena's values were forming. Hans was a middle-age adult male who had completed graduate school whereas Rowena was a preadolescent female entering middle school. They met to help Rowena with several transitions in her life, including the divorce of her parents and her entry into a new school.

Children and adolescents, their families, and their communities vary in their tolerance for diversity. Foster parents, whose religion often differs from that of their foster children, can examine their religious beliefs and consider how they would help such children meet their religious needs (Schatz & Horejsi, 1996). Some youngsters learn to fear or dislike those whose backgrounds or physical characteristics vary from their own. George, a young client, grew up in a small Southwestern town. All the people he had met in his life were Christians. Therefore, when he and his parents came in to the local mental health clinic for an initial screening session with Sue, a woman whose head was covered and who wore a long-sleeved robe, he felt uneasy. Sue sensed her young client's discomfort and immediately attempted to put him at ease.

Social workers' attempt to understand the children and adolescents who are their clients is an important component of the assessment process and is vital in building rapport with them. In attempting to understand their clients, practitioners frequently have to operate on the basis of incomplete information. The focus of social work practice with children and adolescents includes changes of thoughts and actions, but perceptions and attitudes also play a role in working with youngsters and may be the focus of change efforts. Social workers may obtain a glimpse of one or more aspects of the values, preferences, or attitudes of their child clients. The values of professional social workers develop through a course of education and professional socialization. Although for social workers tolerance is a professional value, which is sometimes shared by young clients and their families, it is important for practitioners to tolerate clients regardless of their ability to tolerate others.

Some social workers serve young clients who are referred to them for antisocial actions that reflect intergroup conflict and tensions. Andy was a young client who had participated in the youth section of an organization that had been implicated in attacks on minorities, including the firebombing of African American churches. After a visit to the family in their home, Joanne, the social worker, understood that Andy's views were similar to those of his parents. Andy's parents divorced when he was 3 years old, and he spent much of his time with his mother, who once had been imprisoned for participating in an armed robbery. Joanne's liberal views made it difficult for her to find a common ground with which to communicate with Andy and his family. In tandem with other professionals, including a social worker and a nurse who also were troubled by Andy's views and activities, Joanne used an ecological approach, working with a variety of social systems impinging on the life of Andy.

The values of children and adolescents are intrinsic aspects of their moral and character development. Although values and moral and character development may be analytically distinct, in reality they are integrally and inextricably tied together within the individual child. Alex was a child who appeared to have little superego, or moral, religious, faith, and character development. He had been referred to a social worker after a neighbor complained to authorities that he had been cruel to neighborhood animals. His parents reported being surprised by such activities.

Schools and communities are increasingly turning to issues of character development in an attempt to counteract the risks of violence among adolescents. The principal of a Western school decided to post the Ten Commandments within each classroom. This action was approved by the majority of classroom teachers. However, a parent of one third-grader protested the action, which was ultimately appealed by the American Civil Liberties Union.

Moral and character development are related to personality development. Youngsters who are lacking in socially acceptable types and levels of character development also have the potential to develop an antisocial personality. Such youngsters are more likely to engage in aggressive acts that infringe on the rights of others and cause harm to society. Many of these youngsters have had early abusive relationships with caregivers. They may be charming and manipulative at times while being unable to form a helping relationship. It is very difficult for practitioners to engage such youngsters in treatment.

Anthony savored his meetings with his social worker at the juvenile correctional center. He enjoyed making her cry as he regaled her with tales of his impoverished upbringing. He embellished some of his stories to a considerable degree. However, he believed that she was the key to him leaving the institution and was determined to get her on his side. He even tried to form a love relationship with her, as had Matthew, his best friend at the center. However, none of these strategies seemed particularly effective until one day when he was visited by a student with whom he walked out of the first set of locked doors of the institution before the social worker realized what had happened.

Conscience development among children includes the incorporation of parental values, the development of a sense of guilt at wrongdoing, the ability to inhibit destructive impulses, and the development of morality (Rose, 1999). Lack of proper conscience development is associated with noncompliance, antisocial behavior, and conduct disorder. Work with parents has increasingly been seen as an important means of helping youngsters who lack proper conscience development. Conceptual schemes of the moral development of youngsters involve the consideration of hypothetical situations. Moral development, particularly among females, is related to the development of interpersonal relationships and is also situationally based.

Social workers deal with social issues that have moral aspects. To form a rapport with clients, social workers tend to take a nonjudgmental approach. Social work does not easily promote the moral and character development of young children. Families and communities often are challenged to provide guidance to children and adolescents. Many schools are overburdened with other roles and responsibilities and may not readily be able to address such challenges.

Religious and spiritual values and issues are significant factors in the lives of many young clients and their families (Shor, 1998). The attempt to understand the diverse nature of American society and the influence of cultural variables on the effectiveness of social work practice with diverse ethnic and racial groups, who form the clientele of social work, is increasing. Moreover, the role of religion and spirituality have become more prominent in direct social work practice with children and adolescents.

Frequently, religion is of comfort to young people. Research evidence indicates an inverse relationship between religion and distress in adolescents (Mosher & Handal, 1998). Adolescents' concerns about religion are shaped by their ability to comprehend abstractions. Interest in ideology tends to be pronounced during adolescence. Adolescents often struggle with such issues as whether God exists and, if so, how this can be known. The development of faith in youngsters has normative developmental aspects that encompass a progression of stages involving the conceptualization of, consideration of, and belief in God.

Religious issues are often the focus of adolescents' peer discussions. However, religious discussions and beliefs do not necessarily prevent all acts of violence. Anne was a member of a prayer group at the high school in her small Southeastern town. Adults in the town and well beyond its borders were very surprised when a member of the prayer group came to school one day toting an assault rifle. A violent incident ensued that took the life of Anne and three other high school students.

In adolescent psychosocial development, religion is linked to identity formation through fidelity, which is characterized by commitment (Markstrom-Adams, Hofstra, & Dougher, 1994). Fidelity and identity commitment appear to be greater among religious minority adolescents and among adolescents who frequently attend religious services. World religions underlie social relations and child development. The values of Confucianism are part of the consciousness of Koreans and may be observed in hierarchical social relations, such as those between parents and children (Park & Cho, 1995). Confucian values also underlie the nature and structure of the Chinese family (Hamilton, 1996).

Freedom of religion, an essential aspect of democracies, is limited in autocratic societies. Despite years of repression of religion in the former Soviet Union, research indicates that adolescents were able to maintain their religious and ethnic identity, including thoughts, feelings, and actions (Zisewine, Schers, & Levy-Keren, 1996). Adolescents throughout the world maintain an interest in religion. A study of Dutch adolescents indicated a strong interest in religion and revealed convergence of views among those who were of different religious denominations, and even among those who described themselves as being believers and nonbelievers (Janssen, DeHart, & Gerardts, 1994).

In the United States, the average level of religiousness appears to decrease during adolescence (Donahue & Benson, 1995). African Americans and girls tend to be more religious than whites and boys, respectively. Furthermore, religiousness is positively associated with prosocial values and actions, and negatively associated with suicide, substance abuse, early sexual involvement, and delinquency. Religiosity can have a favorable impact on adolescent substance abuse (Corwyn, Benda, & Ballard, 1997) and adolescent criminal behavior (Benda & Corwyn, 1997) although it has been argued that its effects on the latter are limited (Benda, 1995). Stark (1996) suggests that a contextual effect posits a negative relationship between religious commitment and juvenile delinquency, except for findings from studies conducted with adolescents on the west coast of the United States. Indeed, Benda (1995) found similar effects of religiosity on delinquency in rural Arkansas, urban Arkansas, and Baltimore.

Two studies of Seventh-Day Adventist adolescents examined worship and social problems, as follows. One study of Australian adolescents showed that psychological adjustment, reduced alcohol consumption, less suicide, and increased religious faith were related to higher frequency of family worship (Strahan, 1994). Another study of American and Canadian adolescents indicated that children whose families either did not worship at all or who worshipped daily had high rates of substance abuse whereas those whose families worshipped moderately with high youth involvement had low rates of substance abuse (Lee, Rice, & Gillespie, 1997).

Many youngsters in the United States experience bicultural socialization. Such children and adolescents are in the process of becoming socialized within the mainstream culture as well as within their own ethnic culture. In some respects convergence occurs. However, often times value conflict occurs between American culture and other cultures. Segal (1991) depicted the family conflict between immigrant parents who uphold the collectivist values of the traditional Indian family and their American-born adolescents who engage in individualistic actions.

A research study of Indian families who immigrated to the United States indicated that fathers attempt to maintain continuity with the Indian culture while mothers tend to encourage North American characteristics in their children (Patel, Power, & Bhavnagri, 1996). George grew up in a strict home. However, when his family moved to the United States, he saw that other teenagers were able to stay out late and do what they wanted. When he came home very late one night, he and his father had a loud argument. George was ejected from the home.

Social work with children and adolescents in the United States has been in line with the individualistic Western value system. The effectiveness of universal and wholesale approaches to delivering services to children and adolescents of varying backgrounds may be increased through awareness and knowledge of such backgrounds. U.S. society is becoming increasingly diverse, which has also focused attention on issues of diversity as they affect social work practice with children and adolescents.

Social work with children and adolescents is conducted in sectarian and nonsectarian social agencies. Although the influence of religion is pronounced in sectarian agencies, they tend to serve children and adolescents from varying backgrounds. Many sectarian agencies pay explicit attention to religious issues. Moreover, nonsectarian or nonreligiously affiliated social agencies also encounter issues of whether and how to address religion, how to deal with differences in religion among staff and clients, what is the role of religion and its relationship to constructive citizenship and social interaction, and the prevention of social problems such as antisocial behavior and violence.

Religion and spirituality are a class of variables by which practitioners and their child or adolescent clients are characterized. Such issues may become more complex when youngsters come from families in which the parents are of different religious backgrounds. Additional complexity derives from situations touching on or related to religion, in which children or adolescents are treated by a treatment team whose members come from diverse religious backgrounds. Professional members of treatment teams are trained to minimize bias stemming from personal backgrounds, including religion. Nevertheless, religious background is part of the makeup of the professional.

Social work practice with children and adolescents should pay attention to religious background. A tenet of such practice is that all clients be treated equally regardless of background factors such as ethnicity, race, religion, and culture. Attempts to improve the process and outcome of social work with children and adolescents involve a consideration of matching practitioners with clients in the areas of religion, cultural background, ethnicity, gender, education, and social class. Of course, such variables may be similar or dissimilar between practitioner and client. Various combinations of practitioner and client characteristics may be effective.

Practitioners are often faced with the challenge of using the spiritual or religious beliefs of youngsters to facilitate their work (Aust, 1990). Moreover, such beliefs may be in harmony with and may support social work practice. Social work practitioners often need to accept child or adolescent clients who have engaged in activities considered immoral or unacceptable from a religious perspective.

Working with religious children and adolescents, and their families, differs from working with nonreligious clients. Nonreligious clients may have a variety of attitudes toward religion, ranging from professed ignorance to disbelief to antagonism. Some children or adolescents rebel against their parents' beliefs and become either more religious or less religious than their parents. Some youngsters, particularly adolescents, may seek out or be drawn to other religions.

Religious and spiritual beliefs of clients sometimes contrast with social work values in defining the nature and resolution of the social problems of children and adolescents. Whereas social workers are unlikely to proceed from the notion that the difficulties of children and adolescents stem from religious or supernatural reasons, family members of children and adolescents, and youngsters themselves, may hold such views. Indeed, they may even believe that they are "bad" or have done something to deserve a "punishment" that they have experienced. What they may need, from a social work perspective, is an explanation, perhaps an alternative explanation, that is believable and acceptable to them, for what has happened to them or their children.

Many children and adolescents who come to social workers for assistance have experienced traumatic events. Religious beliefs may be useful to them, and their families, in coping with trauma. They may be faced with accepting difficult situations, situations for which perhaps everything that can be done has been done. They may feel that all that can be done is to pray and ask for divine intervention and assistance. As such, religious beliefs can provide youngsters and their families an element of hope. Anne had childhood leukemia and, although other children had been cured, unfortunately her chances of recovery were slim. Her social worker was grateful to have the assistance of the pastor, who provided additional comfort to the girl and her family.

Adolescents who are interested in religious issues frequently use the framework of the religion with which they are raised as their frame of reference. Some youngsters of course stay with their family's religion and may become either more religious or less religious in regard to observance and belief than their family is. Occasionally, adolescents dabble in spirituality and avoid "organized religion." Their motivations may include one or more of the following factors: a desire to find a common bond with youngsters of other religious backgrounds, a sense of rebelliousness, and a questioning of social institutions and authority. Some adolescents rebel against their family's religion, morality, and codes and standards of conduct and behavior. Some adolescents find comfort in others' religions. Members of religious minorities may be intrigued by or proselytized by other religions. Some adolescents who are spiritually bereft and lost may join religious cults. Social workers may have a reparative role to play with adolescents who joined cults and then attempt to reintegrate into society.

The religious and spiritual beliefs of social workers can facilitate practice with children and adolescents. The advantages include a feeling of kinship with spiritual or religious youngsters, which may improve rapport. Thus, practitioners may readily identify with and understand their clients' struggles to deal with religious and spiritual issues, as well as provide a framework for how to deal with discrepancies between religious and moral ideals on the one hand and human frailty, tragedy, and evil on the other. Oftentimes, such understanding transcends religious differences. Other advantages include the hope of the practitioner, a beneficent worldview, and an interest in the social welfare of the client, stemming from religious and moral sources.

Practitioners who work with children and adolescents whose culture and values differ from their own have the challenge of resolving problems within the youngster's worldview (Holaday, Leach, & Davidson, 1994). Indeed, it is always difficult for people, including practitioners, to transcend their own particular worldview. A developmental factor exists as well. The practitioner must bridge the gap in extending understanding and resolving problems to children whose level of development is less mature, and may otherwise differ, from that of the practitioner.

Some children and adolescents are part of faith communities, such as the Amish and the Orthodox Jews, whose influence extends well beyond religion and encompasses most aspects of their lives, including family and education matters. Such communities tend to have their own systems for helping children and adolescents. Other school-age children have spiritual lives that are distinct from, although they may be related to, their religious lives (Coles, 1990). Indeed, one could conceptualize school-age children in regard to spirituality and religiosity. Kelly (1990) categorizes clients as follows: (1) religiously committed, (2) religiously loyal, (3) spiritually committed, (4) religiously and spiritually open, (5) superficially religious, (6) religiously tolerant and indifferent, (7) nonreligious, and (8) hostile to religion. Such a categorization scheme, which relates closely to content and practice, applies to children and youth. However, one must remember the developmental aspect of the thoughts, feelings, and commitments to religion that children and youth tend to have at an early stage.

Furthermore, Kelly (1990) categorizes how religion may be associated with issues in counseling. Four categories are (1) predominantly or specifically religious issues, (2) nonreligious issues with a significant religious component, (3) nonreligious issues with high potential for a religious and spiritual dimension, and (4) nonreligious issues with little apparent or close connection with the religious dimension. Social work practice with children and adolescents had for many years emphasized the latter category. However, a contemporary interest is exploring religious issues and considering counseling issues in regard to religion.

Along with psychotherapy and counseling, social work practice with children and adolescents is a value-laden process (Grimm, 1994). Bishop (1992) offers seven guidelines for using religious values. One, help clients feel that their religious values are an accepted part of the helping process. Jody was an adolescent who, after a period of alcoholism and drifting away from her studies, had reaffirmed her faith and her belief in God. Marilyn, her social worker, was not a very religious person and indeed was somewhat skeptical about persons who had "found religion." Nevertheless, Marilyn saw that spirituality helped Jody cope with her stressful family life, the changes associated with adolescence, and the demands associated with her school.

Two, view religion as part of the solution, rather than as part of the problem. Frank, an adolescent with paranoid schizophrenia, believed that Simon, his social worker, was a priest. Simon was surprised because his religion did not encompass the priesthood. However, he recognized that his own manner and appearance might appear to be priestlike to a member of another religion. Moreover, Simon understood that Frank came from a religious home and was a religious adolescent. Simon also understood that, along with medication and other approaches used by a team in the mental health clinic where he worked, religion was to be a means of communication, a metaphor, and perhaps even a method of arriving at a way of managing the youngster's serious mental health problem.

Three, become more educated about cultures, religions, values, beliefs, and practices. Abigail was a social worker who grew up in a small west Texas town. She had little contact with members of any religion and culture other than her own. When she moved to Houston, she was astonished at the diversity around her. She was intrigued about how the families lived and attempted to learn more about them in her family service agency position.

Four, become involved on community and professional levels with persons from diverse cultures and a variety of religious views. Heloise, a practitioner, was fascinated by people of other cultures and religions. She decided to form an interfaith social services committee at her church.

Five, explore your own religious values. Frank, a social worker, had dabbled in Buddhism. However, after many years he decided to explore his own Catholicism, from which he had rebelled in his own tumultuous adolescence.

Six, consider the implications and consequences of resistance for clients regarding religious issues. Mary was supervised in her clinical work by Anton, who attended an extensive workshop on supervision and religious issues. Anton began to discuss Mary's work with adolescents in regard to their spiritual, moral, ethical, religious, and faith development. Mary began to see that whenever clients began to discuss such issues, she abruptly changed topics.

Seven, learn to communicate in a straightforward manner about your religious views and your clients' religious views. Angelica worked in a sectarian social service agency helping families of troubled teenagers. Her discussions of faith were straightforward and uncomplicated. In interagency discussions with other social workers, Angelica soon realized that such issues were complex.

Languages and Acculturation

In the United States, many people assume that English is the only language children and adolescents, and their families, need to speak. Consequently, the education of children and adolescents has been in American English, and youngsters, whatever their ethnic origins, have learned it.

However, some children and adolescents living in the United States have a language other than English as their first language. In large urban areas immigrant populations of youngsters speak dozens of foreign languages. Many such children are likely to speak Spanish. Furthermore, many non-Hispanic children and adolescents residing in metropolitan areas with large Hispanic populations have a modest command of rudimentary Spanish.

Social workers who want to work with Hispanic children and adolescents, and their families, also benefit from knowing Spanish. Some social agencies employ practitioners on the basis of their language ability.

Children and adolescents, and their families, who have the opportunity to express themselves to social workers in their first language ("mother tongue") have the advantages of a command of the language and comfort in its use. If their first language is other than English, the clients may look toward one another, the worker, or a translator for help as they struggle to express themselves clearly in English and search for the nuances of language and meaning. The clients are likely to be aware of and uncomfortable about the fact that they are not communicating in English as well as they would in their native tongue. It is the role of the social worker to understand the situation, convey an understanding, provide support, and also attempt to comprehend the client communication.

In immigrant families it is likely that members have different levels of language, communication, and culturally based social competency. Often, children and adolescents learn English from their peers in school and community settings who have better language skills, thus providing a different balance of skills and power within such families. Tilting this balance in the direction of the younger generation may be acceptable in some families yet threatening to very traditional families. In such circumstances, one family member often functions as the translator in communicating with the social worker. However, in circumstances in which language is not shared, the practitioner may rely on translators and pay more attention than is customary to nonverbal communication.

Bilingual and bicultural social workers are in a good position to bridge the language and culture gap for children and their families. The bilingual social worker in the United States may ably communicate with clients whose first language is not English but whose second language is English. Referral to another practitioner, with greater proficiency in the language of the client, may be made by a practitioner with limited non-English language proficiency. The referral process must be handled smoothly to minimize the potential introduction of any feelings of rejection that may arise in association with the reason for the referral. Ideally, clients are assigned to workers who understand their language, thereby minimizing feelings of rejection or other factors related to termination or ending treatment with that worker.

As a nation of native persons as well as immigrants from throughout the world, the United States is a highly diverse society. About one out of four U.S. citizens is a member of one of four ethnic minority groups. Twelve percent of the U.S. population are African American, 9 percent are Hispanic or Latino, 3 percent are Asian and Pacific Islander, and 1 percent are Native American (U.S. Bureau of the Census, 1992). Many children and adolescents who are members of ethnic minority groups are potential or actual social service recipients.

Some children and adolescents who are members of ethnic minority groups are native born and others have immigrated. Both learn the ways of majority culture to participate in the larger society. However, their paths of potential or actual entry into the majority culture vary. Native Americans tend to be resistant to assimilation and integration into the majority culture (Herring, 1989). African American adolescents have a complex challenge in attempting favorable resolution of their identity crisis due to their acculturation patterns (Peretti & Wilson, 1995). Children and adolescents vary in regard to the extent to which they want or need to maintain their native cultures and adopt the majority culture. A study of adolescents who emigrated from the former Soviet Union to the United States indicated patterns of coping with identity issues that were labeled *clinging, eradication, vacillating,* and *integrating* (Berger, 1997).

The family is the chief social agent through which youngsters' adjustment to immigration occurs (Ben-David, 1995). The extent to which immigrant parents accept the prevailing culture impacts their children. A study of predominantly Asian immigrants indicated that children of parents who accepted the majority culture scored higher in social competence than children of parents who did not accept the majority culture (Pawliuk, et al., 1996). Furthermore, many of the children who were reported to have major behavioral problems had rejected their ethnic culture.

In seeking entry into the majority culture, immigrant children and adolescents are faced with many obstacles, including discrimination and lack of understanding from the majority group as well as from other minority groups. They may have special difficulties and social service needs. Native-born groups have special problems in regard to their relative poverty and powerlessness compared to the majority culture. Immigrant groups may have particular problems in regard to acquiring the language, values, and mores of the majority.

The rate at which immigrant children and adolescents become acculturated to the majority culture depends in part on their prior and current level of exposure to majority cultural influences. Indeed, American culture has a worldwide influence, which is present through media, music, food, and clothing, all of which are likely to appeal to children and adolescents. Youngsters who immigrate at an age when they experienced such culture while overseas may more readily accept it on arriving in the United States.

The extent to which youngsters come from families that accept the majority culture is related to the reasons for their immigration. The push versus pull phenomenon, or voluntary versus involuntary emigration are the dynamics that underlie the acceptance of a new culture. Parental attachment to the culture of origin, and parental interest in and ability to accommodate the new culture, also influence the acculturation and adjustment of the children. Youngsters who immigrate with their families acculturate along with them within their new society. A research study of adolescents whose parents had emigrated from the Indian subcontinent to England showed that, in particular, girls had positive attitudes to the adoption of English norms, and Hindu and Sikh adolescents had high levels of acculturation (Ghuman, 1997).

The cultural values of Western societies tend to be individualistic and competitive. Children who are raised in one Western society may find it easier to accommodate living in another Western society. However, children who are raised in more cooperative societies, such as Mexico, may experience culture and value conflict on entering more competitive cultures. They may have a difficult time in school and community settings. Children and adolescents raised in more cooperative cultures tend to try to get along with and be part of their peer group, rather than standing out as individuals who are striving to achieve. Such cultural differences present conflict situations for youngsters that ultimately may result in intervention by a social worker.

As the youngest of six children, Jorge had learned to get along with the members of his immediate and extended family. Jorge, who wanted to do well in school, usually managed to succeed academically. Moreover, he felt he had to get along well with the other children in class. When he was not doing well in his final year in high school, his family did not understand, particularly because in Mexico he had done as well as all the other children. The school social worker and a Mexican American colleague mediated the situation both at home and at school to improve the family's and school's understanding of Jorge and his culturally related school difficulties.

The problems of immigrant adjustment and absorption are especially evident during adolescence. Such problems may affect youngsters who immigrated during childhood and now have reached adolescence, as well as those who immigrated during adolescence. Although many families experience turmoil during the adolescence of their children, immigrant families have special difficulties. According to Baptiste (1993), immigrant families tend to experience five common transitional problems that impede their relationships with their adolescent children.

One, immigrant families who move from one culture to another tend to experience changes in familial and generational boundaries. In their home country and in the United States, the Y family had been one large multigenerational family living together. However, they felt that it was strange that many grandparents in the United States rarely lived with the rest of the family. They began to wonder whether something was wrong with them or with "those crazy Americans."

Two, immigrant families are likely to experience a lessening of parental authority. In Sarah's house the family was accustomed to her father being the boss. Although Sarah's parents restricted her from visiting people who were not her relatives, occasionally she visited other children's homes and realized that their fathers did not always have the last say. As Sarah approached adolescence, she began to speak out and talk back to her father. Her father reacted to the change in his daughter's actions with rage. Her mother became concerned about the safety of her daughter.

Three, immigrant families often fear losing their children to the new culture. Ahmed had come along with his family on a yearlong trip to the United States while his parents were students at school and working. Although the family originally planned to return to the Middle East after the year was completed, they had mixed opinions about when to return to their homeland. During the year, Ahmed developed a taste for fast food and American toys. Moreover, he no longer seemed interested in eating the native dishes that his parents continued to prepare for him and his sister. His parents confided that perhaps it had been a mistake for them to come to the United States.

Four, immigrant families are unlikely to be prepared for the extraordinary degree of change and conflict that usually accompanies immigration. The J family were fairly well adjusted in their native country. However, to their surprise, they began arguing vehemently a few months after arrival in the United States. Ms. J wished to return to her native country and was tearful much of the time. Mr. J disliked his native country and wished to forget about it. He avoided mentioning it in their conversations. Eight months later, Ms. J returned to their native country with their children whereas Mr. J stayed. At that point, Mr. J spoke to a social worker about schooling, the marital situation, and child care.

Five, immigrant families often experience extended family enmeshment and disengagement problems. Indira came from a very large and very close family. Family meant everything to her. Even her most distant cousins were among her closest friends. When Indira and her immediate family immigrated to the United States, her extended family longed for and planned her return. However, as the years passed, they realized that Indira might indeed stay in the United States, a phenomenon that they had seen before among other people in their small town but had yet to accept. Members of Indira's family came to visit her in the United States. However, they did not feel as close as before she had emigrated.

Large differences exist within and between cultures. For instance, Native American children and adolescents have intertribal, interclan, urban-traditional, and individual differences (Everett, Proctor, & Cartmell, 1983). Furthermore, generational differences tend to be pronounced in many cultures. Also, certain cultural groups, such as Hispanic Americans, have many subgroups, including Cuban Americans, Mexican Americans, and Puerto Rican Americans.

Learning about cultural differences and becoming acculturated, which involve both cognitive and experiential aspects, are long-term processes. Learning about another culture encompasses language and cultural learning, including knowing various norms and behaviors considered acceptable in another culture. To relate effectively to children and adolescents, and their families, from another culture requires an ability to enter, become a part of, and accept that culture.

David had clients from Puerto Rico. After a period of time he learned some Spanish, and developed a fond appreciation for the native cooking, to the point that he preferred it over the diet on which he had been raised. His willingness to join his Puerto Rican clients for a meal they prepared fostered a closeness between them, which furthered his work with them. His Puerto Rican clients considered him to be one of them, and invited him to participate in Puerto Rican cultural events.

Knowledge about the ethnicity of child and adolescent clients, including their racial, ethnic, and religious affiliations, is helpful in understanding and knowing how to work with them. It will also be useful for practitioners to understand the impact of such factors on the child's development, experiences, and identity. Sometimes the ethnicity of the practitioner and the young client are similar. When practitioners share the same ethnicity as the client, they may assume that their beliefs and values are in accord (Maki, 1990); however, they must also be aware of potential differences between them. Factors such as how many generations one's family has lived in and been acculturated to a country, society, and culture, as well as geographical or regional factors, can be a source of differences between practitioners and clients. Moreover, ethnicity is but one of many sources of beliefs and values.

When the ethnicity of the practitioner and the client differ, Parson (1993a, 1993b) advocates that practitioners share personal information about themselves and their background with their clients as a way of reducing the gap. Practitioners may share information about their heritage, interests, and family. Such an approach may be particularly apt in working with youngsters who may be curious about who the practitioner is and how the practitioner lives. Such steps can promote rapport between them.

Socialization

Although children are unique individuals, socialization provides a commonality to their experiences. Traditionally practiced in settlement houses, socialization has been an important approach in social work practice with children and adolescents, and their families, and has been especially useful in working with immigrants.

Children and adolescents become socialized through participation in group activities in social institutions. Several components to socialization exist, namely the extent and ways to which youngsters are already socialized both to another culture and to the new culture; the extent and ways to which they wish to and are capable of becoming socialized to the new culture; and the characteristics of the ultimate or end goal of socialization.

Socialization encompasses the acquisition of culturally specific social and conversational skills and competencies. Socialization, a normative social process that occurs among children and adolescents, is facilitated by social workers through two sets of means. One set of means includes cognitive, behavioral, educational, and social skills training that provides direct didactic instruction and vicarious or simulated social experiences, as in role plays. Another set of means includes arranging for youngsters to participate in social activities in the new environment that will provide them with socializing experiences.

How youngsters think about others and social situations is an indicator of their socialization. Cognitive factors include youngsters learning how to think like others in the new culture so that they can then act in accordance with and respond to socially relevant situational demands. Cognitive factors involve the development of five interpersonal-cognitive problem-solving (ICPS) skills within a social environment (Shure, 1994). One ICPS skill is the sensitivity to the existence of an interpersonal problem, which can be challenging as socialization encompasses learning new social rules. Andy was friends with another youngster. However, he never noticed that at some point his friendship was not as lively as it used to be. It was only after the other boy was no longer friendly with him, that he realized something was not right.

Two, means–ends problem-solving thinking involves the application of knowledge of how to put a particular social plan into action. Mary wanted to be friends with another girl. The following day during her morning recess at school Mary asked her to come over to her house.

Three, alternative thinking encompasses some flexibility on the part of children and adolescents. George wanted to ask Sue on a date. When she said that she could not visit him in his house, he thought of asking her to a movie.

Four, consequential thinking entails some experience within a new social environment. It is the skill of thinking what the results might be of implementing certain decisions and actions within the social environment. Marie wanted to join a club at her middle school. However, she realized that if she asked the girl who was the president, her chances of being accepted would be less than if she asked the girl who was the treasurer.

Five, among older children and adolescents, the ability to be aware of the reciprocal nature of social interaction, is a relatively sophisticated skill. It calls up the limits of one actor within a particular social interaction, as well as the notion of social ambiguity. Marco realized that if he was friendly with the boy in his neighborhood who had a motorcycle, the boy might be friendly with him.

Socialization is directly related to the goal of promoting the social and emotional development of children and adolescents. Furthermore, as youngsters develop emotionally, they develop socially, and vice versa. Social and emotional development are also tied in to culturally based competencies. Socialization encompasses social knowledge and its application, so that youngsters know to what extent which emotions are experienced and displayed within particular social situations. Jon had always been an expressive child. However, he learned that Americans in his town did not particularly embrace whooping and crying in large crowds. Social and emotional development are tied to cognitive and behavioral development. Through social learning processes involving observation, imitation, and modeling, children and adolescents normatively develop their abilities to interact within social settings.

Socialization encompasses learning how to live within families and how to get along with others. Many child and adolescent clients come from families that experience high levels of conflict. Often, such youngsters have difficulties in coping with conflict, and their means of resolving conflict are aggressive, violent, or otherwise socially unacceptable. Many young clients have witnessed violence or experienced abuse at home, which provides them with a powerful example of a destructive means of coping with stress and conflict that they may be prone to imitate. Although social learning occurs largely through youngsters' direct involvement with others, the role of technology, including television and the Internet, is also a factor. Such mediated socialization can also impact on the youngster's social and emotional development.

Social workers use social learning processes of observation, imitation, and modeling to influence the socialization of children and adolescents positively. Practitioners provide models with whom youngsters may identify. For ethnic minority populations, modeling is usually most effective when the model is of a similar ethnic grouping (Costantino & Malgady, 1996). Such models have successfully overcome the difficulties they experienced. John was an adolescent who had been socialized into the path of a delinquent. However, he was successful in becoming resocialized as a law-abiding youth who had plans to develop a career in law enforcement. He consented to serve as a model for a residential treatment facility.

Socialization encompasses the ability of children and adolescents to interact with younger children, peers, older children, and adults. Frequently, young clients have developed their social skills to a greater degree with one age grouping than with another. Chris was in middle school and his closest friend was a neighbor who was in elementary school. Chris was more comfortable playing with children who were much younger than himself; he had no peer friends. His mother was concerned about his present and future social life.

The relative impact and influence of parents and peers upon child development has been a matter of debate. Scholars have posited that family members other than parents, and other children, may have a more important role to play in contemporary socialization than has previously been acknowledged. Furthermore, the relative importance of persons varies developmentally. For instance, it is well known that the influence of peers waxes and the influence of the family wanes in adolescence.

Socialization of children and adolescents occurs within family, school, and community settings. In each setting children learn how to cooperate and compete, although these elements are played out differently in each setting. In family settings, within the sibling subsystem, children learn to cooperate with their siblings in a mutually beneficial manner. However, they may compete for parental attention or, in some homes, even food! In educational settings children cooperate as members of the same class, grade, and school. However, they compete in regard to school performance, attendance, achievement, and popularity. In community settings, cooperation and competition occur in neighborhoods, clubs, athletic teams, and other social organizations.

The skills that youngsters develop generalize to family, school, and neighborhood settings. However, contemporary socialization is difficult when discrepancies exist between the norms and values of such settings. Esther was a youngster who was part of a religious community but attended a secular school. When she commented on the fact that other children in her school ate ham, her parents became distressed and considered pulling her out of the school.

Youngsters in urban environments usually have more opportunities for socialization than socially isolated youngsters living in remote rural areas. Youngsters in large families or who live next to kin tend to have greater opportunities for socialization than youngsters in small families or those who live far from kin. Opportunities to interact in social settings enable youngsters to develop their social skills. Of course, some youngsters who have ample opportunities to interact still do not develop their social skills to an adequate level. Youngsters who have social skills deficits require social skills training or interpersonal-cognitive problem-solving training to help them develop adequate levels of social competence.

Positive socialization provides youngsters with models who cope with developmental demands in a manner that is constructive to self and others. Alberta was a member of a religious family who lived in the inner city. Her neighborhood was one in which much crime and drug abuse was present. Alberta's mother functioned well despite having rheumatoid arthritis. Her grandmother had survived the loss of her husband at an early age. Her grandmother's triumph over adversity was a matter of pride to her, her mother, and her granddaughter.

However, some youngsters have models who cope with such demands in a manner that is harmful or destructive to self and others. Jason's father was recently diagnosed with a life-threatening illness. Moreover, he lost most of his money when a correction occurred in the stock market. He attempted suicide which did not succeed but which left him disabled and unable to work.

Contemporary socialization is made more difficult when children and adolescents are exposed to antisocial influences. Social workers help youngsters whose friends and acquaintances engage in illicit activities such as substance abuse. Given the difficulties of successful intervention in such situations, prevention strategies are advantageous. The stage of involvement in illicit activities is also a factor. All other factors being equal, youngsters who are beginning such activities may have more potential for being diverted from such a life than do other youngsters who are further down such a path.

Social work practice in such a situation inevitably involves working with corrections and law enforcement. Social skills development includes the ability to resist joining such a crowd or declining particular dangerous invitations and activities. Through gang work, the practitioner considers the potential for changing the peer group to make it more positive or constructive. Yet another option for youngsters in such a situation is joining another, more socially advantageous peer group, whose social rewards and enticements may draw the youngster to it.

The social systems perspective is useful for viewing the contemporary socialization of children and adolescents. Family factors include the closeness of the youngster to the family, the prosocial modeling available in such a setting, and the support it provides. School factors include the presence of prosocial, nonsocial, and antisocial forces. Community factors, which are broad and pervasive, are difficult for youngsters who remain in such a community to resist. Some geographic communities, and the schools therein, may have a greater preponderance of a certain type of activity, be it prosocial or antisocial, than do other such communities.

Social workers promote the socialization of children and adolescents at the societal level too. Inevitably, social workers exercise social control. Parenting and family interaction, as means of socialization for children, vary on the societal level. In societies that are high in control, such as Thailand and Jamaica, inhibition, peacefulness, politeness, and deference are encouraged (Lambert, Weisz, & Knight, 1989; Weisz, Suwanlert, Chaiyasit, & Walter, 1987). In contrast, the goals of socialization in the United States tend to be independence, competitiveness, and differentiation from the family. The actualization of such goals is seen in youngsters in the United States who are far removed, geographically and otherwise, from their families. Moreover, in Thailand and Jamaica, children and adolescents are often referred for "overcontrolled syndrome," consisting of fearfulness, sleep problems, and somaticizing, whereas in the United States, youngsters are often referred for "undercontrolled syndrome," consisting of disobedience, fighting, and arguing.

Cultural Competencies and Communities

Social workers who help children and youth from diverse sociodemographic backgrounds and characteristics are called on to demonstrate their cultural competencies. Practitioners are expected to be knowledgeable about the traditions, rituals, practices, beliefs, and customs of the children and adolescents they serve. For instance, Hispanic children and adolescents tend to grow up in a culture with an enthusiasm for personal interaction (Curtis, 1990).

It is feasible to attain knowledge of a broad range of cultures and to gather in-depth knowledge about a small number of them. The attainment of cultural competencies is aided by a sensitivity to multiple cultures. Knowledge about the characteristics and features of minority children and adolescents is developed by in-depth experiences working and living in ethnic minority communities. Some practitioners acquire life and professional experience with a number of cultures whereas others' experiences are within a more restricted cultural range.

Youngsters who are positively influenced by social workers whose ethnicity and culture differs from their own may develop an increased tolerance for diversity. Some youngsters relate to peers from diverse backgrounds in integrated schools, international schools, and within mixed geographical and residential communities. Some youngsters relate to people from diverse cultural groups within their own families too. When Jane's mother, who was Italian, died of breast cancer, her father remarried an Asian woman. Jane had difficulty understanding her stepmother and continued to mourn her mother's loss.

The concept of community implies togetherness and sharing. Several assumptions related to community guide social work practice with children and adolescents. Some youngsters and their families may have a difficult time finding their place within a particular geographic or identity community. Some children and adolescents are part of communities in which social problems are severe and impede their constructive growth and development. Other children and adolescents are more isolated and may lack community connections. Some youngsters, including adolescents, seek community. Adolescents, in pursuing their own identity and individuality, seek to find others with whom they can form community.

Furthering the community connections of children and adolescents, and their families, is an important goal of social work. One of the tasks of the social worker is to see to it that youngsters are embedded in or are part of communities that nurture and support their development. The influence of an individualistic value structure, the ascendance of secular values and decline in religious and spiritual values, the high rate of mobility, and the emphasis on the economy are among the factors that have contributed to the change in community in U.S. society.

Traditional communities have remained a feature of life in the United States. Children and adolescents participate in ethnic communities, whose members share an attachment to history, faith, and symbolism. Social work involves allowing youngsters to explore and validate their ethnicity. In religious communities youngsters share their religious views with others. Children and adolescents find solace in making friends with same-faith youngsters. Furthermore, modern communities influence social work practice with children and adolescents. Communities have changed in regard to their meetings and their means of expression. Virtual communities and technology are also part of this trend. Some youngsters seek community via the Internet.

Schools are communities in which young people seek academic and social camaraderie, which may extend beyond school boundaries. Some youngsters attend schools in their own geographic neighborhood, which has the potential to tie school and community settings more closely together. Other youngsters attend schools in other neighborhoods, which may open up a vista of opportunity to them, reveal a neighborhood similar to their own, or show them how less fortunate peers live.

Conclusion

Social work practice with children and adolescents is a helping relationship. Practitioners attempt to understand the culture of their young clients and simultaneously assess the extent to which young clients understand the social worker as a cultural being who delivers a helping intervention. Social work practice with children and adolescents occurs within a diverse world. Social workers practice with children from an array of social, ethnic, and racial backgrounds. Both minority and majority children are clients of social workers.

Children and adolescents vary in regard to their cultural competencies, including their ability to negotiate and understand other cultures. Ideally, they develop attitudes that are flexible and tolerant and allow themselves to value and appreciate other cultures. Some children who grow up in international or cosmopolitan environments learn to appreciate such cultures. Whereas youngsters may be alike in many ways, differences exist among them in regard to values, ethnicity, culture, language, and socialization. The practitioner's task is to bridge those gaps.

The development of children and adolescents encompasses the contemporary languages, acculturation, socialization, and competencies of children. Families and communities, which vary in composition, structure, type, and interaction, serve as the context for the development of children. Values, religion, and spirituality influence children's moral and character development.

CHAPTER

3

Contemporary Social Issues Affecting Children and Adolescents in Family Systems

Changing families are major sources of stress for young people. Marital separation and divorce and the formation of single-parent families and stepfamilies are central issues in the lives of many children and adolescents. This chapter illustrates the ties between family arrangements, distress, and well-being of youngsters. Furthermore, it illustrates how children cope with stressors.

Families as Social Systems

Social workers understand children and adolescents within their family contexts. A social systems view of the family provides a framework for analysis, assessment, and intervention. The family system includes the parent–child subsystem. Social workers improve the individual and joint functioning of parents and of children, improve the relationship between parents and children, and prevent a deterioration in the parent–child relationship.

Siblings comprise another subsystem of the family. The influence of this subsystem on the development of children is greater than previously recognized. Other family members can be important to the development of the child as well. To some extent, this depends on the type of family. For instance, in single-parent families, other relatives, such as grandparents, may have a special role.

Peers are present in neighborhood, community, and school systems. Although the influence of peers on the development of adolescents has been widely recognized, peers also contribute to the development and adjustment of younger children. Adults, especially teachers, also have a significant influence on the development and adjustment of children and adolescents.

Families live in locational communities. In urban environments, families live in close proximity. In supportive social environments, the opportunities for constructive child development are considerable. However, in impoverished social environments, their future development is at risk.

Rural practice tends to be generalist with few specialists readily available (Brownlee, 1994). Specialized diagnosis, assessment, and treatment in health care, mental health care, and education is usually more available in the urban environment than in the rural environment. Because of the scarcity of specialized local resources, rural practitioners often need to refer youngsters to geographically distant practitioners and clinics. Consultation with specialists is also usually available at a distance, and Internet access is likely to improve mediated opportunities.

Great distances are often involved in rural practice. Practitioners often spend a considerable amount of time traveling to observe and work with children and adolescents in family, school, and community settings.

The rural environment is characterized by isolation. Youngsters tend to have fewer opportunities to be socialized to a wide range of social environments than do children who live in an urban environment.

In rural settings, virtually all public and many private aspects of practitioners' lives are often known to clients and their families. Rural practitioners tend to be highly visible and have numerous overlapping, dual relationships with client families. Practitioners who work in a rural environment often have children who attend school and who are friends with clients. Although such relationships can humanize and enrich the experiential aspects of working with children and adolescents, and their families, they can also occasionally pose ethical dilemmas to the practitioner.

Practitioners who grow up in rural settings may be aware of and cope with the special features of practice in such settings. However, practitioners from urban areas may be surprised to experience such events in the rural communities to which they relocate.

Family Composition and Structure

People compose families in various ways; they get married, divorced, and remarried; and they give birth to, adopt, and provide foster care to children. The structure and process of how families are composed influences the youngsters who are part of them.

Much social learning occurs in families. Children and adolescents learn about love, marriage, sexuality, and human relationships. They also learn about power while growing up within their families (Simon, 1990). The power balance of the family partially depends on family composition and structure. Numbers of family members partially influence power balances. Some families, including two-parent nuclear families with one child, have more adults than children. However, other situations, as two-parent families with two children and single-parent/single-child families, involve an even balance between numbers of parents and numbers of children.

By definition, adult-centered families primarily focus on the needs and interests of adults, and child-centered families focus on the needs and interests of children. However, balanced families attempt to meet the needs and interests of all members. Some families are dysfunctional; that is, little attention is directed to meeting the needs and interests of its members. Family interaction is best understood within its cultural context (Kurtines & Szapocznik, 1996). Cultural and ethnic background affects marital and family interaction, communication, and functioning.

Family Types

Major changes have occurred in how families are defined (Pinderhughes, 1995). Indeed, a great diversity of family types currently exists.

Single-Parent Families

Youngsters who grow up in single-parent families are likely to have different experiences than children who grow up in two-parent families or extended families. Moreover, some children are more likely to grow up with one or both parents than other children are. Unfortunately, some children grow up for a period of time without a family of their own, be it nuclear, extended, or stepfamily. Many child clients are in families where parents are missing or deceased (Kranzler, 1990), mentally or physically ill or disabled (Beardslee, 1990), or neglectful or abusive (Johnson & Cohn, 1990). Some such children, however, may be adopted, and eventually become part of another family. Census data consistently indicate that the percentage of African American children up to age 14 who live without either one or two parents is at least twice as high as the percentage for white children (Ruggles, 1994).

Some of the differences between children who grow up in a single-parent family and those who grow up in a two-parent family relate to the lesser financial, temporal, and emotional resources usually present in a single-parent family (Rose, 1989b). The quality of the parental relationship, socioeconomic level, and quality and type of schooling also affect the growing child. Children may have difficulty securing adequate levels of acceptance from single parents who experience inadequate levels of support, guilt feelings, and lack of conformity (Simon, 1990).

Many single-parent families are female-headed families. Single-parent families are likely to be less affluent than two-parent families. Although many male-headed, single-parent families may have less economic difficulties than many female-headed, single-parent families, nevertheless single fathers often experience discomfort. A research study indicated that the discomfort of single fathers decreases as the number of years of sole custody increases, as their satisfaction with their social life increases, if they do not have a religious affiliation, as their income increases, and as their rating of themselves as a parent increases (Greif & DeMaris, 1990). Furthermore, discomfort as a single parent increases if single fathers' relationship with their children deteriorates and if visitation decisions are handled in an ambivalent manner.

Single-parent families often report their stigmatizing experiences to practitioners who work with their children. The stigma of divorce appears to be lessening, given the continuing effect of a high divorce rate and the rising number of single-parent families in the United States. Single-parent families, once very much a rarity, are now common, and in some geographical locales are the majority. Tony felt left out because all the other children in his fourth-grade class had two Christmas trees, and he only had one! His parents reassured him that he was loved as much as the other children in his class.

Whether and how many parents work in and out of the home and earn an income is also related to the availability of parents to their children. Latchkey children who grow up without parental supervision are vulnerable to experience accidents, have difficulty in completing their homework, and are lonelier than other children. In one-earner families, children are more likely to have a parent who is available to meet their needs as they arise than children in two-earner families. Furthermore, how much one-earner and two-earner families earn relative to their needs is yet another factor to consider in conducting an assessment of children and their families.

A distinction exists between earning a living and having a career. It sometimes requires a considerable amount of compromise and flexibility for parents to pursue two sets of careers and provide desirable levels of care and nurturance for their children. Frequently, dual-career parents are able to enlist family members and purchase child care from non-family members to supplement the care they directly provide to their children.

Stepfamilies

Stepfamilies, once relatively uncommon, are becoming the most common type of family in the United States (Pasley, Rhoden, Visher, & Visher, 1996). About three out of five first marriages end in divorce, and about three out of four people who divorce remarry (Bumpass, Martin, & Sweet, 1991; Norton & Miller, 1992). Despite their prevalence, and the possibility of support available from their prevalence, the difficulties in adjustment experienced by members of stepfamilies, including the children involved, remain considerable. Stepfamilies tend to be more complex than other family forms. The difficulties of integration and cohesion are multiplied in the stepfamily. Furthermore, the structure of stepfamilies is often less clear than the structure of biological families.

Four sets of issues have been identified regarding stepfamily integration (Pasley, et al., 1996). One, children who are part of two households are likely to experience boundary ambiguity (Jacobson, 1994). In joint custody arrangements children spend time in two family situations and have two sets of living arrangements, often experiencing some sense of wonderment about where they belong and even who they are.

Two, boundaries that distinguish the stepfamily from the previous marriage ought to be clear (Duran-Aydintug, 1993). The feasibility of establishing such boundaries depends on the nature of the present and the former marriages, and the circumstances of the divorce. Stepfamilies need to create new symbols, rituals, or practices that characterize their present family life.

Three, unresolved past family issues that emerge in the new marriage impede the stepfamily's efforts at integration (Clingempeel & Brand, 1994). Such issues, including feelings of resentment and disappointment are likely to be particularly strong in the early, formative phase of the new marriage. Awareness of such factors by the new family members, and the use of family life education by social workers, may be particularly valuable.

Four, the developmental stages of the children may be at odds with the life cycle stages of the marriage and stepfamily (Mandell & Birenzweig, 1990). For instance, the marriage may be new, yet the children may be adolescents. Such dynamics present challenges, particularly when family members feel that such situations are outside the norm.

The success of the remarried family or stepfamily is related to the resolution of the prior marital relationship, the influence of the parent who is living outside the stepfamily's home, coparenting, the mobility of children between homes, and the absorption of the new marital partner into the family (Morrison & Stollman, 1995). Given so many factors to resolve, it is no wonder that remarriages and the formation of stepfamilies are often more difficult than initial marriage and family formation.

Grandparent-Headed Families

The grandparent–grandchild relationship can be a precious one to both parties, particularly when the immediate family is changing or the parents are insufficiently supportive of the children. However, grandparents who want to be involved in the lives of their grandchildren are not always given the opportunity to do so when parents divorce. At times the noncustodial grandparents are innocent bystanders to the marital conflict that propelled the family into divorce; at other times they are involved in the conflict. The grandparents of the children of the noncustodial parent may lose their access to their grandchildren, which can be stressful to both the grandparents and the grandchildren. Grandparents have sued for visitation rights with their grandchildren.

Whether due to abandonment, substance abuse, imprisonment, ill health, or even death, parents are not always available to take care of their children. When parents are not available to carry out the parenting role and function, other family members, including grandparents, may provide care for children. The grandparent-headed or "skipped generation" family, is increasingly common in various sectors of U.S. society (Burnette, 1997). Although some grandchildren do well in inner cities, issues for grandchildren in inner-city families include developmental delays, undiagnosed learning and neurological problems, and anticipatory loss and abandonment (O'Reilly & Morrison, 1993). Variants on the grandparent-headed family are those families in which children join in as nephews or nieces or cousins.

Extended Families

Contemporary families are highly variable in form. Nuclear families, consisting of parents and children living together, tend to be bigenerational. Although extended families were the norm in Western society for many years, today bigenerational families are more prevalent than extended families. Many nuclear families tend to lack the buffers and resources that help extended families cope with life events. The nuclear family is but one family type, and the social worker is likely to see children from other family types too. Given the emphasis on the nuclear family as the norm, and the prevalence of stepfamilies, it may be difficult to conceive of other family types, such as larger, multigenerational families.

In some cultures extended families consisting of three or more generations living together are common. Asian cultures tend to emphasize the extended family and to consider the individual as part of the family (Chin, 1983). Native American families have traditionally been extended and multigenerational, although as values have changed a variety of family forms have come into existence (Herring, 1990).

Changing Families

Although some youngsters are fortunate in having a stable family, many children experience significant changes in the composition, structure, and functioning of their family.

Family changes vary in duration. At times, a family change that began as a temporary change, such as a marital situation, becomes permanent, such as a divorce. At other times, a family change that appeared to be permanent was temporary, such as a divorce followed by a reconciliation.

Families cycle through changes. Ernestine, who was born with a congenital abnormality, and Sylvia, who was born normal, were twin sisters. Their mother accepted Sylvia but had a difficult time accepting Ernestine. In the decade following their birth, the girls' parents divorced, reconciled, remarried, and divorced again. Eventually, their mother remarried. Their father, who retained custody of the children, remained a single parent who raised the children with the assistance of his own aging mother.

Family changes are first order and expected, or second order and unexpected. As experienced by the child, family changes are the result of loss or incapacitation of one or both parents because of physical or mental illness, abandonment, or marital separation or divorce. Family changes also occur as the consequence of child maltreatment and intervention by child welfare authorities.

Family change has objective or realistic elements and subjective or personal elements. Divorce is an actual event that affects the emotions of family members. In families, objective changes lead to subjective change. Objective family changes are often perceived differentially by family members, including children, based on their family role, chronological age, emotional maturity, and physical and mental health.

Marital separation and divorce is a major contemporary stressor and a significant source of disruption in the lives of many children and adolescents. Indeed, it may be conceptualized as an overlapping tri-stage process. The predivorce stage is characterized by marital conflict and the contemplation of divorce. Children may witness the enactment of family conflicts and are likely to feel the disagreements. Some children may wonder whether their parents will get divorced or, on occasion, whether they will be physically hurt.

The divorce stage incorporates the decision to divorce and its implementation. The decision to divorce, which is made by one or both marital partners, is sometimes arrived at suddenly or quickly. The decision may be explicit or implicit. At some point during this stage, children are informed about the decision. In some families the children are informed early; in others they may learn about the decision at the last possible moment. To some youngsters the information is a surprise or a shock; to others it is expected. For many children, divorce is an unpleasant and unanticipated event that, as much as it may have been thought of or even talked about, confuses them when it actually occurs.

The postdivorce stage involves the emotional accompaniment to divorce and the actual rearranged circumstances of living. In some cases it involves the formation of single-parent and blended families. The child is faced with the reality of a new life and new relationships, and it can be a difficult adjustment.

Divorce

Social and family arrangements are designed to support, meet the needs, and promote the well-being of children and adolescents. Legislation, social policies, schools, communities, and families can be protective of young people. When social and family arrangements are inadequate to take care of children and adolescents, social services are intended to fill the gaps.

Many youngsters are children of divorce. Indeed, it has been conservatively estimated that at least one out of three youngsters are directly affected by parental divorce (Furstenberg, Nord, Peterson, & Zill, 1983). Moreover, many schoolchildren are affected by divorce (Schreier & Kalter, 1990). Whereas in some schools relatively few children have experienced parental divorce, it has been reported that in some schools four out of five youngsters are children of divorce (Baruth & Burggraf, 1983). Indeed, in such schools, divorce is the norm. Furthermore, divorce is a topic of discussion by children in many schools.

Conflict within families, which sometimes escalates to violence and may culminate in divorce (Arnold & Carnahan, 1990), tends to be difficult for the children. In the past, many couples who today would divorce stayed together. Many couples with children who considered divorcing were deterred from doing so because of religious considerations, the stigma associated with divorce, the anticipated reactions of relatives, and the impact of the divorce on their children. Today, when divorce of couples with children is relatively common in the United States, the impact of the divorce on the children is less likely to be a consideration for many couples. Yet the question remains: What is the emotional impact of divorce on children?

Divorce dramatically changes children's lives, tending to frustrate them in their heartfelt desire to live with both parents. Of course, at times children can be close to and be nurtured by both parents after a divorce, yet the bitter feelings aroused by divorce tend to complicate children's emotional lives. Many children of divorce neither comprehend the divorce nor understand why it happened to them. Often, children of divorce question who was responsible for the divorce, wondering what their role was in it, and fear what will happen to them in the future.

Divorce is an emotional event for children. Subsequent to the shock of divorce, children often experience fear of the unknown, guilt, and loss (O'Brien, 1981; Reder & Eve, 1981). Also, many children tend to feel neglected (Segal & Segal, 1989) and helpless (Admunson-Beckmann & Lucas, 1989). Many children and adolescents feel responsible for and blame themselves for the divorce (Kostoulas, Berkovitz, & Arima, 1991). Children of divorce tend to feel that they are different from their peers, and sense that they are not compatible with others (Kurdek & Siesky, 1980a, 1980b). Children from divorced families experience anger at one or both parents, conflicting loyalties, neediness, fear of being forgotten or abandoned, vulnerability, loneliness, loss, sadness, shame about what happened to the family, an agitated identity due to the family change, and a wish that their parents would overcome the separation and reunite (Kanoy & Cunningham, 1984; Wallerstein & Kelly, 1976, 1980).

Divorce tends to interrupt normative family development and impacts the social and emotional development of children. It may result in the interference of a positive identification with the same-sex parent (Williams, 1984). In the most common divorce scenario, the father becomes less available to his children. At ages 5 and 6, children appear to be particularly emotionally vulnerable to the loss of a father through divorce (Williams, 1984). The practitioner is often faced with helping children make the transition, which is experienced as a loss, and helping families provide for the needs of the children. In some instances the practitioner serves as a temporary partial replacement for the lost parent. The practitioner helps find a temporary or permanent replacement, and tries to ensure greater availability of the noncustodial parent.

Children and adolescents differentially perceive and interpret family events, including divorce, in accordance with their own development. Children's perceptions of divorce are related to the impact of divorce, which varies with age and gender (Wallerstein & Kelly, 1976). Two years postdivorce, boys tend to exhibit more difficulties than do girls in controlling their impulses, more conduct disorders, and more difficulties in developing and maintaining friendships (Stolberg & Mahler, 1989). Furthermore, although 5 years after divorce the adjustment of most boys and girls is approximately equivalent, many boys continue to experience peer rejection. Boys are prone to develop problems early in the middle school years whereas girls usually demonstrate problems beginning in adolescence (Kalter, Schaefer, Lesowitz, Alpern, & Pickar, 1988).

Many school-age children in all socioeconomic strata experience parental divorce. Younger children, who are in elementary school, tend to be most vulnerable to the impact of divorce, and tend to demonstrate anxiety, asthma, depression, withdrawal, and poor school performance (Carlile, 1991). Younger children have fears concerning disruption of parental nurturance whereas older children and adolescents are more likely to be enmeshed in conflicts of loyalty between parents (Kaminsky, 1986). Indeed, during and following the divorce, many children experience a substantial reduction in the quality and quantity of parental attention and support (Kaslow & Schwartz, 1987). For instance, the first year following divorce is often marked by unsupportive, authoritarian, and erratic parenting (Hetherington, Cox, & Cox, 1979). Indeed, after a divorce, many women and men take about 3.5 years and 2.5 years, respectively, to regain their stability (Wallerstein & Kelly, 1979). Therefore, when divorce occurs, children are often subject to several years of unstable and ineffective parenting.

Divorce has become, and indeed remains, a widespread phenomenon. It is more accepted in the United States than it was a generation ago. What are the reasons for divorce? High expectations among marital partners and a lack of realism about the course of marriage appear to be partially related to the divorce rate. The discrepancy between what is real and ideal is a source of conflict in marriage and is one of many personal, interpersonal, and social factors that contribute to parental divorce. Few reasons appear to forestall divorce in contemporary strife-torn domestic situations. Although some frame divorce as a moral issue, it is a personal issue to be determined or resolved by the marital partners.

Currently, divorce, more than war or illness, is a primary reason for parent absence in the United States. Changes in social values in individualistic Western societies, such as the United States, have also contributed to the increasing acceptance of divorce. The ascendance of hedonistic and narcissistic approaches to life in such societies accompanies a corresponding acceptance of divorce.

Family structure has changed dramatically to encompass many forms; for many persons its ideal form is nuclear. Indeed, such a viewpoint is basically a romantic one. The role of the social worker is limited by the status associated with romance in marriage in the United States and the relative lack of acceptance for more pragmatic reasons for marriage, such as economic well-being, health, and a context for childbirth and child rearing. Unfortunately, nuclear families tend to be somewhat unstable. Single-parent families are becoming more prevalent in Western societies.

Divorce has physical and mental health, developmental, and educational consequences for children. Children of divorce are more frequently diagnosed as having serious illnesses than are children from intact families (Coddington & Troxell, 1980; Jacobs &

Charles, 1980). Children of divorce have more psychiatric consultations than other children do (Kalter, 1977, 1987). Thoughts of suicide and sexual promiscuity among children have been linked to divorce (Benedek & Benedek, 1979).

Divorce is a stressful change for families. Social problems often ensue as marital relationships become disrupted. Family conflicts, which often culminate in divorce, tend to interfere with the learning, achievement, and academic adjustment of children and adolescents in the school setting (Effron, 1980). The adversarial aspects of the divorce process directly influence children's adjustment (Saayman & Saayman, 1989). Divorce has the potential to impact negatively the self-concept and relationships of children and adolescents with their peers and teachers (Hodges, Buchsbaum, & Tierney, 1983; Parish & Wigle, 1985; Rozendal, 1983). Children of divorce tend to have more school adjustment and achievement difficulties than other children have (Pasternack & Peres, 1990).

Stress

Children and adolescents experience considerable transition and stress due to the reduction in social support that often accompanies parental divorce. Dramatic change and disruptions occur in such circumstances in children's relationships with noncustodial parents and other family members. Social workers identify and enhance sources of stability in the turbulent periods of children's lives. Subsequent to marital separation and divorce, the presence of a parent and siblings in the home are a source of continuity in the lives of children. Other sources of stability include relationships with other relatives, as well as friends.

Nuclear families tend to be prone to stressors that increase the probability of family conflict and divorce. Practitioners work with families that are at various stages of responding to stress. Practitioners see many children whose families are unable to cope well with the stressors they experience. Many referrals made on behalf of families with children reflect high levels of client stress, difficulties in coping, and the limitations of extant support services for families.

By definition, normative stress in children and adolescents varies according to their stage of development (Arnold, 1990). For many children, attending school not only brings many pleasures and rewards, it also brings with it concomitant concerns and pressures. School-age stressors contribute to fears of success and of failure, test anxiety, school phobia and other school fears, and school and community violence (Christie & Toomey, 1990; Sears & Milburn, 1990). Fear of failure tends to be more prevalent than fear of success. Test anxiety is common as children become aware of the consequences of high-stakes testing. Such anxieties can induce other physical difficulties. School phobia often keeps children away from school until the difficulty can be diagnosed and treated.

Violence, the ultimate expression of aggression and conflict, is the focus of prevention. Violence, including severe physical abuse, is expressed within marriages and families, and, as an intergroup phenomenon, appears throughout society in school, neighborhood, and community settings. Violence, which has been a longstanding threat in inner-city schools, is now widespread, often unpredictable, and a major concern in both middle and high schools. Exacerbating the concerns about school violence are the lethality of weapons that have been used by children and adolescents.

Individually or in combination, such stressors can be overwhelming for children and adolescents who lack adequate, readily available coping strategies and skills, self-confidence, and social support. Social workers help young people anticipate and cope with stressors (LeCroy & Rose, 1986).

Often, environmental manipulation and change are useful goals. Sometimes, environmental change is necessary to produce a less stressful social environment for youngsters. Social workers assess the extent to which the environment of children and adolescents is constructive, the costs and benefits to them of the present environment, as well as the anticipated costs and benefits to them of a projected future environment. On completion of the assessment, if and when the benefits clearly outweigh the costs, or the child is in immanent danger in the present social environment, moving the child to an alternative environment on either a temporary or permanent basis, is recommended in some instances, especially following supervision, and interprofessional collaboration and consultation.

Stressors Experienced by Children

Children and adolescents need an optimal amount of stress, a basic component of the life process, to thrive. Intervention to help youngsters cope with stress, often designated as stress reduction or management programs, are meant to help youngsters learn to recover from traumatic stress and reduce the sources of distress in their lives. However, intervention programs should also be designed to develop eustress, namely positive experiences that balance distress by bringing joy to the lives of children and adolescents. Such a philosophy can be shared with parents of children who seek help.

Stress is major or minor in regard to its impact on children. Furthermore, it varies in frequency, as well as in regard to its source. All children and adolescents experience minor, daily hassles. For most youngsters, such hassles represent no more than a temporary inconvenience. David, a middle-class child, attended a middle school with many poor children. After repeatedly being asked by a classmate to lend him a dollar, David came up with an effective reply. He said, "Hey, man, if I had a dollar, it would be in the corner store."

Stress is usually a precursor to anxiety when stressors are traumatic. Children who experience traumatic stressors are liable to develop anxiety disorders. Traumatic stressors are episodic or continual, which can increase their impact. Laura traveled by school bus in a large city along with other adolescents who were very unruly. One day a friend of hers was raped on the school bus. From that time, Laura had trouble sleeping at night and refused to go on a school bus. Consequently, her parents transported her to school. Her parents were thankful that her schooling was otherwise unaffected.

Children vary in their responses to stress. Some children, including youngsters who develop schizophrenia, are highly vulnerable to stress and require a considerable amount of help in learning how to cope with it. Most children cope with stress in a satisfactory manner. The nature and degree of their responses to stress are considered to be within an acceptable range by others. Preventive social work is aimed at further improvement of their abilities to cope with potentially traumatic circumstances.

Children differ in regard to their type and methods of coping with stress, as well as the consistency of their coping methods. Resilient children are highly resistant to traumatic stressors. They thrive in the most adverse circumstances, including wartime. Their ability to cope is awe-inspiring. Many children tend to use constructive, beneficial, and effective methods of coping with stress, including thinking positively, believing in themselves, and accessing support and help from family and friends. However, under circumstances of fatigue and illness, many children resort to harmful and ineffective methods, including engaging in self-defeating and self-denigrating self-talk as well as denying and avoiding others.

Children vary in their acquisition, knowledge, and application of cognitive, social, and behavioral skills for coping with stress. Cognitive coping skills build confidence and reduce anxiety. Social coping skills involve forming and maintaining supportive social relationships. Behavioral coping skills involve engaging in actions, including relaxation, to cope with stress successfully.

Although many children have a variety of means of coping with stressors, some children have a constricted range of methods. When Fabio became overcome by stress, he retreated to his room, locked the door, and listened to his favorite music for many hours. Despite the entreaties of family members to open the door and despite his inability to complete his schoolwork, Fabio would remain in his room.

Social workers assess the coping capacities of their child and adolescent clients. The assessment domains include the methods and effectiveness of their coping skills. Furthermore, social workers can help youngsters, particularly adolescents who develop ineffective or destructive means of coping, such as abusing alcohol and other drugs, develop more effective, constructive means of coping with stressors.

Stressors Experienced by Adolescents

Some stressors tend to be shared by children and adolescents. However, given differences in development and in the types of social situations they tend to encounter, children and adolescents vary in regard to their responses to the stressors they experience. For instance, the family of origin may be a source of stress to both children and adolescents. However, adolescents who experience the divorce of their own parents are likely to be concerned about the impact of parental divorce on their own nascent relationships. Judy, whose parents divorced in her sophomore year of high school, tended to ruminate during the day about what would happen to her and whether she also would divorce.

Many adolescents feel stressed about being pressured into developing romantic and sexual relationships, and need help to cope with them. Adolescents who become pregnant unexpectedly experience a major disruption in their life, which may be of concern to family members, guardians, and friends. Some of the many factors that contribute to teenage parenthood include the early age of onset of sexual activity, undeveloped partner communication skills, irregular and unreliable use of birth control, and the need to be loved by another person, including an infant. Social changes, such as the prevalence of single-parent families and the availability of alternative educational programs, make teenage pregnancy a more viable option.

A few years after reaching puberty, some adolescents have children and form their own families. Some pregnant teenagers who desire to leave their homes and attain adult social status enter into early marriages. The high divorce rate alarms many adolescents considering marriage. Parenthood and marriage are sources of stress that have the potential to change dramatically the course of the lives of adolescents and influence their chances of having a satisfying adulthood. Some adolescents who are about to become parents are unready for the changes that await them. As they form new families of their own, they may simultaneously have to deal with difficulties with their family of origin.

Interventions

Referral

Social workers address the social problems of divorce directly, providing services to young clients who are identified as children of divorce whose difficulties are perceived as centrally related to their parents' divorce. They also address the problems indirectly, in which divorce is either one of many issues that are addressed regarding the life of the child or is a secondary issue to the problems related to the divorce. How children's problems are addressed is based in part on how they are referred for help as well as how services are provided. For instance, some parents who want help for their youngsters throughout the emotionally difficult divorce process have their children participate in divorce mediation.

Children and adolescents are frequently referred for treatment as a function of maladaptive family interaction, as in cases of child maltreatment and family violence. Indeed, difficulties in children can contribute to, be part of, or stem from difficulties in family interaction. Children are usually in treatment on a nonvoluntary basis. However, some youngsters become willing participants. Because of their cognitive development, young children, who have limited comprehension of their difficulties and of treatment methods, may need to be motivated to enter and participate in treatment. With the help of social workers, families can, will, and should support treatment efforts. Social workers can help promote positive and beneficial family interaction.

Assessment

Social workers assess and address the emotional distress that accompanies divorce. Determining whether a child has experienced parental divorce is usually straightforward because many social service delivery settings, including schools, have records of such basic facts. When parents accompany their children to the agency during the intake process, they provide information relating to family status.

Children of divorce may present with social-emotional or mental health problems, which are consequences of parental divorce. Although the presenting problems of children of divorce might be other than divorce per se, social workers must recognize the involvement of the divorce phenomenon in the difficulties that children face. Of course, they must be wary of inferring that a child is experiencing emotions characteristic of children of divorce, for example, loneliness, solely because the child's parents are divorced.

Prevention and Intervention

Social services for family problems are provided in many agencies, including juvenile courts, family service agencies, child guidance and evaluation clinics, counseling centers, mental health agencies, and schools. Providing social services that address family problems, including the impact of divorce, at the school makes it easy for children to receive such services because they are already there and do not have to be transported elsewhere (Schreier & Kalter, 1990). Moreover, schools are natural places to children, in that they provide support and education for children and adults in a nonstigmatizing manner (Strauss & McGann, 1987).

To a large degree social work practice that is responsive to family problems is based on clients seeking social services for their felt needs. Often, the point of contact between families and social workers is relatively late in a chain of disruptive and distressing family events. Many times, by the time families approach social workers, they have already sought help from other family members, friends, acquaintances, neighbors, the clergy, and family physicians, who have been unable to stem the chain of family conflict, disruption, or abuse.

Much social work practice with families, including those on the verge of, in the midst of, or after a divorce, is interventive. However, to forestall many of the social problems of children and adolescents that are associated with divorce, families in conflict could seek the help of the social worker sooner, that is, before their difficulties become overwhelming. Indeed, social services for children and adolescents should be preventive to a greater extent.

At times, feasible prevention is a matter of goal setting. For instance, in some circumstances the prevention of family breakdown is a desirable yet unattainable ultimate goal. In such cases, divorce mediation might be useful in achieving a more feasible intermediate goal of facilitating a more constructive divorce arrangement.

Marital and family checkups with social workers can be a useful preventive intervention. The goal of such checkups would be to promote satisfactory marital and family relationships through the assessment and treatment of difficulties when they occur. Such checkups could be timed to coincide with norms pertaining to the frequency of divorce, so that checkups would be more frequent early on in the marriage when divorce tends to be more prevalent, and less frequent in subsequent years. Another approach would be to conduct such checkups annually.

To promote healthy family functioning, assessment, treatment, and education should be provided as early as possible, that is, prior to the occurrence of a major catastrophe, crisis, or point of no return. A combination of strategies designed to forestall and minimize the magnitude, impact, and occurrence of future problems as well as help with current difficulties of children from families in trouble can be optimal.

Problem Solving

Helping children and adolescents is a bilevel problem-solving process. At one level, problem solving is a method of addressing youngsters' current difficulties. The source and reasons for referral are considered. For instance, many children are referred by family members who believe they need assessment or treatment services. Some adolescents are self-referred.

The initial step of the problem-solving method is problem definition. The problem of the child or adolescent is defined in terms made by the referral source. However, additional problems are defined or conceptualized by the social worker.

The magnitude of problems that can be managed is subject to constraints of client and agency resources. Social workers prioritize client problems in regard to urgency and significance. They consider implementing alternative means of solving problems, including direct services, which encompass providing care to individuals, families, and small groups, and indirect services, including working with the community, social organizations, and engaging in advocacy efforts for social change.

Clinical decision making includes assessment, diagnosis, and prognosis, as in the predicted likelihood of juvenile offenders with severe mental illness recommitting illegal actions. Decision making is used to determine the most efficient and effective strategy to undertake with young clients in need of services. It involves a consideration of the potential consequences of implementing a helping strategy.

Social workers establish goals and objectives for services, and consider action strategies to implement treatment approaches. To determine success they evaluate the effectiveness of their interventions on behalf of particular children or adolescents. Let us consider how social workers evaluate their own practice. Sometimes, success is defined by determining whether child and adolescent clients return for services. A limitation of this approach is that they may seek help from another practitioner or agency. Furthermore, mere attendance does not necessarily indicate participation, which does not necessarily signify attaining treatment goals and objectives. Single-system evaluation designs are useful means of evaluating treatments and programs.

At a second level, social workers develop the problem-solving skills of children and adolescents so that they will be better able to solve their own problems both in the present and in the future. This is the level of empowerment that is particularly useful for children who, when they first approach a social worker, are unable to solve many of their own problems. Social workers help promote children's skills at coping with difficult family situations. In a supportive educational approach, children learn to identify difficult social situations. They also learn that other youngsters experience similar difficulties.

Children and adolescents acquire generalizable knowledge about problem solving that they learn to apply to their own lives. Through problem solving, they ascertain the effects of stressful situations they have experienced. They learn to set cognitive, emotional, and behavioral goals to cope with stressful situations, including thinking of how to reach such goals in steps. They learn to identify and understand their emotions. Depending on their age, their educational background, and their cognitive capacities, they learn to identify and develop coping strategies.

Children and adolescents who lack a desired direction in problem solving need to consider alternatives and, through a decision-making process, select a particular alternative. After implementing their choice, they evaluate its effects, with the assistance of the social worker. Goal attainment scaling is a useful way of evaluating the effectiveness of their efforts. If it is successful, the process is complete; otherwise, the young people continue the process by choosing another direction.

Child and Family Treatment

Conceptualizing child and family treatment yields three levels. Family therapy attempts to modify family interaction patterns; child-in-family therapy focuses on the child and yet understands the role of the family; and child therapy is a more individually oriented approach (Wachtel, 1994). When the entire family is implicated in the child's difficulties and it is feasible to work with the entire family, family therapy is desirable. When the locus of the child's difficulties are largely yet not entirely located in the child, child-in-family therapy is preferable.

Practitioners who use family therapy tend to conceptualize and treat children's problems in terms of the family. However, in a family therapy approach that also emphasizes child therapy, practitioners recognize the potential value of meeting individually with the child in addition to meeting with the whole family (Kuehl, 1993). Furthermore, the practitioner who conducts family therapy uses a multifaceted self, which includes an ethnic self based on ethnic heritage (Ben-David & Erickson, 1990).

Group Work

Although much help is provided to children and adolescents through individual and family treatment, group work is another useful way of working with young people who have family difficulties. Group work is an efficient means of helping children in settings such as schools where practitioners are often hard pressed to find the time to meet the social and emotional concerns of many individual youngsters.

The type and membership of group work varies as a function of the setting. In some settings practitioners refrain either from directly involving individual children and adolescents in psychotherapy for their own particular difficulties or from even directly and extensively discussing their families. In regular schools group work is often conducted with nonclinical populations.

However, in other settings therapeutic approaches are normative. In special schools, and in special education programs within regular schools, group work is conducted with children and adolescents who are behaviorally disordered or seriously emotionally disturbed. In child guidance and mental health settings, psychotherapy groups are offered to highly disturbed youngsters.

Group work has many advantages. The group experience mitigates against children's sense of isolation stemming from the parental divorce. A supportive group promotes normalization (Mervis, 1989). Youngsters see that their peers are struggling with similar problems and feelings. Discussion activities promote empathy, insight, and shared understanding of the nature of family difficulties. Many children and adolescents become more comfortable discussing upsetting events with peers who have had similar experiences.

Practice Principles

In planning how to help children and adolescents, social workers decide which combination of interventions is most suitable to their purposes, how to work with collaterals, and how to manage the youngster's school, community, and family. They also consider the method, provision, sequence, structure, and timing of therapy.

Composition is an important factor in determining the effectiveness of group work. A common sociodemographic characteristic and a theme that the group can relate to help promote cohesion. Ordinarily, a range of member personalities promotes group interaction. Ideally, practitioners have some choice in composing the group. However, in some social agencies, the demands are great enough to include virtually all clients in group work programs.

Working with children and adolescents individually and in groups, and working with their families, is an interactional process. Social workers are responsible for leadership in the interaction. At times social workers lead and at other times they allow the clients to lead. The stylistic dimension of leadership is related to the degree of structure of the helping approach. Often, an intermediate amount of structure provided by the practitioner helps promote interaction. In group work, leadership style has an impact on the productivity and satisfaction of the group.

Process and Methods

The process of working with children and adolescents incorporates family issues for practitioners to be aware of and potentially resolve. Young child clients frequently relate to practitioners as if they were their parents. Practitioners represent or symbolize custodial parents to child clients.

Practitioners socialize children and adolescents into the client role. They explain the goals, norms, methods, and activities of treatment to prepare youngsters for productive therapeutic interaction. For both children and adolescents, activity is an essential aspect of social work practice. Children and adolescents are often satisfied with movement. Activity can serve as a context for the representation and discussion of the child's issues in treatment.

The activities selected by practitioners vary as a function of the age and development of the child. For young children, three levels of play activities are beneficial, particularly for assessment purposes. One, relatively unstructured activities include playing with sand, water, and clay materials. Two, semistructured activities include drawing families and constructing genograms. Three, highly structured activities with rules include board games and sports.

The establishment and formulation of rules, by and for children and adolescents, is an essential aspect of group work. Rules serve the function of keeping members on task and help reduce conflict and aggression in the group. Typical rules center on attendance, sharing, respect, listening, responding and giving feedback, and confidentiality (Cole & Kammer, 1984).

Practitioners guide discussions and tell stories to promote problem solving. Role playing is employed either with individuals or small groups. Young children can participate in role playing, and many adolescents enjoy acting-out scenarios. Youngsters can read and prepare parts in vignettes, plays, and skits.

Phases

The process of working with children and adolescents consists of beginning, middle, and ending phases. The beginning phase typically focuses on developing a rapport with child and adolescent clients. Rapport is a crucial, initial step toward forming a therapeutic alliance with clients, which is often explicit with adolescents. Developing a contract and setting goals and objectives is either formal or informal and varies in specificity according to the treatment method.

Given the nature of referral processes, practice with children and adolescents often entails working with collaterals. Practitioners are also likely to be very involved with conducting an initial assessment, which encompasses requesting information from education, health, mental health, and social service providers. The middle phase is work oriented and focuses on productive goal attainment. The middle phase is likely to be stable in regard to process and treatment. Helping activities usually take place with little interruption. The ending phase involves a review of progress. Clients are usually asked to contribute their views about their progress. Although young children are usually unable to provide very much direct knowledge, observations of their behavior, drawings, and other creative activities, as well as reports from their parents and collaterals are informative.

A consideration of termination issues occurs in the ending phase too. Sometimes, such issues are emotional. In working with children and adolescents who have experienced dramatic family changes, as in parental separation or divorce, termination can be particularly poignant. Children of divorce may have a difficult time in separating from members and practitioners to whom they have become attached. The practitioners attempt to model a constructive separation experience at the end of the group.

Practitioners decide when to end their work with their young clients. Ideally, it will occur when the goals of treatment have been reached. However, treatment sometimes ends prior to goal attainment because of resource constraints or lack of support for treatment.

School-Based Group Work Models

The form and process of children's groups devoted to issues of divorce are determined, to some extent, by the age of the members. Within divorce groups for elementary school–age children, early and later elementary school models exist. An early elementary school model (Kalter & Schreier, 1994) consists of 10 sessions. Session 1 is the introduction to the group. Session 2 is devoted to the group story. Session 3 concerns parent fighting. Session 4 involves the parents telling the children about the separation. Session 5 is devoted to the meeting with the father following the marital separation. Session 6 concerns visiting the nonresident parent. Session 7 is about parent dating. Session 8 concerns remarriage and stepfamilies. Session 9 is devoted to the group newspaper. Session 10 is about the group party and saying good-bye.

A later elementary school model (Kalter & Schreier, 1994) consists of 8 sessions. Session 1 provides an introduction to the group. Session 2 concerns predivorce fighting between parents. Session 3 is about telling children about the divorce. Session 4 concerns custody issues. Session 5 is about visiting issues. Session 6 is about remarriage and stepparenting issues. Session 7 is devoted to the divorce newspaper, which is prepared by the children. The divorce newspaper is distributed in session 8, which is also the last session.

Group Work with Adolescents

Group work with adolescents is distinguished from group work with children in regard to the activities, issues, and development of members (Rose, 1998). Group work provides time-limited support for adolescents and assists them to develop their support systems beyond the group. It helps them deal with a myriad of social and educational problems. Group work helps adolescents resolve issues relating to their personal relationships, assists those adolescents who are contemplating marriage, and serves adolescent parents in a variety of school and community settings. It also helps pregnant adolescents who are in the process of forming single-parent families.

Group work is a method and context that is well suited for exploring issues and developing skills related to personal relationships. Leaders serve as or provide models for adolescents who are dealing with couple issues or who are contemplating marriage. Group work with adolescent couples contemplating marriage aims to increase commitment and maintain morale. Such group work, along with group work with adolescents who are about to become parents, is supportive and educational. Health information is provided for first-time parents.

Group work for pregnant and parenting teenagers has several advantages. It provides acceptance, reduces isolation and stigma, and gives them a place to share a range of emotions. It provides them with a socialization experience that validates their personal status. In working with pregnant teens, the timing of the group in regard to the stage of pregnancy is also crucial. As more adolescents are finding ways of having and raising their children, the need for group work to help adolescents with issues involved in forming their own families is likely to continue into the future.

Conclusion

Social work with children and adolescents occurs in a family context. Families are social systems and function in urban and rural environments. The composition and structure of contemporary families and changes in family functions, interaction, and issues influence the well-being of children and adolescents.

Children and adolescents are liable to experience many stressors. The social and emotional impact of divorce can be particularly pronounced. The nature, scope, and objectives of social work with children of divorce are influenced by developmental factors. Practitioners frequently provide social services to children of divorce in their caseload as well as deal with related problems. Divorce groups for children and adolescents promote better relationships, mental health, and adjustment for youngsters within newly restructured families. Problem-solving approaches, prevention and interaction, and practice principles are key elements of helping youngsters dealing with difficult family situations.

CHAPTER

4 The Process of Helping Children and Adolescents

Children and adolescents, and their families, need a variety of services throughout their lives. Complex forces and pressures in society and the environment surround young people today. Some children live in a world of poverty, violence, drug use, and unsafe schools and neighborhoods. All are faced with developmental issues and must cope with stressors and transitions in their living environment. In recent years with the violence that has occurred in schools, children in all geographic areas and socioeconomic classes are potentially in need of help. According to LeCroy and Ryan (1993), more emotional disturbances exist in children and adolescents today than in the past. Many in the United States view this as a national problem requiring immediate action.

A broad view of the need for services, types of services, risk factors and resilience, and examples of practice are illustrated in this chapter. This is followed by a description of the phases of practice from referral through termination and evaluation, using case examples.

Enhancement Services

Let us initially consider the purposes of services for children and adolescents and their families. Five main goals have been identified for intervening in children's problems. They are to reduce overt problems, promote normal development, foster autonomy and self-reliance, and to generalize therapeutic gains and foster continued improvement (Rutter, 1985).

Services provided are categorized as enhancement or developmental assistance, prevention, and rehabilitation. Often, these major service areas are subdivided into subsystems of service, such as primary prevention, secondary prevention, indirect prevention, and into prevention focused on specific problem areas, such as child abuse, teenage pregnancies, and many others.

Enhancement services do not assume a problem but rather a need for growth and amplification in social living. Many believe that services that enhance social development and enrich daily living should be available as a matter of human rights. Developmental services are often used in helping people who are at transitional or developmental points in the life cycle. The purpose of these services is to promote social competence and to assist people to find new ways to deal with new relationships and roles.

Children need continuous support throughout childhood and special support that changes as their developmental needs and capacities change. Enhancement services often are focused on assisting the parents to help the child. For example, enhancement programs address the everyday problems of parents in giving support to their children. Some parents need assistance as their child enters school or as their child moves into adolescence. Problems in development can be prevented by educating the public or providing adaptive behavioral skills.

Children need to be given opportunities for achievement in cognitive, academic, and developmental milestones. Enhancement services are helpful in bridging racial, ethnic, and class divisions. The concept of enhancement services implies creating a culture of community responsibility for children. Enhancement services are usually implemented when broad areas of risk factors are identified and studied.

Major Risk Factors

Kirby and Fraser (1997) identify developmental risks ranging from prenatal biology to broad environmental factors, including racial discrimination, injustice, and poverty, which limit opportunities for children and adolescents in school, work, and other settings. Racial discrimination has caused people of color to experience a large portion of the burden of poverty and unemployment in the United States (Nettles & Pleck, 1994). As a result, children are vulnerable to the effects of poverty and low socioeconomic status. Children living in poverty are at risk for being subjected to multiple stressors, including family stress, medical illness, parental depression, and inadequate social supports. Poverty is a risk factor for children because of inadequate food, lack of availability of preventive services, and living in unsupportive, unstimulating, and chaotic households (Hart & Risley, 1995).

Other areas of risk for children and adolescents are family, school, and neighborhoods (Kirby & Fraser, 1997). Maltreatment, both abuse and neglect, are factors that are believed to produce risks. Two major mechanisms that help to produce these risks are problems in children's attachment to their parents or caregivers and their maladaptive cognitive schemas resulting from abuse. Maltreated children are likely to view the world as hostile and are prone to develop aggressive interpersonal styles that put them at risk for delinquency and other social problems.

Interparental conflict has been found to be another risk factor for children (Emery & Forehand, 1994; Office of Juvenile Justice and Delinquency Prevention, 1995). Frequent interparental conflicts are believed to desensitize the child to conflict and model a poor example of problem solving.

Parental psychopathology is a risk factor for children. Substance abuse and mental illnesses, such as depression, place children in jeopardy of developing psychosocial problems (Watkins & Durant, 1996). Consistent care may be unavailable to such children because of parental problems.

Inadequate parenting is a risk factor for children that can lead to delinquency and substance abuse. Poor communication, monitoring, and problem-solving skills are likely to produce coercive family interactions. Often this teaches the children to use aversive behavior to meet goals in the home, school, and neighborhood (O'Donnell, Hawkins, & Abbott, 1995).

Another area of risk includes individual psychosocial and biological problems. Biomedical problems in children may impair cognitive abilities or create emotional disorders. A supportive family is essential to help prevent developmental lags for these children.

Gender also has been found to be a risk factor. Research has shown that boys are more severely affected than girls by stressors such as divorce, discord in the family, and out-of-home daycare (Luthar & Zigler, 1991). On the other hand, girls have more difficulty in some aspects of schooling and with some mental disorders (Werner & Smith, 1982).

Often, specific populations of children who are vulnerable and at risk are potentially simultaneously subjected to multiple risk factors. For instance, homeless children have elevated risks of academic delays, chronic illness and other health problems, behavioral problems, and emotional problems. Being aware of risk factors and the way they impact child development and adaptation is essential in developing treatment plans. Often, changing interactions in the environment, in others, or within children is required to alleviate problematic situations.

Another crucial consideration is the resiliency of children and ways to support and undergrid their strengths and capacities. To help children, understanding risk factors and ways to support their adaptive capacities is essential.

Resilience

Resilience is the capacity to exhibit positive outcomes despite being at significant risk (Masten, 1994; Rak & Patterson, 1996). Some children, though exposed to identifiable risk factors, are able to overcome and avoid academic difficulties, behavioral problems, psychological maladjustments, physical complications, maltreatment, and poverty (Brooks & Goldstein, 2001).

Masten, Best, and Garmezy (1990) delineated three major groups of resilience phenomena related to the capacity for successful adaptation despite challenging or threatening circumstances. One group consists of people from high-risk groups who have better-than-expected outcomes. A second group has good adaptation despite stressful experiences. Finally, some people sustain competence and recover from trauma much faster than others.

Masten (1994) identified factors that influence the degree of adaptation made by children and adolescents. One ingredient is the child's developmental path or history. The focus on the past needs to examine competence in psychological functioning over time. Another important factor in adaptive abilities is the nature of the adversities faced by children, that is, the number and severity of simultaneous hardships. Other ingredients of adaptation are youths' social assets and risks and their characteristics that function as vulnerabilities or protective factors. Environmental factors and the content for adaptation are also ingredients for resilience.

Some specific factors and conditions that support the resiliency of children have been gleaned by research, but this knowledge is fragmented and not yet complete. The importance of relationships throughout life has been found to be a supportive condition for resiliency. Secure and supportive personal attachment early in life, especially during the first year, makes it likely that individuals will be protected against adversity in later life (Werner, 1984). This relationship correlates directly with self-concept, which also undergirds resiliency (Rutter, 1990).

Radke-Yarrow and Sherman (1990) found that the direction of development in children at risk depended on interaction. Resilient children sustained relationships with their disturbed parent or family. Even maltreated children who had good relationships with their caretakers in childhood were found, in later life, to be good parents (Kaufman & Zigler, 1989). Supportive networks were also found to be conducive to maintaining resiliency. A longitudinal study conducted by Werner and Smith (1982) found that vulnerable children with support networks of parents, grandparents, neighbors, or relatives can escape adversities without lasting harm.

In potentially emotional or stressful situations, reactivity, which is considered to be a temperamental or a personality trait, is related to the quality of social-emotional functioning. Some temperamental or personality traits of children have been found to be significant for resiliency. Intelligence is one characteristic found important to children living in adverse situations (Herrenkohl, Herrenkohl, & Egolf, 1994; Radke-Yarrow & Sherman, 1990). In research on children living with parents who were emotionally unavailable, unpredictable, and negative, assertiveness and high achievement motivation were found to be important for successful adjustment. Radke-Yarrow and Sherman (1990) noted that assertive children are better equipped to reach out for support and to draw out something supportive from depressed parents. Many problem-solving attempts were found to be made by children facing chronic adversity.

Even maltreated children were found to be able to sustain resilient striving. Maltreated children who pulled back from conflict, detached from high-intensity affect in the family, and were compliant with the wishes of their caretakers were more likely to escape abuse and achieve competent adaptation. In contrast, the more affective, expressive style of resilience may provoke attention and reactions from others, resulting in greater risk for maltreatment (Rutter, 1990).

In summing characteristics, Benard (1991) found that resilient children have high expectations and a belief that life has meaning. They are goal directed, and have problem-solving skills. These qualities together are desirable to produce the best outcomes. An even broader conclusion drawn was that a higher proportion of resilient children are firstborn, recover quickly from illnesses, and are remembered by their mothers as good natured. Wang, Haertel, and Walberg (1994) found that resilient children were those who had easy temperaments.

Special skills have also been found to be conducive to resiliency. The ability to shift and focus attention is an important mechanism for emotional and behavioral regulation. Children who can regulate their attention are resilient to stress. Consequently, they are better liked by peers and are viewed by adults as being socially appropriate (Eisenberg et al., 1997). Attention control is positively related to both social status and socially appropriate behavior.

Another skill, identified by Chess (1989), is adaptive distancing. This psychological process is one in which a child can stand apart from the distressed family members and friends and can accomplish constructive goals and continue with psychological and social development.

Focus on enhancement of factors that help to promote resiliency is essential in helping children with less ability to adapt to negative environments and relationships. Identifying the need for both enhancement and prevention requires some assessment of both the risk factors and presence of resources that may be supportive to the resiliency of children and adolescents.

Enhancement services are usually provided for groups or cohorts of children. Exceptions to this occur in tutoring or mentoring relationships. However, selecting an individual child or adolescent for services suggests that they have been identified as either currently having or potentially developing a problem. Social agencies, such as Boys Club, Girls Club, settlement houses, and community centers, provide enhancement services to children on a one-to-one basis through the use of volunteer services.

The following is an illustration of services provided for the enhancement of groups of preteen children. The event occurred in a settlement house in an isolated community of multiple nationalities and ethnic and racial groups within a large urban area on the west coast of the United States. The children lived in a low-income neighborhood. Many parents worked in low-paying jobs in nearby fish canneries. In the settlement house, groups of young boys and groups of young girls were recruited with the purpose of exposing them to new experiences and to new geographic areas, neighborhoods, ways of life, cultures, and people. It was believed that knowledge would allow them to have a broader perspective of their possible choices as they matured.

One group of girls went to swim in the pool of a community center. They noted the type of nearby housing as different from most of their homes, since the center was located in an upper-middle-class area of the large city. Indeed, the center was newly constructed, large, and in a beautiful setting. The girls were unsure of how accepted they would be in the center. They were acting shy and a little afraid as they donned their swimsuits and entered the pool area. Few others were in the pool. After playing in the pool for some time, Christina, a Mexican American girl, said that she wanted to learn to swim. As no instructor was immediately available to teach her, Christina approached an older woman who had been swimming back and forth across the pool and asked her whether she could help her learn to swim. The woman indicated that she could try. Christina learned that the woman was a member of this center and lived around the corner.

The significance of this interaction became clear as the group of girls traveled back to their own community. Christina was delighted with her experience. She had been unsure about whether she would be accepted outside of her own community by people who were different from herself and lived in this higher-income neighborhood. Christina discovered that the lady she selected to give her instructions was willing, friendly, helpful, and interested in knowing about her as a person. She felt accepted, cared about, and important to a stranger living in a very different community, from a different culture, and a different socioeconomic class. This experience gave Christina new confidence in herself. Christina excitedly shared the details of this experience to the others as they returned home. The girls listened intently as she described it.

Another enhancing experience occurred as adolescent girls and boys from the settlement house took a trip into the mountains to play in the snow. Few of these teenagers had ever seen snow. As the bus approached the area selected for sledding, it began to snow. The teenagers were fascinated by the drifting flakes. One teenager wondered how snowflakes felt as they hit you: "Did it hurt you?" Soon they opened the windows of the bus to try to experience how snow felt. Later, several youths ran around barefoot in the snow. They explained that they had removed their shoes and socks because they were wet. They had only experienced shoes wet with rain, so they responded in a similar way to shoes wet with snow. They did not know about the possibility of frostbite.

The preceding examples demonstrate services provided for the development or enhancement of children and adolescents. The youngsters were provided opportunities to experience interactions with people differing from themselves and in other geographic areas and environments, giving them a broader perspective on possibilities for living. Other types of enhancement programs commonly used are units of a curriculum or the use of small groups to teach skills for problem solving, Head Start programs, and school breakfast and lunch programs.

Although conceptually distinct, a relationship exists between preventive and enhancing services. Prevention implies the danger of becoming a problem or causing pathology. Developmental or enhancing services are intended to promote health or development. Even if services begin at one level, they may move to another level as needed.

Prevention

Tudor (1996) states that some think of prevention as having multiple levels of differentiation. The first level is preventing first occurrences; the second level is preventing avoidable consequences; and the tertiary level focuses on prevention of avoidable complications of an irreversible disease and finally preventing recurrence of disease. In this chapter the term *prevention* is used only for primary or secondary prevention.

Primary prevention precedes the onset of a defined problem. Secondary prevention occurs as soon as possible after the identification of the problem. Remedial services are used when an existing problem is acute and chronic and needs to be resolved (Northen, 1982). Sometimes the levels of help giving overlap. As discussed previously, development, or enhancement, is concerned with the promotion of health or development. Primary prevention implies the danger of a problem developing. The idea of prevention is tied to concerns about pathology. Primary prevention is an attempt to change the incidence of cases either by enhancing competence or decreasing problems in the targeted population (Braden & Hightower, 1998).

Prevention occurs either through indirect or direct means. Indirect prevention focuses on social conditions that require change and addresses gaps in service, licensing, certification, and consultation through social action, social legislation, and community planning and organization. Licensing or certification is a preventive measure in children's services intended to ensure that certain standards are met. For example, foster parents and adoptive homes are certified before children are placed. Consultation is also a means of primary prevention in that it assists personnel to provide more effective services to children and families.

Primary prevention through direct services to client systems are directed toward the future. For example, such services are intended to prevent a psychological breakdown by enhancing the youngster's skills and abilities. In prevention, the focus is primarily on need. The goal of prevention is to change the incidence either by enhancing competence or decreasing problems in targeted populations. Direct means of primary prevention include improving social, academic, or vocational competencies through education. Primary prevention is a central theme of elementary school guidance programs and government preschool programs, such as Head Start, family preservation, and community-sponsored programs.

Training to improve coping strategies of those who experience stressful life events and crises is also useful. Preventive interventions characteristically target populations rather than troubled individuals. This is the hallmark that distinguishes prevention from treatment activities. Some common areas for preventive services are teenage pregnancies, substance abuse, child abuse, eating disorders, illness, and injuries. Another method of primary prevention is modifying the environment to reduce or counteract unfavorable circumstances. Primary prevention programs intend to rid neighborhoods of drugs, provide more police protection, and improve safety conditions.

Understanding risk factors is not the same as understanding the mechanisms by which children and adolescents are affected (Braden & Hightower, 1998). For example, household poverty is a risk factor for school failure. However, this much information does not identify the specific mechanisms of risk. Prevention programs must be based on risk mechanisms such as attendance at underfunded schools, poor health and nutrition, and lack of parental assistance with children's homework. The prevention effort for each of these mechanisms would be different. Prevention programs are driven by a conceptual base that provides underlying assumptions dictating the content and methods to be used.

Following are two examples of a primary prevention program in a school setting. It was discovered that many girls who graduated from elementary school began to have a variety of problems in adjusting to middle school, especially peer social pressures. These conditions appeared to contribute to dropping out of school and fighting among girls. Consequently, during their last semester in elementary school, all girls participated in groups to orient, educate, and support them as they entered the new environment of middle school. The other instance of primary prevention was a program using field trips, developed for 9- to 13-year-old boys. Sessions were devoted to discussions of sexual issues, job opportunities, responsibility, and decision making.

The hallmark of secondary prevention is early diagnosis and prompt treatment. Problems are identified, and preventive components outweigh the remedial aspects. Secondary prevention programs deliver services to young people who are at risk of developing disorders. Dropout prevention programs target children with unexcused absences and low grades.

A social agency that worked with gangs in a large metropolitan city recognized that younger siblings of their clients were likely to become gang members in the future without some intervention. As a result, groups of these younger siblings received intensive preventive services in an attempt to forestall such an outcome. The children were seen in groups and individually. Often, family work was provided too.

The children were involved in discussing and planning enjoyable activities, which were the primary focus of the groups. In doing so, they learned to resolve conflicts peacefully, make decisions, schedule time, assign responsibilities, and carry out tasks in a dependable way. The children developed skills essential to relating successfully to others in the community. As viewed by the children, the learning that was required to have fun was secondary for them.

Preventive efforts are also offered to children and adolescents who have suffered together in disasters, such as hurricanes, earthquakes, or school shootings. Often, children of divorce and young people who have experienced a death of a significant person in their lives are targeted for preventive efforts. Braden and Hightower (1998) note that these situations tend to cause stress reactions, rather than pathology, so the emphasis is to reduce the immediate effects of stress.

Therapy and Treatment Services

Therapy or remedial services are provided to children and adolescents after they exhibit chronic or severe evidence of a disorder. Remediation is designed to assist youngsters to alter emotions, thought processes, and actions that underlie their difficulties. The remedial perspective views young clients as capable of solving their problems with the help of others. It helps young people overcome their disorders. It also involves altering environmental conditions that contribute to their problems.

Webb (1996) identified the following criteria indicating the need for individual work with children:

- When clients' behavior is so extreme as to interfere with their ability to interact with others
- Unable to continue with age-appropriate tasks and growth
- When individual work is needed to alleviate clients' anxiety or help them to modify behavior (for example, child abuse or neglect)
- To help children who have low self-esteem and children who have disabilities (pp. 141–143)

Direct work with children and adolescents is useful in helping to change personal and environmental factors that cause breakdown or impairment of psychosocial functioning. The practitioner–client relationship clearly becomes an important factor for bringing about change.

Physically abused children require treatment. Although a plethora of research and literature on sexually abused children exists, relatively little focus is on those who have been physically abused. The literature often combines these populations and does not always clearly differentiate treatment approaches for each of them. Often, it is assumed that treatment of physically abused children only requires that they be removed from the abusive family situation and be put into an ostensibly safer home. Many times the family becomes the client who receives services with little attention given to the needs of the child (Altstein & McRoy, 2000).

According to Finkelhor and Berliner (1995), child abuse is an experience rather than a disorder or syndrome. Symptoms presented by these children can differ by the form of abuse; the child's developmental age, gender, and adjustment prior to abuse; the relationship of the child to the perpetrator; and factors related to family conflict, cohesion, and support of the child (Becker & Bonner, 1998). Nevertheless, aggression toward peers, decreased self-esteem and social withdrawal, depression, anxiety, and academic difficulties have been identified in the literature as consequences of child abuse (Crittenden & Ainsworth, 1989; Fantuzzo, 1990; Fatout, 1990a,b; Hoffman-Plotkin & Twentyman, 1984; Wodarski, Kurtz, Gaudin, & Howing, 1990). Adolescents who have been abused are subject to demonstrate alcoholism, mental illness, or premature death (McCord, 1983) and are more likely to be arrested for delinquency, adult crimes, and violent behavior (Widom,

1989). Awareness of these potential consequences of child abuse provides a beginning point for understanding the meaning of the behavior of abused children and adolescents.

The Case of Tommy

Background

Tommy is an 8-year-old boy who had been abused, neglected, and rejected. He was placed in a foster family at the age of 2 and then placed in a succession of six different homes. Child abuse was reported in one foster home and suspected in another. The last foster home was expected to be Tommy's adoptive home. However, without making the reasons for their decision clear, at the last possible moment the foster parents decided that they were unable to adopt him.

Tommy had been hospitalized five times and was expected to have another operation to correct his harelip. He was insecurely attached because of the lack of continuity in his life. The level of his academic performance was minimal, and he was described by his teacher as a loner.

Current Situation

Tommy is a blue-eyed, blonde-haired boy who is small in stature. He is immature and appears to be much younger than 8 years of age. He appears to be sweet, soft, and childlike. At the present time, he is still living with his foster parents, who decided not to adopt him.

As Tommy and the child welfare worker entered the practitioner's office, he looked around the waiting room and office in a guarded, suspicious manner conveying his concern about what was going to happen to him. He was withdrawn as he was introduced to the practitioner. He did not look at her and was distracted by his surroundings. He saw the toys in the next room and started to leave the room through the door. The child welfare worker called him back. When he ignored her request, she went to retrieve him. He reluctantly returned still looking toward the toys as she held his sleeve.

The child welfare worker indicated that she would be leaving but would return to take him home. He seemed very unconcerned about what was being said as he continued to look into the next room. The practitioner went into the playroom with Tommy. He quietly picked up one toy after another, glancing at each one before moving on to the next toy. After Tommy viewed everything of interest to him, he stood quietly swinging his leg and scuffling his feet against the floor. He seemed totally oblivious to the fact that the practitioner was there. When she attempted to communicate with him, he did not look at her and often did not answer her at all except for an occasional one-word response.

As Tommy looked at the toys, the social worker attempted to join in and engage him by commenting often as he picked up a toy and discarded it. Usually, he ignored her and did not respond. While he wandered around the room aimlessly, the worker attempted to identify who she was and what was the purpose of their meeting. Again, Tommy made no response. The worker asked Tommy whether he wanted to return the next week. He nodded his head in the affirmative.

Assessment of the Session

Tommy was unable to interact with the social worker in a meaningful way. He was frightened, suspicious, and almost totally distrusting of others and their intents. Even his response to objects was very unsure as he picked up and replaced the toys. Some of his behaviors, such as wandering around the room and swinging his leg and kicking the floor in a meaningless manner, indicated his withdrawal from the world. The few times Tommy appeared to try to respond to the worker, he seemed to be too confused. He appeared to be unsure of what was expected from him.

The purpose for seeking services by the child welfare agency was to help Tommy to become "less depressed and more outgoing." They also indicated that Tommy seemed to express his anger in foster homes by doing "sneaky" little things to upset others in the home, which had, at times, created chaos. Due to Tommy's level and ways of functioning, he was unable to participate in goal setting at this time. Initially, the social worker needed to identify the goals of working with Tommy. The major purpose of working together was to help Tommy begin to develop a sense of trust in an adult. This would take time and as his living situation became more stable, the social worker could work with his new family to build on his developing sense of trust and belonging with them. The following goals were set for working with Tommy:

1. Refer Tommy for testing as soon as possible.
2. Engage Tommy in interacting with the worker even at a minimal level.
3. Encourage Tommy to begin to interact with peers.
4. Provide experiences for Tommy to try his abilities with adults and children in the community.

The initial task of the social worker was to engage Tommy and develop a trusting relationship. This process was very slow as Tommy needed to test the safety of the relationship step by step. One of Tommy's strengths was his willingness to attempt to be in the presence of adults. He was willing to test their acceptance of him and his safety in their presence. Resilience was also a strength. Tommy had survived abuse, neglect, and rejection in a variety of situations and was still ready to try again.

Building a Trusting Relationship

At first, Tommy did a great deal of touching of things that belonged to the worker. He examined her earrings, patted her head, rubbed her arm, and looked at her pin. It was clear to the worker that this touching was his way of testing the worker's response to him, rather than an interest in the objects. Often, as Tommy touched an item, he looked at the worker's face, waiting for a response. He also kept an eye on the door, making sure there was a quick way out, if he received a violent response from the practitioner. When the worker did not respond negatively, he seemed ready to move on with his physical contact, for which he sometimes received verbal permission and assurance.

The next step for Tommy was to test some aggressive behavior on the worker, which he did surreptitiously. He played with the puppets, especially those with a big mouth, such as the alligator and a big bird. He often became the voice of the puppet as he attacked the worker's arm or hand with the puppet's mouth. Occasionally, Tommy used the puppet to pinch and sometimes to twist her arm. The practitioner responded to this very quietly, saying that this kind of attack hurt and was not okay to do. She continued by telling him that touching her arm was fine, but hurting her arm was not. Through this experience, Tommy found that the worker did not respond by hurting him even when she was being hurt by him.

After several weeks, Tommy was more comfortable in making physical contact with the worker. He often sat next to her and finally very close to her as they read stories together. After determining that physical proximity to the social worker was safe, he finally showed his desire to sit in her lap as they read. She allowed this to happen as long as he needed, for about two sessions. She felt that this was very important to him in developing their trusting relationship together. Now Tommy was ready to become involved in activities with the worker and begin to express his feelings through his pictures and play.

Much work still needed to be done to continue trust building. Tommy was manipulative of the therapist as he had been initially. He was inclined to maneuver the worker to do what he wanted. Sometimes he took her finger and directed her to what he wanted. He dealt with her almost as if she were an object rather than a person. He seemed to take the role of the controller, just as he had been treated in the foster homes where he had been maltreated. It is noted in the literature that some physically abused children use their abuser as a role model and play out this behavior with others.

This role was further confirmed when the worker took Tommy to a fast-food restaurant. As they sat drinking their sodas, a customer recognized the worker and came over to talk with her. Tommy tolerated this for a minute or two, then he poured part of his soda on the worker when she was not looking, an act that immediately got her attention. He had again focused attention on himself and taken control of the worker through manipulation. Tommy participated in the consequences of his behavior by helping the practitioner clean up the spill.

Work with Tommy continued primarily through the helping relationship, with special attention given to the process, and focused on interactions and their meanings. Adjustments were made as a need or opportunity arose. As these processes were worked through, step by step, Tommy was able to develop more trust, and they were able to focus on his behavior and feelings resulting from the abuse and neglect he had suffered.

In working with Tommy, the interaction had been primarily physical contact. With Sylvia, an adolescent girl, the focus of the process was more on verbal communication. Sylvia had recently been released from a juvenile facility and was referred to a mental health center in her community.

The Case of Sylvia

Background

Sylvia is 14 years old, the second of six children still living in the home with her mother and her mother's current boyfriend. Sylvia had run away from home on many occasions and returned again of her own volition. This time she had been gone for a month. Her mother was reluctant to report Sylvia to the authorities because previously she had made multiple reports. The school social worker discovered that Sylvia had continued to attend school on a regular basis during the month that she was away from home. This seemed to indicate that the focus of Sylvia's concerns might be related to the home environment or other personal problems she might be experiencing. She was referred by the school social worker to the mental health center.

Current Situation

Despite her reluctance to attend, Sylvia kept her first appointment at the mental health center. She entered the office in a subdued, hesitant manner and conveyed an attitude of "I'm here, but you can't make me talk." When the social worker attempted to talk with Sylvia, her responses were one-word answers. Finally, Sylvia directly said that she did not want any help. The worker said that was up to her, but that she seemed to be unhappy in her own home and perhaps they could work on some things together.

Sylvia stated that she doubted anyone could help yet went on to talk about school and her friends. By the end of the session, Sylvia was communicating in a more relaxed manner and made an appointment for the next week. Sylvia, the school social worker, Sylvia's mother, and the mental health social worker decided that Sylvia could continue to stay with her friend for a "little while" and not yet return home.

After several sessions, the mental health social worker and Sylvia were able to identify communication and situational problems in the home that caused Sylvia to leave. Having identified the issues of primary concern, a treatment plan could be developed. A variety of theories and approaches for working with adolescents and children have been identified in the literature (see Chapter 6) and could be appropriately used for helping Sylvia and her family.

A General Approach for Helping Children and Adolescents

Helping children and adolescents consists of three broad stages, namely the beginning, middle, and ending stages. The beginning stage includes the initial interview(s), assessment, and development of a treatment plan. Initial interviews focus on the problems and needs that prompt children and their families to seek help. These interviews provide an excellent opportunity for observing and hearing youngsters and their parents relate the problems of concern. Material gained from these sessions along with information gathered before the first contacts provide the practitioner with the basis for an assessment. Awareness of assessment as an ongoing process that continues throughout the three stages is important. As new information is discovered, the initial assessment is subject to modification as needed. After information has been gathered and negotiated with the parents, child, and social worker, a treatment plan, consisting of goals to be met and strategies to be tried is developed and agreed upon by them.

The middle stage is the period in which the major work is done. During this time the accomplishment of previously set goals is the focus. Methods and strategies for treatment are implemented, expanded, and modified as needed and approved by the child and parents.

The final stage includes evaluation and termination. Goals and accomplishments are reviewed and evaluated with the parents and child. Preparation is made for stabilizing the gains that are made. Rehearsals of gains made and sometimes referral to other resources support the changes already made by the child.

Professionals working with children and adolescents need to expand their knowledge base and their methods of practice because of the focus on the psychosocial developmental patterns specific to healthy growth of children and adolescents and sometimes the unique methods to bring about change with this population. Helping youngsters involves two major processes. One is the practitioner's use of procedures and techniques and the other is the client's growth process. Sarri (1986) notes, "these two processes occur interactively and simultaneously in practice" (p. xii). Emphasis on the growth process is especially important in working with children and adolescents because they are in a continual period of transitions in all realms of development, including physical growth and motor development, psychological states, cognitive and language development, social and emotional development, moral and ethical development, and sexual unfolding.

Immediate awareness, understanding, and application of knowledge regarding expected developmental markers is essential in working with children and adolescents. It would be more feasible for a professional to discuss a complex situation with an adolescent than with a child who has not yet developed an ability to think abstractly. It is only as the social worker understands transitions made, or not yet accomplished, that beginning decisions about methods of giving help can be determined.

The other requirement in working with most children and adolescents is the use of play and activity as a context and a method for helping them understand and often resolve problems (Fatout, 1996). Both structured and unstructured play are used in working with children. Unstructured play is a means of communicating and expressing oneself. Young people from infancy through adolescence use play to express themselves and their individual needs and to relate to people with whom they are in contact at a given time. Garvey (1977) identified five criteria that define unstructured play: (1) it is pleasurable, or has positive value for the player; (2) it is intrinsically motivated, without external purpose or required action; (3) it is spontaneous and not compulsory; (4) it requires active participation by the player; and (5) it has a definite relationship to what is "not play" in the real world.

Children and adolescents need a means of expressing themselves. They usually communicate both verbally and nonverbally with the practitioner. If they lack verbal skills, play is often substituted for this purpose. Sometimes play is used to engage the client or practitioner either initially or when the relationship has developed and is comfortable. An example of this type of play occurs when an adolescent boy brings a balloon, yo-yo, or football to the session and attempts to involve the therapist in playing with him. Unstructured play is very much a part of the interactions when adolescents are seen in groups.

Other types of play that are very useful in working with children and adolescents are structured play or activities, such as storytelling, games, role playing, crafts, and drawing. Often, these activities are used in helping children attain their goals. This type of play is often called developmental. Sometimes practitioners use the limits or boundaries of the game or the roles intrinsic to the activity to bring about behavior changes in the child. For example, in playing checkers, rules help to provide boundaries and limit interactions. For some children, this provides a constraint on large body movements and helps them control themselves. Other children feel that they are freed up to participate by the very fact that structure is provided. The structure helps set the boundaries for them on what is acceptable behavior and allows them to have some choice between possible responses. Just as role playing is used, some limits and boundaries are used to identify and center interactions between participants.

These levels of communication and interactions are primary tools used by the social worker in relating to children and adolescents. Play is also helpful in assessing youngsters' developmental level and competence. Settings and workers tend to differ concerning the amount and type of play used.

The Beginning Phase

Referral

Children are usually unaware that they have a need or problem. Usually, they come to the attention of social workers as their parents or guardians refer them for services. Often, children are referred by school personnel. Other sources of referral include physicians, psychologists, psychiatrists, police officers, recreation personnel, workers in religious institutions, neighbors, business persons, community members, teachers, and other helping professionals.

Children are often in denial and engaged in survival efforts. Often, children interpret referral as an indication that they are "bad" or that someone does not like them. If careful explanations and clarification are not provided, this situation may create anxiety for children that may result in them initially perceiving sessions with practitioners as punishment. Anxiety is alleviated as children become aware of the reason for seeing the social worker (Rauch, 1993).

Once the referral is received and the child and parents have given permission to attain further information, background information is sought. Having the parents sign a form giving permission to seek information from other sources is essential. The specific source and the dates for valid requests for information must be identified. In addition to the clients themselves, usual sources for background material include reports from other school personnel, medical reports, police reports, and any prior social work evaluation of the child and the parents.

Once the background information has been received, analysis of all the information is useful in beginning to develop a picture of children and their environmental situation. Often children respond differently to diverse situations depending on the setting, the expectations, and the specific persons involved. Children's behavior in the school setting may differ from behavior observed in the home or with children in the neighborhood. Social workers, having experience with specific resources, evaluate the expected accuracy of reports received. Sometimes information given by the referral source may be inaccurate and distorted. Regardless, obtaining the perceptions of others is useful to social workers in preventing potential distortion of their own view of the situation (Geldard & Geldard, 1997).

Often, communication with sources of information is advantageous for the child. Clarifying the referral information with the source of the information is often beneficial. This is especially true when working with school employees. Often the communication focuses the interest of teachers on the well-being of the individual child. Over time, the referral sources benefit from feedback about children's movement throughout the helping process.

The purpose for sharing this material needs to be clearly identified by the social worker. The information given must be general so that it does not violate confidentiality. With older children and adolescents, encouragement to "sit in" on a feedback conference with selected referral sources further develops confidence and trust in the practitioner as a helping person. If participation of the child is not feasible, sharing the expected content of the session with the child may be useful. This allows the child to clarify and understand the type of information that is shared and provides an opportunity to negotiate changes of content.

Initial Sessions

In most situations, when working with children, parents are an important part of the therapeutic process. A decision must be made regarding the format of the first interview. Early on, the practitioner decides whether the parents and children are to be seen together or separately. In the latter case, the practitioner decides who is to be seen first. The characteristics of the child, the parents, and the situation are useful in making this determination.

Initially, considering the age of the child is important. Usually, at least during the first part of the interview, younger children feel safer and more comfortable staying with their parents than they do staying with the social worker who is new to them. Given that children may be unaware that they have problems, seeing the parents and child together allows the child to hear the reason for coming for help. The child also has an opportunity to observe the manner in which the parents and the worker interact. This type of format also supports the expectation that children are permitted to develop a relationship with the social worker and that they have more direct power in problem solving and making changes they desire.

Geldard and Geldard (1997) suggest another arrangement that may be useful at times is one in which the parents are first seen alone. In contrast to the format suggested previously, this structure for the first interview may allow some children to feel safe and comfortable and still in the care and control of the parents. The interview usually continues as the therapist asks the parents for permission to talk with the child alone. With some older children, this arrangement may lead to feelings of secrecy and distrust by the child. The "real" problem of concern may still be unclear to the child.

Special caution must be used in interviewing adolescents. Detecting the views of the youth and the parents concerning the problems for which they are seeking help is essential. Frequently, seeing the adolescent and parents together may be the most desirable format. However, if great differences of opinion exist, considering another structure may be more advantageous. To decide requires the worker to consider the potential dynamics of the situation. If the parents are seen first, the adolescent may be inclined to believe that the practitioner has already "taken their side." This situation may make it difficult for a helping relationship to develop between the worker and adolescent. Seeing the youth first can promote the relationship with the practitioner. It suggests that the worker is interested in the adolescent's view of the situation and it empowers the youth. The parents may be seen later, either in the presence of the youth or alone.

It is sometimes useful to start with the adolescent. Many teenagers do not want family members to be present at the initial session. Their presence may be humiliating to the adolescent (Aiello, 1999). At times, an adolescent may make an appointment for help without parental knowledge. In these instances, it is essential that the agency and practitioner are cognizant of the laws regarding seeing an adolescent without the permission of the parents. Often agency policies determine whether and how many times youth can be seen before the parents are made aware of the situation.

Content of Beginning Interviews

The first sessions are intended to clarify the specific reasons for seeking help and to discover whether the practitioner is the proper resource to provide that help. A usual first step in determining whether help can be provided in this service setting is taking a developmental history, sometimes referred to as an intake interview. An outline used for this purpose includes the parents' relationship, the physical and emotional state of the mother during the pregnancy, the situation after birth, early childhood, and school years. Reasons for seeking help by the parents and child are explored and the worker describes the purpose of the available services simply, clearly, and accurately. A discussion and sharing of ideas, further exploration of the situation, and exchange of ideas about the way assistance can be given is a part of the agreement among the parents, child, and practitioner. If the parents are seen first, it is essential that the child know why he or she is there. The parents or guardians are asked to tell the child the reasons. If the explanation is inadequate, the worker needs to complete the reasons.

If an adolescent is seen first, often the problems are identified before the session with the parents. After the session with the adolescent, parents need to be aware of the nature of the problem and to know some general information regarding the situation. Sometimes teens and their parents request to be seen together. This permits the family to discuss mutual concerns and plans and to negotiate differences.

When the child and parents do not continue with family therapy but instead choose to be seen separately, confidentiality may become a difficult issue to resolve. Ethically, the child has a right to confidentiality and the practitioner must determine what is in the child's best interest. Orton (1996) notes that professionals are divided on how to satisfy the parents' request for information and still maintain the child's right to confidentiality. The practitioner must try to balance the child's right to confidentiality with the parents' legal right to know.

Often this dilemma is the easiest to resolve with young children and older adolescents. Young school-age children often want their parents to be aware and concerned about what is happening in their lives. A conference may take place from time to time with the worker and the parents, sometimes with the child also present. In contrast, many older adolescents do not want their parents to know anything about the content of their sessions with the worker or about their lives. In this situation, negotiating with older adolescents and their parents about expectations regarding sharing information is important. Many parents are aware of the importance of allowing adolescents to learn to make their own decisions and may be more willing to relinquish some of their right to know about treatment. Social workers affirm to adolescents and parents that ultimately adolescents determine how their lives proceed, but that practitioners can offer help in the process.

Decisions to Be Made

Parents, children, and practitioners must come to an agreement about working together. During the initial interview the potential clients and social worker determine whether needed services can be provided in this setting. The parents and child gauge the worker, the setting, and methods of treatment to be used. Consideration must be given to the purpose of the agency, available resources, the required methods and techniques necessary to work with this client system, and the worker's level of skill.

An immediate consideration is the purpose of the agency. Some client problems, which are unsuitable for the setting, can be dealt with more appropriately in another agency. For example, children who are very withdrawn and depressed are referred to an agency that works with delinquent and predelinquent children. The physical facilities, setting for interviews, and orientation of staff are focused on accommodating children who are hostile and aggressive. The agency does not have resources appropriate for working with socially withdrawn children who are referred to a mental health service.

Resources available are also related to the type of client expected to be seen in the agency. For example, well-equipped playrooms are an important resource for agencies that mostly serve young children. Games and activities available are related to the type of client served in the agency. Skills of the practitioner are often honed to help a child with similar broad areas of problems. Networks for consultation and referral have been developed to help meet the need of the population served by the agency.

These elements need to be taken into consideration by the parents, child or adolescent, and social worker in determining whether they should begin work together. Initial interviews allow for this decision to be made. If it is determined that they can work together, a beginning oral or written agreement is established.

Building a Relationship

A primary concern in beginning work with children and adolescents is the development of a helping relationship. The tone for the relationship needs to be warm and friendly so that the child is not intimidated by the sessions. Some children may be difficult to engage in treatment for a variety of reasons, including lack of trust of adults, hostility, silence because they are frightened, acting up, and behaving inappropriately. An atmosphere that conveys that they can talk about thoughts or worries is conducive for developing a caring relationship.

Characteristics of the agency, physical environment, and the practitioner can affect the development of a relationship. First, the building in which the agency is housed and its neighborhood location affects the child's perception of what to expect. A building that seems very large and sterile, like an office of a physician or dentist, may seem frightening to a young child. The same building may give adolescents a sense of anonymity, as well as a feeling of protection from awareness of peers.

The neighborhood in which the agency is located also contributes to beginning expectations. It may provide a warm and friendly setting, or it may be frightening and intimidating. It is important for practitioners to be aware of how clients may be feeling as they arrive. This cognizance allows the worker to more carefully tune in to the child and family and what they are thinking and feeling. For example, if the agency's parking lot is filled and the child's parent has had a confrontation with another person attempting to park, it can be expected that a beginning attitude may be negative. In addition, if the office of the professional is difficult to find within the building, the negative attitude may be exacerbated. The child or adolescent may have had a bad day at school and may not be in a very receptive mood.

Characteristics of the social worker are also very important in developing a helping relationship. Practitioners need to show that they are receptive, trustworthy, and reliable, and that they can help clients feel comfortable enough to express their feelings. Nonjudgmental acceptance is important in developing a helping relationship. It implies that children are entitled to their feelings and that they can risk expressing them without fear of rejection or humiliation. An attitude of nonjudgmental acceptance can be communicated by listening carefully to the child or adolescent and by responding verbally or nonverbally. Other important worker characteristics are a genuine caring for children, respect, honesty, empathy, and understanding of the child's culture. The child needs to be viewed as a fully participating person in the helping relationship.

Webb (1996) notes that the child's experience with adults until this time has been primarily with parents or teachers. Children have learned a role and have been expected to behave in prescribed ways in relating to these persons. To develop a helping relationship it is essential that the child becomes open and free to express him- or herself without these usual constraints. To do this, a practitioner must be clear about whom he or she is and the purpose for working together. This gives the worker an opportunity to know the child in a way different from most other adults.

Giving the child options and choices about the first treatment session is desirable. The child may be allowed to explore the building. This may be especially useful if the child's anxiety level is high. With young children, inviting both the child and the parents into the playroom to look around may help the child feel more comfortable in strange surroundings. The practitioner may point out that toys and games are available to be used because children do not always express themselves verbally. Sometimes the child and worker talk, at other times they play. Stating this to both the child and parents helps reinforce the purpose of play as a therapeutic tool. Young children may tell their story through play or other suitable media, and older children may sometimes be engaged in a game or other activity.

A quiet room for interviewing children and communicating through play needs to be arranged. Low chairs and a table are important both for interviewing and engaging in play activities. Often a rectangular table is useful because it allows the practitioner to position himself or herself in relation to the child. When communicating, a table may create a barrier between the child and worker. To counteract this, the practitioner may sit on the same side of the table as the child or sit away from the table. In contrast, when the child is playing with clay or involved in another craft activity, it may be more useful for the worker to sit across the table from the child. This allows the opportunity to listen and communicate as well as to display interest in the child's play or project and to help as needed.

Ideal settings for working with adolescents include a room with comfortable chairs relatively free from barriers that might impede open communication. Games and other conversation items appear on a shelf in the room.

Clues for beginning a conversation with a child may be taken by noticing the clothing, jewelry, hairstyle, well-worn sneakers, a T-shirt message, or from the design on the lunchbox. In orienting the child, it is important to tell the child that this is a place where he or she can talk about things that are of concern. With young children, the practitioner may suggest that the child look around, examine the toys, and explore the room. Paper, crayons, and colored markers need to be available so the child can draw pictures of his or her home, family, or other subjects of interest. The child is asked to draw a picture of the whole family in any manner desired. Often, verbal communication alone will not be productive. This is especially true when the child has poor communication skills or is emotionally distressed.

Older children are often more prepared to talk with the practitioner than younger children. The practitioner invites children to tell their stories. As the social worker participates in this process, he or she is aware of the dangers in asking too many questions before sufficient trust has developed. The child may fear being asked to reveal information that is private and too frightening to share at this time. The child who feels intruded on may withdraw into silence or some behavior intended to be distracting. To alleviate the possibility of misunderstanding or misinterpreting what the child means, she or he must be told that nothing the practitioner says is "written in stone," and the child can let the worker know whether or when they disagree.

In beginning work, exploring the adolescent's understanding of why they are present and what their life experience has been is often useful. Some techniques for accomplishing this might be to ask the young person what a typical day is like for him or her or what is the weirdest experience they have ever had. Often adolescents have been referred by others to get help. They may still feel very angry with adults generally and the source of referral particularly. Successfully exploring these feelings helps to open communication and to begin establishing a helping relationship.

Directly using material that has been gathered during the referral process with the child or adolescents is risky. Using material gathered from others may cause the child or adolescent to feel threatened, vulnerable, exposed, and uncertain about how much more information the worker has. This may cause the child to feel resentful that information has been given by others secretly and without consent. Even though confidentiality has been discussed with the child and parents together, clarifying this issue in the first few sessions with the child alone is still important. The child must understand that not all information can or should be kept confidential.

Sometimes, supervisors, secretaries, receptionists, and others, as a part of their job, may see or hear information regarding the case. An honest and easily understood message to assure the child is a clear statement that the social worker is only trying to make the situation better, not to hurt or get the child into trouble. Later, when a clear understanding of this issue has occurred, and the parents need to be made aware of a situation, it is important that the child is allowed to participate in determining how this is to be done. Possible ways of doing this and potential consequences need to be discussed. Geldard and Geldard (1997) suggest this discussion might involve questions such as the following:

> Would you like to tell your parents yourself?
> Would you like me to be present while you tell them?
> Would you like me to tell your parents with you present?
> Would you prefer me to tell your parents without you being present?
> Would you like this to happen today or at another time?

Allowing children to make choices, even if all the solutions are undesirable to him or her, gives the child a sense of empowerment and autonomy.

Beginning interviews with adolescents usually involves more direct communication than beginning interviews with children. The worker may begin by clarifying the adolescent's knowledge about why they are present. This is usually followed by further exploration of their view of the identified problems. Sometimes adolescents are reluctant to talk with the practitioner. Techniques for engaging adolescents are to ask about a typical day in their life, to encourage them to talk about their concerns even if they appear to be unrelated to the identified problem, or to involve them in a game or activity.

In working with a shy, withdrawn adolescent girl, a social worker found it useful to play the board game Sorry. The adolescent saw the game in the practitioner's office and asked about it. It was decided that they would try it. The object of the game is to draw cards and count squares on the board in an attempt to reach the end of a path first. If the player lands on the opponent's square, he or she sends the opponent back to square 1.

It was evident in the first few games that this adolescent girl could not bring herself to send the practitioner back to the beginning. In contrast, the worker sent the adolescent back to the beginning when required, and in doing so she attempted to model a caring and concerned attitude. The adolescent enjoyed the game and asked to play it almost every session. Over time she progressed to the point that she could send the opponent's piece back to the beginning, sometimes with great glee. The interaction between the practitioner and the adolescent was enjoyable. It allowed the young person to develop a trust of the worker and it helped to empower her to function in her best interest. The game helped the social worker to show caring, assess problem areas, and to observe progress in resolving them.

Adolescents often attempt to distance themselves by talking about someone else or by asking questions in the third person. If this occurs, the worker should respond by answering in the third person. Previously it was noted that the life experience of the child affects his or her view of the role and expectation of adults. Now the adolescent has experienced relationships with peers and with adults in a variety of roles. Distancing may be a way of testing the trustworthiness of the social worker.

Often, adolescents are angry with school personnel, the police department, the juvenile court system, their parents, or any source that referred them for services. They come to the social worker's office with a hostile attitude that tests the worker, serves as a defense against anxiety, or is a displacement of rage against parents. Adolescents customarily express hostility through silence. They may come into the office, slouch down in a chair, and refrain from making eye contact with the practitioner. Any questions or attempts to talk with a hostile teenager may receive no response or at best a very brief response. Silences must be interrupted soon to prevent power and control issues from erupting.

Many techniques may be used in attempting to break the silence. The worker may attempt to get the adolescent to express the anger they feel. Sometimes, the anger is an expression of their denial that they have a problem. If so, engaging the adolescent in exploring problems that are seen as important to themselves may be a useful technique. Alternatively, the worker may suggest a game or a task that the therapist and teen can carry out together. Keeping some games and objects of interest on the office shelves may promote the adolescent to initiate some discussion.

As the practitioner and adolescent begin to engage each other and some mutual understanding of the purpose and process becomes evident, the social worker may need to suggest a conceptualized hypothesis of the issues to the youth. Broad treatment goals may be offered as a place for the adolescent and worker to begin. The goals as discussed may be changed completely or modified.

As the helping relationship develops with the child or adolescent and the parents, the social worker gathers more information and understanding about the persons and situations of concern. A partnership is developed in which both the child or adolescent and practitioner have a stake. The child or adolescent brings a problem or need, emotions, conflicts and fears related to that concern, and expectations about the contact and the social worker. The worker brings a body of knowledge, access to resources, methods and skills of helping, and an orderly way of proceeding. Not only is the helping relationship a context for treatment, but it is also a dynamic element of treatment.

Assessment

Assessment, which is "the process of gathering, analyzing and synthesizing salient data," is especially difficult for school-age children (Rauch, 1993, p. xiv). It involves examining developmental stages, personality patterns that are just developing, and pathologies that are less crystallized. Assessment is not only a beginning of the helping process, but a process that continues throughout the relationship with the child or adolescent until termination. For the social worker, assessment begins even before the first client contact. When the client is referred by others or telephone calls are made for the first appointment, some information is given that begins the assessment process.

A mother may call requesting an appointment for her 8-year-old son, who is having difficulty in school. This may be the extent of the information given about the client. Even with information this brief, the practitioner begins to prepare for the ongoing assessment. Knowledge about the psychosocial development of an 8-year-old boy is necessary to compare the boy's functioning with other children of the same age, similar circumstances, and with the same attributes (Lucco, 1993). In preparation for the sessions with the child and the parents, questions are formulated about the circumstances of the difficulty in school, first thinking about the potential reasons for the difficulty. Is the child having behavior problems and learning problems? No firm answers to the questions are developed, only a readiness to begin to put facts together after interviewing the child and parents.

During the first sessions, further information is sought. Information gathered over the first few sessions provides the basis for formulating a multidimensional view of the child and circumstances as a basis for ongoing work together. In assessing children and adolescents, many areas of functioning are examined and evaluated, such as biological, cognitive, psychosocial, and others. (For further discussion, see Chapter 5.) The nature of assessment tasks varies depending on the type of setting in which help is to be given. This comprehensive evaluation is the basis for determining the specific interventions to be used with this child.

Two major types of information, namely objective and subjective, are sought in assessing children and adolescents (Garbarino, Stott, & faculty of the Erikson Institute, 1992). Objective information is observable, such as aggressiveness, symptoms of depression or hyperactivity, and other behaviors. This information may be gained through observation or formal assessment tools using a variety of psychological tests. Information of this type is provided by those having an opportunity to observe the child in various settings, such as the playground, in the home, in the neighborhood, and in social interaction. Areas for observation are the child's general appearance, behavior, mood or affect, intellectual functioning and thinking, speech and language, motor skills, play, interactions with the parents, and relationship with the social worker. More refined observations include facial expressions, posturing, gestures, and proximity to the practitioner.

Subjective information involves the child's experiences and perceptions in life. His or her perceptions may not be totally based on reality and must be recognized, evaluated, and sometimes changed by a sensitive therapist. Play or conversation with the child provides the primary content for an awareness of these views and attitudes about reality. An illustration of this is a child's perception that he or she is the cause of the split up between the parents and their decision to divorce.

It is important to understand as much as possible about the child and family. Often beginning information is gathered with the use of an intake interview with the parents and child or by using a form filled out by the client. Information gained in the first sessions includes the identity of the child and parents, their major concerns, medical history, developmental history, learning development, emotional development, special concerns, family relationship and history, and relationships with peers and others.

The environment of the child is another area for assessment. Home visits, where feasible, provide even more understanding of the client situation configuration necessary for assessment. Some environmental factors that are especially significant are adequacy of the housing, the school environment, safety of the child, social support systems, financial resources, health care, and available recreational resources. Any environmental change affecting the child and family is an area of concern. Some potentially significant changes would be moving to a foster home, requiring homemaking services, using visiting nurses' resources, referral of a family member to hospice care, parents attending Alcoholics Anonymous programs, and requests that the parents work more closely with the school.

In working with children and adolescents, interviewing, combined with observations and other kinds of interactions, allows the social worker to piece together a picture of the child's inner world. In some settings, the social worker conducts an independent assessment.

However, in other settings, such as schools, hospitals, residential settings, and other agencies that employ multiple professionals for services, a team working together makes the assessment. In these agencies, several professional persons with specialized knowledge can provide a comprehensive understanding of the child and the circumstances.

In beginning interviews the practitioner is looking for three elements, the need or problem situation of concern, feelings about the problem, and the expectation held by the child and the social worker (Thompson & Rudolph, 1988). Specific information is essential:

- The appropriateness of the child's or adolescent's behavior for the age level
- Considering the circumstances, the appropriateness of the child's behavior
- The frequency of occurrence of the problem behavior
- The duration of this behavior
- Suddenness of the behavior's occurrence
- Interference in the child's or adolescent's functioning

Broad areas to be aware of in assessing children and adolescents include developmental delays, organic disorders, conflicts and anxieties, psychosomatic disorders, mental retardation, reactive disorders, and genetically predisposed disorders (Aiello, 1999). Assessment with children is a hypothesis-generating opportunity. The core question is, Why is this child engaging in this behavior? The focus is to understand why the problem behavior is happening at this time and what can be done about it.

The search for an answer to the core question is illustrated in the case of Elena, who was present with a small group of preadolescent girls who had been referred because of delinquent behavior. Four members were present. Elena seemed to be very angry with the social worker, calling her names in Spanish. Because the worker did not know Spanish, she could only guess what was being said.

The worker questioned Elena as to why she was so angry. Elena's response was more name calling, which continued for some time with the worker trying to think of anything that had happened between sessions that could have angered Elena. Finally, one of the other members told Elena that if she did not stop, the worker would "kick her out." When Elena was reassured by the worker that this would not happen because the purpose of the group was to help the participants with behaviors that got them into trouble, the reason for her anger became evident. Elena's mother had told her that she would never leave her; however, her mother had taken the younger children and left the home the night before.

Elena became less tense and began to cry as she told the group what had happened the previous night. She had felt betrayed by her mother and now questioned whether she could trust the practitioner. Previously the group had been assured that "the group existed to help them." Elena was testing to see whether the worker would keep her word. When she found she was not rejected, she talked about what was really bothering her.

Another area of focus important to the treatment of children and adolescents is culture and ethnicity. Culture and societies determine how symptoms are defined in many cases and the type of treatment required. Even the nature of the therapist–patient relationship is determined by cultures and their beliefs. In a society that sanctions possession by devils as the principal etiological base for emotional problems, exorcism would be viewed as effective treatment and the therapist would have a magical role. On the other hand, in a society in which personal achievement and independence are valued characteristics, the practitioner tends to promote mutual investigation into the way the individual relates to others (Group for the Advancement of Psychiatry, 1982).

Ethnicity affects characteristics such as style of dress, language, holidays and ways of celebrating them, and more subtle factors, such as family structure, styles of relating to others, communication of feelings, attitudes, values, and behaviors. Lieberman (1990) suggests that cultural sensitivity be thought of as a form of interpersonal sensitivity and attunement to specific idiosyncracies of another person. Attunement will result in practice that attempts to understand the subjective world of the client. It also accepts and respects the client's ethnic and cultural traditions. In working with children and adolescents, it has been found that communication and understanding of the child's culture creates trust and reduces defensiveness (Westwood & Ishiyama, 1990).

Assessment of Special Concerns

The problems of children and adolescents often occur because of difficulties in the functioning of their families. For the practitioner to make an assessment, to help identify goals, and to prepare a treatment plan, it is essential for the worker to be aware of specific family problems known to affect the child. Some specific conditions of concern are families that are violent, those affected by drugs and alcohol abuse, those in which parents have divorced, stepfamilies, those in which a recent death has taken place, and many other conditions.

Substance abuse problems touch most persons in the United States (Watkins & Durant, 1996). Substance abuse in the home has been strongly related to violence in all forms of spouse and child abuse. Neglect can be expected in many families in which a parent is addicted and may result in lack of attachment and inability of the child to fully function in the future. Children who have been exposed to an atmosphere of drug use are more impulsive, deficient in play skills, less goal oriented, and less securely attached than nonexposed children (Combrinck-Graham, 1995). In research, Youngstrom (1991) concluded that children exposed to cocaine use in the home had more serious behavior problems than those who had been exposed in the womb.

Often, the parent's use of drugs and the guilt that follows produce negative conditions for healthy development of children. These conditions may result in the child's exposure to extremes of sudden harsh punishment, perhaps child abuse, along with guilt-ridden overindulgence and gentle kindness. It is important for the social worker to focus on the symptoms and the underlying causes for the child's behavior. If addiction is occurring in the home, therapy for the whole family is desirable. Although family therapy is not always feasible for a variety of reasons, oftentimes children in these situations can be helped.

In exploring the child's problem through talking and playing, the social worker may discover that the child, who is living in an addictive situation, can be helped. If the home is dangerous for the child, he or she may be removed and placed with relatives or with foster parents after a report has been made to the Office of Community Services.

Most children of addicted parents continue to live in their own homes. The child may need help to achieve developmental tasks that have not yet been accomplished. For instance, a child who is 7 years of age and in the second grade has difficulty in getting along with peers and needs some help in developing peer relationships. If lack of play skills or inability to identify goals and accomplish tasks is the deficit, these areas may be the specific focus for the social worker. Being aware of problems expected in children living in homes in which substance abuse is occurring provides a starting point for assessment of the child.

Determining the child's strengths and resources is a major part of the assessment. The child is first viewed in comparison with other children of the same age, then he or she is individualized to develop a treatment plan. The practitioner develops a plan for a particular child in a particular situation.

Assessment occurs at the beginning of the helping process and is also a continuing activity for the practitioner throughout the helping relationship with the client or adolescent. As the child's situation changes, the social worker notes this and alters the evaluation. Because assessment occurs from moment to moment, it helps to decide the kind of relationship to form, both with the child and others in the environment; "hence it determines the intervention itself" (Bisman, 1994, p. 112). In summary, the nature of assessment tasks varies in differing settings, but the process used is similar in the differing settings.

Planning and Goal Setting

Planning is the bridge between assessment and work toward specific goals in the treatment process. It translates assessment content into goal statements that describe the desired results (Johnson, 1992). The plan identifies both process and outcomes by specifying intermediate objectives and end goals. Assessment develops from the observations of the child and the situation. This material is conceptualized and from this we create treatment hypotheses. Then treatment strategies can be planned and applied to the child in the situation.

Planning calls for a complex set of decisions. These decisions are informed by a broad body of knowledge that links purposes to action. Components of the plan are stated in terms of goals and objectives. Planning includes the means to reaching goals. It encompasses the unit of attention, strategies to be used, and roles and tasks to be used. It sequences the tasks, specifies the time frame, and considers the cost. A goal is the overall, long-range expected outcome. To reach the end result, intermediate goals or objectives are identified. An objective is a miniplan within the overall plan. The objective is expressed in terms of the desired outcome. The following case of Louis is an example of planning.

Louis is a 7-year-old boy living with his mother and his 13-year-old sister in the family home in a middle-class residential area. Louis was an outgoing, happy child until his parents divorced. Since he has been aware that his parents are divorcing, he has become very quiet, withdrawn, and openly expresses little feeling about the situation. He seems unable to concentrate in school and withdraws to his room when he returns from school.

After an assessment of Louis and the situation, the social worker began to conceptualize this information. A first step for Louis may be to understand what and why the family change is occurring. Strategies, which are planned attempts to influence persons or systems in relation to a goal, are identified. The purpose of the strategy is to stimulate discussion, allowing Louis to express feelings and to clarify the reality of the situation.

Louis and his mother help the worker develop goals to assist Louis with his adjustment:

- Accept the fact that his parents are divorcing.
- Understand that he is not alone.
- Help him reconnect with his peers.
- Involve him in after-school activities.

Intermediate goals or objectives for the first goal are:

- Express feelings about the divorce to the practitioner.
- Talk with his mother and father about what this means for him and discuss this content with the worker.

Strategies for the first objective follow:

- After a discussion about the meaning of divorce, ask Louis to draw a picture of his family before the divorce.
- After a discussion about the "old family," have him draw a picture of the "new family" and discuss differences including both the good things and the bad consequences of the change.
- Read a book about divorce written from a child's point of view and discuss it.
- Role play with him a situation in which he tells his best friend about his parent's divorce.

Planning calls for a complex set of decisions informed by a broad body of knowledge. The plan must be relatively complete, but at the same time must be flexible and permit changes as the process develops. After a plan is completed, it is presented to Louis and his parents for agreement and modification, if needed. Together they contract to follow through on this plan.

It should be noted that some goals identified for Louis's treatment could probably best be accomplished in a group setting. After several sessions with the social worker, Louis may be referred to a group of children having similar problems, if available. Louis might be seen concurrently by the worker individually and still participate in the group, or he may move from individual sessions to ongoing participation in a group.

The Middle Phase

From the beginning phase, a basic concern of the practitioner is the need to establish trust with the child or adolescent. This is not always an easy task. Children have a wide range of abilities to trust adults, depending on their psychosocial development, age, and experiences. If a child has not previously experienced a trusting relationship, the development of complete trust in the social worker may be difficult if not impossible. The other factor that may affect the development of trust is the age of the child. Often, adolescents are more peer oriented and may be reticent to communicate with adults, fearing that information revealed may be shared with their parents.

To cultivate trust, it is essential for the practitioner to be attuned continually to any nuances that may indicate the child's concern in this area. It is not unusual for the child actively to test the trustworthiness of the social worker in a variety of ways. He or she may tell the worker shocking accounts to discover whether they will be shared with the parents. Another method of testing the social worker's trust is to talk about subject areas that are taboo. This type of behavior occurs often and over a long period of time with children who have not learned to trust.

A primary way of developing trust is through communication, both verbal and non-verbal. During the middle phase, the focus of helping is clearly on the problems or needs that brought the child and parents to the social worker. The child must be allowed and encouraged to tell his or her story, sometimes in words but often in behaviors, or through the use of activities and games. If the child is able to recount what is happening in his or her life, the practitioner listens for the child's latent as well as manifest messages and interprets the concerns, meanings, and manner in which the story is related. Being aware of the tempo, stress, intensity, articulation, and quality of the communication provides clues about the child's functioning.

Verbal Communication

Child clients frequently need some help in communicating. Often, the social worker asks questions to help fill in the gaps and create a fuller understanding of the situation. Children are easily influenced by adults and the way questions are asked. Sometimes the child answers what he or she thinks will satisfy the questioner. The child's answer may also be influenced by the preceding question, what he or she thinks the question means, and what answer the interviewer will accept. Answers are often affected by what the child or youth thinks the consequences will be of providing the information (Garbarino, Stott, & faculty of Erikson Institute, 1992; Geldard & Geldard, 1997).

Usually, open-ended questions are more appropriate than closed-ended questions, which can be answered by one or two words. Understanding the specific question from the perspective of the child is important. Using empathy, which means "the ability to understand a particular thought, feeling, or behavior by seeing it through the child's eyes" is the essence of true communication and understanding of the situation (Orton, 1996, p. 180).

Time may be needed for the child to feel comfortable and safe in this new environment. A sense of control in the interview may be especially important for some children. "Telling the story" provides an opportunity for the child to clarify and gain a cognitive understanding of events and issues (Geldard & Geldard, 1997). It is an active means for the child to ventilate painful feelings and to deal with anxieties. The worker uses active listening skills made up of major components such as matching the body language of the child, using minimal responses, using reflection, and summarizing.

Communicating through Activities

For children who are unable adequately to verbalize the problems and issues of concern, play, games, or other activities may be used. Play allows the child to deal with anxiety-producing or sensitive material as if it were someone else's problems. Symbols may be used through taking different roles, and transferring feelings or emotional states either as real or pretend play. It also allows the child to reverse roles and deal with taboo subjects (Fatout, 1996).

An attempt is made to help the child gain mastery over issues and events and empower him or her to enhance self-esteem and social relationships. This can be accomplished by reenacting past events and traumas or simulating an event that was not experienced previously to experience power and control. Materials and activities used to accomplish this include books and stories, drawing pictures, imaginary journeys, painting and collages, pretend play, puppets and soft toys, symbols and figurines, and sand trays.

Some specific materials are especially helpful in encouraging a child to express emotions. Clay is an especially useful medium for expressing sadness, fear, or worry. Drawing allows the expression of a variety of emotions. Sometimes, finger paints aid in expressing the emotions of joy, happiness, and celebration. The physical use of some materials helps make the child feel powerful. Punching a lump of clay or play dough, engaging in mock battles between good and evil puppets, or burying objects in the sand tray, all allow aggression and related feelings to be expressed.

A variety of activities help the child develop problem-solving and decision-making skills. Storytelling and books are useful materials for exploring and thinking about alternatives. Storytelling allows the child to distance him- or herself from frightening or unacceptable emotions. Puppets, toys, and tape recorders are useful in promoting ideas for the child to make up dialogue to solve problems. Children may need to visualize the situation through the use of dollhouses, miniature cars, figurines, and sand trays.

Social workers need to learn and understand the meaning of play and activities just as they learn verbal communication. Purposefully planned use of activities requires the worker to think through the use, required skills, degree of necessary control, appropriateness to the issue of concern, cultural sensitivity, and timing. Attention is also given to past activities, their purposes and success, the present needs of the child, and how this is expected to move him or her toward the contracted goals.

To begin each session, the social worker selects materials to be made available for play or other activities. Planning is based on assessing the child's abilities and problem areas that are the focus at that time. Awareness of the impulse control and attention span of the child partially determines what and how many toys, games, books, or other materials are available in the room at one time. For example, Louis, who needed to accept the fact that his parents were divorcing, was asked to draw a picture of his family before the divorce. Crayons and paper needed to be immediately available for the boy's use.

Because the practitioner expects to have a discussion with Louis about divorce, a storybook might be useful for concentrating attention on this area. However, because Louis has been found to be very focused, other material in the room is not expected to be distracting and may be useful in expressing some of his feelings nonverbally. For example, if stories and storytelling are to be used in working with Louis, it may be important to have toy cars and balls available. Often, the expression of feelings may be expressed verbally but may also need to be expressed by actions. Causing wrecks with toy cars or throwing a ball at the wall may help to vent some of the anger or frustration that the child is unable to express verbally.

Other Interventions

A variety of alternative interventions can be used in working with children. Often, children are seen in groups. In addition to play, teaching new skills, rehearsing new ways of interacting, reinforcing new or desired behaviors, and conducting trips in the community are all intended to help the child develop more appropriate thinking and functioning. For the social worker to help the child or adolescent facilitate a change, options must be explored. Once an option has been selected, rehearsing and experiencing new behaviors provide a way of testing new behaviors.

Sometimes the child or adolescent needs help in developing a plan to control behavior and to use the newly acquired knowledge and skills in coping with situations in the future. Regardless of the intervention used, summarizing at the end of each session provides some clarity about the thinking and accomplishments at that time. It helps the child or adolescent recognize and repeat their accomplishments and learn and understand how they occurred.

The overall helping process is a problem-solving process that Compton and Galaway (1994) have described as follows: "The problem-solving process may be understood as a series of interactions between the client system and the practitioner, involving integrating feeling, thinking, and doing, guided by a purpose and directed toward achieving an agreed-upon goal" (p. 43). The problem-solving process, regardless of setting, is used in accomplishing a variety of objectives, including prevention, mediation, rehabilitation, and enhancement for both children and adolescents.

Intervention Skills

The helping relationship, verbal communication, and communication through activities are all necessary in working with children and adolescents. The social worker's major activities with the client may vary with the child's age and the particular situation. Usually, the practitioner attempts to increase clients' understanding of themselves and their situation, develop social competencies, resolve identity issues, overcome obstacles, and enhance opportunities in the environment (Northen, 1982). These aims are particularly applicable in working with adolescent clients. Often, the focus in practice with children is enhancing current functioning or helping them through fantasies, stories, and other means to work through developmental issues.

It is often difficult for children to modify their behavior and understand their problems and situations due to their level of development. For example, a 7-year-old girl was unable verbally to work through her understanding of her situation because of her inability to think abstractly. For several weeks, she continued building a house out of blocks and each time pretended that the house burned down. As she talked about the house burning, she was very gleeful. This is most understandable in reviewing her background. She had been abused and terribly damaged in her home. Feelings she had experienced and the relief of separation were displayed in her repetitious play. Some of the feelings about what had happened to her were worked out and put away without her being aware or understanding why she had been behaving in this way. This "working through" only became evident as the child no longer needed to continue this type of play.

The practitioner uses his or her personality, values, knowledge, and skills in help giving. With knowledge and sensitivity the practitioner must also use herself or himself to provide the interventions, experiences, and interactions to help accomplish the predetermined goals. In the middle phase the social worker is expected to have a clear understanding of the goals. It is important to plan possible sequential intermediary goals, which are expected to lead toward the final outcome. This plan must be very flexible because of the spontaneity of the children and their relatively short attention span. For example, if the practitioner has set the scene for using dolls and a dollhouse for a session to help the child with family relationships, but the child has found a turtle on the way to the session, the turtle will no doubt become the focus of attention. If the worker is creative, he or she may be able to move the child to talk about turtle families and their relations with each other. The interaction between the worker and child and resources available provide the primary means of change and goal accomplishment.

Ending Phase

Termination is a vital part of the treatment process. As the child or adolescent becomes aware of changes that have been made, how they were accomplished, and how to repeat the skills and behaviors learned, they can duplicate this experience in relationships outside the therapeutic setting. Specific goals must be accomplished in preparation for ending the helping relationship. This is the time to summarize and evaluate progress and to finish tasks that have not yet been completed. In addition, preparation must be made to put to use this newly acquired knowledge.

A goal that is especially important in working with children is resolving ambivalence about leaving the relationship. If this is not done successfully, it may be perceived by the child as a negative experience and a loss, to be avoided in the future. The result of this type of negative experience is illustrated by Karen, a child in a residential treatment center. A social work intern reviewed case recordings with her supervisor to determine which children needed special help. Karen was selected and arrangements were made to meet her in a social work office.

However, Karen did not come at the appointed time, so the student went to her living unit to see what had happened. She found Karen lying on her bed and asked whether she could talk to her. Karen reluctantly agreed. When Karen was questioned about missing her appointment, she turned to face the wall with her back to the worker and said she did not want to talk to her. She said that in the past she had too many "friendships that were bad." Karen went on to say that when they had gotten close, the person "just disappeared," and that hurt too much. So she was not going to do this again. Obviously, Karen had not been terminated previously in a helpful manner and perceived that the outcome expected would be hurt rather than help.

Endings may stir up a variety of feelings, both positive and negative. Termination should be a meaningful and growth-producing experience. Children and adolescents need to leave the social work experience with a sense of achievement and a belief in their ability to function in everyday life at home, in school, and in their community.

The way the termination process is planned and conducted depends on the nature of the relationship, duration of treatment, and the reasons for termination. Termination of a helping relationship may occur for a variety of reasons (Rose, 1989a). Ideally, the reason for ending is that goals have been accomplished and the child is ready to move on. However, a variety of other causes for ending, such as the worker's caseload is transferred, the worker leaves the job, or the child discontinues treatment, or moves from the area, are not uncommon occurrences. When the number of sessions has been determined in the beginning, accepting the end of the relationship is easier for the child or adolescent. An awareness of the time for ending allows children or adolescents to recognize the importance of accomplishing their goals in a timely way.

Generally, ending the relationship is easier if there have been fewer sessions rather than many sessions over a long period of time. If the number of sessions is limited, the focus of work is directly on the goals. If the relationship occurs over a longer period of time, it is expected that the relationship may become more important. Sometimes the longer-term relationship may promote more dependency than empowerment.

Preparation for Ending

As part of the ambivalence felt by the child or adolescent, both positive and negative feelings are usually present as endings occur. Although termination or ending is often predominantly characterized by positive feelings, a sense of sadness and loss may also be present. Adolescents are often anxious to end treatment and may have a sense of achievement about gains that were made.

In preparation for termination, it is helpful occasionally to mention the time of ending. Often, denial is used as a defense, and time needs to be allowed for working through feelings and preparation for separation. Although the ending is decided on in the beginning, reminding the child about two-thirds of the way through that the social worker will not be meeting after a specific date helps the child and worker refocus on problem solving, using the remaining time profitably, and prepare for separation. Young children demonstrating the impending ending in a concrete, visual manner is especially helpful. One way to help the child visualize and understand the approaching ending is to place items such as pennies or candy in a box or jar, removing one each session and counting the items that remain. With older children and adolescents, a calendar is used to help visualize the amount of time left for work. In one of the last few sessions, it may be important for the social worker to clarify, in discussion with the child or adolescent, what he or she will be doing after the sessions end. This is intended to help them understand that in the future they will no longer be coming to the sessions.

Loss and separation are common themes during termination. Forms of expression of dependency are common. Through words or actions the child may express the need to continue with the social worker. Regression may be used for this purpose. Issues that seemed to have been resolved earlier may reappear in an effort to demonstrate that he or she still needs services.

Mack was very sad and upset as he came to the session. He had originally come to the agency to get help because of his bullying in school. Today, he told about getting in trouble in school. He gave details of the incident and assured the practitioner that he still needed help. At the previous session, Mack and the worker discussed the fact that they would be ending in 2 weeks. Later, as the practitioner talked to Mack's teacher, she found that the incident had been minor and was quickly resolved. Mack was attempting to get the social worker to extend the number of sessions because he did not want to end the relationship. He was trying to show that he still needed services.

Many children and adolescents are ready to end the sessions with the social worker. They feel that they have made significant gains and are ready to go out into the community and use their new skills. So ending is viewed as a time for celebration. Usually, the client and practitioner plan a ritual to break the ties, to mark the ending of the sessions together. They may have refreshments, receive a certificate, or celebrate in a way that is meaningful to the child or adolescent.

The social worker too has feelings about terminating the relationship. These feelings may be similar to those of the child. He or she may feel sad at ending the relationship. At the same time, the worker may feel excited and relieved regarding the outcome. After evaluating the experience, the worker may have a great sense of satisfaction. Experiences that were helpful and those that might have been done differently can be identified.

Along with ventilation of feelings and at least partial resolution of ambivalence, the social worker engages the child or adolescent client in a review of progress. This is an attempt to help the young person understand that problem-solving skills that have been learned can be applied to new situations. As the practitioner and client review the experience together, the practitioner needs to be secure enough to listen and respond nondefensively to any of the latter's criticism of practices and processes used.

The ending phase involves an informal evaluation. Examining and expressing feelings of both parties promotes attention to successes, failures, and work still to be done. In addition, more formal means of evaluating progress made is imperative. Examining progress or lack of progress in accomplishing goals is often the first area to be explored.

In working with children and adolescents, gathering information about the current functioning of the client in the home, community, and school is useful. Often, determined by the length of treatment, collateral contacts may have been made throughout the period of work. Sometimes collaterals are only contacted before termination to assess changes in functioning of the children or adolescents that they have observed in their setting. As indicated earlier, the child or adolescent may be encouraged to take part in these contacts. An important aspect of this process of evaluation, which is useful in evaluating goal achievement, includes the observations of any changes that the parents or guardians have observed.

Sometimes, parents also express concern about the child or adolescent maintaining the gains made. As the sessions are ending, part of the work to be done is to stabilize gains that have been made. One means of doing this is conducting an evaluation of the progress that has been made with the children or adolescents. Seeing where they were in the beginning and where they are now is useful for empowering them and increasing their self-confidence. Fuller stabilization of gains may occur as the child or adolescent and the social worker discuss how future situations might be handled. The social worker and the young client may role play possible situations to further test the child's or adolescent's ability to deal with persons and situations that might be expected to occur.

In some settings, termination requires the referral of the child or adolescent to another service. A child or adolescent being seen by a social worker in a hospital setting for physical injuries may be referred to a rehabilitation setting on discharge. A child treated in a mental health center because of relationship problems with peers may be referred to a youth agency where social skills learned can be immediately applied in new relationships. If a referral of this type is made, it is important that the social worker follow through and make contact with the new service provider. Sometimes a meeting is set to make necessary connections with the new provider and the child or adolescent.

Often, the social worker may assure the child and parents that they may return to the agency later if further help is needed. In most cases, if the current worker is no longer there, another person in that agency could be of assistance. Often children and adolescents who have had a productive relationship with a worker in an agency ascribe helpfulness to everyone in the agency, sometimes including the receptionist and building maintenance personnel.

Follow-up may also be done by social workers in some agencies. Perhaps a month or two following termination, a call is made to the client to make a brief assessment. This contact can remind the client of the gains that they have made and encourage them to use these skills in current situations.

Evaluation

An ethical principle of social work asserts that social workers are accountable for what they do and the method of doing it. They along with their clients are accountable for the degree of attainment of goals. Social workers are expected to evaluate their own practice and to be accountable for the choice of practice models used. It is expected that the theoretical approach used in working with children or adolescents takes into account needs, capacities, culture, and problems.

The evaluation is based on the overall plan for service and on the contract made with the child or adolescent and the parents. Adherence to basic ethical principles such as informed consent and confidentiality is essential. Social workers are responsible for using the best knowledge available through research and practice experience.

Records are essential to determining progress made by the child or adolescent and the interventions that have been helpful. Increasingly, social workers are held accountable for their practice by clients and the public at large. Third-party payers and managed-care organizations require that practitioners meet standards that they have determined. Records are required for this purpose.

Outcome evaluations are very important in determining appropriate use of helping skills by the social worker and also for advancing knowledge about the effectiveness of specific interventions. This type of evaluation includes the definition of the problem area, methods used to resolve the problem, the desired outcome, and the criteria for measuring attainment. Single-subject designs are useful for measuring progress made by clients. In working with children, developmental issues need to be taken into account in interpreting change.

Many standardized measures of evaluation are available for use. The social worker is responsible for selecting the appropriate one. Some standardized measures are questionnaires, checklists, rapid assessment instruments, personality tests, interview schedules, and sentence completion tests.

Conclusion

Working with children and adolescents is complex because of the many facets and dynamics of behavior immediately evident to the social worker. At the same time it is very challenging to interweave the open, unguarded revelations of the child and adolescent into a more complete and accurate picture, allowing needs and problems to become apparent and available for resolution.

Social work practice and research of outcomes is dependent on a complete and comprehensive exploration of the areas of problem or need. Assessment, which is explored in more detail and described in the following chapter, is the basis for successful practice in working with children and adolescents.

CHAPTER

5

Assessing the Competencies and Difficulties of Children and Adolescents

Assessment is an integral component of social work practice with children and adolescents (Chethik, 1989) that often precedes and guides active intervention. Although most assessment activity occurs at the beginning phase of practitioner–client interaction, assessment continues on as an ongoing activity through the middle and ending phases too.

Assessment entails participation in a series of information collection activities about child and adolescent clients, and observation of the child or adolescent, which encompasses viewing the interaction with the client and gathering observational data. At some point in the assessment process, participation and observation merge. During interaction with their young clients, practitioners simultaneously participate in the interaction and observe themselves, their clients, and the dyadic interaction.

Social work practitioners form assessments that are formal or informal, written or unwritten, explicit or tacit, objective or subjective, and specific or global. Practitioners assess the social and emotional, cognitive and language, moral and ethical, and physical and perceptual-motor domains of development of children and adolescents. They determine the extent to which youngsters exceed, are within the norms, or lag in particular developmental domains.

This chapter examines the assessment of the functioning, behavior, and development of children and adolescents as a primary role of direct service practitioners. This chapter describes the assessment roles of practitioners; diagnosis and assessment including referral processes; practitioner perspectives; and the development, competencies, and problems of children and adolescents that are subject to assessment.

Problem Recognition and Referral Processes

Problems tend to have real and perceived aspects. Family members are key players in the assessment of children's difficulties. Parents, and other family members, may recognize the child's difficulties.

When parents and children share related difficulties, four possible situations may occur stemming from the interaction of two problem recognition dimensions. Moreover, problem recognition encompasses recognition of the existence of the problem, understanding the nature of the problem, and assuming a readiness to act on behalf of the child to remedy the problem.

On one dimension, the parents do or do not recognize their own problem. On a second dimension, the parents do or do not recognize the problem of their child. The interaction of these two dimensions results in four possible problem recognition situations. In one situation, the parents recognize their own problem and recognize the problem of their child. In a second situation, the parents recognize their own problem and do not recognize the problem of their child. In a third situation, the parents do not recognize their own problem yet recognize the problem of their child. In a fourth situation, the parents neither recognize their own problem nor the problem of their child.

Of the four possible problem recognition assessment situations, the two most common situations appear to be those in which congruency exists in problem recognition between parent and child. In those instances in which parents perceive their own difficulties as worthy of remediation, they may also see the difficulties of their own children as being worthy of remediation. Moreover, in those instances in which parents have difficulties that they tend to deny, they are likely to deny similar difficulties in their own children.

At times, astute parents notice developmental problems of their children. Furthermore, in some instances a developmental problem is brought to the attention of the parent by another family member, or a school or agency representative. The parent is more likely to accept the difficulty that has been brought to their attention if it is presented tactfully and appropriately. Ideally, problem recognition is accompanied by a decision in favor of help seeking.

The service location of screening assessments is determined by the social agency that receives the referral. Social work practitioners who work in an information and referral capacity are responsible for determining the best setting for the assessment of the child or adolescent. Practitioners in the intake section of an agency are likely to be responsible for conducting an initial problem screening. They determine the seriousness of the young person's problem and the urgency of an assessment. Situations in which the health and well-being of the child or adolescent is in danger require rapid assessments and intervention.

Some assessments are preventive. Public health officials in the community may conduct mass screenings that determine the incidence of developmental problems of many youngsters. Pediatricians also assess children, especially preschool children, for developmental difficulties.

The Smith family, who lived in a rural area, were delighted with the birth of their second child, Susan. However, their pediatrician was concerned about the development of the infant and requested that the parents seek a consultation. The Smiths brought Susan to the local mental health center where their child was assessed by a pediatric social worker. The social worker reviewed the records, interviewed the parents with Susan, and consequently made an appointment for her to be seen by an experienced pediatric neurologist, Dr. Singer, who flew in once a month for a day of assessments and consultations. Two months later Susan was seen by Dr. Singer. Although Dr. Singer immediately recognized that Susan had moderate mental retardation, he patiently and extensively examined her before offering his diagnosis to the parents. Although the Smiths were shocked, they accepted the diagnosis and began planning for appropriate social and health services.

The Perspective of the Practitioner

Social work practitioners tend to perceive children in one of two ways, corresponding to deficits and strengths models. Each model is associated with a cognitive style of the practitioner. In both models it is assumed that the child has the potential to improve wellness and health. However, the strengths model tends to be more optimistic about potential improvements whereas the deficits model tends to be less sanguine and more realistic about such improvements.

The traditional role of social work practitioners has been to determine the nature and extent of the deficits and difficulties children experience to ameliorate them. The deficit model derives from the perspective of medical practitioners who attempt to locate pathology to treat disease. The deficit model, which is widely used in health and mental health care practice settings, is most useful in conjunction with a categorical system for diagnosis and assessment.

The severity or seriousness of the identified problem is assessed by the practitioner. In the deficit model one of two assumptions may be held by practitioners, depending on whether the identified problem is minor or major. An assumption, which usually is held when the identified problem is minor, is that aside from the identified problem, the child or adolescent is presumably largely or completely well or healthy. Another assumption, which usually is held when the identified problem is major, is that because the child or adolescent has the identified problem, he or she is presumably largely or completely unwell. Reactions to the latter assumption have contributed to the development of the strengths model.

The strengths model tends to accentuate the positive aspects of children's development and functioning and assist youngsters in their overall development. The more newly developed strengths model involves focusing on abilities, that is, determining the strengths or competencies of children and adolescents to build on them. Competence refers to the capacity of the child or adolescent actively and effectively to manage environmental demands and opportunities (Van Aken, 1992). Primary features of the strengths model for practitioners are that child and adolescent clients have healthy characteristics and have the potential to increase their health and well-being. Such expectations are useful in setting the goals of social work with children and in guiding the treatment process.

The deficit model and the strengths model are complementary. Practitioners usually choose either the deficit model or the strengths model as a function of their professional and agency philosophy of care. However, each model has its limitations. For instance, the strengths model is most useful in areas of practice in which global approaches to assessment are held. However, it may lead to a disregard of problematic aspects. To address the limitations of each model, practitioners may need to employ a balanced perspective in which they consider both the presence and lack of abilities among clients. Ideally, practitioners simultaneously maintain a balanced perspective of assessing all areas, including those in which the child is functioning well and those that are problematic. Practitioners thereby form bilateral assessments that encompass both competent and problematic aspects of children's and adolescents' functioning, behavior, and development.

The Diagnostic Practitioner Role

Social workers Joan and Jane had a debate about diagnosis. Joan, who prefers to use the strengths model, would rather look at children's existing abilities than their difficulties. She dislikes labeling children and feels that labels are negative and stigmatize children. She says diagnosis is labeling. She feels that labels stay with children for a long period of time. She feels that children's difficulties are rarely serious enough to warrant using a label.

Jane says that although she makes diagnoses, she does not label the children with whom she works. She believes that she is a realist and just does what she needs to do. She recognizes that not all children are absolutely well and healthy all the time. She feels that they come to her for help for a reason and she believes that making a diagnosis allows her to focus on an area that needs to be attended to for her work. She feels that it is better to label a disorder and treat it than avoid the disorder. She likes the medical model, believes working on a team with medical personnel provides a stimulating experience, and works well with health professionals. She is comfortable looking at difficulties, knowing that in most cases she is able to be helpful in ameliorating them.

Julia overheard the debate between Joan and Jane. She agreed with some of what each had to say. However, Julia said that a balanced model encompasses both perspectives. Diagnosis as well as an assessment of strengths are parts of the total picture. She said that the glass is both half full and half empty. She indicated that Joan and Jane do not have to disagree if they are moderate and if a balanced perspective is used.

Diagnostic Accuracy

The assessment process, which encompasses a consideration of the strengths and limitations of children and adolescents, also includes diagnosis, a hallmark of contemporary social work practice with children and adolescents. The strengths of children and adolescents can be addressed in a global assessment of their functioning. Occasionally, a diagnosis reveals strengths, which also tend to be revealed through the social history process.

Practitioners are most likely to function as diagnosticians in the early phase of the process of working with children and adolescents (Combrinck-Graham, 1990). Indeed, they are often called upon to formulate a diagnosis in the first few meetings with their young clients. They proceed to practice based on their initial diagnostic formulation, which they may subsequently revise. Occasionally, they provide an early provisional diagnosis, which is clarified in later meetings.

Social work practitioners are careful in diagnosing children and adolescents. They may consult with other professionals to arrive at the most accurate diagnosis. In their assessments of children and adolescents, practitioners aim to be accurate in determining problem presence, type, importance, and intensity. They wish to determine that a problem is present when it actually is present, and not present when it actually is not present.

However, obstacles exist in conducting and arriving at an accurate diagnosis. Inaccuracies include seeing a problem when it does not actually exist, as in making a diagnosis when the condition is not present. Another inaccuracy is not seeing a problem when it actually does exist, as in not making a particular diagnosis when the condition is present. A "true" diagnosis may exist even if the practitioner does not make such a diagnosis because of a false belief that the client is healthy and has no diagnosis, because of an unwillingness to make any diagnosis, or because of arriving at an erroneous, alternative diagnosis.

Diagnostic aspects of assessment tend to emphasize the investigation of perceived limitations. Unfortunately, diagnostic labels have the potential to stigmatize children and adolescents. Diagnoses vary on a public/private dimension such that some disorders are more socially noticeable whereas others are less noticeable. Stigma is associated with disorders based on people's belief systems about the causation of disorder. To minimize stigma, practitioners strive to maintain confidentiality in regard to the diagnosis.

Children and adolescents tend to label themselves in the same way others label them. If others label them in positive ways, they may label themselves in positive ways. Unfortunately, if others label them in negative ways, they may also label themselves in a correspondingly negative manner. Practitioners tend to distinguish between the child and the diagnosis so that the child is neither referred to nor thought of as being the diagnosis.

Diagnosis is a necessity in health and mental health services, and in some other arenas as well, such as in special education. In health and mental health settings, practice is closely keyed to diagnosis (Simeon & Ferguson, 1990). The diagnoses of children and adolescents are many. The diagnostic systems used include, yet are not limited to, the DSM-IV (American Psychiatric Association, 2000).

Diagnoses of children and adolescents vary in terms of their importance, severity, and prognosis. Importance of diagnosis is related to the comprehensiveness of the potential impact on the developing youngster. Whereas some diagnoses, such as schizophrenia, tend to be important in their own right, other diagnoses, such as eneuresis, which nevertheless require assessment and intervention, may be less important. Moreover, each particular diagnostic category may also vary in severity. For instance, mental retardation may be mild, moderate, severe, or profound.

Children and adolescents, and their families, may experience psychosocial reactions to the diagnosis, prognosis, and treatment of health and mental health disorders. Prognosis varies as a function of diagnosis and treatment. Diagnoses of serious physical health disorders, which may carry implications of pain and suffering and issues of life and death, are often fear arousing to parents and their children.

The meaning and implications of physical health diagnoses may be clearer to children, adolescents, and their families than mental health diagnoses. In physical health care, social work practitioners attend to the correlates and consequences of the disorder, including its diagnosis and treatment. In mental health care, practitioners tend to be more integrally involved in treating the disorder per se than in physical health care. Practitioners provide support to diagnosed children and adolescents, and their families, and refer them to support groups as needed.

In health and mental health settings, diagnosis is often based on team work (Plenk, 1993). Moreover, the team that carries out the diagnosis is often the team which carries out treatment. In child guidance and evaluation clinics, practitioners carry out assessments of youngsters through a data-gathering process that can be lengthy. Often, assessment is carried out by a team. Team members assess family dynamics and may make mental health diagnoses. Following their assessments, team members usually treat the children and families. Treatment team members have responsibilities in accordance with their professional strengths. In addition to working with children and adolescents, social workers are responsible for working with parents, families, schools, and community resources.

Social work practitioners in school systems have a range of professional responsibilities. In many school systems, the social worker's primary responsibility is to conduct assessments of pupils' educational development and behavior. Assessments are carried out by social workers as members of pupil personnel teams. Generally, children and adolescents in school systems who are referred for treatment are those who have engaged in some disturbed or disturbing behavior that has brought them to the attention of school officials. Most assessments culminate in a recommendation for treatment. A potential outcome of an assessment, which rarely occurs, is that a child is not in need of treatment.

In the past, many adolescents were referred for treatment outside the school setting. Today, depending on the nature of the problem and the resources available to treat it, children and adolescents may be referred for treatment either within the school system or at a social agency in the community. Social work assessments may involve separate interviews with each parent and with the child or adolescent who has been referred for social services, as well as conjoint interviews with both parents and interviews with the entire family (Gardner, 1993; Semrud-Clikeman, 1995; Wachtel, 1994). In families of divorce, the interview process may include biological parents and stepparents in multiple families. Or, the social worker may interview individuals and subsystems of entire families, as in a parent and child together.

Child Development: Norms and Lags

A major goal of social work practice is to help youngsters develop as normally as possible given their social situation. Normal development, which encompasses an approximation to average development, primarily refers to statistical or numerical norms. As such, a wide range of development is considered normal.

By definition, most children, including youngsters in primary prevention programs, develop normally. In regular education programs in schools, most children who are assessed are within the normal range of development. Even among children who are normal in overall development, however, it is likely that at least some of them will be assessed as lagging in one or more domains of child development. Delays or lags are measured in terms of statistical differences that suggest that particular children are behind their age group in one or more developmental domains.

Moreover, in secondary and tertiary prevention settings, such as special education programs and rehabilitation centers, many youngsters are assessed to be lagging in one or more developmental domains. Fewer children in treatment programs in such settings are expected to develop normally than are children in primary prevention programs. However, it is expected that treatment will increase the proportion of children who develop normally. It is reasonable for most parents to expect their children to develop normally. Moreover, some parents expect their children to develop perfectly. Social work practitioners attempt to modify expectations of parents given the developmental status of their child, projected future development, and intervention programs.

Practitioners are responsible for determining when child and adolescent clients experience delays or lags in development. Parents of child and adolescent clients may expect practitioners to search for and detect delays in children even if they may initially deny such findings in their children. Whether practitioners are directly responsible for the assessment of developmental delays or have other responsibilities in working with children or adolescents, they are expected to be able to determine substantial delays in development.

Social workers are also expected and required to identify factors, such as child abuse and neglect, that contribute to or exacerbate developmental delays. Practitioners' detection of developmental delays are subject to confirmation by other professionals and team members and further assessment and diagnostic procedures. A psychoeducational assessment specialist helps determine whether a child has a reading problem, what the nature of the problem is, and what kind of treatment might be useful. Further testing determines whether an adolescent client who appears to be very nervous indeed has an anxiety disorder, the type of anxiety disorder, and potential remedies.

Practitioners often have a reference group in mind that serves as a basis for comparison, when they are assessing children, and as a means of considering the peer group and age group. The reference group is based in part on the practitioner's actual and vicarious life and clinical experience with children and adolescents. In assessing the client, the practitioner may think of youngsters who are of related age, mental status, gender, or other sociodemographic characteristics. The reference group may also involve the application of formal assessment tools. Indeed, the practitioner considers the measurement domain and measurement instruments in regard to considering the child's peers.

For the purpose of a comparative assessment, two sets of peers are of comparative utility. One set consists of a group of normal peers, matched on sociodemographic variables, who are a comparative group. Another set is youngsters who are a clinical sample. Professional values indicate that practitioners accept child and adolescent clients as they are, respecting their individuality and worth. Such values temper the implications of assessment of children, yet ought to allow professionals to implement assessments in a rational manner. Furthermore, use of such values along with the need to provide treatment will guide practitioners to make comparative assessments. Such assessments are useful for helping individual children, are conducted with dignity and respect toward individuals, and with the goal of maximizing the competencies and development of children and adolescents.

Assessment consists of decisions and expectancies. In some situations that provide the potential for effective assessment and service delivery, a match occurs between practitioner expectancies and the reality of developmental delays. In other situations a mismatch between such expectancies and reality may occur, which may result in overlooking children with actual developmental delays or in the error of spotting such delays when they do not actually exist.

Children's development is either within norms, or a delay actually exists. Two factors exist in regard to the assessment of developmental delays. One, the assessment of the presence of developmental delays among children and adolescents may vary by setting. Practitioner expectancies about the presence or absence of developmental delay among children and adolescents are a factor in their assessment. Practitioners must be tuned in to the detection of possible developmental delays in a variety of settings.

In normative settings the mind-set of many practitioners is that most children are within developmental norms. In many schools, most children's development is within acceptable norms. In such settings, practitioners may be unlikely to have the cognitive set of seeking developmental delays. However, in some normative settings, such as public schools in impoverished neighborhoods, many children may have developmental problems.

Effective practitioners have realistic expectations about developmental levels. They must attend to finding and assessing the following types of children and adolescents for developmental delays. Children at risk include those who have participated in early intervention programs for infants and toddlers with special needs and their families. Children who have speech or learning problems, or sensory impairments are also at demonstrated risk. Children who receive special education services are subject to ongoing assessments. Dropouts may also experience developmental delays. Migrants and homeless children, who may be harder to find, may also benefit from developmental assessments.

In some specialized settings, where most of the children are assessed as having a developmental lag, many practitioners may expect that most children are outside of developmental norms. Many children are referred to specialized settings by generalist practitioners who have conducted a prior assessment and suspected that the youngsters have a developmental lag. Practitioners who conduct assessments in specialized settings expect to find and indeed actively seek developmental problems. Joe, an unruly 9-year-old, was brought into treatment for a conduct problem. The practitioner perceived a language delay that resulted in referral to a speech and hearing clinic.

Two, the practitioner assesses the existence or absence of a problem. In accurate assessments, the practitioner actually assesses an extant problem or determines that a presumed problem is not present. In inaccurate assessments, the practitioner assesses the presumed occurrence of a nonexistent problem or assesses normative development when a problem actually exists. When assessment is geared to diagnosis, potential mistakes of identifying problems when none exist can be mitigated by using reliable and valid instruments to supplement the clinical diagnostic interview, and by using objective diagnostic criteria. Furthermore, valid assessments can be obtained by using multiple interviewers who each conduct multiple interviews. When team members conduct independent assessments, check their work, and compare their ideas, they are able to develop sound assessments. Teams must guard against the potential for groupthink, which can interfere with arriving at sound assessments due to an overriding influence of social desirability phenomena (Janis, 1982).

Many youngsters are brought to social workers for assessment because of difficulties that are disturbing to others (although not necessarily to themselves). Indeed, many children and adolescents have relatively little understanding of the nature of social work assessment or of the necessity of seeing a social worker. The emotional aspects of the assessment process can be aided for child clients by the practitioner's use of an optimistic viewpoint, pleasant interaction, and a focus on any positive findings. The child's self-esteem may be affected by the assessment process.

Competencies and Difficulties
of Children and Adolescents

Practitioners assess children and adolescents in regard to cognitive and language, physical and perceptual-motor, social and emotional, and moral and ethical development (Monkman & Allen-Meares, 1985). Cognitive and language delays are diagnosed more straightforwardly in children for whom English is their first language than for those youngsters for whom English is a second language. The development of physical and perceptual-motor skills is tied to youngsters' overall health. Children and adolescents who have physical disabilities may require specialized assessments to determine their skill levels. Social and emotional development may be delayed due to family factors or child abuse. Moral and ethical development may be delayed in families where one or more parents engage in criminal behavior.

Social Interaction and Emotional Competencies

Social development refers to youngsters' ability to relate to others whereas emotional development refers to their ability to experience and express their feelings. Facial expression reflects emotional state, and each emotion has unique features at experiential and expressive levels (Cole, 1991).

In assessing children's emotional development, the Emotional Development Interview (EDI), which focuses on six emotions, is a useful guide (Dupont, 1994). Anger, shame, guilt, and sadness are considered to be negative emotions. Anger consists of threats to well-being or identity that the child considers to be unfair. Shame is the youngster's feeling of being inferior or flawed. Guilt is the child's feeling associated with having done wrong or otherwise harmed others. Sadness is the child's feeling of having lost a significant other or failed in a significant way. To assess negative emotions, the EDI consists of the practitioner asking questions to provide an understanding of the situation in which the child feels such emotions; the child's reasons for feeling that way; what the child does when feeling that way; and the reasons for doing whatever she or he does when feeling that way. Then, the child is asked how the situation turns out and whether this is the way he or she wanted it to turn out.

Pride and happiness are positive emotions. Pride is the child's feeling of having accomplished something or having a valued identity. Happiness is being well and doing well. Using the EDI entails the practitioner asking the same questions for the positive emotions as for the negative emotions. Moreover, for the positive emotions the EDI involves asking the child whether he or she ever deliberately does anything to feel proud or happy.

Moral and emotional development are related. Emotions are experienced by children and adolescents as morally induced when they are consistently associated with a sense of oughtness (Stilwell, Galvin, Kopta, & Norton, 1994). Moral emotions include negative emotions, such as fear, guilt, anxiety, contempt, and shame (Callahan, 1991), as well as positive emotions experienced in the face of moral challenge, such as excitement, pride, or elation.

Moreover, social and emotional development are directly related, with content areas of overlap, as well as connections to cognitive development. Children's awareness and understanding of their emotions reflect their levels of social-cognitive development. Moreover, youngsters who are highly developed in one domain usually tend to have high levels of development in the other domain. Furthermore, social development can be inferred through assessments of emotional development and vice versa.

When youngsters are referred to social work practitioners for treatment of emotional difficulties, an assessment of their social skills is essential. Indeed, given the importance of social skills to social and emotional development, children should be routinely assessed for their social skills functioning. Two measures are particularly useful. The Social Skills Rating System (SSRS) is a psychometrically sound, comprehensive, standardized measure of the social skills functioning of young children (Gresham & Elliott, 1990). The Interpersonal Competence Scale (ICS-T) is a set of brief rating scales for teachers and parents that consists of items that assess social and behavioral characteristics of children and adolescents (Cairns, Leung, Gest, & Cairns, 1995).

Social and emotional development, including relationships and feelings, are closely and directly related. Social and emotional competencies reflect children's age-related development. As infants grow, they develop their emotional repertoire. They begin to realize that others exist in the world in addition to themselves and their mothers. As children grow, their social world extends beyond the mother–child relationship to encompass the rest of the family. Furthermore, as infants move into and beyond childhood, their social world widens beyond the family and encompasses friends, acquaintances, and community members. Correspondingly, the nature of their requisite social and emotional competencies change. They learn that different actions are expected in a greater variety of social situations. Youngsters learn the norms of appropriate emotional expression. Older children and adolescents are expected to have mastered such norms.

Children's understanding of friendships, coordination of social perspective, strategies for interpersonal negotiation, and the processes and themes inherent in friendships progress through developmental periods (Selman & Schultz, 1990). The developmental periods are preschool through early elementary school, upper elementary school, middle and high school, and late adolescence (Gallagher, 1993).

Children and adolescents who have not mastered the social and emotional norms and skills may require assessment and intervention. Youngsters are often referred to practitioners for emotional problems, including lack of impulse control, aggression, violence, and depression. Negative and socially undesirable emotions are often either internalized by children or expressed by them as antisocial actions.

Social work practitioners assess emotional development through obtaining and interpreting parental, peer, and teacher reports of youngster's actions, such as excessive sulking. Practitioners obtain self-reports from children and adolescents in interviews, through the administration of instruments, in discussions of social situations that involve peers, and through play. In some situations, reports become available from community members or even through law enforcement authorities. Practitioners may also keep anecdotal records of unexpected incidents and social interactions (Oosterhof, 1994). Running records, which are comprehensive, descriptive accounts of everything that a child says and does, tend to be written as the child is observed (McAfee & Leong, 1994).

Another useful instrument, the Psychosocial Assessment of Childhood Experiences (PACE), is a standardized investigator-based interview of children and their parents (Sandberg, et al., 1993). The types of information assessed include acute life events, long-term psychosocial experiences, and major happenings over the child's lifetime, including prolonged separation, illness, and family breakdown (Glen, 1993).

Social competence, which has been conceptualized in a number of ways (Siperstein, 1992), refers to appropriate social behavior that fits particular circumstances, the presence of peer relationships, and specific prosocial behaviors (Guralnick, 1992). From a social-cognitive perspective, social competence relies on underlying cognitive competencies, including perspective taking, encoding, social cue interpretation, strategy generation, and evaluation of consequences (Leffert & Siperstein, 1996). It also encompasses language facility. Social competence refers to the ability of children to reach their interpersonal goals (Guralnick, 1990).

Emotional regulation refers to the processes by which children and adolescents monitor, evaluate, and modify their emotional reactions to attain interpersonal goals (Thompson, 1994). Children who form secure attachments to their parents have greater peer social competence than other children have (Contreras & Kerns, 2000). Peer social competence of children is the single best childhood predictor of adult adaptation (Hartup, 1992). Emotional regulation is an important mechanism that accounts for the link between parent–child attachment and the quality of peer relationships. Social competencies of children and adolescents include many cognitive, affective, and performance skills at varying levels of specificity. Many social competencies exist ranging from global social skills, such as making friends, to microsocial skills, such as maintaining an intermediate amount of eye contact.

Children and adolescents may need to learn new social skills, such as how to make a friend or how to begin a conversation, or they may need to expand the rudimentary social skills they possess. Entering or joining an existent social group is an important skill for children who seek to make new friends (Weissbourd, 1996). It consists of the child making an introductory statement, speaking in a voice that is audible to the other children, and looking directly at them.

Advances in socioeconomic status and improvements in housing, health care, and education bring an increased capacity to provide for a wide range of children and adolescents with disabilities (Wright, Sugden, Ng, & Tan, 1994). To assess school-age children for disabilities and determine their eligibility for special services, the practitioner considers multiple sources of information, including school records, student work, prereferral procedures, observational techniques, interviews, testing, ecological assessment, direct assessment, dynamic assessment, task analysis, outcome-based assessment, and learning styles assessment (Waterman, 1994). The primary areas of assessment include intelligence, language, perceptual abilities, academic achievement, and behavior and emotional/social development.

Social skills deficits are a specific learning disability (LaGreca & Vaughn, 1992). Most studies have indicated that children with learning disabilities are at greater risk to be socially rejected or neglected (ignored) than are their higher-achieving classmates (Bryan, 1991). Children with learning disabilities who have social difficulties should be assessed for their affective status, self-efficacy, social status, social skills, and absence of destructive behaviors (Bryan, 1997). A study of elementary schoolchildren showed that youngsters with learning disabilities and pupils who are low achievers have similar social competencies; however, the latter tended to experience greater loneliness (Coleman, McHam, & Minnett, 1992).

A broad definition of mental retardation includes social competence (Luckasson et al., 1992). The quality of life of children with mental retardation is directly related to their social competence. A research study of the social competence of children with mild mental retardation revealed their responses to simulated social conflict situations (Leffert & Siperstein, 1996). The children were accurate in interpreting simulated hostile intentions, yet showed difficulty in accurately interpreting benign intentions. Moreover, children who experienced difficulties in their social-cognitive processes were more likely to display extreme patterns of behavior than other children with mental retardation.

Whereas practitioners may chiefly receive information about the social competence of children and adolescents from a single source, such as one parent, ideally, practitioners assess social competence through multiple persons (sources) in multiple settings using multiple methods. To assess social competence, practitioners rely on the direct observation of children and adolescents in clinic, school, family, and community settings (Compher, 1993). Practitioners observe the social interaction of youngsters with peers, teachers, and family members.

The Assessment of Social Competence (ASC) instrument provides a sound measure of social competence for children who have moderate to profound levels of mental retardation (Meyer, Cole, McQuarter, & Reichle, 1990). The ASC subscales are initiate, self-regulate, follow rules, provide positive reinforcement, provide negative feedback, obtain cues, offer assistance, accept assistance, indicate preference, cope with negatives, and terminate interaction. The social competence subscales of the well-established Child Behavior Checklist (Achenbach & Edelbrock, 1983) have been shown to differentiate clinic-referred from nonreferred children, children within different diagnostic categories of disruptive behavior, and nonreferred boys from boys with learning disabilities (Frankel & Myatt, 1994).

Children's developmental difficulties are assessed in family, school, and agency systems. Each setting has the potential to provide the social work practitioner with unique insights on the social competence of children and adolescents. Observation in multiple settings provides practitioners with a richer and fuller picture of the young person than observation in one setting. Few practitioners have the opportunity to observe children directly in all settings; however, they may obtain reports from persons in most or all settings. All practitioners have the capacity to observe children directly in at least one setting, which is usually the clinic or office where the youngster is assessed and the interviews take place.

Unobtrusive observations are invaluable for making assessments of the young client's social relationship skills in a way that is unlikely to affect their representation. At times, practitioners can visit and observe the child or adolescent in school and home settings. In school settings, practitioners may be able unobtrusively to observe the child on the playground and, in some instances, in the classroom. Observations of family interaction at home may provide realistic information. Occasionally, practitioners observe the child or adolescent in other community settings, especially in rural settings. Indeed, practitioners in small towns and rural settings may have many opportunities to observe children and adolescents informally.

Observation in the clinic can also be useful, such as seeing the client before and after the interview. Practitioners may observe their own dyadic interaction with the youngster in the interview. Children and adolescents may participate in structured interviews in which they respond to videotaped vignettes of social situations, for example, conflict. Furthermore, it may be feasible for the practitioner to observe the child directly or to obtain observations from others if the child is in treatment in another treatment program in a clinic.

Practitioners are also able to rely on anecdotal reports of the social competence of children and adolescents, which may be relayed by letter, telephone contact, or interview.

For instance, Mary, a school practitioner, heard from Beth's teacher that Beth had few friends in the classroom. She subsequently observed Beth's interactions with other children on the playground.

Formal instruments can help in the assessment of children's social and emotional functioning. Some of these instruments are scales completed separately by children, parents, and teachers within broad-based assessments of children's functioning (Achenbach, 1982). Other measures include sociometric measures, which tend to be completed by peers (Oden & Asher, 1977); the Children's Assertive Behavior Scale (Michelson & Wood, 1980), which is a self-report; and the School Behavior Checklist (Miller, 1972), which is completed by the teacher.

Practitioners assess the social lives of children and adolescents. They determine whether the peers and social situations of child and adolescent clients are appropriate and constructive, considering factors such as their age. Maxine was a 10-year-old girl who was referred to a clinic for antisocial behavior and poor school achievement. The practitioner conducted a community-based assessment and discovered that Maxine socialized extensively with older neighborhood adolescents whose activities came close to breaking the law.

Adolescents with serious, chronic illness face extra challenges to their social and emotional functioning. A study of adolescents with cystic fibrosis, their parents, and health care providers revealed that the youngsters experienced a wide range of problematic situations (DiGirolamo, Quittner, Ackerman, & Stevens, 1997). Such situations occurred within the domains of eating and weight gain, dating and pubertal development, medications and treatment, future plans, health concerns, clinic and hospital visits, friends, physical activities, parent–teen relationship, and school. The behavior-analytic approach employed in the study has wide applicability in working with adolescents. For instance, it formed the basis for a self-management program for emotionally disturbed adolescents (Ninness, Glenn, & Ellis, 1993).

Practitioners assess the quality and quantity of social interaction, which is essential for health and well-being. The three types of social interaction of children and adolescents assessed by the practitioner are nonsocial or asocial, prosocial, and antisocial interaction. Social skills are developed through social interaction. To assess children's social skills practitioners employ multiple assessment methods, including self-report and other-report instruments, observation, interview, and sociometric measures (Lachar, 1993; Rost & Czeschlik, 1994).

Checklists of social skills and role-play tests of simulated social situations are useful means of assessing social skills. Self-reports of youngsters depict peer networks, social interaction, and social problem solving. Likert scales used by teachers, parents, and peers provide accurate assessments of the social skills of children and adolescents (Gresham & Elliott, 1990). Touchscreen videodisc computer technology has been shown to be useful in assessing elementary schoolchildren's perceptions of and responses to social scenes (Walker, Schwarz, Nippold, Irvin, & Noell, 1994).

Abell, McDonell, and Winters (1992) have developed the Prosocial Tendencies Scale for Children (PTS-C), which uses brief vignettes to stimulate responses descriptive of children's prosocial orientations across behaviors and contexts. The two subscales of the PTS-C are measures of attributed responsibility and of reported tendencies to behave in a prosocial manner. The social statuses of children are assessed by the practitioner. Practitioners may make a visit to the school where observations of children on the playground and other settings are informative. To aid in observation, practitioners use categorical systems and checklists for noting interaction in social domains. Reports from parents, teachers, and guidance counselors are also useful in assessing peer social status.

When given a choice, children and adolescents appear to gravitate toward peer groups that are attractive to them. Some peer group settings are voluntary. For instance, in school settings, although the classroom may be involuntary, the playground peer group may be voluntary. Some children have one social status in one peer group and another status in a different group. A desirable social status implies few peer interaction difficulties. However, even popular children can have social difficulties. Occasionally, popular children are referred for help.

More commonly, however, neglected, isolated, or rejected youngsters are referred for help. On sociometric measures, neglected children receive few votes for either popular or rejected roles. Rejected children receive many scores that indicate dislike by peers and few scores indicating that they are liked. Children who are referred for help may experience social withdrawal and lack friends. Some such children tend to be ignored and unnoticed by other children whereas others tend to be noticed yet are actively pushed away by their peers. Such children vary in their emotional difficulties as well.

Moral and Ethical Competencies

Social work promotes the moral and ethical development of children and adolescents. Moral and ethical development is intertwined with social and cognitive development. Older children and adolescents are likely to be involved in complex moral situations encompassing social interaction with peers in neighborhood and school settings. Practitioners seek to determine whether their clients understand such complex situations and are able to cope with related conflicts.

The moral and ethical development of children, which is related to religion and the family, reflects community values. However, the influence of religion and views of acceptable moral behavior vary between communities and have changed over time. Many families undergo changes that make it difficult for them to socialize their children with moral and ethical behavior. Schools are expected to carry out socialization functions. However, schools have become preoccupied with helping pupils meet academic expectations and preventing and coping with school violence committed by pupils.

Social work practitioners can make inferences about moral development of children from observing their play in group situations, and in family, school, community, and neighborhood settings. By being a member of a family and participating in family situations at home, children and adolescents develop their sense of morality, ethics, and justice. Through playing with children at school and in the neighborhood, by being a member of a peer group, and by working in classroom settings, children also develop morally and ethically. The practitioner observes children in such settings and obtains the views of those who are in a capacity to comment on the actions and activities of the youngster.

The parent–child relationship is essential to proper conscience development. Social workers assess parenting, particularly among children who are engaged in socially unacceptable behavior. Extremes in discipline, consisting of overly harsh or very laissez-faire parenting, have been implicated in childhood behavior problems. Staff at a child guidance and evaluation clinic were perturbed to see the antisocial behavior of young Billy who was referred for fighting with peers. However, the situation became much clearer when Billy was picked up by his biker dad who indicated that he didn't see anything wrong with Billy's behavior. Social work practitioners assess moral and ethical development according to age norms (Kohlberg, 1978). As children mature, they give thought to rules and their applications in play, games, and social situations.

Psychoanalytic thinking has had a profound influence on conceptualizations of the development of morality, ethics, and conscience. Moral and ethical development of children, including the sense of right and wrong, the acquisition of conscience, and the development of a sense of guilt, varies by sociodemographic factors, including gender and age. Conscience conceptualization in nonclinical children and adolescents progresses through five hierarchical stages (Stilwell, Galvin, & Kopta, 1991).

During the preschool external conscience stage, the child explains moral learning in terms of behavioral consequences. In the brain or heart conscience stage, the school-age child recounts concrete moral mandates that have been internalized from the commands and behavioral reinforcements of elders. The heart/mind or personified conscience stage of the older child consists of efforts to coordinate emotional and empathic factors with cognitive moral mandates resulting in greater sensitivity and personality to the conscience. The confused conscience stage in midadolescence consists of trying to resolve differences among mandates derived from older authority and newer choices derived from peers and popular culture. The integrated stage consists of the older adolescent emphasizing an awareness of personal responsibility in choosing values.

Moral and ethical behavior is a function of moral and ethical development. Moral and ethical problems related to the character development of children and adolescents appear in significant interpersonal conflict, conduct problems, and violence. Such problems are often the focus of referrals from law enforcement and legal authorities to social workers. The nature and source of referrals provide a clue to practitioners about the seriousness of the problems. When children and adolescents are involved in immoral or unethical behavior, they come to the attention of potential and actual, primary and secondary referral sources in the family, at school, and in the community. Adults serve as referral sources to practitioners although other children or adolescents may prompt referrals.

Violations of social and legal norms of moral and ethical behavior by children and adolescents prompt referrals for assessment and intervention. Social workers often assess children and adolescents who have broken society's laws, who have been involved in acts of violence, and who are in institutions because of delinquent behavior. Assessment is frequently implemented because of an infraction by the child or adolescent that has come to the attention of legal, child welfare, health, and educational authorities. Social workers in juvenile justice settings focus on the assessment of moral and ethical development.

The risk of violence toward self or others is assessed during, entering, and leaving inpatient and outpatient facilities during processes of intake, evaluation, and treatment. Six factors are considered in the assessment of violence and suicide (Nurcombe & Partlett, 1994). These factors include demographic factors; the nature and expression of violent threats; past history of violent threats or actions; psychological factors; the social environment; and entering, losing, or terminating a therapeutic relationship.

Young children who may have limited moral knowledge, as well as adolescents whose moral knowledge is adequate, may engage in illicit actions, such as theft. Some children and adolescents are referred to social workers for assessment and intervention because of their illicit actions. Repeated or serious offenses are likely to be detected and result in referral. Local law enforcement agents, teachers, and social workers may detect lawbreaking, and may engage in informal diversion, in which they warn youngsters to abstain from further illicit and destructive activity.

In moderately serious instances of lawbreaking, youngsters are referred to a formal court diversion program for assessment and intervention. Adolescents may be required to appear before the board, agree to a contract, make an apology and restitution to a crime victim, and engage in community service. For those young persons who have committed very serious offenses, formal court diversion is not an option. In such situations, youngsters are assessed and treated through the juvenile court. The juvenile court was originally set up to provide adolescents protection from the adult court. However, the juvenile court may label, stigmatize, and formalize a criminalization process, hence the development of formal court diversion programs for lesser offenses.

Social workers assess whether their child or adolescent clients have any overall moral and ethical developmental difficulties. Practitioners determine whether such difficulties are broad based, generalized, and occur in multiple school and community settings. Practitioners are also aware that some such difficulties are focused, situational, and tend to occur in one setting.

The moral and ethical development of children and adolescents is related to their mental health. Many children and adolescents referred to practitioners for assessment and intervention have significant behavioral disorders. Clusters of problem behaviors, including a combination of cruelty to animals, fire setting, and enuresis, are indicative of potentially serious mental health difficulties. Mental health agencies assess moral and ethical development, which may be framed or conceptualized in medical, cognitive, and behavioral terms.

Assessments of moral and ethical development are part of a broader assessment of child or adolescent development. In mental health assessments, moral and ethical development are considered part of the social history of the young client. Furthermore, many children acquire formal instruction in morality through religious education, which is revealed through social histories. Although assessments of youngsters' moral and ethical development may be comprehensive, most are brief and focused. Practitioners seek to determine to what extent youngsters have developed their conscience and are functioning according to ethical and moral norms, given their sociodemographic and age characteristics.

Assessment of moral and ethical development is implemented by interviewing children and adolescents, and collaterals. Practitioners may ask children and others questions to elicit moral reasoning and experiences. Reviewing information about behavior that indicates lapses in moral and ethical development is also useful. Furthermore, the moral and ethical development of children and adolescents is assessed through the use of stories that indicate abilities and deficits in moral reasoning. Youngsters are asked how they would respond to and resolve ethical dilemmas and conflicts in scenarios. Practitioners determine to what extent the youngsters understand the moral aspects of the stories and are able to make moral and ethical decisions.

Social work practitioners assess both development and behavior. Practitioners use guidelines for assessing and determining the moral and ethical development of their young clients. The absence of severe behavioral difficulties, which often implies normal moral development, is a partial indicator.

Two issues that are directly related to customary ways of conducting social work practice have served as deterrents to considering the moral and ethical development of children and adolescents. One issue is the reluctance to address religious issues in practice with children and adolescents. More recently, however, social workers are beginning to consider the issue.

Moral, ethical, and faith development, which proceed in stages, have objective and subjective aspects. Individuals of various religious faiths and secular persons have varied ideas about what is moral and ethical. Social workers consider the religious and cultural backgrounds of clients to understand their moral and ethical development and behavior. The social consensus on such issues, however, is embedded in the law.

Another issue is the nonjudgmental stance taken by social workers. Many practitioners have steered away from considering the moral and ethical development of young clients. Social workers need to accept their young clients while considering and assessing their moral and ethical development and behavior.

Cognitive and Language Competencies

Cognitive and language development are closely intertwined. Delays in cognitive development may hamper language development and vice versa. Infants with language delay tend to have delayed social and cognitive development (Carson, Klee, Perry, Muskina, & Donaghy, 1998).

Moreover, language and behavior development are linked as seen in the joint presence of language disorders and behavior disorders among school-age children and adolescents (Walker et al., 1994). Children with language disorders frequently have problems in social interaction (Tallal, Townsend, Curtiss, & Wulfeck, 1991) and mental disorders (Beitchman, Nair, Clegg, Ferguson, & Patel, 1986).

Cognitive competencies include the demonstrated ability of children to think, organize, reflect, analyze, and synthesize information. Such abilities represent the physical growth and maturation of the brain and the central nervous system. Input from persons in family, school, and neighborhood environments can stimulate the development of cognitive competencies. School readiness tests are given to measure the readiness of first-grade students to begin the formal school curriculum.

Potential or actual cognitive difficulties include youngsters' ability to process information (Rutter, 1988). In some instances, the practitioner assesses the level and causation of mental retardation. Whereas mild and moderate levels of mental retardation pose real limits on youngsters' abilities, those children with severe and profound levels of mental retardation have considerably greater difficulties in living. The practitioner may also examine developmental disorders, learning disorders, attention deficit and disruptive behavior disorders, and psychotic disorders in regard to the presence of cognitive difficulties. Developmental disorders appear throughout infancy, childhood, and adolescence.

Communication disorders, which may be detected through interviewing the child, include expressive language disorder, mixed receptive-expressive language disorder, phonological disorder, and stuttering (American Psychiatric Association, 2000). Such communication disorders may be diagnosed by health and mental health practitioners, including speech, hearing, and language therapists. Social workers who detect language problems may refer children on for specialized assessment. Practitioners may also see children who have already had such an assessment and who may have begun speech therapy. Bishop (1998) has developed a useful Children's Communication Checklist (CCC) to assess social communication.

Children and adolescents develop within speech, language, and hearing environments. Many children have monolingual environments in which, by definition, the language at home, at school, and in the neighborhood are literally one and the same. However, bilingual and multilingual youngsters may face other challenges. For instance, their parents may speak one or more languages at home. The children may use a language at home which differs from the mainstream language taught at school and used in the neighborhood.

Furthermore, some children are expected to speak one form of English at school and another language at home. The language that they are expected to speak in the neighborhood may either be the language of the school or of the home. Immigrant children, and children who move from one geographic region to another within a country, may face social issues, including stigma and discrimination, related to their limited knowledge and use of mainstream language, verbal pronunciations, accents, and dialects.

Bilingual and multilingual practitioners may readily assess and comprehend such language issues. Monolingual practitioners may develop their competencies in the languages of their clients. They also may work with translators who are familiar with the languages of their young clients. In community, school, and family observations and interviews, practitioners are likely to determine how children and adolescents function within the language developmental domain.

Language competencies refer to children's ability to express themselves in verbal and written ways, each of which are communication methods and abilities subject to assessment. Ordinarily, practitioners are attuned to psychosocial factors underlying difficulties of children and adolescents in communication. However, practitioners also must assess difficulties in communication that reflect children's speech and language problems. At least two classes of language problems may be distinguished. One class relates to the production of language. The other class represents an ability in one language along with a lack of familiarity with the mainstream language of the predominant culture.

Speech and language development are closely related in children. If speech or language difficulties are present, their origin and nature may need to be assessed. The practitioner seeks to determine whether the child has difficulty hearing, understanding, or communicating a particular language. Some children have medical impairments that interfere with their speech and language functioning. Speech difficulties that may be of a physical nature, such as a hearing difficulty, also need to be considered and assessed.

Deafness poses challenges to the social and emotional development of deaf children (Greenberg & Kusche, 1993). Deaf children are bicultural in that they must find ways to contact and communicate within the worlds of the deaf and of the hearing. They need to learn to master sign language. Ethnic minority deaf children have an additional cultural experience within the majority culture. Children who experience deaf-blindness or autism have severe communication difficulties. They are subject to being misdiagnosed as having severe to profound levels of mental retardation (Wolf-Schein, 1998). Such children may benefit from nonintrusive assessment.

Practitioners assess the cognitive and language abilities of their child and adolescent clients through observations, interviews, and reports (Christie, Newson, Newson, & Prevezer, 1992). Interviewing clients is useful in assessing their cognitive and language development. By listening to children recount an incident or situation, practitioners gauge the acquisition, processing, and communication of information as well as determine whether cognitive problems exist. Through interviews, practitioners seek to deduce youngsters' thinking abilities and patterns (Memon, Cronin, Eaves, & Bull, 1993; Saccuzzo, Johnson, & Guertin, 1994). Practitioners become attuned to youngsters' vocabulary, word choice, and interrelationship of ideas. If practitioners notice any gross disturbance in their young clients' cognitive functioning and use of language, they may refer them to a specialist to determine the origin and extent of the difficulties. Moreover, practitioners may receive reports about cognitive and language functioning from school and health officials, referral agents, and specialists to whom some children are ultimately referred.

Practitioners who assess the cognitive skills and functions of their child and adolescent clients seek to address six sets of questions (Hughes & Baker, 1990). One, questions about the information processing of clients include the following: To what extent does the child recognize, attend to, and scan diverse types of information? How accurately does the child process information? How broadly does the child generalize information that has been gathered? Does distortion of information or overgeneralization occur?

Two, questions about cognitive level include the following: At what cognitive level does the child function? Is the child's cognitive development at the same level as her sociodemographic peers?

Three, questions pertaining to intelligence include the following: What is the child's general intelligence level? Does the child's assessed level of intelligence represent his true level? What types of intelligence are the child's strengths? What types of intelligence represent limited functioning?

Four, questions pertaining to education include the following: Given the child's cognitive development, is she in an appropriate school and class? What is the child's level of academic functioning in school?

Five, several questions emerge in regard to children's acquisition of information. To what extent does the home environment provide the child with mental stimulation and the information needed for cognitive development? How many books are in the home? Is there a computer at home? To what extent do parents discuss ideas?

Six, some questions apply to the communication of information. How verbal is the child? How expressive is the child? How communicative is the child? How does the child express his ideas and emotions?

Physical and Perceptual-Motor Competencies

Assessing the physical and perceptual-motor development of children and adolescents encompasses an awareness of changes in the youngsters' features, including stature, mobility, and skill development over time (Carmichael, 1990). Health and allied health care practitioners, including pediatric physicians, nurses, and social workers, observe youngsters as they mature. In some communities, practitioners see youngsters whom they have known professionally for an extended period of time, including periods of intensive professional contact and other periods of little or no contact. Over time, they are able to see changes within children. When practitioners see a child whom they have previously served, they are able to compare the child's prior and present development and functioning, and may attempt to predict the child's future development and functioning.

Practitioners consult their own records and also use reports from those persons, including parents and pediatricians, who have known the child for a longer period of time. Practitioners examine each child's records, gather data from others, and observe each child over a time period that minimally includes the assessment phase and often extends to the treatment phase. In child guidance and evaluation clinics the focus of study of the child may begin with the prenatal period. The practitioner assesses the health, psychosocial functioning, and environment of the mother preceding, at the time of, and following the birth of the child.

Social workers are responsible for assessing the extent to which children's physical changes are normative. If physical anomalies or developmental difficulties are noted, social workers refer the youngster to health care practitioners for diagnosis and treatment. Practitioners compare children's physical and perceptual-motor development to age norms to determine whether their development is normal. Such norms provide an overall indication of physical status from which gross deviations may be noted. However, such norms must be used with caution because they tend not to reflect regional and sociocultural differences.

The time period available for comparison is based in part on the availability of data on the youngsters' physical and perceptual-motor development. Pediatricians regularly record such development of children in their care. Difficulties in such development are assessed through observation as well as reports from health care providers in school, clinic, and community settings. In addition to medical, social scientific, and quantitative data or reports, practitioners may also rely on the interview.

The reference points for comparison are limited by a number of factors. In a managed-care environment in which the cost of services is carefully monitored and controlled, many practitioners see children and adolescents for a brief period, both in terms of the time for the actual interview as well as the length of treatment or number of sessions. Some physical and perceptual-motor developmental changes are due to genetic endowment and environmental factors, including a traumatic event, abuse, or accident. Difficulties in physical development include the presence of anomalies, deformities, and disabling conditions, including mental retardation, which may be present at birth (Handen, 1997; Szepkovski, Gauvain, & Carberry, 1994).

Physical developmental problems are of concern to practitioners because of their psychosocial consequences, including stigma, shame, and embarrassment. Social workers assess the social and emotional impact of physical changes (Lucco, 1993). Indeed, many practitioners may initially detect physical changes of children by becoming aware of the social and emotional consequences of such changes. Social workers seek to determine how the social and emotional development of children and adolescents is related to their physical and perceptual-motor development. In many cases, the least complicated social and emotional developmental course for many children occurs when they are similar to their peers in physical and perceptual-motor development. However, wide variation in the physical and perceptual-motor development of children, as well as peer groupings, exists.

Culturally approved differences in appearance may actually result in higher self-concept. However, children who are dissimilar in appearance to most of their peers may be prone to have a lower self-concept in comparison to such children and to develop depressive or aggressive reactions, for which they may be referred for treatment.

Practitioners who work with families may compare child or adolescent clients to their siblings (Lucco, 1993). Although most such family comparisons involve age differences, they provide other valuable information as well, including the opportunity to see how heredity and environment appear to influence the development of clients and their families, as in the cases of fraternal and identical twins.

Inevitably, practitioners compare children to peers in school and neighborhood settings. Experienced practitioners have the opportunity to compare youngsters to two types of peers, namely children whose difficulties have caused them to be referred for assessment, and children without clinically significant problems.

Children normatively acquire gross and fine perceptual-motor skills, which they learn to combine in their movements. Developmental coordination disorder is a motor skills disorder (American Psychiatric Association, 2000). As a result in part to unevenness in physical development, some adolescents appear to be ungraceful, clumsy, awkward, or "gawky." The practitioner must determine how much of such gawkiness is normal, and whether other difficulties related to physical and perceptual-motor development are present.

The Movement Assessment Battery for Children is a comprehensive assessment and intervention package (Movement ABC) (Henderson & Sugden, 1992) that has been validated for use in the United Kingdom and Singapore (Wright et al., 1994). It consists of the Movement ABC Checklist, the Movement ABC Test (formerly the Test of Motor Impairment [TOMI]), and guidelines for remediation.

A social component of the assessment of children's physical and perceptual-motor development exists. Practitioners assess how other children and adults react to the appearance and movements of their child clients. In situations where a child is physically disabled, such reactions can be extreme. Most visually impaired children proceed through perceptual-motor development in a normal sequence although they tend to be delayed in comparison to sighted children (Sleeuwenhoek, Boter, & Vermeer, 1995).

Some youngsters, including those who have been maltreated, tend to be smaller than their peers. Some children with physical and mental health disorders are either thin or obese. Eating disorders can be difficult to assess because adolescents with such disorders often attempt to mask them. However, due to their prevalence in Western societies and the potential risks to the life and well-being of sufferers, practitioners should probably inquire about eating patterns, consider weight, and make a differential diagnosis for the potential existence of eating disorders for all adolescent female clients.

Difficulties related to physical and perceptual-motor development of children include deviations in weight or height. Social workers are sensitive to clients' weight in part because obese children in particular tend to be stigmatized. Practitioners who initially tend to categorize children in regard to weight may consult tables keyed to gender and body frame to determine appropriate weights. Again, caution must be exercised because such tables usually do not reflect regional and cultural norms.

A range of developmental difficulties may be experienced by children. Failure to thrive (FTT) consists of organic, nonorganic, and mixed types. Comprehensive and interdisciplinary assessment of FTT is necessary because of the breadth of child populations as well as the multiplicity of factors that appear to lead to a severe and persistent lack of normative weight gain (Bithoney, et al., 1991). The child's affect and actions toward family and others, and physical and developmental status, should be assessed. Poor nutrition and inadequate growth and development of nonorganic FTT children appear to be exacerbated by poverty, dysfunctional parent–child relationships, improper education, and a lack of developmentally enabling experiences (Heffer & Kelley, 1994).

Practitioners may have child or adolescent clients who are either considerably shorter or taller than their peers. Major differences in stature may result in social and emotional difficulties. Children of unusual stature may be treated differently than other children in home, school, and community settings. Adults sometimes perceive youngsters who are very short as being younger than their taller peers. Very short children have many social difficulties. Structures are built for people of a certain minimum height and those who are shorter than that height may have a difficult time maneuvering and navigating easily. Furthermore, short children have more difficulties in regard to their own safety and security. They are also subject to considerable prejudice from a taller world that tends to label them pejoratively.

Ralph had been well adjusted as a young child. As Ralph got older, he grew little. Unfortunately, growth hormones did not help Ralph grow. Furthermore, he was not a good candidate for medical treatments that involved promoting bone growth through stretching. Although Ralph performed very well academically, he was taunted mercilessly by his peers at school and in the neighborhood. Ralph became sensitive to and bitter about his height and antagonistic to others. Eventually, Ralph confided his hostile feelings to his teachers at school, who were concerned that he might commit an act of violence. Ralph was counseled by a social worker. Although still perturbed by his shortness, he remained nonviolent. In high school, Ralph's interests turned to medicine. He planned to do medical research on disorders pertaining to growth and stature.

Like children who are very small, children who are very tall may sometimes have a difficult time being socially accepted by their peers. Alice, who was the tallest child in her sixth-grade class, was referred to a social work practitioner for having low self-esteem. She was remarkably self-conscious about her height, particularly on one occasion when a substitute teacher asked the children to line up in size order. When another tall girl entered the school, Alice felt better. The social worker focused on many of Alice's fine features and talents, discussed other tall girls she knew, and attempted to compose a group for tall girls.

Children may have multiple interacting developmental difficulties. Furthermore, just as a strength in one domain may be linked to a strength in another domain, a difficulty in one domain may exacerbate a difficulty in another area. For instance, children may have cognitive difficulties that are organic or physical in origin. They may distort and misinterpret social events and develop emotional problems. Christian was a very tall boy who had been academically retained. When Christian entered the fifth grade, it was obvious to the other children that he was much older than they were. The other children at school snickered at Christian for being academically retained, hurt his sense of pride, and enraged him. One day outside of school, with his physical size and age on his side, Christian responded to their snide comments by attacking some of the boys. Consequently, he was suspended from school. Ultimately, a social worker was summoned to help Christian with the social and academic difficulties he experienced.

Conclusion

Many of the problems of children and adolescents that social workers attempt to redress are best understood in a developmental context. Periods of rapid developmental changes among children signify the importance of timely assessment.

Although primary prevention entails work with children who are mostly or entirely within developmental norms, many of the children who are social work clients depart from developmental norms in one or more aspects. Deviations from physical and perceptual-motor developmental norms may have adverse social and emotional consequences for the youngster. The practitioner is responsible for noting delays or lags in development.

Developmental domains tend to be interrelated. Social and emotional development tend to be closely intertwined, and a close link exists between social and cognitive development. Cognitive and language development are closely linked, as are moral and ethical development, and physical and perceptual-motor domains.

Several developmental domains influence the child or adolescent's communication patterns. The practitioner is responsible for assessing the child's ability to communicate socially, to communicate emotions and cognitions, and to use speech and language.

Practitioners conduct an overall assessment in which they pay attention to all domains. They assess developmental domains separately, in interaction, and in terms of their meaning and significance for the whole child. Practitioners focus on specific developmental domains in depth when a difficulty is noticed or brought to their attention. The detection of children's developmental difficulties increases the probability of remediation. Indeed, in some instances, referral processes may be considered to precede assessment.

Practitioners are engaged in diagnostic, participant, and observer roles in assessment. Their perspective may be to focus on client strengths, deficits, or their combination. The balanced perspective allows practitioners to assess the competencies and problems of children within developmental domains. Practitioners may use comparative methods in conducting their developmental assessments. They compare the child or adolescent client with other clients who have similar sociodemographic features, including age and gender. Practitioners may also rely on comparisons based on interviews as well as on report data. In the following chapter, theories, strategies, and techniques for practice are considered.

CHAPTER

6

Theories, Strategies, and Techniques for Practice

After assessing the child, family, and situation, a treatment plan must be developed. The social worker helps the child cope with the issues and concerns that have been identified. This chapter focuses on the theories that have the best fit for assisting the child. One option is to select an approach that addresses most of the child's concerns. For example, the child's identified areas of dysfunction are specific behaviors at school that need to be changed. The approach that one might expect to be most useful would probably be behavioral methods. Another option is to select the strategies, procedures, and techniques from multiple bodies of thought that have been shown to be most useful in helping to change those specific identified behaviors (Turner & Jaco, 1996).

The social worker is in an enviable position with a variety of treatment modalities to assist children and adolescents in making desired changes. Andreae (1996) noted that the social worker's domain has a "contextual understanding of the holistic nature of human functioning" (p. 601) that allows the worker to select and apply various methods of treatment. To develop this blend of helping strategies, it is necessary to understand both the bodies of thought and the individual concepts and constructs that best fit the child or adolescent. The approaches for practice that are believed to be most useful in working with children and adolescents are discussed and examples of possible interventions and applications are provided in this chapter.

Cognitive Theory

Cognitive theory is based on the idea that a child's thinking is the principal determinant of emotions and behavior. "Cognitive life and emotional life are inseparable" (Weiner, 1985, p. xix). This therapy is intended to provide a therapeutic experience by implementing a balance between thought and action so that the young client can gain maximal corrective feedback. The social worker directs and helps the child or adolescent to identify, challenge, and change thinking patterns that result in dysfunctional forms of emotion, behavior, and problem solving.

"In a cognitive approach to social work practice, the central concept is that most human emotion is the direct result of what people think, tell themselves, assume, or believe about themselves and their social situation" (Lantz, 1996, p. 98). Albert Ellis (1977) developed an ABC theory to explain the relationship between the activating event (A), what the person believes (B), and the consequences (C). Cognitive theory was used with Cindy, an adolescent girl who had just been rejected by her boyfriend the previous night. At his suggestion they had broken up (A). She was crushed and came to see her therapist. She was first encouraged to tell the therapist of the event. What she believed (B), as a result of the break-up, were the following: I'm no good, I'll never have another boyfriend, and I'm hopeless and awful. She was feeling very depressed and wondering whether she should just kill herself (C).

According to cognitive theory, most dysfunctional behavior and emotions of children and adolescents are a direct result of misconceptions that they hold about themselves or about various environmental situations. Correction of the emotion occurs when the misconception is changed. Often, young people are not aware of their misconceptions. Many misconceptions, irrational thinking, erroneous beliefs, and cognitions are outside the young person's conscious awareness. An exception is that some dysfunctional emotions are the result of organic physiological, neurological, or clinical problems. An assumption that must be corrected is that not all unpleasant emotions are dysfunctional and not all pleasant emotions are functional. A much broader view was held by Maultsby (1975), who defined rational cognition as any thought, idea, belief, attitude, or statement to the self that is based on objective reality, is life preserving, is productive for achieving one's goals, and decreases significant internal conflict and conflict with others (Lantz, 1996).

In the cognitive approach the personality of the child and adolescent is believed to be flexible—capable of being influenced by both physical and social factors. Differing from the Freudian view of competition, which occurs between people, this approach views young people as equals, collaborators, fellow human beings, and cooperative throughout life. Young people were viewed neither as good nor bad, but rather as creative beings who ultimately can decide how to live their lives.

Producing Change

The change process occurs when the young client identifies, challenges, and changes misconceptions, faulty beliefs, distorted cognitions, and irrational self-talk. Faulty beliefs create dysfunctional self-talk, which results in dysfunctional emotions and behaviors. The helping process of the cognitive approach is primarily educational. An attempt is made to empower the young client to bring about change.

Dysfunctional emotions and behaviors such as beliefs, conceptions, misconceptions, and self-talk are primarily learned through the young person's social experiences. Some cognitive therapists believe that the past is unimportant whereas others believe that it is helpful to talk about the past to discover some of the situations that led to the learning, emotions, and behavior. One unresolved concern is whether race, class, and gender experiences may have an impact on the client's beliefs and cognitions.

Treatment Principles

Judith Beck (1995, pp. 5–9), a major proponent and theorist of this approach, identified 10 principles of cognitive theory:

1. Cognitive therapy is based upon evoking a formulation of the client and a problem based in cognitive terms.
2. This approach requires a sound therapeutic treatment relationship.
3. Cognitive therapy emphasizes collaboration and active participation.
4. This method is goal oriented and problem focused.
5. This approach initially emphasizes the present.
6. Cognitive therapy is educational. It helps to make the client his or her own therapist.
7. This model is time-limited, when possible.
8. Cognitive therapy sessions are structured.
9. This approach teaches clients to identify, evaluate, and to respond effectively to dysfunctional thoughts and beliefs.
10. This method uses a variety of treatment techniques.

Relationship and Techniques

The treatment relationship is expected to help in two ways. First, it gives support to the young client. The treatment relationship helps the client know that the therapist believes in his or her ability to grow and function in a healthy way. It helps correct the low self-esteem resulting primarily from negative misconceptions of the self. A second contribution of the relationship is that it allows distortions in the relationship between the young client and the social worker to be examined so client misperceptions can be corrected. The relationship is used to check on distortions that may be present.

A technique used by the cognitive therapist is clarifying internal communications. It involves providing feedback on what the young client is thinking and telling him- or herself. Everyone has automatic thoughts, which are streams of thinking that coexist with more manifest streams of thought (Beck, 1964). For example, Tom was reading his science book and having an automatic thought: "I don't understand this." He was feeling anxious. He may respond to this thought either in an unproductive way or in a productive way. An unproductive way is to think, "I'll never understand this stuff." He accepts this thought as correct and feels sad and frustrated. A productive response to his feeling that he does not understand is, "I do understand part of what I am reading. Let me just reread this section." By using cognitive therapy, he can look for, identify, and evaluate his thoughts and develop a more adaptive response.

Explanation also is identified by Lantz (1996) as a treatment procedure. The social worker helps to explain the dysfunctions in thinking and behavior of the young client through the use of the ABC theory, which later is used to make homework assignments. Basically, the form of this assignment is presented so that it allows the client to use the ABC theory in his or her daily life to analyze beliefs and self-talk that are creating dysfunctions. A form that helps the adolescent clarify this process can be used in this assignment.

Experiential learning is also used to provide feedback to the young client. A primary technique is to use the cognitive dissonance principle. The social worker may set up a treatment situation in which the client's behavior is incongruent with the client's misconceptions. A commonly used technique in this approach is the paradoxical intention. Lantz (1996) believes that this procedure is most appropriately used with people who are experiencing anxiety. An example is an anxious adolescent, who, although in good physical health, has vomited on his way to his new high school. Each morning he is concerned that he may do this again. He is instructed to try to vomit on his way to school. When the youngster is unable to vomit, it helps him to stop thinking about this behavior.

In the cognitive approach, the emphasis is on automatic thoughts, namely those closest to conscious awareness. The major goal is to make the process of therapy understandable to the therapist and the patient (Beck, 1995). The final element in each session is feedback and summary of new ways of thinking about self, others, and situations.

Careful consideration needs to be given to the maturity level of the child or adolescent before attempting to use this approach. This methodology emphasizes abstract thinking, which may not yet be available to the young child. However, Reinecke, Dattilio, and Freeman (1996) have shown the application of cognitive theory to attention deficit hyperactivity disorder, oppositional defiant disorder, chemically dependent adolescents, childhood depression, social competence, separation anxiety disorder, low self-esteem, adolescent survivors of child sexual abuse, adolescent eating disorders, students with learning disabilities, adolescent inpatient treatment, family problems, academic problems, and high-functioning adolescents with autism.

Crisis Intervention

Many definitions of crisis exist in the literature. Focusing on the individual experiencing the crisis, Ell (1996) defines a crisis as "an acute emotional upset of the individual's steady state that occurs in conjunction with a perceived breakdown in coping skills" (pp. 169–170). Roberts (1991) defines crisis more broadly "as a period of psychological disequilibrium, experienced as a result of a hazardous event or situation that constitutes a significant problem that cannot be remedied by using familiar coping strategies" (p. 4). Most definitions involve similar steps in the crisis process. These include (1) a stressful life event, (2) a perception of the event as meaningful, (3) disorganization or disequilibrium responses to the event, and (4) coping and resolution.

Another characteristic agreed upon is that crisis is time limited. In 4 to 6 weeks the young person in crisis experiences a turning point when things are resolved, either positively or negatively (Parad & Parad, 1990). In regard to the number of sessions required to help the young person, some practitioners see one session as short term and others view 6 weeks as short term. This determination is partly influenced by the nature of the crisis.

Gilliland and James (1997) identify three domains of crisis:

1. *Developmental.* For children, crisis may be starting school, and maturational problems in all areas of functioning.
2. *Situational.* Moving to a new school and neighborhood, parental separation or divorce, sudden illness of the child or the caregiver, accidents or death of a parent are all potential crises for the child or adolescent.
3. *Existential crisis.* For children, a crisis may be inner conflict about parental separation or changes in relationships, anxiety or tension related to trauma or sudden changes in living conditions.

Some crisis situations are personal family matters. Others are triggered by a tragic occurrence, such as an earthquake, plane crash, or other traumatic event affecting large numbers of people. A number of characteristics of crisis can be identified (Gilliland & James, 1997).

First is the presence of both danger and opportunity. If the crisis is not resolved in a positive way, negative effects may continue. Even if the crisis seems to be resolved, when stress breaks out in the future, the crisis may reemerge. Second is the condition of a complicated symptomatology, with no clear cause and effect relationship. Gilliland and James (1997) describe the symptoms as becoming a tangled web "that crisscross all environments of the individual" (p. 4). Third is the existence of seeds of growth and change. Anxiety must reach a boiling point before a desire for change occurs. Regardless of the circumstances, a choice must be made; not choosing is also a choice.

Transcrisis states, or what happens immediately after the crisis, are very important. This aftermath determines the effect of the crisis. If it is submerged, new stress may cause the matter to reemerge. Transcrisis points are benchmarks that are critical to progressive stages of positive therapeutic growth. Both universality and idiosyncrasies exist in the nature of responses to crisis; however, disorganization and disequilibrium are present in every crisis.

Specific professional skills are required for working with children and families in crisis. An important skill is poise. The social worker is often confronted with shocking, threatening material, and the client is often out of control. A stable, rational atmosphere is important for crisis practice. An essential attitude of the worker is faith that the client can be pulled through. Relaxation techniques may be needed to relieve the buildup of tension for the worker.

Other professional crisis management skills are creativity, flexibility, and energy. Organization, direction, and systematic action are required. The social worker needs to have quick mental reflexes because more activity and directiveness are required. Other useful characteristics are tenacity, courage, willingness to delay gratification, a clear sense of reality, and strong resilience (Gilliland & James, 1997).

Various crisis intervention models are used by practitioners. Six or seven steps are used, with a great deal of commonality among the models. The first three steps, whose order may be interchanged in practice, involve assessing the lethality and safety of the young client's need, establishing rapport and communication, and defining the problem. Then, the sequence of steps include dealing with feelings and giving support, examining alternatives, making plans, and obtaining commitment. Sometimes, a follow-up with the client by phone or in person at a later time is offered.

To be able to assist young clients from varying cultural groups, the social worker must examine and understand the world from the client's view and look for alternative roles that are more appealing and adaptive to the background of the client (Cormier & Hackney, 1987). It is also desirable to help the client make contact and elicit help from indigenous support systems.

Broad areas for assessment of young persons in crisis are their cognitive states, affective states, and their psychomotor activity. Specific areas to be assessed are whether the current crisis is an acute or chronic condition, the client's emotional strength, and his or her emotional status. The client's alternatives, coping mechanisms, support systems, and resources must be discerned. In many cases, assessment of suicide potential is very important.

Issues of Greatest Concern for Children and Adolescents

Specific types of crisis that children and adolescents experience are abuse, potential suicide, loss, bereavement, grief, and family violence. Often, children and adolescents who have been abused, either physically or sexually, suffer posttraumatic stress disorder (PTSD).

Abused Children.   With abused children, assessment must be done to determine whether PTSD is present. Specific strategies and techniques have been developed to assist with this problem. To diagnose PTSD, certain criteria must be met as specified in DSM-IV-TR (American Psychiatric Association, 2000, pp. 467–468). The young person must have been exposed to traumatic events and experienced, witnessed, or was confronted by an actual or threatened death or serious injury.

Young children engage in repetitive play in which they express themes or aspects of the trauma; they may have frightening dreams; and they may reenact specific traumas. The young person persistently avoids certain situations, thoughts, dialogue, or feelings about the event. They may also avoid activities or people that arouse recollection and may be unable to recall important aspects of the trauma as well as other identified behaviors. Symptoms of PTSD are difficulty in falling or staying asleep, irritability or anger outbursts, difficulty concentrating, being watchful for threats, and exaggerated startle reactions.

Techniques for treating persons with PTSD include multiphasic treatment, which treats the crises as they occur one after the other, and extinguishing intrusive images, which involves going back to the original event and finding new adaptive responses. Other techniques used are flooding and implosion, thought stopping, gestalt, and a more recent promising strategy of eye movement desensitization/reprocessing (Gilliland & James, 1997).

Treatment for children who have been sexually abused differs from that for children who have been physically abused. A major focus in therapy for sexually abused children has been to encourage ventilation of the experience and to find new coping and adaptive skills. This process has often been used in small groups. Treatment for physically abused children has not usually been focused so directly on past experiences. The emphasis often has been meeting needs and overcoming some developmental lags that occur as a result of the physical abuse. Learning new skills and developing more trust of adults has often been the focus. Behavioral modification has been a major technique used for helping to develop and learn new skills.

Suicidal Children and Adolescents.   One myth about suicide is that children under 5 years of age never commit suicide. All children, especially adolescents, are at risk for suicide. Shneidman (1985, pp. 121–149) identified six sets of characteristics of suicide:

> *Situational characteristics:* the common stimulus is enduring psychological pain; a common stressor is frustrated psychological need.

Conative characteristics: the purpose of suicide is to seek a solution; a common goal is the cessation of consciousness.

Affective characteristics: hopelessness/helplessness; the internal attitude is ambivalence.

Cognitive characteristics: cognitive state is constriction.

Relational characteristic: interpersonal act is communication of intention; common act is egression.

Serial characteristic: consistency in lifelong coping patterns.

Some strategies and suggestions for persons coming into contact with a child or adolescent who may be suicidal follow (Gilliland & James, 1997). Trust your suspicions that a young person may be self-destructive. Tell the young person that you are worried about him or her. Ask direct questions about thoughts of suicide. Do not act shocked. Do not leave the youngster alone. Ensure that the youngster is safe, and assure him or her that something is being done. Assume an active role in the child's protection. After the situation is resolved, monitor the progress closely. This crisis model is effective in working with children having thoughts of suicide.

Loss, Bereavement, and Grief as Crisis.
Children of all ages are capable of grieving. Sometimes the grief is covert; at other times it is overt (Norris-Shortle, Young, & Williams, 1993). Some overt signs are aggression, irritability, eating changes, disobedience, and nightmares. Covert signs of grief are guilt, depression, or confusion. Children at different ages experience grief differently because of developmental considerations. All children need to be truthfully informed about deaths that have occurred. Adolescents may not know how to express their feelings about death, particularly the first time it occurs. They may feel excluded from the family and yet need to be a part of the family at this time. They also need some privacy to grieve on their own.

Separation and divorce create a loss in a child's life that causes feelings of grief and mourning. Often children are fearful, angry, guilty, confused, insecure, and feel unloved. Psychosocial hazards associated with separation and divorce are the parents' quarreling, communication issues, the child's feeling that he or she is a passive victim, feeling the need to take sides, abandonment, loss of one parent, a one-parent home, and loss of parent's income.

Some techniques for dealing with bereavement in young children are the use of puppets, artwork, sand play, and psychodrama. For adolescents more appropriate strategies are individual counseling and intervention and group grief work. The adolescent who has just lost her best friend needs to have an opportunity to ventilate feelings and discuss their experiences together. Often, small groups of friends discuss the experiences and thoughts they have about the deceased friend and their relationship with her.

Sometimes, the major intervention for a crisis among students is conducted in the school setting. Often, when a traumatic event has occurred, a team of adults comes into the school to work with the student body. A typical crisis intervention team might include school counselors, school administrators, school psychologists, and school and mental health social workers. Issues to be dealt with by the team are the nature of the school crisis, the emotional needs of the students and faculty, identification of the high-risk populations, parental involvement, and long-term crisis interventions. Methods of helping with the grief process include setting up minicounseling centers, small grief groups, and large groups as needed, leading classroom discussions, and meeting with faculty.

Task-Centered Social Work

Goldstein and Noonan (1999) identified the task-center approach as having originated in research conducted by Reid and Shyne (1969). Findings demonstrated that short-term interventions in a briefer time were as effective as long-term ongoing services. Over time, this research had a major impact on social work treatment. The task-centered approach underwent testing and development during the 1970s and 1980s (Epstein, 1992).

Epstein envisioned a more inclusive approach, one in which all problems are appropriate for task-centered interventions. It has continued to develop and Epstein has delineated a more detailed prescriptive approach to the model. She identified four sequential overlapping steps. First, the client's target problems are identified. The second step is developing the contract, including the agreed-upon goals, focus, tasks, scheduling interviews, and time limits. Next, problem solving, or task achievement, is implemented. Finally, termination occurs.

Major Characteristics of the Model

Task-centered social work is characterized by an empirical orientation (Reid, 1996). The hypothesis and concepts about client systems are grounded in a case search. This approach draws on a number of empirically based theories and methods, such as cognitive-behavioral, problem-solving, cognitive, and family structural methods.

Clearly, the focus for service is the client's acknowledged problems, rather than the worker's belief about the client's problem. The client must need help with a specific problem or set of problems. The task-centered approach can be used with both voluntary and involuntary clients (Doel & Marsh, 1992; Reid, 1996; Rooney, 1992). Help may be given by assisting the young person to solve problems; sometimes the context needs to be changed (Reid, 1996). Contextual change may be needed for problem resolution, or resolution may have a beneficial effect on the context. For example, George's grades may lead to positive changes in the teacher's attitude, or a change in the teacher's attitude may lead to a more positive grade for George. A need for significant contextual change is not always an objective of this approach.

Task-centered practice is usually limited to 6 to 12 weeks. Research has indicated that the effectiveness of interpersonal treatment is relatively short lived, that is, most of the benefit of interpersonal treatment emerges within a few sessions (Garfield, 1994; Johnson & Gelso, 1982). The relationship of the client and practitioner is a collaborative but caring one. Assessment information is shared by the practitioner and client. They avoid hidden goals and agendas, and the client's participation is very important in developing treatment strategies. It is the client who will be the primary change agent, so his or her ideas are especially significant.

Purpose and Method

The purpose of task-centered practice is to help the young client resolve problems by planning and using problem-solving actions. The practitioner helps the client move forward with solutions to problems that they have defined and hope to solve. These actions may occur both within and outside the sessions with the social worker. Mobilizing the client's action is the intent of problem solving.

Reid (1996) states that the task-centered approach can be used in child welfare, public social services, medical settings, in industry, geriatric, and mental health services. Problem classifications used are problems in family, interpersonal relations, problems in social roles, decision making, resources, and distress that is reactive to situational factors. It is assumed that the problem is a temporary breakdown in coping skills. Forces to cause change are motivation to relieve distress and use resources in the client's environment.

A primary function of the session is to lay the groundwork for actions. A means of effecting environment change is jointly planned by the social worker and client. The time limit established is expected to enhance the effectiveness of mobilizing efforts. The number of problems for focus is also limited.

Exploring the Problem

Psychosocial problems are expressions of something the child or adolescent client wants that they do not have. The problems are defined by the young client rather than the practitioner. Problems are explored, pointing out difficulties and possible obstacles or negative outcomes that the client has not acknowledged. The problem is identified by the client with the guidance of the practitioner. It is expected that by the end of the first or second interview, the client and practitioner will come to an agreement on the problems for focus. The problem is clearly defined and the terms are specified. For instance, John is constantly out of his seat and creating chaos in the classroom. He has been suspended from school on several occasions. He wants to go to college in the future, so he wants to change his behavior and reputation. In the past week he has been removed from the classroom four times because he talked and bothered other students while they were doing their work.

The practitioner and client explore the context of the problem and identify the causes that could be manipulated or the resources that could be used to alleviate the problem. An effort is made to understand the dynamics and contextual features and the frequency and severity of the problem. Causal factors are determined by the client and practitioner working together. The practitioner contributes professional knowledge, and the client shares his or her personal knowledge of the problem and context. Problem exploration is a data-gathering assessment activity. Efforts are made to understand the dynamics of the problem and the contextual features.

Contracting and Planning

An oral or written contract is developed that explicitly states acknowledged problems. There must be an agreement to work on the problems together, even if the young client is not highly motivated to work on the problem. Both the client and practitioner are expected to operate within the agreed-on contract. The contract may be renegotiated.

A task identifies what the youthful client is to do to relieve the problem. Often at this time a broad task is identified; specific tasks are identified later. Some thought is given before specific tasks are developed. Finally, a plan is developed so that the client can begin to work on the task before the next session.

The client must be clear about the tasks to be completed. Questioning, reviewing, and summarizing the needs before the session ends is important. It must be clear to the client that the practitioner expects the tasks to be accomplished. The worker may leave the client with the statement that they will check next time to see how it went.

Tasks are also planned for the practitioner to carry out before the next session. He or she will be exploring resources to help create changes in the client system. The practitioner's task may be discussed with the client to create an awareness and an understanding that he or she too is keeping the contract.

A reason and a purpose for accomplishing the task must be established. Potential benefits are suggested. John is made aware that by carrying out his task, he may receive better grades and be better prepared to attend college. Discussion with John may help him see some special benefits to be gained by accomplishing his task.

Implementing the Tasks

It is also important to be prepared for obstacles that may prevent task accomplishment. The social worker talks with John about what obstacles he might see to task accomplishment. If he identifies potential blocks, this can be discussed, identifying means by which they can be overcome. The practitioner also must be aware of potential obstacles, such as the fact that John is already so angry with his teachers and principal that he may not be able to control his outburst. If this is the case, the social worker needs to provide a resource to help John express his anger in nondestructive ways.

During the session the young client and practitioner may role play and rehearse what the client is going to say and the possible choices of responses. The practitioner takes a coaching or teaching role in the role playing and rehearsal of communications with other students who stimulate and provoke part of John's acting-out behavior in school.

Reviewing Progress

As the social work practitioner meets with the young client at the beginning of each session, progress on task accomplishment and problems are reviewed. If tasks are not completed, Epstein (1980, p. 234) suggests a checklist of the areas that need to be examined:

1. Are you working on a problem of high interest to the client?
2. If you are working on a mandated problem, does the client understand the consequences of ignoring, avoiding, or failing to change?
3. Does the client understand the task?
4. Is the goal specific?

5. Have you reviewed the target problems and task sufficiently, adjusted the task often enough to fit the client and the situation?
6. Have all the available resources been fully provided?

At times, it may appear that no movement has been made, but rather new problems may have appeared between sessions. However, progress may have been made. What the practitioner does next depends on the result of the review. If a task has been completed, the practitioner may assign another one. If the task has not been completed, possible obstacles are reviewed and plans are made to overcome the obstructions. Different tasks may be assigned, or the problem may be reformulated. The practitioner takes a leadership role and pushes for contextual change to help the client work through the problem. He or she may use a variety of techniques, such as encouragement, advice giving, role playing, modeling, and exploration

Practitioner tasks are also examined in a similar way. Three types of such tasks are identified by Epstein (1980). One task is getting information the young client needs to perform his or her task. With written consent of the child and the parents, another task is conferring with other agencies to develop a positive attitude and commitment to provide social services for the client. With clients' permission, another worker task is conferring with those involved, such as parents, teachers, and officials, on behalf of the child.

Practitioners help remove obstacles and help clients use resources. The practitioner explores, examines, and explains factors and reasons for lack of success. Distorted views or expectations of the client must be modified. The practitioner may search for other resources in large systems, such as child welfare services or school settings, if the client is having difficulty in accomplishing tasks.

Because task-centered practice is a short-term approach, termination is already determined in the first session. A thorough review of the progress made throughout the sessions is a focus in termination. Often, the task may only be approximated rather than completely achieved. Attention is focused on ways in which the client can continue to work on their tasks. On occasion, extensions of service are made for a few more sessions.

The task-oriented approach was used with Mike, a 13-year-old living with his mother. Since the death of her husband a year ago, Mike's mother had been depressed and reclusive. Recently, Mike began to get into trouble. He often stayed out all night, was truant from school, and dabbled in drug use. He and his friends had recently been caught breaking into a house, and he had been placed in a juvenile facility.

Mandated Problems

The court ruled that Mike was a minor in need of supervision.

The mother believed that he needed a father figure.

The agency thought that he needed supervision and a better relationship with his mother.

Social Context

Mike had never been in trouble before and was very frightened about the possible consequences. He readily admitted that he needed help and that he had become involved with a bad crowd. He talked of how his father's death and his mother's grief had affected him.

Target Problems
1. Grief and loneliness because of the death of his father
2. Lack of a sound relationship with his mother
3. Mike staying out all night; Mike not attending school

Tasks
1. Seek counseling for dealing with grief.
2. Find times to communicate with his mother.
3. Be in by curfew time.
4. Attend school regularly.

Specific Tasks
1. The practitioner negotiated for Mike to receive counseling for grief. Mike agreed to keep appointments as scheduled.
2. Mike would talk to his mother at least once a day. The practitioner would refer the mother for grief counseling and encourage her relationship with Mike.
3. Mike would keep a curfew.
4. Mike would return to school. The practitioner would negotiate with the school for his return.

Time limit: 12 weeks

The practitioner and Mike met on a regular basis to discuss progress toward task accomplishment, obstacles, and ways to overcome the impediments.

The task-centered approach can be used in families or with groups and with individuals. It has been used to help families deal with problems stemming from divorce, death, and serious illness, and to help severely emotionally disturbed children and their families (Ewalt, 1977). Many believe that it can be used with all types of problems. As reported by Reid (1996), research has demonstrated the effectiveness of this approach with a number of differing populations. The major area of concern continues to be the durability of the approach. Research results are mixed regarding how long the positive results continue to be effective. Reid (1996, p. 634) indicates that the approach cannot be used with the following types of clients:

1. Clients who are uninterested in taking action on their problems
2. Clients who are unwilling to use the structure of the model
3. Clients who have problems that are psychogenic and motor difficulties
4. Clients who do not wish to be helped

Age of the client may be a limiting factor in its use because a major procedure is encouraging autonomy and empowerment of the client.

The task-centered approach can be used either as a whole or for the activities of planning, implementation, and review by the social worker using other methods. If it is used in the latter way, it has a much broader application. The approach can be used in almost any form of treatment to identify and carry through on a desired action. A long-term psychosocial approach may be used to carry through on a problem.

As noted earlier, the task-centered model is closely related to behavior modification, cognitive therapy, and problem solving. Task-centered practice and behavior modification could easily be combined. Behavior modification could be used to count and verify progress in resolving agreed-upon tasks.

Behavior Theory

Outcome research has demonstrated the effectiveness of behavior therapy in bringing about change with various populations of children and adolescents and their families in a wide range of organizations and environments. "Behavior therapy refers to systematic application of techniques intended to facilitate behavioral changes based principally, but not exclusively, on the conditioning theories of learning" (Thomlison & Thomlison, 1996, pp. 39–40).

The development of behavioral practices can be traced to Pavlov, who studied respondent or classical conditioning in the early twentieth century. Operant conditioning was advanced by Thorndike, Hull, Watson, and B. F. Skinner, and social learning was established by Bandura (1976). Beck (1976), Ellis (1977), and Meichenbaum (1977) advanced the cognitive behavior approach that is viewed as part of the behavioral paradigm.

A primary assumption made in the behavioral model is that all behavior is learned and can be defined, measured, and changed. So, personal and social problems can be viewed as behaviors that can be seen, measured, and changed. The means of changing behavior is to alter what happens before and after the target behaviors. Behaviors are changed by changing environmental events and reinforcement by significant others. Social learning theory formulates ways that behavior can be changed.

Three major elements of learning theory are target behaviors, antecedents, and consequences (Bandura, 1976). Target behaviors are behaviors that are the focus for change. Antecedent behaviors or events precede the target behaviors, and events that follow are the consequences. The focus of assessment is the consequences. These three elements of learning theory are referred to as the ABC paradigm, as described in the preceding chapter.

The first step in changing behaviors, using learning theory, is to identify the target behaviors. Then, the antecedents and consequences can be identified. Assessment is usually accomplished by direct observation. An example of a target behavior to be changed is Anne's tardiness in arriving at school. The antecedent behavior is Anne staying in bed when she is called. The consequence is that Anne gets in trouble and is sent to the principal's office. To change the target behavior of being late to school, Anne must get out of bed the first time she is called. By doing this, the antecedent—getting out of bed—is changed. This action, in turn, changes the consequence—being sent to the office, and positive change has occurred.

To assess the problems to change and the desired outcomes, the following steps must be taken:

1. Identify the behavioral problems and their maintaining conditions.
   a. What are the antecedent behaviors?
   b. Identify the consequences of those problem behaviors. What are the consequences of those events that occur after a target behavior?
2. Identify the behaviors that are to be targeted. These behaviors must be observable.
3. Set the conditions for a baseline measure. Record the frequency of occurrence of the targeted behavior.

The next steps are implementing the plan as follows:

1. Clearly identify the target behaviors.
2. Establish new antecedent events for the targeted behaviors.
3. Establish new consequences that are to be provided for each occurrence or nonoccurrence of the targeted behavior.
4. Formulate a written contract. Specify the following:
   a. Target behaviors for change
   b. New antecedents for each targeted behavior
   c. New positive consequences
   d. What happens if the contract is violated
   e. What consequences act as bonus reinforcers

In each session the tally is examined by the social worker. The worker needs to provide positive reinforcement by acknowledging change and hard work. If little change has been made, it may be necessary to reexamine aspects of the program design and, if needed, make changes in some part of the process. If behaviors have been achieved, move toward termination.

In preparation for termination, the family needs to be instructed to continue the tally. An appointment is made for termination and follow-up. At that time, it is determined whether the behavior changes have been maintained. If not, the program may need to be reinstated. If the behavior has been maintained, termination takes place.

Typical child problems that are the focus for behavioral procedures are hyperactivity, chore completion, sleep problems, enuresis, eating disorders, noncompliance, interrupting, and fire setting (Butterfield & Cobb, 1994). Behavior therapy techniques have been found to be effective with conduct disorders and antisocial behaviors.

It is especially important to be aware of the family's culture, because different behaviors may be more acceptable in one family than in another. So behavior therapy needs to be focused on the family in a given culture.

Behavioral approaches can be used for individuals, groups, and now is being used in community organizations. It is used with pharmacology approaches for attention disorders, depression, and obsessive compulsory disorders. Often, this methodology is combined with task-centered practice and can be used with psychosocial approaches.

Person-Centered Therapy

Originally, the person-centered approach, in contrast to social casework and social work generally, had no interest in a psychosocial history of the client. More recently, as the approach began to be used in a more eclectic form, history taking has become more acceptable. In the beginning the concept of diagnosis was not used but, over time, has become more acceptable to some (Rowe, 1996).

The person-centered model, sometimes called the client-centered model, was developed by Carl Rogers in the 1940s and has been expanded throughout the years. This theory is aimed at the incongruence between the young person's experience and his or her self-concept. Rogers believed that there is an inherent tendency in each person to grow toward self-actualization. This tendency is present at birth, and each person has the ability to reach his or her potential, which is innate to the organism. Another important belief in this approach is that the human organism is innately good and naturally wants to behave in healthy ways. To grow, nurturing qualities must be present in the environment. The therapist's task is to create the conditions that allow and encourage growth.

Roger's personality theory developed from his own theory and his research in counseling. He found that once the child's self-concept is formed, two needs develop. One is a need for positive regard from others; the other is the need for positive self-regard. These two needs, along with the person's experiences, begin to shape the nature of functioning. This occurs whether movement is toward actualization or not.

Self-concept is based on the individual's perceptions and evaluations of his or her experiences and what they convey in regard to his or her worth. One way of developing self-regard is based on the positive regard of others. This may create problems in development and growth when the positive regard of others becomes more attractive to us than actualizing ourselves; then incongruence develops. When this occurs, young people are controlled by others rather than by themselves and their goal of actualization.

The child may first experience this evolution of incongruence when the parents impose specific conditions on the child being loved by them. For example, a 7-year-old child, who was seen as a good child, sat quietly, not making any noise while other children were noisily running around and having fun. Behaving in this way made the quiet child feel good about receiving the admiration of adults who were present; at the same time, she was angry that she was not having fun as the other children were. These contradictory feelings between receiving regard from others and self-regard can bring about conflict for the child.

Rogers noted that three conditions, namely genuineness, unconditional positive regard, and empathy, help to free the actualizing process. Children need to experience these three conditions to actualize themselves. The role of the social worker is becoming the companion to the child in the journey toward self-discovery (Rogers, 1986). In displaying genuineness, the worker does not put up a "false" or professional front, but rather reacts and responds as he or she truly feels. Unconditional positive regard involves caring and accepting the other person, that is, being positive and nonjudgmental.

The final major attitude needed is empathy. This involves understanding the young person's frame of reference, including the meaning and feelings being experienced and communicating these understandings to the individual. The primary function of empathy is to free up the young person's ability and willingness to become involved in self-exploration.

This approach has had a significant impact on all social work with children and families. Axline (1947) developed an approach that drew from these nondirective principles, which became the basis of nondirective play therapy (Rowe, 1996). The primary assumption is that "the individual of any age has within him or herself, not only the ability to solve his or her problems satisfactorily, but also a striving for growth which makes mature behavior more satisfying than immature behavior" (Guerney, 1983, p. 23). Axline (1947) suggested self-direction as a focus on the source of the child's own growth.

Client-centered play therapy, more than any other play therapy, grants the child the freedom to be himself or herself without facing evaluation or pressure to change. By playing, the child is believed to bring feelings to the surface, face them, and learn to control them or abandon them. With these experiences, the child realizes his or her power to be an individual, to think for him- or herself, and to make decisions to become psychologically more mature and thus to realize selfhood.

Principles and Practice in
Client-Centered Play Therapy

A primary method of client-centered play therapy involves the participation of the therapist in play, as directed by the child. Most behaviors of the play therapist are intended to facilitate the child's self-direction, self-exploration, and self-growth. The therapist is expected to participate in play, be warm and friendly, develop close relations with the child, and nonverbally place limits on their behavior. The therapist reacts to the child instead of initiating action.

Ages of children suitable for play therapy were studied and suggest that toys were suitable to use for children up to the age of 12 years. Ginnott (1961) recommended toys that lend themselves to acting-out behavior, not toys that evoke diffuse hyperactivity. Other desirable toys were identified as those that would permit reality testing, allow the child to express feelings symbolically, and encourage catharsis and insight. Older children might use tape recorders, equipment such as stethoscopes, and other office equipment.

This type of play therapy was taught to volunteers and parents so that it could be used at home or in other settings. Play therapy led to the development of filia therapy, which is conducted by the parent in the home.

Adolescents would participate in person-centered therapy as adults, with the therapist using the same types of techniques as with adults. This theory as used with adolescents and parents is closely related to reality therapy and task-centered therapy. All these approaches require the client's use of autonomy as a part of the process. A primary difference is that the client-centered approach is much more self-directing than the task-centered model or reality therapy. In the client-centered approach, the therapist is more responsive to the direction of the child. However, the therapist is much more directive in task-centered and reality therapies.

Communication Theory

The presenting problem in this approach is concern with identifying the redundant communication patterns that serve as the rules that govern interactions. Communication theory is the major underpinning of various forms of strategic therapy. Primary versions of this model developed from professionals working together at the Mental Research Institute (MRI) in Palo Alto, California. Some proponents for this approach were Segal (1991), Haley (1984, 1987), and Madanes (1991).

A primary assumption of this approach is that communication affects behavior, and all behavior, including but not limited to speech, is communication. Information is a result of contrasting phenomena with each other and distinguishing between them. Facts may not be information. When the facts fit one's existing assumptions about the world and oneself, they may still be facts, but they are not information. How social systems mutually behave is communicated through information and feedback.

A single unit of communication is a message; a series of messages between two people is interaction. Over time, communication feedback processes become redundant and patterned; as a result, these patterns of interaction become the rules for interaction. Watzlawick, Beavin, and Jackson (1967) identified a number of axioms of human communication:

1. One cannot not communicate (silence is communication).
2. Every communication has a content and a relationship aspect. The relationship aspect classifies the content and is therefore a metacommunication.
3. The nature of a relationship is dependent upon the punctuation of the communication sequence between the communicants. Each person views a situation in his or her own way.
4. People communicate both digitally and analogically (verbally and nonverbally).
5. All communication interchanges are either symmetrical (between equals) or complementary (from a one-up or one-down position).

Possible difficulties in communication between people is the double bind. The common elements of a double bind follow:

1. A one-up or one-down position is an intense relationship. The child in a one-down position must be able to interpret the message of the one-up person. This view of the world is usually learned in the family of origin.
2. The parents in the one-up position constantly use punishment or threats of punishment, not rewards, which creates a learning context based on avoiding punishment rather than on receiving rewards.
3. Conflicts exist between verbal and nonverbal messages.
4. The child is unable to escape the situation or to clarify the conflicting messages.
5. For the child to learn to see the world through a double-bind lens, the learning must have been repeated and pervasive.

The symptomatic behavior involves incongruent levels of messages. Having experienced the double-bind communication, the child comes to the point of not believing the communications of most people, even when no such double-bind messages are communicated.

A first order and second order of change exists. First-order change is attempted according to the rules or assumptions of the client system. Second-order change is outside the young client's current rules. The catalyst for change is the introduction of a novelty.

This order of change is beyond the youngster's assumptive world. The social worker is looking for information on which the young client's functioning might be based. "Some clients encounter a block in processing particular information that conflicts with what they already believe, with their own rules for information processing, or with operating rules within their social groups" (Nelsen, 1980, p. 69). The social worker needs to develop and implement interventions that interrupt the rigid problem-maintaining patterns.

Underlying the MRI approach is that if what one is doing is not getting results, one needs to stop doing it and try something else. The second order focuses on making changes in the attempted solutions rather than the presenting problem. Greene (1996) identified six stages of treatment: (1) join the client's system, (2) define the problem, (3) define the outcome goal, (4) identify the attempted solutions, (5) develop and implement change strategies, and (6) termination.

Strategies for Change

According to Greene (1996), several strategies for change are used in this approach. One of the techniques for change is *reframing,* which is offering plausible alternative meaning to some aspect of the young client's problem. An illustration of this is an honor student who was about to receive his diploma and was looking for summer work. He came to the social worker's office complaining that he had too many choices and what a terrible decision it was to make. He was really agonizing over this decision, and he seemed to feel depressed. He felt he was in an unfair situation. The social worker reframed his view by talking about how lucky he was to have so many choices and to be so sought after by so many potential employers. With this change in perception expressed, the young man's face brightened and he left the office pleased with himself and with his situation.

Another technique is *restraint from change.* The social worker may suggest to the young client that presently the client should go slow in attempting to make a change. This is a useful technique for dealing with clients who are compliant and yet attempt to keep things from happening. Complying with the restraint short-circuits the problem-maintaining pattern.

Positioning is another way to encourage change. A child, Nita, is experiencing difficulty in adjusting to a new school. Those around Nita continue to tell her that things will get better and that soon her new school will feel just as comfortable to her as her old school. The more optimistic they become, the more sure she is that the situation is impossible. The social worker may join her in her pessimistic view that things probably will never be the same. They then can work together to help Nita make the adjustment to the new school.

Behavior prescriptions can also help the child or system to change. The child may be receiving a verbal message to change but a nonverbal message not to change. This technique prescribes either a change in the pattern or sequence of the problem or the frequency or intensity of the problem. A mother may be overinvolved with her young son whereas the father is observant and detached. One way to change the family interaction is to alter the situation in which the family meets or the activity in which they participate. If the father and son are mechanically inclined, they might spend a session putting together a model plane or car.

Some of the behaviors are indirect prescriptions such as to advertise rather than conceal, the great effects of small causes (suggesting the perfectionist child purposefully make mistakes). Others are the devil's pact (get an agreement to perform a behavior before being told what the behavior is), odd-day/even-day rituals, and using qualifying language (refuse to take a definite position) (Greene, 1996). Populations served by this approach include adolescent substance abusers, behavior problem children in schools, persons in crisis, children in child protection, and children with eating disorders (Amatea, 1989; Nelson, 1980).

Problem Solving

Problem solving is an approach that was primarily developed in social work by Helen Harris Perlman (1957). It was an attempt to make social work practice with children and adolescents and their families more pragmatic and here-and-now oriented as opposed to the diagnostic school's position of a formal diagnosis and treatment plan. Gelfand (1988) defined problem solving as "a systematic step by step thinking and acting process that involves moving from an undesired to a desired state" (p. 1).

Problem solving is a process that is very natural for young people. Children and adolescents use their natural capacities of the cognitive powers of reasoning and logic to attain their goals by solving problems. In fact, Perlman (1957) thought of daily living as a problem-solving process. Only problems that could not be solved alone sent young people and their families seeking help from a social worker. When the problem was resolved, the young person continued with his or her life and problem-solving ability.

The problem-solving process is a way of drawing a conceptual map to guide the social worker and young client through the steps involved in the change process. This process is intended to move the youngster from the problem to the solution (Compton & Galaway, 1994). Emphasis is on the effectiveness of the decision itself, learning a problem-solving process, and implementing and evaluating the results. It is assumed that every young person has the ability to make changes and choices about themselves and their environment. The social worker supplements the skills of the young person to solve the problem. Problems are outcomes of a natural process of human change and growth. If problems are seen as a part of life, the capacity to solve them is also ascribed to young people. Perlman saw problem solving as a process, not as a goal in itself.

The problem-solving process may be blocked by a number of factors, including a lack of knowledge, inadequate resources, or experiencing emotional responses that impair the young person's ability to solve the problem (Turner & Jaco, 1996). Using the problem-solving method, the social worker and young client develop a collaborative relationship that can be used to motivate and support the client's effort. Together, they use a rational, cognitive process of identifying, evaluating, choosing, and implementing a solution from among a range of alternatives. Bedell and Lennox (1997) write of communication and problem-solving training as a means of helping children gain competence.

The problem-solving method of helping has also been used in working with groups over a long period of time. In 1976, Somers indicated that problem solving characterized the formulation of social group work practice across the spectrum of 50 years. Over time, this approach has been expanded and changed. Haley (1987) used a focus on problems with families and identified a problem as a sequence of acts among several persons. The problem-solving approach is described as linear in nature but a circular process in application (Compton & Galaway, 1994). It is a flexible approach that can be looped back to a beginning stage at any point, either by the client or worker.

Steps in the Problem-Solving Process

Request for Services.   The first phase of the problem-solving model is when the young client and the social worker meet. They develop a collaborative relationship and begin the exploration of problems. Often, problems are multiple, sometimes in clusters. The problems and their interrrelationships are explored. After exploring the problems and their configuration, a single problem or at most a few problems selected for focus are partialized or broken down to make them more manageable. Generally, the problem for focus is selected by the young client but with the guidance and agreement of the social worker.

Identifying the Problem.   In working with children and adolescents, the selection of the problem may become very complicated. In most cases, the child or adolescent has one opinion of the problem whereas the parents (or guardian) have a differing version of the problem. Also, it is not unusual for the referring institution or social agency to have its own version of the child's problem.

In an institution for mentally challenged adolescents, the referring institution requested assistance in helping the child relate better with his peers in the living situation. Alex wanted to make contact with his family and relatives and to return to the community. The parents and relatives wanted no contact with Alex; they just wanted him to remain in the institution. As a way of beginning to identify the problem, it quickly became clear that no issues were going to be resolved until Alex had pursued his concern. Why did Alex need to learn to get along with peers in the institution if he could leave and go back to his family? So a sequence of problem resolution needed to be accomplished before the reason for referral—poor peer relationships—could become the focus.

Once the problem or problem configuration has been selected, the young client and the social worker identify long-term and short-term goals for the focus of their work together. The emphasis during this process is to help the client determine what is needed and how it can be attained. A focus is on the resources of the client and other resources in the community that might be made available to him or her. A preliminary agreement is sought by clarifying the resources of the social agency and other resources in the community that might be made available. Knowledge of such resources allows further study and refinement of the problem.

The next step is assessment of the young client in terms of his or her motivation, capacity, and opportunity. Motivation is viewed in terms of the client's desire or drive to solve the problem or attain the goal. Motivation is greatly affected by the client's hope that the problem or issue can be resolved and the goal can be attained. This expectation of success can be further enhanced by the social worker's belief in the client's potential. In the process of partializing the problems, one may want to begin with a goal that is expected to be relatively easily attainable. This is expected to help the client gain confidence and motivation by his or her proven ability to accomplish goals.

Opportunities are focused on the resources available to be used with and for the young client. This may include resources known to the client and the social worker's supplemental help in providing resources in the form of services. Alex wanted to begin by exploring the resources that could be made available for him to return to the community.

Capacity, a third area of assessment, was a primary concern in attempting to resolve the problem identified by Alex. His desire to resolve this problem was strong; he was focused and was able to make suggestions about how contact could be made with his relatives. However, Alex's ability to function outside the institution was very limited, and he would need continuous supervision. He had a low IQ and did not relate well to others. By resolving his primary problem first, even though the outcome was negative, Alex became more motivated to work on the problem for which he had been referred originally. Both his capacity and opportunity had been assessed in this process.

Contracting.   The next step in the problem-solving process is the development of a contract and further assessment and evaluation of the young client and his or her situation. One must determine how the identified problems are related to the needs of the client system. In this assessment it is important to look at what factors contribute to creating and maintaining the problem and what strengths and resources are available for problem solving.

A concern of the worker is what principles and knowledge of social work practice could be applied to the resolution of the problem. A plan must be made to help the client move systematically toward the agreed-on goals and the resolution of the problem. A specific plan of action is made and agreed on by the client and the social worker. This includes reachable goals, after an exploration of alternatives and an evaluation of their likely outcomes. An appropriate method of service is determined to accomplish the goals. In this process both the roles of the worker and the young client must be identified for working together toward this change. Part of this process is an evaluation of the prognosis or the expected and hoped-for success for the child or adolescent, and the family, as a result of this plan.

Implementation of the Plan.   The point of intervention must be decided and tasks assigned both for the client and the social worker. Resources and services to be used with the problem-solving intervention need to be identified and made ready for use. A plan of action must be made clear by deciding what, when, and who will carry out the assigned roles. With the accomplishment in resolving one problem, it may have been planned or requested that they move on to another problem for resolution.

Termination.   A primary focus during this time is the accomplishments of the young client. It is important for the client and the social worker to evaluate how progress was made and why some problem areas were not successfully resolved. The social worker, alone, also needs to spend some time evaluating the success of the particular interventions she or he used.

During termination, other areas need to be evaluated and stabilized. First, it is important to evaluate the gains that have been made by the client and how these can be maintained by the client in the future. The worker–client relationship must be ended. Preparation must be made by the worker to cope with his or her own feelings about termination and also the feelings that the client may experience. Finally, the client and worker need to review the possible natural supports in his or her network within the family, friends, and community that can be used to support the gains and help the client deal with new problems as they arise.

Evaluation.   It is important to evaluate the progress of the client and the interventions used throughout the total contact of the worker with the client. A continuing evaluation needs to be made of the purposes of the interventions and their success and appropriateness to induce the change required. Another area for evaluation is whether the client has learned problem-solving skills that can be used in attempting to resolve problems in the future. The worker needs to be aware of what has been learned that can be used successfully with clients with similar problems in the future.

Assumptions and Thinking Underlying the Approach

Problem solving as a process was expected to involve and engage the client in recognizing and taking ownership of the problem. These ideas were very much influenced by John Dewey and his belief that learning was problem solving (Perlman, 1957).

Perlman attempted to move away from pathology and find a method that was applicable to all people with problems. Problem solving is a here-and-now, reality-based way of helping young people who need assistance. An expectation exists that children and adolescents are able to work toward solving problems and that perhaps they need a challenge to be engaged in more effective ways of coping in the future.

Work must begin "where the client is" is another assumption in the problem-solving approach. Young people are always believed to be in the process of becoming. This method has been found to be helpful with multiproblem families and crisis-oriented clients. By focusing on the problem as a focus for intervention, the young person is able to reduce anxiety and mobilize energy. This method allows the client to experience success in one area, thus encouraging him or her to proceed with larger problems.

The problem-solving method focuses on the present and uses the power of the helping relationship to motivate the client. Authenticity is important in the relationship between the social worker and the child or adolescent. It is especially useful in working with this population because of the close relationship between education and therapy. The child may need to learn the steps of problem solving to deal with issues in the future. The social worker assesses the client's motivation and decides how to engage him or her in the process.

Problem solving is a part of the ecological systems approach and the task-centered model. Dubois and Miley (1996) have integrated it into a cognitive base and written about it as an intentional client-empowering operation.

Limitations

Turner and Jaco (1996) state that one of the limitations of the problem-solving model is that it is not suitable for all clients. It has been suggested that it is not applicable to all ethnic groups. It is inappropriate for use with strong people working on unfinished business, and with transitional situations, such as marriage, separation, or death.

Problem-solving is no longer seen by Turner and Jaco (1996) as "the current predominant conception of practice" as it was by Siporin (1975, p. 51). Instead, it is now so absorbed into much of social work methods and processes that it "essentially becomes the basic method that underlies much of practice in addition to the generalist approach" (Turner & Jaco, 1996, p. 519).

Existential Social Work

For the existentialist, young people discover their own uniqueness in the way they relate to the objective experience of life. Subjectivity is a young person's freedom. It exists as a unique responsive relationship to the world. "Its primary activity is the conveyance of meaning through thought and feeling, intuition and sensation, and the assertion of this unique perspective through creative arts" (Krill, 1996, p. 252).

Through limits set up by life, a young person's inner objectivity is challenged in terms of certain beliefs and meanings that they have concluded about him- or herself. In a similar way, young people realize their potential. The young person senses that the world wants and needs some response from him or her. It is this awareness of both limits and potentials that is the foundation on which young people judge their own unique perspective and readjust this view when necessary.

The encounter between subjectivity and the outside world is a continual struggle. If the child or adolescent values his or her subjectivity and its uniqueness, development, and expression in him- or herself, it must be valued in others. "Human love is the effort to understand, share, and participate in the uniqueness of others" (Krill, 1996, p. 253). The young person as existentialist attempts to understand self and immediate surroundings and, in a lifelong process, may incorporate the principle of the joining of humanity and the universe. The origins of the existentialist point of view in social work, which was rooted in the work of Otto Rank, was developed by Jessie Taft (1937) as she wrote of the functional school of thought.

Krill (1996) identifies five organizing principles of existentialist philosophy: (1) disillusionment, (2) freedom of choice, (3) meaning in suffering, (4) the necessity of dialogue, and (5) the stance of responsible commitment. Change can occur by relinquishing defensive beliefs, judgments, and symptoms that interfere with the natural growth process. A therapeutic task is to help the young client experience disillusionment with security efforts that block growth.

The young client has freedom of choice about changes. The critical ingredient for change is his or her desire to change. The client receives a message of positive affirmation by the social worker's belief in the client's capacity to change. The social worker affirms the suffering of the young client. Anxiety and guilt are seen as necessary and directional for a young person. The potential for changing orientation often requires normalizing pain as a natural consequence of the child or adolescent's conclusions about adjusting to life.

The young client's growth is concerned with continual reassessment and depends on feedback from the environment. To gain honest feedback, she or he must allow others to be free in their expression. In therapy it is important to help young clients be open and to encourage free responses from others. The social worker attempts to get the young client's recognition and commitment to his or her own "inner, emerging unique lifestyle." To do this, therapy must be client centered. The social worker helps young clients become aware of and respect their own unique lifestyle—to discover that they are intricately involved in the life process itself.

Krill (1996) states that existentialism claims no technique system of its own. It is viewed as compatible with reality-oriented and cognitive-oriented therapies that emphasize heightening the client's awareness through actions in the "here and now" (Ellis, 1977; Glasser, 1965; Reid, 1979; Werner, 1982). In the helping relationship the social worker affirms the inherent value of the young client as a unique person with a lifestyle that is his or her own. Clients have the power of free choice and the power to decide how to shape their own lives. Among the existentialist social worker's values are the following: human beings have a capacity for free choice; they are of worth in their own perspective of life; they require open interactions with their surroundings to grow; suffering is an inevitable part of growth; and self-deception is a potent force.

No matter how emotionally disturbed a child or adolescent may appear to be, within the youngster is an integrative core that prompts him or her in the direction of experiencing and expressing uniqueness. This belief suggests that a conflict-free part of the personality survives and transcends dysfunctioning.

Components of Change

Two components, rational and experiential, are required for change to occur. These two components are both valued because one reinforces the other. Krill (1996, p. 266) identifies five therapeutic activities that help clarify self-understanding and experiencing:

1. The attitude of the therapist toward the client can be a new type of affirmation by this significant other that the client has never before experienced.
2. The therapist's skill with empathy may provide the client with an experience of being understood more intensely than by any others in his or her life.
3. The therapist's openness about him- or herself is an invitation for the client to dialogue experiences. In this way the client may experience a candid honesty that may not be available in everyday interactions.
4. Here-and-now techniques heighten awareness. Techniques such as Gestalt, encounter groups, psychodrama, and transferences between the therapist and client stir new areas of individual awareness.
5. Tasks to do, outside the therapy session, provide new behavioral experiences.

It is more important for the social worker to understand the dynamics of the young client's present struggle than to attend to historic data. It is important to understand the client's unique worldview, such as ways of relating to meaningful others, beliefs about oneself, and both positive and negative judgments.

The three principles of treatment used for the therapeutic approach of the existentialist social worker are a client-centered orientation, an experiential change emphasis, and a concern with values and philosophical or religious perspectives. The existential stance provides a philosophical perspective that can be related to many avenues of social work practice. This model is clearly more appropriate for use with adolescent clients or children who have a high level of psychosocial development.

Role Theory

Despite debates and disagreements about whether role theory is, in fact, a theory, it provides an approach to analyze social behavior that is absent from many other theories (Davis, 1996). Role theory has become very important to social work practice with children and adolescents, and their families, because of its emphasis on the person–situation configuration.

Social work literature is replete with references to role, its meaning, uses, and functional/dysfunctional consequences. Definitions of central terms is essential for understanding and providing common terminology for application of role theory. Definitions used here are those identified by Davis (1996) and in agreement with terminology commonly used by others.

Positions are classifications of persons, such as teachers, fathers, women, children, and social workers. *Ascribed positions* are those positions dependent on accidents of birth, for example, being child, being an adult, or having a disability. *Achieved positions* are attained through skill or effort. These positions include social worker, doctor, politician, and teacher. Ascribed behaviors have primacy over achieved positions. These are the positions that lay the foundation for subsequent socialization. Children and adolescents eventually enter most positions in their lives through a combination of ascription and achievement.

Status is the value placed on the position (Biddle, 1979). High status indicates more prestige and can take the form of wealth, strength, or power. *Role* refers to characteristic behaviors performed by persons occupying a social position. Role is a "patterned sequence of learned actions performed by a person in an interactional situation" (Sarbin, 1954, p. 225). A *role set* consists of roles potentially associated with a single position. One may speak of a woman in one set of roles for a child, a second set of roles for her husband, and a third set of roles for her boss.

Role expectations are sets of expectations from generalized others. Expectations include rights and obligations. These are the "oughts" and "shoulds" to which young people are subjected. *Role complementarity* is said to occur when role behavior and role expectations are harmonious. This results in satisfactory role relationships. *Norms* are role expectations that prescribe behaviors that ought to be performed by the person in that position. For example, traditionally, it is a norm for mother to take care of the children and a norm for father to support the family financially. *Social identity* is the sense that young people have of themselves, which emerges from the positions they occupy and the adequacy with which they perform their roles as judged by significant others. Self-identity may change as children and adolescents enact changes in their roles.

A variety of terms have developed to describe role-related difficulties. *Role conflict* is a difficulty that young people experience in the performance of their roles. Role conflicts occur when young people experience incompatible demands in the performance of their designated role. *Interrole,* or *interposition, conflict* occurs when the role expectations of one role are incompatible with another role. The role of a woman leaving for work at

7:00 A.M. may be incompatible with the role of the mother getting her child ready for school at 8:00 A.M. *Intrarole,* or *intraposition, conflict* occurs when expectations associated with a single position are incompatible with another. *Role ambiguity* occurs when expectations for a role are unclear or incomplete, usually when new roles are developing or when old roles are being redefined, as when housewives went to work in factories during World War II. *Role overload* suggests that roles are too complex. It tends to occur when roles are discontinuous and lack similarity.

Role behaviors are learned through processes such as modeling, identification, and reinforcement. These processes make roles dependent on social learning theory. A major part of understanding the functioning of a young person relies on an awareness of the roles that he or she is expected to play and how adequately they are played. Role induction of the child or adolescent into the client role is a vital part of the beginning process in the helping relationship. The induction primarily consists of an educational process of the youngster.

First, the young person must be able to verbalize what he or she expects of the client role and the social worker role. The social worker may teach the child or adolescent other possible parts and nuances of the two roles as a beginning orientation to the helping process. The social worker "starts where the client is." Explicit areas for evaluating role performance are identified during assessment (see Davis, 1996, pp. 590–591), including (1) the ways the client's problems are created out of incomplete and inadequate socialization into the roles that they are expected to play; (2) difficulties that stem from insufficient contemporary support for the roles expected of them; and (3) the interactive nature of many client problems.

An assessment of roles focuses attention on the relationships between position, status, and access to resources and power (Germain & Gitterman, 1980). The perspective of role theory provides for an analysis of the social determinants of behavior. It helps social workers discover the status/role demands that are the most stressful for children and adolescents, and their families.

Within our ever-changing world, roles are changing too. The rate of divorce, the child's position in the family, and the adoptions of children have created new roles without clear expectations and often without clear boundaries. These new roles and their boundaries often are seen as deviant and unacceptable. These areas often are a part of the problem for which the client seeks help. The new role definitions have greatly affected couples and parent–child relationships and have required new definitions within practice.

A focus on role clearly removes the problem as residing within the individual and locates it in the transactions of the young person with society. The emphasis for the social worker is likely to be providing models for learning new behaviors, supporting child and adolescent clients who choose to deviate from the model approved by society, and lobbying for antidiscriminatory legislation for stigmatized persons. Intervention with young clients experiencing role conflicts that result in guilt or related feelings is also an appropriate area for social workers using role theory. The social worker explores the client's feeling about not meeting the expectation of the role and helps the client to appraise his or her current role performance.

Role playing is a commonly used technique with children and adolescents. It can be used in individual, group, and family therapy to teach, practice, and learn new roles. It is also very helpful in promoting an understanding of complementary roles. This is usually accomplished by role reversal, when one person takes on the role of another. This process assists the youngster in seeing the situation from the perspective of the other. In working with a child in the playroom of a mental health center, the child directed the social worker to play the part of the student and he would be the teacher. This role play helped the social worker gain some understanding of the boy's view of the power, authority, and rudeness of his teacher. It also helped explain the negative role the boy had taken with the teacher.

Role reversal has a somewhat different meaning when working with children and adolescents who have been abused or neglected. As a result of their maltreatment, the child may take on the role of the parent. If that child is removed and placed in another living environment, role conflict often occurs. In this case an attempt is made to teach the child to participate in the role of a child to complement the role of the caregiver.

A variety of techniques for exploring and understanding roles have been developed, such as on-the-spot interviews, doubling, mirroring, and sharing (Toseland & Rivas, 1995). A common practice in social work and in educational settings is to break down components for learning new behaviors and for teaching them to children. The practitioner is not limited to focusing on role; the young client's feelings about the adequacy of role performance is also a topic for discussion.

Using Multiple Bodies of Theory

In working with children and adolescents, multiple bodies of thought, strategies, procedures, and techniques can be very useful. Several approaches employ techniques borrowed from other approaches. Often, techniques from task-oriented, problem-solving, cognitive, and behavioral approaches are all used with the same youth for the same problems. In many ways these approaches overlap and require the use of some of the same techniques. Crisis theory utilizes many strategies taken from models. In regard to actualizing the self, existential practice has many commonalities with client-centered practice. Although the methodology of existential and client-centered practices differ, their basic purposes are closely related.

Social work with Leo, a 14-year-old boy who dropped out of school, required strategies and techniques of several models. He had been in minor trouble—fighting, drinking, and staying out all night. His parents brought him to the mental health center for help. Leo acknowledged that he is unhappy with life but does not know what to do about it. His parents wanted him to return to school. It was going to be important first to help Leo find his direction in life.

Turner (1996) developed a useful classification of practice theories. With an understanding of a variety of theories, strategies, procedures, and techniques for practice, the social worker can selectively choose interventions that have the best fit for Leo and his problem. Leo needs to discover more about whom he is and how he relates to the world. Procedures and techniques that are client centered, with an emphasis on person and society; existential, focused on the person's attributes; and cognitive, stressing the person's attributes, could all be helpful in beginning to assist Leo to discover whom he is and in what direction he wishes to move.

It is important that Leo begin to actualize himself, gain some understanding of his relationship to the world, and change his behavior. Then problem-solving and task-oriented procedures and techniques focused on using the young person's attributes could be used to help Leo identify situations he wants to change and how he wants to accomplish this. The use of a variety of procedures and techniques that match the client's needs allows both breadth and flexibility in helping the client move toward goal attainment.

In another case, 8-year-old Tessie came to the attention of the social worker as a result of physical abuse and subsequent placement in foster care. Strategies and techniques from crisis and client-centered theories that focused on the young person and society would be important in beginning work with Tessie. Later, as a result of Tessie's experiences and her misperceptions about herself, strategies from communication, existential, and problem-solving techniques emphasizing the young person's use of attributes could be helpful. Role and client-centered interventions, which are person and society focused, could help Tessie begin to relate to her new home, school, and environment.

After meeting with the child or adolescent and parents and identifying issues that need to be explored and changed, goals are determined and the social worker begins to make a treatment plan. The treatment plan is focused on the goals, strategies, and techniques to be used in helping this youth. The interventions need to be identified and analyzed by the social worker. The worker may decide to use a unitary approach that is most appropriate for the problems or techniques and procedures from various theoretical systems to provide a closer fit to the variety of issues of concern to the youth.

Clearly, the most beneficent means of helping the young client is to use interventions that fit most closely with the client's needs. This often requires the social worker to possess knowledge and skill in using a variety of techniques derived from multiple approaches to practice. Often, working with organizations and agencies supplements interventions with children and adolescents and their families. Some possible social services and strategies are discussed in the next chapter.

7 Using Agency and Organizational Systems

This chapter has two purposes. One purpose is to analyze the impact of social agency and human service organizational systems on social work practice with children and adolescents. A second purpose is to explicate ways of working within such systems that can be helpful to children, adolescents, and their families.

The scope of direct social services for children and adolescents is examined within their organizational context. To understand the social agency, the social worker considers the dynamics of the agency, its climate, organization, structure, functioning, staffing, and resources. Baglow (1990) observed that only recently have the dynamics of agencies working on child abuse cases begun to attract academic and professional attention.

Social work practice with children and adolescents, and their families, occurs within the context of three aspects of social organization. One, as members of society, youngsters and their families normatively participate in social organizations, such as clubs and religious groups. Two, children and adolescents are members of families that possess a certain degree of organization. Three, children and adolescents receive social services that also have a degree of structure and organization.

Social Systems

Social work practice with children and adolescents, and their families, occurs within the context of agency and organizational systems. Practitioners have contact with agency and organizational systems in meeting the needs of young clients. Private practitioners also interface with agency and organizational systems.

However, some programs and agencies operate outside the realm of other agency systems. For instance, family support programs, which build on family strengths, operate outside state public child welfare systems (Downs & Nahan, 1990). The family support model is a collaborative model that has eight features (Leon, 1999). The first feature is services across the life span. The second feature is utilization of a strengths perspective and community empowerment frameworks. The third feature is integration of services. The fourth feature is collaborative partnerships between government, service agencies, and communities. The fifth feature is neighborhood-based and family-friendly services. The sixth feature is local government fiscal support. The seventh feature is identification of the formal and informal strengths and resources within a community. The eighth feature is integration of specific and measurable goals and objectives to measure outcomes.

A functional analysis of child-serving agencies is related to their purpose. Three sets of purposes, goals, and objectives of child-serving organizations exist. One, the survival of the organization is a paramount goal. However, many child-serving agencies must modify their mission over time to continue to survive. Two, in regard to programs and groups, the purpose of the organization includes carrying out helping activities. Service provision is important for children and adolescents in need. Three, in regard to individuals within the organization, including practitioners, professional goals include advancement, achievement, and effectiveness. As social systems, social agencies and human service organizations tend to be interacting wholes consisting of subsystems. Active efforts by practitioners keep them viable, balanced, and well organized.

Social agencies and human service organizations are related to larger systems, including the community and society, and to smaller systems, including small groups, families, and individuals. Most social agencies and human service organizations are large groups that tend to be fairly bureaucratic in nature. Regardless of their size, all child-serving human service organizations comprise large groups with relatively impersonal dynamics. However, within child-serving organizations are many small task groups, including teams, committees, and case conferences whose dynamics tend to be somewhat more personal. Large and small work groups within human service organizations tend to be task oriented.

Contexts of Practice

Eight contexts of social work practice impinge on the social agency and human service organization serving children, adolescents, and their families. One, the political context determines the priority given to social service delivery for children and adolescents. The priority is also reflected in the resources allocated to such services. Within the social agency and human service organization, the political context includes the power that personnel have in regard to the definition and delivery of social services for children and adolescents.

Two, providing social services to children and adolescents has a considerable financial cost. The economic context refers to how factors such as funding for services, cost of services, payments for services within social agencies, managed care, insurance, and governmental contributions affect the adequacy, quality, availability, utilization, coordination, efficiency, and effectiveness of services for children and adolescents (Morrissey, Johnsen, & Calloway, 1997).

Managed care consists of a variety of financing and service delivery arrangements (Hughes & Luft, 1998). The one characteristic such arrangements have in common is that enrollees are encouraged or required to obtain care through a network of participating providers who are selected by the managed-care organization and who agree to abide by the rules of that organization.

Heflinger and Northrup (2000) conducted a survey of community agencies in one area that provided or interacted with behavioral health services for children and adolescents. They reported the following changes under a capitated managed-care contract:

(a) problems in service delivery experienced by the target population increased; (b) quality of behavioral health and related services available decreased; (c) service system performance decreased, (d) the extent to which goals of an effective behavioral health service system were being attained was also rated as significantly decreased; and (e) coordination of services for the target population and collaboration among providers declined. (p. 175)

Three multiple-funding models exist for the modern family service agency (Martin, 1993). One, the community-care model is akin to the traditional model of the family service agency. Payers of service include a fiduciary agent, such as United Way, which is the first payer. Two, the targeted-care model focuses on a particular population, such as children in schools. Demand exceeds resources, creating waiting lists. Three, the specific-care model focuses on specific clients who seek social services. Such clients have the resources to pay for services through an employee assistance program, an insurance plan, or out of pocket.

Benefits refer to the anticipated, expected, and obtained outcomes available to child or adolescent clients. Indigent young clients and their families receive government benefits or entitlements. With the input of economists, cost–benefit analyses are implemented as part of program evaluations.

Public and private social agencies and human service organizations provide social services to children and adolescents. Governmental organizations, which are in the public domain, are universalistic in their approach to serving children and their families. Private services are nonprofit, for profit, and private practice. Private nonprofit agencies provide specialized in-home and group-living services for children.

Residential treatment centers for children and adolescents are confronted with challenges in regard to changing funding systems, information management needs, human resource environments, and client requirements, as well as demands to redesign service delivery systems (Gunn, 1998). Total quality management (TQM) provides tools to create organizational changes to meet such challenges. Moreover, TQM is used to improve quality of services, improve intra-agency cooperation, reduce operating costs, increase trust in management, advance consistency in accountability, and improve effective flow of communication in residential treatment centers (Cozens, 1997; Hodge-Williams, Doub, & Busky, 1995).

For-profit child-serving social agencies and organizations include private psychiatric units for children and substance abuse centers for adolescents. However, the boundaries among the sectors overlap. The public sector, which is a service system, is a funding source for the other sectors (Lourie & Katz-Leavy, 1991). Public child welfare agencies purchase services from all sectors, especially the private nonprofit sector.

Social workers help children and adolescents while working with managed behavioral health organizations (MBHOs) and managed-care organizations (MCOs). Social workers face dilemmas in working with young people who need more services than MCOs authorize. Ethically, they must continue to provide such services while advocating for the MCO to authorize additional care.

Three, the social context reflects the extent to which child and adolescent services are embedded within society. Whereas Western cultures tend to view the child and adolescent as an individual, Eastern cultures tend to view the child and adolescent as a member of the family. Child and adolescent services, including assessment and treatment, are individualistic or family centered. The two sets of variables pertain to the culture and the services. The juxtaposition or interaction of such variables yields four possible contingencies.

In the two convergent scenarios, the culture and the services are either both Western or are both Eastern. The child and family receive similar messages in regard to the nature and definition of the problem and its treatment from cultural sources and the agency. In two additional, divergent scenarios, the culture and the services are Western and Eastern, respectively, or vice versa. The child and family receive dissimilar and conflicting messages in regard to the nature and definition of the problem and its treatment from cultural sources and the agency.

Four, the values context refers to preferred choices in social service delivery. The structure of values is present in societies, organizations, the social work profession, child and adolescent clients, and their families. Ideally, all such values are consistent with one another. However, within social agencies or human service organizations serving children and adolescents, professional value conflict sometimes occurs. For instance, in a child guidance and evaluation clinic, the professional values of a behaviorally oriented practitioner differed from the rest of the psychodynamically oriented staff.

Five, the religious context refers to social and family issues pertaining to family types, marriage, intermarriage, divorce, family planning, abortion, child-raising norms, child abuse and neglect, and education of children. Religiosity varies by region such that the population of children and adolescents and their families is more likely to be religious in some regions than in others. Moreover, some agencies may be affiliated with a larger religious organization, may receive funding from a religious foundation, and may have a mission that is religious in nature. Social workers may have religious views that are consistent with the organization. However, if their views are not in accord with the social agency or organization, they are likely to experience internal conflict.

Six, service delivery patterns are in a period of change. The historical context refers to the extent to which current patterns of social service delivery to children, adolescents, and their families are influenced by how services were organized and delivered in the past. The future of the organization of service delivery is determined in part by technological and societal changes and the demographics of childhood. More short-term and technologically based patterns of service delivery will be developed in the future. Human service organizations are also affected by staffing patterns, such as the extent to which professional social workers supervise paraprofessionals, and the extent to which social workers practice with families whose structure is changing. Moreover, as societal attitudes and beliefs change, so do agencies. For instance, public child welfare agencies now provide postlegal adoption services (Watson, 1992).

Seven, the social work practitioner must consider confidentiality, legal issues, and ethical issues. Confidentiality has advantages in protecting the privacy of child and adolescent clients and their families. Nevertheless, it tends to restrict the flow of information that could be beneficial to clients. Professional social workers who are members of the National Association of Social Workers follow the Code of Ethics whose ethical standards apply to clients, colleagues, practice settings, professionals, the profession of social work, and the broader society.

The legal context influences professional ethics, the sanction for social services, the extent to which services can be delivered, who is eligible for services, the way in which society allows social work practice with children and adolescents to take place, and the consequences for failing to observe such guidelines. Legal issues include the duty to warn others if a person's life is in danger, as in the case of an adolescent who is threatening suicide or homicide. In a litigious society, instances of conflicts and their potential resolution are affected by state as well as federal law. Legal issues permeate child welfare and adoption, mental health, and school social work. Family courts in one jurisdiction or state rule in favor of adoption rights for one party, yet in another state another judge rules in favor of an opposing party. Furthermore, national conflicts occur as in the case of Elian Gonzales, which involved symbolic issues as well as the real needs of the child and his family. Immigration and Naturalization Services were involved in that complex child custody case, which became a widely publicized issue.

Eight, the professional context refers to the profession of social work, as well as other professions that serve children and adolescents, including physicians, nurses, psychologists, counselors, and teachers. The child-caring professions each have an organized body of knowledge based on their research activities. The professional context also influences the organization and delivery of social services. It affects such organizational issues as the culture of the organization, knowledge for practice, prestige, power, allocation of resources, clinical decision making, cooperation and competition, and intradisciplinary and interdisciplinary teamwork.

Resources

Four types of resources undergird the provision of social services to children, adolescents, and their families. One, many social agencies provide material resources to children, adolescents, and their families. Indeed, social agencies are involved in procuring, utilizing, disbursing, and accounting for material resources. Material resources encompass many items, including new and used clothing, furnishings, and appliances that have been donated for distribution to needy children and their families. Agency personnel are involved in soliciting, securing, and managing material resources. All such efforts occur within the legal context. Appeals for material resources involve publicizing both the needs of children and their families and the successes of agencies in meeting such needs.

Two, human resources include the professional and paraprofessional staff, who plan, supervise, implement, and evaluate direct and indirect practice. Personnel decisions are realized: agency staff are hired, trained, supervised, promoted, assigned, and evaluated. Practitioners, programs, and agencies are evaluated formally and informally on an episodic and periodic basis. Moreover, staff work together in intradisciplinary or unidisciplinary teams as well as in interdisciplinary or multidisciplinary teams.

Three, fiscal resources are used for compensating staff, purchasing equipment, maintaining extant physical plant, constructing new facilities, funding programs, paying insurance, and transferring resources to needy children and their families. Sources of funds include federal, state, and local governments, as well as private foundations and individuals. Funds consist of construction and program grants for social agencies, as well as grants for special, innovative projects.

Social agencies serving children and adolescents vary in terms of their financial resources. Some agencies have many resources. Other agencies attempt to help children, adolescents, and their families with a very limited budget. The more affluent agencies have more resources for employing and training staff, as well as providing them with modern equipment to carry out their tasks and functions. Fiscal resources for state agencies are based on the fiscal health of the state. More affluent states have more funds available to provide for the needs of children through social agencies.

Through mail and telephone solicitations, many social agencies engage in a process of fundraising, which includes mass appeals to the public and targeted appeals to selected constituencies. Fundraising occurs at various times of the year, including the end of the calendar year when many people are in a festive and generous holiday mood, as well as when they are considering fiscal matters.

Four, the architectural features of social agencies, including their physical plant and layout, affect the functioning of staff and clients. Promoting cheerfulness in children through a treatment program is facilitated when the building in which services are provided is brightly painted and well lit.

Many social service programs require a physical plant. Services for children require part or all of a building—in some instances, a physical entity—that is separate from adult services. Services for children and adolescents require special furnishings and equipment for play and athletics. Buildings must be kept in good working condition compliant with building and housing codes for a jurisdiction. Residential services require considerable additional resources for housekeeping, security, and food.

Interorganizational Environment

Occasionally, social services for a child and his or her family are provided in one clinic setting. Usually, however, the vast, interrelated array of needs of children and their families exceed the scope and capacity of any one agency to meet such needs (Voydanoff, 1995) and require the provision of multiple services (Golden, 1992). Social agencies serving children function in a broad interorganizational environment. However, the current array of social and health services systems for children and their families are fragmented (Kagan, 1991).

Interorganizational relationships progress from cooperation to coordination to collaboration (Daka-Mulwanda, Thornburg, Filbert, & Klein, 1995). Cooperation refers to organizations working together. Coordination involves sharing information and joint planning between organizations. Collaboration refers to organizations in which resources, power, and authority are shared and where people are brought to achieve common goals that exceed the capacity of any one organization or practitioner to accomplish. Critical issues in collaboration include turf issues; multilevel systems; leadership; funding; location; role of parents and youth; culture, ethnic origin, and special needs; confidentiality; and lack of common terminology.

Case managers coordinate the social services that children and families receive from multiple social agencies. Multisystem children need services from multiple social agencies or departments. Some children with severe emotional or behavioral problems have needs that are even greater than the capacities of multiple agencies to meet. In such cases, difficulties may arise because of differing perceptions of need, multiple and conflicting case plans, and lack of community resources (Van Gorder & Hashimoto, 1993). The National Commission on Children (1991) indicated that families require integrated and sustained help by professionals who recognize, assess, and respond to multiple problems and needs. The development of services that are responsive to the multiple needs of children and their families is services integration (Agranoff, 1991).

Organizational systems and programs are integrated on two levels (Kahn & Kamerman, 1992). One, on the administrative or management level, linkages are made to improve planning, budgeting, and management operations. Strategies to coordinate programs, organizations, and policies include interagency councils or committees; colocation of services; single point for intake and assessment; flexible, pooled, or decategorized funding; coapplication procedures; coordination or consolidation of programs, budgeting, planning, and administration; and comprehensive management information systems.

Two, on the case or client level, linkages are made where children and families come in contact with the service delivery system. Strategies include case management, case conferences or case review panels, individualized child or family case assessments and services plans, case monitoring or outcome monitoring, a focus on the family as the treatment or service unit, home units, and flexible funds or resources at the disposal of the frontline worker.

Meyers (1993) has identified three sets of variables that serve as incentives or barriers to successful social service coordination for children. The first set of variables is structure and technology. Conditions fostering coordination include professional values and organizational norms that support the overall goal of service coordination as well as the specific objectives of the collaborative project. The second set of variables are interagency networks and resource exchanges. Conditions fostering coordination include strategies that are well matched to expectations and resources. The third set of variables are agency and line staff discretion. Conditions fostering coordination include the goal of the collaboration, which is analyzed in regard to the actual changes in decisions and behaviors of staff.

Collaboration may be promoted through formal and informal strategies. Establishing cross-system model programs, pooling funds, offering cross-system training, preparing joint proposals, and submitting joint fiscal requests are formal collaboration mechanisms. Interagency advisory groups help in referrals, program planning, and development. In comprehensive collaborative efforts, multiagency groups plan and implement services.

The Child and Adolescent Service Systems Program (CASSP) promotes the development of systems of care for young people based on the involvement of the community and collaboration between agencies (Stroul & Friedman, 1986). Four principles exist for promoting effective collaboration (Homonoff & Maltz, 1991). The first principle is mobilization of concerned and influential community and agency members. The second principle is respect for the autonomy and interdependence of systems. The third principle is appreciation of divergent perspectives. The fourth principle is commitment to shared goals. The realization of these principles is based on support through staff training, flexible agency structure, sanction from a strong community, and state and federal legislative support. Glisson and James (1992) state that federal legislative efforts have sometimes inhibited the development of coordinated service systems.

Interdependence of social agencies serving children and their families consists of three types. One, pooled interdependence consists of each organization making a distinct contribution. Two, in sequential interdependence the output of one organization forms the input of another organization. Three, reciprocal interdependence involves mutual adjustment and feedback.

The interorganizational field of social service agencies for children and adolescents consists of social networks. Social workers participate in networking to maintain and increase their professional contacts. Networking provides informal ties with colleagues that are useful in making referrals, sharing information, and collaboration. Networking occurs at the local, regional, national, and international levels. It is facilitated by contacts through face-to-face meetings, as well as through the written word and electronic communications.

Referral

The agency field consists of input, throughput, and output. Children and adolescents and their families proceed through and are processed by agencies. Referral, intake, assessment, treatment, and evaluation are the processes. Programs have intake committees composed of representatives from different agencies. The referral process is an important aspect of agency functioning. Within the larger interorganizational field, social agencies seek, receive, and provide referrals. Referral sources for children and adolescents include family members, as well as health and allied health care, education, and law enforcement service providers.

Children who experience vague feelings of discomfort or distress rely on others, especially family members, in actively seeking and obtaining help. Older children and adolescents are often better able to articulate their concerns than younger children. In working with children, practitioners virtually always have contacts with other persons, for referral, support, and change. Family members are the most frequent sources of collateral contacts.

Referrals range from voluntary to coercive. Referrals of adolescents to mental health services tend to be coercive. Coercive referrals result in less utilization and less favorable treatment outcomes than other types of referrals (Bui & Takeuchi, 1992). A research study of the referral of minority adolescents to community mental health clinics indicated that poverty was the most significant factor in coercive referrals (Takeuchi, Bui, & Kim, 1993). African American adolescents are frequently referred to community mental health centers by an external social or legal agency. Occasionally, adolescents refer themselves for social services. Their motivations for seeking services are diverse and include problem solving, as well as avoiding prosecution.

Children and adolescents are referred to social agencies because of problems they are experiencing that are disturbing to themselves or others. In seeking help referral agents act on their sensitivity to the existence of a potential or actual problem. Parents and other family members expect a resolution of such problems.

Social workers in agencies, along with parents and family members, engage in a process of problem solving. They identify and clarify the nature and extent of the problem, consider a means of rectifying the problem, encourage the use of an identified means of solving the problem, and evaluate whether indeed the problem has been solved. If the problem has not been satisfactorily resolved, the problem-solving process is restarted, perhaps at a later date.

Although clinical problems are the primary focus of social agencies, a host of administrative and maintenance problems are likely to surface as well. Agency administrators attempt to resolve problems related to staff, resources, organizational directions, priorities, and maintenance.

Social workers gather information about their young clients from a variety of sources, including the children and their families, as well as the professionals and agencies that have served them. At the beginning stage of interaction with children and their families, practitioners seek to obtain the quantity and quality of information relevant to their professional needs. Comprehensive case records are ideal to many practitioners yet may not be readily available. Usually, most information is received. Rarely is all requested information received. Most practitioners have to work with incomplete information and use their judgment to compensate for a lack of such information.

Subsequent to information collection, social workers and agencies engage in information processing. Much such activity is assisted by the use of computers. Information processing is often a key aspect of decision making within social agencies. Decision making serves as a key to action. Indeed, agencies and organizations serving children are faced with many yes–no decisions, beginning with whether the agency can serve the client.

Management information systems, which provide a useful means of organizing data on clients and clinical services, are vital to the operation of the modern child-serving human services agency. Such systems provide a rational basis for clinical decision making. Social workers are increasingly using computer-based systems to exercise judgment and make decisions in regard to diagnosis, prognosis, treatment, and risk pertaining to children and adolescents.

Conflict and Crisis

The relationships between social agencies serving children, adolescents, and their families consist of cooperation and competition based on agency missions, needs, interests, politics, economics, and power. Competition and cooperation are potent forces in intraorganizational and interorganizational environments. Social agencies set and work together to achieve common social service goals on behalf of young people and their families.

Although peaceful relations are an ideal of the social work profession, interagency conflict regularly occurs when organizations with different mandates interact to provide social services to children and adolescents. Conflict stems from competition for scarce resources, including power, prestige, and economics. Sources for conflict among human service organizations managing sexual abuse cases include differences in socialization, goal incompatibility, task uncertainty, differences in performance expectations, and resource limitations (Baglow, 1990).

Fargason, Barnes, Schneider, and Galloway (1994) developed a model for managing conflict that involves the three steps of problem characterization, acknowledgment of relevant goals and interests, and negotiation when interests are in conflict. The model is vulnerable to difficulties relating to training, resource limitations, frequent changes in team membership, hidden costs, large groups, poor follow-through, and outcome measurement.

Many types of conflict exist within social agencies. Conflict is seen in differences of professional opinion about how to proceed with case assessment, treatment, management, and evaluation. Cognitive conflict is related to differences in thinking style, attitudes, and perceptions of staff members. Professional conflicts occur between members of different helping professions.

Young clients who receive social services experience intrapersonal or internal conflicts and interpersonal or external conflicts with others in their environment, including parents, teachers, and friends. Children and adolescents who receive social services are also likely to experience conflict with practitioners! A goal of practice is for young clients to acquire and develop their conflict resolution skills.

Social agencies and human service organizations serving youngsters undergo crisis when faced with overwhelming threats to their stability, legitimacy, mission, resources, and support. Crisis occurs when violence threatens, conflict becomes unmanageable, and when the agency loses focus and becomes adrift in regard to its purpose. A crisis is caused when an emergency endangers the safety, lives, or well-being of children or others within the agency. Crisis also occurs when a large amount of turnover occurs within the agency or when an agency executive leaves because of scandal or financial mismanagement. For instance, a crisis occurred in a social agency because of an investigative report that revealed unethical conduct in the treatment of children.

Crisis presents both a danger and an opportunity to change for those involved in the crisis as well as for the agency. Conflict management and crisis resolution within agencies promotes the maintenance and functioning of the social agency. The agency is challenged to overcome the crisis, become stronger, and position itself to predict and meet future crises.

Organizational Structure

The distinguishing features of human service organizations, relative to other types of organizations, include ambiguities associated with their means of helping people and of evaluating their work. Many social agencies serving children and adolescents, and their families, tend to have a unique culture, depending on the type of child-serving agency and the extent to which it is nested in another type of social agency. Agencies with voluntary clientele tend to be understanding of and receptive to addressing the needs and issues of children and families. Many such agencies attempt to have a warm, friendly, and welcoming climate. However, agencies with an involuntary clientele, such as juvenile detention centers, generally have a harsher and more foreboding climate.

The organizational structure of most child-serving social agencies tends to be formal, with an organizational chart that lists the position, title, and function of each office. Formally organized child-serving human service organizations also have informal aspects. Indeed, the dynamics of child-serving agencies vary in regard to amplitude, direction, and intensity.

Formal and informal communication occurs in human service organizations serving children. Formal communication tends to follow the chain of command and is related to organizational structure and tasks. The chain of command is an important aspect of communication within formally organized and highly structured human service organizations, including social services for families in the military. Formal communication that expresses and influences decision making includes calls for action and encompasses mail, such as memos and letters. Informal communication tends to follow circles of acquaintanceship and friendship and includes gossip, rumor, and innuendo.

Leadership

Leadership in an organization can have significant effects on the availability and delivery of social services for children and adolescents. Leadership within child-serving organizations is exercised at many levels, including the task or work group levels, and is also used in other group work within the agency. Practitioners, supervisors, and administrators are designated, appointed, or elected as leaders. However, as a distributed function, leadership is exercised by all agency practitioners. Furthermore, practitioners can encourage the development of leadership among child and adolescent clients.

In child-serving agencies delegation of duties and responsibilities is a management tool. To some extent, delegation can also be used as a practice tool in group work, when children or adolescents learn to take on selected leader responsibilities as a way of fostering their own skills. (Nevertheless, the leader is ultimately responsible, even if certain duties are delegated to a group member.)

Leadership has a stylistic dimension. Some leaders tend to be autocratic, others democratic, and yet others laissez-faire. Democratic leadership, which is probably best accepted by staff in many child-serving social agencies, involves soliciting and using input from staff in decision making. Transformative leadership can change the culture of an agency. Organizations need guidelines to educate staff about their interorganizational roles and responsibilities (Briggs & Koroloff, 1995). The roles and related responsibilities of organizations include initial facilitator, fiscal agent, organizational mentor, and independence consultant.

In contrast to social service agencies for children and families, which are staffed by professionals, family advocacy organizations are staffed by family members (Koroloff & Briggs, 1996). They form family advocacy organizations at the local, state, and national levels. Family advocacy organizations address major goals, decision making, financial support, staffing, and issues as they proceed in the entrepreneurial, collectivity, formalization and control, and elaboration of structure stages in their organizational development.

Management of resources and personnel is exercised in child-serving human service organizations. Some clinicians become managers. Human relations is a vital aspect of leadership and management. Whether the professional is a supervisor, program director, or executive director, human relations skills, which include tact, diplomacy, and the exercise of influence, are essential.

Accountability and Expectations

Accreditation is designed to provide uniformity of care that meets minimum national and regional standards. Regulatory bodies that accredit child and youth services, such as the Council on Accreditation for Children and Family Services, visit agencies and review records.

Innovative programs tend to have an evaluation component to determine their effects. Moreover, some agencies, including clinics and hospitals, have a regular research program. Agency-based research is becoming more acceptable as more practitioners become trained in an expanding array of quantitative and qualitative social research methods.

Funding agencies expect that their capital will be accounted for and used properly. The federal government has issued guidelines to eliminate improper billing in health care, including upcoding, submitting claims for unreasonable or unnecessary services, and billing for noncovered services (Foxhall, 2000).

Accountability is exercised through both formal and informal methods. Formal reports are used to judge the extent to which professional performance is maintained. The service provision of social workers occurs within the context of the agency's evaluation. Evaluation of programs such as the child services program of a large agency or the adolescent services unit of a multiservice agency is useful in determining aspects that are acceptable and those that need improvement. Moreover, informal and casual impressions, experiences, observations, and discussions form the basis of and influence the judgment of multiple constituencies.

Child and youth agencies are accountable for the quality, efficacy, effectiveness, ethical delivery, and results of service delivery. A variety of constituencies, including children and their families, the agency board of directors, professional associations, and legislators, hold the agency, its director, and the professional staff accountable for such aspects of service delivery. Social agencies use agency policies and procedures to guide the provision of social services to children and their families. Professionals are expected to engage in ethical conduct and provide effective service delivery. Professionals govern themselves because they know that if they do not do so, others will. They work together on teams and within programs, and they engage in peer review.

Supervision is a major component of social work practice with children and adolescents. Supervision style varies and includes didactic, therapeutic, and task-oriented approaches. Supervision entails control of social workers and their practice. The span of control refers to the limited number of practitioners whom a supervisor oversees. Technology has impacted on supervision, with the use of electronic mail and educational material.

Supervisors expect that their supervisees discuss their work and develop their professional competencies in delivering humane, ethical, and effective social services to children and their families. Program and agency directors expect treatment to be offered in an efficient and effective manner. They speak directly to supervisors. (Even supervisors have supervisors!) Occasionally, they speak directly to practitioners about how they handled a case if it raises competency or liability questions.

Through intake and referral processes, children and adolescents develop a set of expectations about social services. Young children with little familiarity with social workers think of education and health care professionals from whom they have previously received services. Family members have their own perceptions, needs, and difficulties, which they expect to be addressed. Adult family members have a combination of parental, adult, and, occasionally, even childlike expectations of how they will be treated and of the success of treatment.

Scope of Direct and Indirect
Services for Children

Social agencies and human service organizations provide direct and indirect services to children, adolescents, and their families. They formally define the populations of children and adolescents that they serve in terms of factors such as geographical areas.

Agency auspices play a significant role in the definitions of service populations. Nonsectarian agencies tend to be universalistic; that is, they serve all persons regardless of religious background, although they impose other restrictions on eligibility. Sectarian agencies tend to be particularistic; that is, they seek to serve children and families with a particular religious background although they also serve others.

Public agencies are nonsectarian and universalistic whereas private agencies tend to be more particularistic. Economic factors, including the family's socioeconomic status or social class, influence where they seek to obtain social services for their children. For instance, whereas poor families largely seek public services for their children, some middle-class and many upper-class clients can pay for and seek private services, which they perceive will offer them greater responsiveness. Furthermore, some families first seek help at a private agency that is covered by their insurance for a limited period of time. If the child continues to require social services, families often seek services at a public facility.

Despite the availability of social services to children and their families, barriers exist that restrict access to services. Barriers include the visibility of services; the location and accessibility of services; the cost of services; ethnic, language, and cultural barriers; residence and citizenship; the complexity of services; the cumbersomeness of the requirements of application for services; and the use of waiting lists.

Four barriers exist to the implementation of cross-system initiatives to increase the availability of nonresidential services for children and their families through child welfare and mental health systems (Knitzer & Yelton, 1990). One, professionals in such systems, as well as legislators, have a proresidential preference. Two, professionals in such systems doubt the strengths of parents. Three, child welfare agencies are skeptical of the capabilities of mental health systems, particularly in regard to knowledge about the child welfare system and permanency planning. Four, service funding is mostly inflexible.

Social agencies use inclusion and exclusion criteria to determine which children and families they will serve and which they will refer elsewhere for services. Formal inclusion and exclusion criteria are explicit; informal criteria are tacit. Inclusion and exclusion criteria are a matter of preference and are based on history, tradition, funding sources, perceived efficacy in serving the population or treating particular problems, and a limited capacity to respond to requests for services. Inclusion and exclusion criteria are operative at agency and practitioner levels. That is, both agencies and practitioners prefer to work more with some clients than with others. Practitioners often choose to work with children and families on the basis of those with whom they feel they can empathize, develop rapport, and be effective.

Operational definitions of eligible child and family service recipients are useful in many situations because they clarify whom the agency helps. However, they can also become restrictive. Some individual children and adolescents are deemed ineligible for services from social agencies due to residence, age, diagnosis, or behavior problems. Moreover, a combination or constellation of such factors emerge.

Social agencies serving children and their families make use of mandates and contracts to coordinate service delivery (Woodard, 1994). Some youngsters live just outside the geographical or catchment area for which an agency is mandated to provide services. Some children are deemed to be too young for some agencies while being too old for other agencies. Moreover, in some communities fewer services are available to treat older adolescents approaching adulthood than are available to treat children and younger adolescents.

Diagnoses are frequently used as inclusion and exclusion criteria. Some agencies serve children with mental retardation but not those who also have other mental disorders, and vice versa. Occasionally, social agencies do not serve children who have a mental or physical health diagnosis that is more commonly seen and treated in adults. Unfortunately, some agencies do not have the resources to make an accurate diagnosis or arrange appropriate proper treatment. Some children and adolescents are deemed to be too difficult to manage in some settings. For instance, a child whose behavior is not well controlled at home or in community settings has a difficult time receiving social services in such settings and is referred elsewhere for treatment.

Social workers may provide services to children in conjunction with law enforcement authorities. They may provide protective services for children and adolescents. Many youths are placed in secure juvenile detention facilities. However, these conditions are often unsuitable for children, many of whom are best served by home detention. A home detention project in Broward County, Florida resulted in many youths being permitted to stay in their own homes without jeopardizing public safety at a considerable financial cost savings and with strong community support (Schwartz, Barton, & Orlando, 1991).

Some agencies, such as housing authorities, deliver indirect services to children and adolescents. Indirect services on behalf of young people consist of administration, management, supervision, consultation, evaluation, and research. Administration, which includes a range of activities, comprises agency and program components. Management includes a consideration of effectively using resources within an agency framework. Gustafson and Allen (1994) have proposed a management model of child welfare that involves a mission statement, covered population, program modules, service tracks, service inputs, performance standards, and preferred client pathways.

As noted previously, supervision encompasses different styles and approaches. For instance, the focus of supervision is educational. Consultation involves professionals sharing their expertise in assessment, diagnosis, and treatment of children. Evaluation involves the determination of whether programs are successful and goals have been reached. Methodologies include goal attainment scaling. Research that is clinical, programmatic, and organizational in nature addresses generalizable questions.

Practice Settings

The location of services for children within an agency and the process of social work vary as functions of the type of agency. Two types of social agencies exist. One, in child-serving agencies whose entire mission is devoted to helping children, services for children are located throughout the agency. Clearly, such services are designed for children. Agencies such as child abuse prevention centers are predominantly focused on helping children and their families. Sheppard and Zangrillo (1996) have developed three joint investigations of child abuse program models. The models are improved agency-based joint investigations using existing agency resources, multidisciplinary interview centers, and child advocacy centers.

Two, in social agencies whose mission is to serve a wide age range of clientele, services for children are located within one age-defined unit, such as a children's unit or an adolescent unit; are components of other, non-age-defined units, such as medical specialty units; or, occasionally, are a component of adult services. At times, social workers attempt to meet the needs of children and adolescents within settings that are primarily designed for other purposes and clientele. For instance, employee assistance programs focus on helping adults, yet also help children. Some parents receive social services from vocational rehabilitation offices, benefits from food stamp offices, or reside in jails. Some older siblings receive assistance at college mental health counseling programs. Family service agencies, settlement houses, and Y's have special programs for children and youth.

Furthermore, missions change such that social agencies that once served only children subsequently serve a wider age range of clientele, or vice versa. For instance, a program offering social services for battered women expanded to include services for the children who have witnessed and experienced domestic violence.

Settings for social work practice with children and adolescents have distinct organizational features and vary according to the level of stigma young clients experience in receiving social services. Many social agencies attempt to destigmatize services. Children experience a variety of emotions as clients in social agencies, and shame tends to accompany stigma. Some service delivery settings and offices, such as private practice, that are homelike, are congenial and comfortable for very young children. Social workers must see to it that receiving services bolsters the child's sense of accomplishment and self-efficacy, namely their belief that they are competent.

Schools, health, mental health, family service, and child welfare agencies are practice settings for social work with children and adolescents. Such organizations include child development centers, mental health and retardation offices, community mental health centers, juvenile probation offices, children and youth service agencies, drug and alcohol offices, family abuse councils, adolescent treatment units, special education programs, Head Start programs, and private agencies serving children. Although the helping process emphasizes direct interaction between practitioners and children, referral and networking on behalf of children occur, and collateral contacts with family, school, social, and community agencies also takes place. Confidentiality and ethical issues are related to the age of the child and the child's relationships with family members.

Child welfare, probation, mental health, and special education are the public systems that place children. Some children are placed in correctional settings. Residential and non-residential settings, as well as in-home care and out-of-home placement, are used. Many children are placed in out-of-home care by child welfare and mental health agencies (U.S. House of Representatives Select Committee on Children, Youth, and Families, 1989). The greatest proportion of children who are in out-of-home care are in foster homes. Out-of-home care, particularly residential placements, is costly.

Child welfare and mental health agencies share a common goal of serving children in home and community settings. Intensive Family Preservation Services (IFPS) programs work toward preventing unnecessary out-of-home placements of troubled children. Three approaches to cross-system IFPS programs exist, namely separate, parallel programs; partially integrated programs; and completely integrated programs (Robison & Binder, 1993).

Child welfare and mental health agencies serve virtually the same children and families (Knitzer & Yelton, 1990). Child welfare agencies frequently receive referrals from mental health agencies, and vice versa. Many of the adolescents in foster care have major emotional and behavioral problems. In some states, child abuse teams include mental health professionals, and foster care units have mental health crisis teams attached to them.

Schools are normative, nonstigmatizing settings for children to receive social services. Many types of schools exist, including public, private, and parochial; elementary, middle, and high school; and regular and special education settings.

Health and mental health services are provided on an inpatient and outpatient basis, include hospitals and clinics, and encompass prevention, intervention, and rehabilitation. Children and adolescents may participate in full or partial hospitalization programs. They may use grief counseling programs. The extent of stimga in health settings varies depending on the setting and the physical disorder. Children with AIDS are likely to be stigmatized. Mental health settings, including child guidance and evaluation clinics, tend to be relatively stigmatizing settings.

Social services for children and adolescents may be delivered in home or community settings. Social workers engage in gang work in community settings. They visit children and their families in their homes. They work with children and families who live on the streets and in homeless shelters. American Family Inns are residential education and employment-training (RET) centers for entire families (Nunez, 1995). Their family services include needs assessments, case management, health care services, crisis nurseries, family preservation and reunification, housing assistance, and postplacement and follow-up. Their child services include child development daycare centers, prekindergarten programs, accelerated after-school programs, recreational and cultural programs, and summer camps.

Conclusion

This chapter has considered the organizational context of social work practice with children and adolescents, and their families. The intraorganizational environment refers to the internal organization of a social agency serving children whereas the interorganizational environment refers to the relationship between child-serving social agencies.

Resources, and strategies to obtain and disburse them, are a crucial factor in successful human service organizations. Child-serving organizations vary in regard to the size of their budget, scope of programs, numbers of clients served, and numbers of professional staff. The scope of direct services for children and adolescents is influenced by resources available and the niche that the agency fills. Group and organizational factors are important because the agency is a large group comprised of small groups.

The scope of indirect services for children and adolescents is broad. Administration, management, supervision, consultation, evaluation, and research play important roles in the human service organization. Information is the basis for decision making and action in social work practice with children. Settings for social work practice with children are many and encompass those where children are the primary clientele, as well as those that attempt to meet the special developmental and other needs of children within a broader agency environment.

CHAPTER

8 Methods and Practices in School Systems

The purpose of this chapter is to examine the nature of social work practice with children and adolescents in regard to their participation in school systems. The involvement of social workers in a range of practice issues, including health concerns, social and academic performance, and violence, are considered. This chapter analyzes issues in schools that are directly related to education, including the nature of intelligence.

The purpose of social work in school systems is to further the child's ability to learn, to adjust to school, and to become a constructive member of society. Social workers in school systems enable children and adolescents to learn by attending to social problems that interfere with the learning process. Much contemporary social work with children and adolescents is school based or school linked. Although most school social work is with children who are in grades K–12, opportunities also exist for practice with infants and toddlers who have developmental delays or established risks (Radin, 1990).

Social Context of Schooling

Family transitions significantly affect many of the children and adolescents for whom school social workers provide services. Germain (1991) has identified two types of family changes. Whereas virtually all families experience first-order changes, which are normative and expected, second-order changes, which are unexpected, appear to affect fewer families.

Surprisingly, perhaps, poverty persists in the United States. Although poverty rates fluctuate, it is estimated that approximately one of four U.S. children live in poverty. Poor children are disproportionally minority children living in single-parent families. School social workers are likely to see many poor children who are at risk of experiencing and developing many social problems. Conditions associated with poverty are major factors in children dropping out of school (Duttweiler, 1995).

Many of the nation's homeless are families with children. Homeless families are more vulnerable to crime and illness than are sheltered families. Without an address, it is difficult for homeless children to remain in school and receive social services. However, some programs are especially designed for homeless families and children.

Many children in the United States who have sufficient access to food do not eat properly and do not receive adequate nutrition. Moreover, many do not get enough exercise. The combination of poor nutrition and lack of exercise poses threats to children's immediate and long-term physical health.

An essential aspect of readiness for learning is nutrition. Children who are well fed are more likely than hungry children to be able to attend to and participate in instructional activities. School nutrition programs provide free or low-cost breakfasts and lunches to poor youngsters who are at risk for having inadequate nutrition at home. Such meals provide benefits to increase the attraction, cohesiveness, and value of coming to school for the child and family; dealing with hunger so that it is not a distraction from learning during school; minimizing behavioral problems associated with hunger; and improving the physical health and development of the child. However, children's access to food and food security decline during the summer months. In addition to being concerned that children receive proper nutrition in school, social workers are also concerned that families use food benefits in the community for which they are eligible, including nutritional programs for pregnant women, food stamps for poor families, low-cost food outlets, food drives, food banks, and food cooperatives.

Many children are not enrolled in health insurance programs. Furthermore, active attempts to locate children who are eligible for health insurance programs have not always been successful.

Many of the nation's children do not receive adequate physical and mental health care, including preventive screenings, inoculations, regular examinations, and professional care when they are ill. Many poor children do not receive regular care that could obviate the need for urgent care. They are more likely to receive urgent care in hospital emergency rooms, and receive little preventive care and routine care. Neonatal care is a significant health factor as well. Children of poor mothers who have received inadequate care during pregnancy are more likely to be born with physical difficulties than are other children. Many such children have ongoing health problems.

A primary goal of education is the attainment of literacy. Nevertheless, many schoolchildren have considerable difficulty attaining adequate reading and writing skills. The lack of such skills hampers them in understanding the world around them, succeeding in school, and ultimately limits their future employment opportunities.

Many illiterate children and adolescents have illiterate parents who are unable to help them with their schooling. School social workers attempt to get illiterate parents involved in adult literacy programs. Such efforts increase the likelihood that their children attend school and receive the maximum possible educational benefit.

Mobility and Diversity

In the United States, families are highly mobile. It was once estimated that the typical U.S. family moves, on average, once every 7 years. Geographic moves affecting children range from a move within the same neighborhood to a move to another country.

The impact or consequences of the move are likely to be both positive, in regard to new opportunities for personal development, and negative, in regard to losses of friendships and social support. Often, the greater the physical distance of the move, the greater the impact of the move on the developing child. The impact of geographic mobility, which can range from insubstantial to traumatic, depends in part on the age and development of the child. The impact of moving as perceived, experienced, and expressed by the child is likely to be greater for older children and adolescents than for younger children and preschoolers. For preschool children, if the family moves intact, the adjustment is usually satisfactory. The impact of the move is most noticeable on children's immediate and long-term social and emotional development. Moving can be particularly difficult for adolescents.

In the United States, the reasons for moves are often economic, such as a parental employment or career opportunity. Moving can also be subsequent to a family change, including loss of a parent, separation, or divorce. Moves, which can vary in duration, can be temporary or permanent. The impact of either type can be significant. Parents are not always aware at the time of a move whether it will be temporary or permanent. Furthermore, they do not always communicate their knowledge of the expected duration of the move to their children. Often, young children have little input into the decision to move.

School social workers become aware of a child's move from the child, peers, family, or others at school. Practice opportunities revolve around scenarios in which youngsters leave school because of a geographical move, because youngsters are left behind when a classmate makes a geographical move and leaves the school, and because youngsters have moved to a new school.

Geographic moves also usually entail school moves. School moves are of several types. Voluntary school moves are those that are initially acceptable to the pupil. Involuntary school moves are initially unacceptable to the pupil. School moves include graduations and moving to a higher-level school, namely elementary to middle to high school, as well as moving to a different or new school. Reasons for school moves include geographic moves, family changes, and changes in school policies that shift students from one school to another within a particular district. The impact of school moves on children varies with their frequency. Children who move between schools frequently are more likely to have peer relationship difficulties, including making friends, than other children.

Emigration from one country and immigration to another country is a type of geographic move that also involves a school move. Immigration ranges from movement between countries and regions that share similar languages and cultures, for example, England and the United States, to movement between countries and regions that have disparate languages and cultures, for example, Saudi Arabia and Sweden.

U.S. schools play a vital role in assimilating immigrants (Pryor, 1992). School social workers help children and adolescents from countries whose languages and cultures are markedly different adjust to a new language and culture. The presence of family change may exacerbate the child's difficulties in accommodating the new language and culture. Children from many different countries attend schools in urban areas. In rural schools, cultural dislocation is usually a less frequent event; the immigrant child represents a rare case to many rural school social workers.

School populations reflect the diversity of a country. Unfortunately, tensions between ethnic and racial groups are often present in community schools. Hostile interracial and interethnic conflict has the potential to culminate in violence. School social workers are involved in improving relations and fostering understanding between children from majority and minority groupings within schools.

The demographic composition of the United States is changing such that cultural groups that previously were in the numerical minority are becoming the numerical majority in some regions and vice versa. The actual composition of a school system and a school varies such that the majority in one school and school system is a minority in another school and school system.

The pupil populations most at risk for difficulties in school performance include African Americans, Native Americans, and gay and lesbian students. African American male students have disproportionately high rates of corporal punishment, school suspensions, and special education placements (Gregory, 1997). The most frequent causes for school disengagement among African American students are suspensions and expulsions (Jordan, Lara, & McPartland, 1996).

Typically, ethnic and racial minority pupils, and gay and lesbian students, experience a relative sense of powerlessness and isolation from the majority. They experience concerns about discrimination and persecution, and safety and well-being in the school. School social workers attempt to empower these students. Practitioners encourage them to support one another, formally and informally, and form clubs or social groups.

To succeed in learning at school, children and adolescents must acquire and develop their language competencies. Native language speakers have a marked advantage at school over children for whom the language of instruction is a second language. School social workers assist bilingual and multilingual children, children with learning disabilities in the area of language, children with speech and hearing disorders, and children with mental retardation and other developmental disabilities (Vigilante, 1990). Social workers identify and refer such children, seeing to it that they receive the diagnostic and remediation services they need within and outside the school, and work with family members to promote understanding and support of the child. As outside intervention does not always adequately address pupils' educational needs (Kardon, 1995), intervention programs must be developed and offered within the school.

Attendance

Children and adolescents whose emotional needs are met and who are in safe and stable home, school, and community environments have a great advantage in learning. However, three additional factors should be met for them to succeed. One, they must come to school on a regular basis to engage in the types of learning activities the school provides. Two, they must be motivated to learn and be rewarded for learning. Three, they must receive support at home, in the school, and in the community for their efforts at learning.

School social workers help children and adolescents cope with chaotic and unstable home environments, including divorce, by offering programs such as divorce groups for children. They monitor, investigate impeding factors, and reduce obstacles to attendance. They provide motivation and support to youngsters who have difficulty fitting into a school's academic and social environment.

Children and adolescents leave schools because of moving, graduating, and dropping out of school. Adolescents who leave compulsory schooling early, who are also known as school leavers, decrease their life chances. For instance, they usually have a difficult time subsequently obtaining satisfactory employment. School social workers attempt to reduce and prevent dropping out of school. They attempt to return youngsters who have left school, or who are absent or truant from school, to school to graduate. To meet such goals, school social workers assess the reasons for and circumstances surrounding the child who has left school.

All children who are in grades K–12 in U.S. schools are required to attend school regularly. In most jurisdictions, they also are required to attend school in the district where they live. Furthermore, they must attend a specified minimum number of days, which depend on whether they are attending elementary, middle, or high school. Students who have not met such attendance requirements are at risk to experience academic failure and grade retention. Chronically tardy students face disciplinary action.

Truants are students, 6 to 16 years of age, who do not attend school. Parents, legal guardians, and the public are encouraged by child welfare authorities to call truancy centers to report students suspected as truant. Students who are found to be truant are eligible to be transported to a truancy center by law enforcement personnel during regular school hours.

In many areas, absences require written documentation to be excused, and such excuses must be returned to the school within a specified number of days following the child's return to school. Excused absences are usually granted for personal illness, serious illness or death in the immediate family, recognized religious holidays of the student's own faith, and natural catastrophe and disaster. Exceptions to attendance requirements are occasionally granted by school authorities following a review of the student's record. Students with extended illnesses are eligible for homebound service programs. In some areas, students who are suspended from school are assigned to discipline centers. Attendance at such centers is mandatory. Nonattendance counts as unexcused absences. Middle and high school students who are expelled are assigned to alternative centers. Transportation is provided. Nonattendance results in referral to the juvenile court system and the district attorney's office.

Students with Disabilities

Schoolchildren are required to demonstrate that they have acquired, mastered, and learned academic material. However, some students suffer from disabilities that interfere with their learning. Within schools, minorities with disabilities are a particularly vulnerable population whose sense of powerlessness is compounded by their disabilities.

Many types of disabilities exist, including cognitive, learning, behavioral, emotional, social, and physical disabilities. Students with emotional and behavioral disabilities have the lowest grades and academic achievement, highest dropout rates, and highest rate of restrictive and out-of-home placements of all populations of students with disabilities (U.S. Department of Education, 1994). The wraparound process for planning the delivery of services within a system of care is useful for helping students with emotional and behavioral disabilities in schools (Eber & Nelson, 1997).

Through special education services, children with disabilities are assessed for and receive individually tailored services. Portfolio assessments serve as valuable alternatives or supplements to standardized tests (Karoly & Franklin, 1996). Consistent with social work values, practitioners ensure that all students, including those with physical disabilities, receive the maximum amount of consideration and respect to which they are entitled. School social workers help children with disabilities receive the equipment, assessment, and testing services they require for optimal studying, learning, and social interaction. Practitioners aim to provide each child with disabilities with access to health care both as a developing child and pertaining to her or his disability. In collaboration with educators, school social workers ensure that children are in optimal educational environments where they are educated to the maximum extent of their abilities. Through a process of mainstreaming, children with disabilities are educated in classes along with other children. Fostering social and academic relationships among children with disabilities and their nondisabled peers is a goal of school social workers.

Community Factors

To succeed, children need supportive school, home, and community environments that reward their efforts at learning. Adequate equipment and supplies, including access to and use of a computer at home and at school, are beneficial. For the child who is at risk of academic failure, an assessment of the home environment encompasses the conditions at home that allow for doing homework. It will also consider family factors that contribute to or detract from a student's success at school.

Schools, which are communities, are also part of other communities. School social workers attempt to work with multiple communities to help children and adolescents overcome social problems and succeed in school. Furthermore, school social workers promote the sense of community within a school.

Communities are marked by shared identity and experiences. In regard to geographic communities, neighborhoods vary in demographics, safety, substance abuse, mental health, literacy, homelessness, stability, and poverty. Schools consist of children and adolescents who live in various geographic communities. At times, school-age children's participation in communities is synchronized. However, some children find that they live in one geographic community, but their school is located in a distant geographic community. For some children of divorce, geographic community becomes more complex.

As members of ethnic and racial communities, children and adolescents share traditions, languages, and experiences. As members of faith communities, children and adolescents share beliefs and customs, observe similar holidays, and attend places of worship. The social work practitioner who serves children and adolescents, and their families, is a member of the social work professional community.

The Nature and Goals of Schools

Schools are human service organizations that vary in size or scale, level and degree of complexity, layers of administration, span of control, climate, and effectiveness. Despite their diverse structure, schools share common goals that pertain to the education of children and adolescents. Some salient goals, such as organizational survival, are not always recognizable. Furthermore, goals change. A school whose primary goal was the education of children in basic academic skills became an organization whose primary goal was the education of children in a wide range of academic and social skills within a family and community environment.

Although education remains the major goal, schools and their programs have other goals and objectives as well. For instance, the objectives of school-based probation programs include improving attendance rates and academic performance, as well as reducing disciplinary referrals in school, frequency and length of detentions, dropout rates, recidivism, and out-of-home placements resulting from delinquent behaviors.

Each individual school is part of a formally organized school system consisting of multiple schools, and is a part of other social systems too. All social systems, of course, have numerous characteristics and interrelated components. The school social worker often attempts to reduce entropy and maintain equilibrium in the system during periods of crisis.

As a system, schools consist of many groups that impact children and adolescents. The school social worker observes and participates in many groups in schools too. As human service organizations, schools are large groups that also contain many small groups. Formal small groups in schools, such as classroom groups and clubs, are devoted to academic and social learning and skills development. Informal small groups in schools include the peer groups and cliques that become prominent during adolescence.

Adolescents frequently want to be accepted by a particular social group in middle school and high school. Those who are accepted by their chosen peer group may appreciate it. However, some adolescents are not accepted by a desired peer group. Such adolescents often experience feelings of social rejection and anxiety. An ethnographic study of socially isolated middle school students indicated that they had a characteristic that was viewed negatively by peers that was related to their rejection (Evans & Eder, 1993). Furthermore, rejected students were assumed by peers to have other negative characteristics, were likely to be labeled as sexually deviant, and on this basis were further rejected, ridiculed, and stigmatized.

High school cliques or social groups are associated with distinct value systems and patterns of social and academic performance. Although most peer groups within most high schools are prosocial, many high schools contain one highly problematic type of peer group whose members have more school attendance, academic performance, mental health, and substance abuse problems than have the other peer groups (Downs & Rose, 1991). Indeed, the highly problematic peer group, which can also be organized as a gang, requires the most remedial intervention from school social workers. Some school social workers promote prosocial and benevolent activities of formally organized antisocial groups. Alternatively, school social workers influence individual adolescents to leave the antisocial group and meet their needs for belonging and participation in constructive group contexts within the school.

Academic Performance

Academic performance, which refers to formal learning, grades, and achievement, is a subset of school performance, which encompasses all aspects of participation within the school environment, including social activities at the school, leadership, and participation in clubs and organizations. A research study showed that social workers who work together with teenage girls, teachers, and parents improve attendance and academic performance (Reid & Bailey-Dempsey, 1995).

Young people whose academic performance is acceptable have the support of parents and school officials to participate in school activities. Children and adolescents who have difficulties in academic performance also need to receive such support. They need to focus on their academic work to meet minimal standards at the school.

School social work aims to promote conditions that facilitate and ameliorate interference with teaching and learning. Two overlapping processes occur simultaneously in school social work. One, school social workers support the academic process of teaching and learning in schools. Two, school social workers implement teaching and learning processes.

Learning theory is essentially a behavioral theory that includes elements of response acquisition and repetition. Its central idea is that learning is accomplished through rewards. Learning theory explains many kinds of learning phenonmena, including overlearning, mastery, and unlearning. From a learning theory perspective, it is more feasible for social workers to correctly teach children and adolescents something new than to teach them to unlearn something incorrect and subsequently attempt to teach them something correct.

Learning theory provides the underpinnings of social learning theory, which explains social behavior. Social learning theory has cognitive and behavior elements, and emphasizes that children learn through a process of imitation, observation, and reinforcement (Bandura, 1976). Social work interventions in the school, such as social skills training (Elliott & Gresham, 1992), are guided by social learning theory.

Intentionality of learning is experienced by teachers and learners. Learning is intentional and unintentional. Fortunately, children and adolescents learn things that social workers and other adults think they should learn, such as desirable ways of making friends. Unfortunately, they also learn things that social workers and other adults think they should not learn, such as coping with stress by smoking.

School social workers coordinate learning in, promote communication, and reduce conflicts between school, home, and community environments. Occasionally, parents have difficulty talking with their child's teacher. School social workers serve as intermediaries between parents and teachers. They help parents understand the role of parents, teachers, and social workers to promote the child's adjustment at school. School social workers help parents of school-age children understand the rights and responsibilities they have for their child's education.

Parents who maintain a supportive relationship with their child's school and teacher promote the child's well-being at school. Parents should attend open house meetings, particularly at the beginning of the year. They should introduce themselves to their child's teachers, visit the child's classroom, and actively listen to the information that is presented. Parents should consider volunteering their time and skills to the classroom. They should actively maintain communication with the classroom teacher and understand what is happening in their child's classroom.

Social workers are involved in working with children and adolescents at school to promote school-based academic and social learning. If a conflict exists between teacher and pupil, the school social worker assesses the nature of the conflict and determines whether it is a cognitive conflict or personality conflict (Fatout & Rose, 1995). School social workers help mediate the relationship between the teacher and the learner, and resolve the conflict. School social workers work with children and their families at home and in the community to promote academic and social learning. They assess conditions at home for doing homework, help families provide proper conditions for study at home, and link students to resources so that they continue to progress in their studies.

As children grow and mature, they become more aware of and participate in learning within community settings. The school social worker brings knowledge of community resources for learning too. Such resources include persons and facilities that promote child and youth development; support prosocial attitudes; and help in acquiring study skills, developing academic habits, and completing homework assignments. Children and adolescents learn from many sources that impact on them to varying degrees at different points in their own development. They value each source of learning differentially. Children and their families have different degrees of comprehension of sources of learning.

Schools are formal sources of learning that provide systematic instruction for children and adolescents. Families are powerful sources of modeling and substantial, informal sources of social and academic learning to children and adolescents. Friends, who provide support and help children learn, supplement the learning available from other sources. Peers, who afford a basis of social comparison to children, are present in classroom and community settings. Moreover, children and adolescents are engaged in a long process of self-instruction. Children and adolescents receive modeling and information from a variety of mass media and Internet communication sources. In addition to acquiring content from other sources, which depends in part on active participation in learning activities, children also learn to learn.

School social workers often teach children how to learn to cope with stressful situations. A research study was conducted of a school-based primary prevention program designed to teach children coping skills to apply to five stressful experiences, including moving to a new school (Dubow, Schmidt, McBride, Edwards, & Merk, 1993). Fourth-grade children were able to generate a range of effective solutions to stressful situations, and they improved their self-efficacy.

As an academic setting, the focus of the school is teaching and learning, which are directly related. Learning is a byproduct of teaching. Although teaching and learning are primarily the roles of the teacher and student, respectively, in the broadest sense teachers also learn and students also teach. Furthermore, school social workers teach children and adolescents, and their families, and school personnel too. Much of the teaching done by social workers is informal and by example, and utilizes dyadic, small-group, and workshop settings.

Children and adolescents have particular learning styles. Social workers can help students who are having difficulty learning by assessing and promoting the compatibility between teaching style and learning style. Many styles of teaching and learning exist. Teaching styles relate to leadership styles and occur in a variety of school and community contexts. Every student has a particular style of learning. Some pupils are more active learners whereas others are more passive learners. Some youngsters learn by doing; others learn by observing.

Learning styles, which are based on many factors, including the age, maturation, and cognitive development of the learner, are related to the learner's senses. Kinesthetic learners learn best through manipulation and movement. For example, young children learn to count by moving blocks. Visual learners learn best by seeing pictures of presented information. For example, they learn by seeing the teacher's instructions on a chalkboard or observing the demonstration of a laboratory experiment. Auditory learners learn best by listening to information. For example, they learn well by listening to songs or audiotapes.

Three domains of learning exist. The first and traditionally most highly valued domain of learning is the acquisition of knowledge. In the academic realm, this refers to knowledge of subjects such as literature, geometry, and Spanish. In the school social work realm, the adolescent learns about the dangers associated with using illicit drugs.

A second learning domain is the attainment of constructive, prosocial attitudes and the unlearning of destructive, antisocial attitudes. In the academic realm, this refers to a reverence for learning. In the school social work realm, this refers to a value of nonviolent means of conflict resolution.

A third learning domain is the skill domain. Children and adolescents learn how to learn. In the academic realm, this includes skills involved in using personal computers. In the social work realm, this encompasses skills in making assertive requests. Social workers promote youngsters' ability to learn how to think about social situations at school.

Although virtually all children and adolescents have an aptitude for learning, they vary in regard to the degree of their aptitude. School social workers consider a variety of factors related to aptitude for learning, including intelligence, motivation, and academic skills, as well as prior schooling and preparation for learning.

The concept and measurement of intelligence has been widely debated. Intelligence and education are cultural values ascribed to by parents. However, traditional viewpoints about intelligence have been used to discriminate against racial and ethnic minority groups, particularly in regard to their access to education.

School social workers practice with parents, who have a variety of viewpoints about their role in the development of their children's intelligence. Some parents believe that intelligence is mostly inherited. If their children are highly intelligent, they take pride in their offspring. If their children have low intelligence or have a degree of mental retardation, they believe that their physical constitution played a role; moreover, they ascribe responsibility or blame to their partner.

Some parents believe that intelligence is largely a matter of environment. If their children are highly intelligent, parents take pride in the upbringing and education they have provided them. If their children have low intelligence or have a degree of mental retardation, they believe that their upbringing played a contributing role.

Some parents believe that intelligence is a matter of both heredity and environment and that the environment determines to what extent the biological potential with which children are endowed unfolds. Parental pride or shame is related, at least in part, to the degree to which they feel they have contributed to their child's level of intelligence.

Intelligence is related to self-esteem such that children and adolescents who believe they are unintelligent have low self-esteem. Social workers counter such feelings by considering the broad range of intelligence. A contemporary view of intelligence is that it consists of the mental abilities that are required to adjust to, shape, and select one's environments (Sternberg, 1997). Intelligence is multifaceted and encompasses artistic, intellectual, kinesthetic, mechanical, physical, and social types. Young people, who have various gifts and talents, need to be valued for the kinds of intelligence they possess. Social workers help them recognize and develop various kinds of intelligence.

Intellectual or academic intelligence is highly valued in most school systems. Children and adolescents manifest it by participating actively in class discussions, writing good-quality papers, completing their homework accurately and promptly, receiving high grades on academic and achievement tests, and participating in intellectual activities and school organizations.

School-age children are tested regularly on achievement tests, each of which provides a single picture of children's abilities. Standardized tests are given in ways that are identical in regard to how answers are recorded and in regard to the tools used by the children to take the test. However, the children's learning environments, including home life and other conditions for learning, are not standardized.

Standardized tests are used to help school officials make decisions about school systems, programs, and students based on their strengths and weaknesses. The results provide information about how students who take the standardized test compare to one another. Standardized achievement tests measure what students have already learned about subjects such as math and science. Standardized aptitude tests measure their ability to learn and cover areas such as verbal ability, creativity, and reasoning. Three methods of reporting standardized tests scores are stanine (standard nine), percentile, and grade-level equivalent scores.

Although intellectual or academic intelligence is necessary, it is not sufficient for children and adolescents to achieve success at school and in life. Social competence, which encompasses the ability of youngsters to relate to and interact with peers and adults in a positive and assertive manner, is also required for effective school performance. School social workers design and deliver programs to improve social competence. Comprehensive school-based social competence promotion programs have the potential to improve youngsters' social and physical well-being (Weissberg, 1990; Weissberg & Elias, 1993). Beginning in kindergarten, children benefit from programs that promote social competence and problem-solving skills. Such programs consist of language development, feelings identification, and social thinking and problem-solving components (Marshall, 1996). A minimum level of social competence is required for children to interact and work with others, including classmates and teachers, and to conform to the social and behavioral norms of the school. Many schoolchildren have acceptable levels of social competence. Some even have exceptionally high levels of competence.

Two types of young people can improve their levels of social competence through social skills training delivered by the school social worker. One type are children and adolescents who are aggressive at school and bully other children. They resort to violence as a habitual way of resolving conflict situations in school. Although their aggressive actions appear to provide them with an immediate solution to their problems, they create significant immediate and long-term social difficulties for the youngster. Another type are shy and unassertive youngsters who neither make appropriate requests nor refusals. Such children attempt to please others and suppress their needs. However, they are often beset by anxiety and are unable to share all their abilities with others.

Education

Most schoolchildren are enrolled in regular education programs that provide normalizing experiences through mainstream courses. Access to regular education is a routine matter through a registration process encompassing place of residence and routine health information.

Children and adolescents whose educational needs are not readily met in regular education programs are eligible to be placed in special education programs. Gifted and talented children participate in honors courses. Youngsters with disabilities participate in resource classes and special education school placements. Entry to special education is a formalized assessment process encompassing testing.

Inclusive education is the education of students with disabilities in age-appropriate general education classrooms with the support of special education (Pryor, Kent, McGunn, & LeRoy, 1996). School social workers use the following six strategies to promote inclusion. One, they prepare students to celebrate human differences. Two, they facilitate the transition process for newly included students. Three, they consult collaboratively with teachers. Four, they help revise school curriculum to address social and emotional needs. Five, they provide services to students in general education settings. Six, they expand inclusive education concepts throughout the school.

School social workers practice with a variety of special education populations. Many of the children and adolescents who are in special education programs have physical or behavioral handicaps or disabilities for which they are stigmatized. Also within the rubric of special education are intellectually gifted children who function at levels significantly above their nongifted peers, and children who are talented in one or more areas, such as in the performing arts.

Social workers are involved in determining appropriate schools for children. Moreover, social workers within a variety of settings help children and adolescents. Some specialized children's residential facilities in child welfare or child mental health have special schools. For children whose limitations or disabilities preclude their participation in schools, a training experience is generally useful. Occupational training is useful for older adolescents. Some children who have extensive limitations benefit from rehabilitation. Vocational rehabilitation is useful for some older adolescents.

Types and Conditions of Schools

The design, architecture, and layout of schools, which vary according to scale, influence human behavior, safety, and social and task interaction. The physical surroundings of the school affect the morale, health, and safety of the persons who use the facility. Often, the physical condition of public schools is not satisfactory.

Social workers attempt to obtain resources for improving conditions at the school, including the physical plant. Funding, which is used for attaining social work goals in schools, covers salaries, materials, and supplies, and makes it feasible to carry out innovative projects. Budgetary items for school libraries, including print and audiovisual material, are costly. Schools rely on computers, along with access to the Internet. School social workers support efforts at modernization such that all children have the opportunity to participate in these learning experiences.

The geographical or physical location of schools has a significant impact on their functioning, including the need for and provision of social services. Schools exist within socioeconomic and community systems. Although social problems exist within all communities, schools in poor communities have a higher proportion of social difficulties and social service needs. Moreover, some schools have children from a range of socioeconomic classes.

Of course, children travel to and from school. Some children have short distances to travel to school and arrive there in minutes whereas others spend several hours traveling long distances each school day. Although some children and adolescents are able to walk, bike, or drive to school, many youngsters depend on others, such as a family member, to transport them. Some children rely on public transportation to get to school whereas others ride school buses. Moreover, transportation is related to school busing, which in some communities is used in association with school integration.

Transportation is also related to safety issues. Social workers are concerned that children are able to travel safely to and from school each day and that they are in a safe school environment. Parents are concerned about the safety and well-being of their children on school buses and in school. Safety includes freedom from harassment, intimidation, threats, violence, assaults, and coercion. Safety is an issue that encompasses the school and community environments. The ideal is a safe school within a safe community.

Schools vary in size. In large schools, although many children are unlikely to know one another, they sometimes utilize strategies to organize structures within the school to generate a smaller scale. Social workers become familiar with many of the children who need social services. Small schools are potentially more personal environments. Social workers are familiar with many of the children in the school. However, social workers are more likely to be assigned to several schools, perhaps of different scales, than to be assigned to work with one small school.

Urban schools tend to be beset with many social problems. Suburban schools, which are usually affluent, also have social problems, including adolescent substance abuse. Rural schools currently have many of the same social problems that once characterized urban schools.

Public education, which is served by school social workers, is universalistic. Some schools, particularly sectarian or religious-affiliated schools, are particularistic. The secular nature of public schools in many areas determines the definition and treatment of social problems.

Regional variations in religiosity affect schools such that in some areas, such as the Bible Belt, the religious culture is present in public schools. Needs and opportunities exist for social work in religious-affiliated schools. The religious affiliation of parochial schools determines the conceptualization and locus of social problems and permissible interventions. Parochial schools are likely to use social workers from sectarian social agencies.

In some instances private schools utilize social workers on a consultative basis. Charter schools serve many children who need social services. Children who are schooled at home rarely receive school-based social services. One exception involves some youngsters who are tested for special education services. Moreover, children who are home schooled receive social services from nonschool sources too.

Some children reside in and receive schooling in residential treatment centers. They receive school social work services that concern behavioral and family issues. Some adolescents receive schooling and related social services in juvenile correctional facilities.

Violence

Conflicts, which are a natural and inevitable aspect of social interaction, are a common occurrence in schools. Conflicts are perceived as positive in their potential for resolution and negative in their accompanying stress.

Social workers in schools identify and seek to resolve many types of conflicts, including those related to school discipline, violence, and substance abuse. Cognitive conflicts, which refer to different ways of thinking, regularly occur in academic situations at school. Intergroup conflicts, which refer to conflicts between members of different racial and ethnic groups, occur regularly in schools marked by a diverse student body and sometimes precipitate violence. For instance, a youth who is an ethnic minority within a school was assaulted at school by a youth who is an ethnic majority within the school. School social workers help teach interracial and interethnic tolerance, understanding, and appreciation of group differences.

Conflict resolution, mediation, and negotiation are useful strategies for resolving problems that occur in most elementary school classrooms, including teasing, put-downs, pushing, hitting, cheating, gossiping, and refusing to share (Porro, 1996). When resolved, conflicts lead to better interpersonal and intergroup relationships in the school setting, as well as improved academic and school functioning. Most conflict resolution training and process consists of school-based peer mediation programs. Nevertheless, some schools have programs that include a formal process for resolving conflicts between parents, students, staff, school, and community; a referral system of trained specialists; and workshops, curriculum, printed materials and other resources (Gallus & Stinski, 1994).

Families, school districts, and state agencies need assistance in resolving disputes concerning the provision of appropriate early intervention or special education and related services to children with disabilities. Dispute resolution is ordinarily handled through mediation. Mediation is a voluntary structured process that attempts to resolve disputes by bringing together the disputing parties and an impartial third party who serves as a mediator. In early intervention and special education, mediation brings together the parents of a child with a disability and school district or state agency officials to resolve disputes about the child's early intervention or special education program.

The physical safety of school-age children is a continuing concern of their families, social workers, and others who work in schools. The vulnerability of children in a compulsory attendance setting and their need to feel and be safe and secure are two contextual aspects of school violence. No schools are immune to violence. Violence in schools is a serious contemporary social problem because of its effects on the physical and mental development and well-being of children and adolescents, including the potential for trauma.

School social workers are involved when community violence spills over into the school or affects schoolchildren. They plan, organize, and participate in community crime prevention projects, including neighborhood watch programs, working in liaison with community police efforts, buddy programs, and citizen patrols.

School violence is an extension of youth violence. During years in which more adolescents are in the population, the potential for crime and delinquency is greater. Violence committed by juveniles comes to the attention of school social workers for one or more of the following reasons: (1) juveniles and their accomplices are or should be in school; (2) the violent activity or crime took place at school; (3) a victim of violence is school age; (4) school-age children have witnessed the crime.

As suggested earlier, adolescents value the sense of belonging and protection of being in a gang. In some high schools, violence is committed by groups of adolescents in gangs. Many large cities have many gangs. The goals of social workers who conduct gang work vary and include making a gang more prosocial in nature by developing social alternatives to gangs for current members or by dissolving a gang.

School social workers seek adolescents who want to take leadership roles and participate in comprehensive community efforts to prevent juvenile crime. Social programs designed to keep children from turning to crime include positive after-school, weekend, and holiday activities; positive role models and mentors; school-based community services and activities; police efforts to reach out to children with prevention services; drug-treatment and drug-education programs; family-support and family-prevention programs; and treatment, counseling, education, job training, and discipline for children who already have broken a law (U.S. Congress, 1994).

School social workers become involved in family violence issues when children are abused or relate that they have observed family violence, and when the child's family environment becomes destabilized as in parental divorce. They organize and conduct groups at the school for children of divorce.

Physical abuse, sexual abuse, and neglect of school-age children are major social problems. School social workers are responsible for detecting and reporting suspected child maltreatment to child welfare authorities. Poor children are more likely than other children to be assessed for maltreatment. Assessment of physical abuse or nonaccidental injury involves noting signs of the child being hurt in ways that are suspect. For example, a social worker observed in an interview that a young boy who was wearing shorts had cigarette burns behind his knees. Assessment of sexual abuse involves an initial observation of young children behaving in an inappropriately sexual manner toward others. For example, in an interview situation, a social worker observed a young girl behaving in a seductive manner. Assessment of neglect involves noting that a child's basic needs are not being met. For example, a social worker noted on three successive occasions that a young child was unwashed and unkempt.

School social workers are concerned when aggression is expressed in an antisocial manner, as in the formation of externalizing behaviors and mental disorders. The expression of aggression can be channeled constructively within athletic and other physical activities that promote the development of social skills and social competence. Entrenched patterns of disruptive behavior during the first years of school increase the risk of later antisocial behavior (Farrington, 1991). Research has demonstrated the effectiveness of a combination of home-based parent training and school-based social skills training in preventing future delinquency among disruptive kindergarten boys from poor, inner-city schools (Tremblay, Pagani-Kurtz, Masse, Vitaro, & Pihl, 1995).

Research has further indicated that social-cognitive processes are deficient and distorted for violent and moderately aggressive preadolescent and early adolescent boys (Lochman & Dodge, 1994). More boys than girls get into trouble at school for antisocial and destructive behavior associated with oppositional defiant disorder and conduct disorder. Some girls, particularly adolescents, express their aggression in an antisocial and destructive manner. Although some girls also have such difficulties, they are more likely to suffer from internalizing disorders, such as anxiety and mood disorders.

Special efforts at understanding and working effectively with teenagers are useful in addressing school violence. Identifying and helping children and adolescents who are experiencing trouble, including children who are bullied, as well as those who have mental health, social, peer and friendship, and academic and school performance difficulties, is important too. Many youngsters who commit acts of school violence have serious mental disorders, including conduct disorders, for which they should receive proper assessment and treatment. Adolescents with conduct and learning disorders benefit from interventions designed to influence their attitudes, aspirations, and behaviors, as well as their peer, school, and family systems (Brier, 1994). Interventions include problem solving, parent management, educational remediation, daily life, weekend recreation, and case management.

School violence, which appears in many forms, is direct or indirect and is often accompanied by hostility. Physical aggression, including actual attacks, the use of weapons, assaults, and battery, which may be accompanied by written or verbal aggression in the form of derogatory terms, racial epithets, and threats, are prevalent features. Although some violence is displayed by individuals, much of it appears to occur in gang format.

Moreover, dating violence, including date rape, is perpetrated and experienced by many adolescents. Low self-esteem and tolerant attitudes to violence are predictive of dating violence (Sugarman & Hotaling, 1989). The use of alcohol and drugs is a frequent accompaniment to dating violence (Burcky, Reuterman, & Kopsky, 1988).

Violence is an everyday occurrence at some schools; at others it is an unusual or episodic event. When violence occurs in an otherwise peaceful school, the nation is likely to take heed of it and be concerned that it does not recur. During the past 2 decades, the types of very serious violent crimes committed by children and adolescents, including murder, caught the attention of the public in the United States. Some such felonies have occurred and do occur on school property, and involve harm to children and adults at the school. Along with young people committing crimes has come a concern with how to manage and administer justice. All states now have the provision to have the most serious crimes committed by children be considered by adult courts.

Social workers fulfill professional roles related to the prevention, intervention, and postvention of school violence. They assess school-age children who appear to be violent, and identify and remediate situations in which violence could occur. Children benefit from interventions that provide them with peaceful models who demonstrate nonviolent means of resolving conflict. Peace Begins with Me is a violence prevention program for children in grades K–6 which combines time-out, self-talk, empathy, gender-neutral attitudes, feelings awareness, assertiveness, conflict resolution, health, and parent appreciation (Whittington, Crites, Moran, Kreidman, & Beck, 1989).

Multiple interventions, including peer helpers and anger management training, are useful. The effectiveness of interventions to prevent violence among young people of color is increased by a consideration of the social and cultural factors that affect oppressed groups (Delva-Tauili'ili, 1995). Many youth of color learn aggressive behaviors to survive in a hostile environment.

Some, yet unfortunately not all, acts of school violence are preventable. School social workers alert police to outbreaks of violence in schools, work with youngsters who have been involved in violent incidents, and engage in crisis intervention during and shortly after an incident of violence. In extreme forms, violence at the school includes suicide, homicide, or a combination of both. Multiple interventions provided by professional and peer helpers are useful. Anger management training is beneficial for adolescents who have difficulty controlling their anger. Postvention encompasses work with mental health professionals in and out of the school setting as well as work with survivors to reduce the potential development of traumatization, including stress-related disorders.

Four roles pertaining to violence involve social learning that increases the probability that the child or adolescent who has experienced violence will become involved in violence in the future: by definition, (1) school-age perpetrators commit the act of violence; (2) accomplices participate in it; (3) witnesses observe it; and (4) victims are physically hurt by it. In some situations one child experiences multiple violence roles, which further complicates treatment. Children who are victimized by violence are at risk for experiencing debilitating effects to their physical and mental health, including posttraumatic stress disorder, for which they will require immediate and subsequent care. They can benefit from crisis intervention or critical incident stress debriefing.

Many practical measures maximize the safety of schools. Many schools have a dress code and require students to wear uniforms as a way of promoting conformity and discipline, as well as minimizing social class differences. Schools attempt to empower children to report trouble. Schools develop rapport and trust between children and principals, teachers, coaches, social workers, guidance counselors, security officers, and youth resource officers. Schools have policies of no tolerance for drugs, weapons, fighting, disruptive classroom behavior, and disrespect for authority along with consequences for policy violations. Schools use hand-held metal detectors and conduct random searches or inspections along with specially trained dogs.

Schools have building-level crisis plans describing a course of action for staff to follow if a violent event occurs. Schools concerned about violence develop teams to deal with incidents that occur. Moreover, school social workers assess, record, and report the nature and type of the violent incident. They estimate whether a violation of school rules and a law violation have occurred. They consider whether they are dealing with crimes against persons, including assault and battery, substance abuse, extortion, robbery, sex offenses, trespassing, and the use of weapons. They also consider whether they are dealing with crimes involving property, which could also injure persons, namely arson, bomb threats and other explosive devices, burglary, larceny and theft, and vandalism.

Resources in preventing school violence include parent organizations, volunteer mentor groups, crime prevention organizations, and student advisor/advisee programs.

School staff, namely pupil personnel team members, teachers, and principals, as well as law enforcement officials, are useful resources too. Some schools have probation officers who meet with juveniles on probation in school classrooms, hallways, and cafeterias. All such resources are useful in promoting communication with children and adolescents to lessen the probability of violent acts.

School-Based Health Clinics

School-based health clinics have extended the role of the schools beyond education to encompass health concerns. School-based health clinics provide comprehensive services including health services, counseling, and education (Harold & Harold, 1991). Health services at clinics are provided on school premises during the school day. Services, which are adolescent focused, are provided by an interdisciplinary team. Social workers in school-based health clinics have a variety of responsibilities including psychosocial assessment, crisis intervention, ongoing counseling or therapy, education, group work, advocacy, referral and coordination, networking, and services to families. Some of the clinics have been supported by the Robert Wood Johnson Foundation.

Children in poor communities, including underserved and underprivileged African American youngsters, have needed and benefitted from school-based health clinics. Such youngsters might otherwise have inadequate access to social workers and health care providers. A wide range of problems, including physical and mental health concerns, family issues, substance abuse, and interpersonal conflicts within the school setting, are dealt with in school-based clinics. Nevertheless, some communities have resisted having health clinics in their schools because of fears that the clinics would provide adolescents with sexual information and counseling, and birth control materials.

The predominant method of helping young people in school-based health clinics is brief individual counseling or treatment, including crisis work. In some cases, including crisis intervention situations, families are seen by the social worker. Often, to make it feasible for parents to attend, such meetings are held at the clinic in the late afternoons or in the evenings. Some school-based health clinics offer group work for children and, occasionally, group work for parents. In some schools a large number of children have a disorder that is the focus of school-based health clinics. Clinical groups are formed for children who share a health or mental health disorder, such as adolescent eating disorders.

Administering case management is also a social work role in the clinic. Even though children may be seen in schools, they often require help from outside social agencies. The social worker at the school-based health clinic coordinates such care. At times comprehensive psychosocial assessments and evaluations are conducted. Social workers see children who are homebound because of illness, visit family members, and observe the child's home. Such visits are related to school programs using visiting teachers.

In schools, children and adolescents benefit from informal support from classmates and friends. Moreover, school social workers use formal peer counseling programs to help young people with academic and social problems that become apparent at school. Peer counseling programs have a number of advantages. They can supplement the work of the school social worker. In addition to the benefits that youngsters receive from being participants in peer counseling programs, through the helper principle, peers can benefit from providing help to others. Young people feel more on an equal level with age peers than they do with adults. The opinion of peers can be powerful; it is more readily accepted by many adolescents than the perspectives of adult practitioners. Children and adolescents are able to listen to peers who have recently experienced the difficulty under discussion. Peer counselors talk to youngsters who consider drastic solutions to their difficulties, such as dropping out of school and suicide.

Although much of the focus of attention of school-based health clinics is on the provision of direct services to school-age children and adolescents, indirect services should receive greater emphasis. Indirect services encompass consultation and collaboration to meet the overall goal of improving the health and well-being of school-age children and adolescents. Consultations to public school faculty and staff can be invaluable in preventive work. Consultation involves establishing reciprocal relationships between social work consultants and teacher consultees (Early, 1992). School social workers who develop sound working relationships with educators give their professional opinion about the nature of the difficulty experienced by a particular child and methods of handling a difficult situation, as well as provide information and education about topics of recurring concern in the school.

School social workers collaborate with health center teams to evaluate and develop treatment plans and measure overall effectiveness. Collaboration is an aspect of intraprofessional and interprofessional practice and represents an indirect service that can provide benefits in addition to the direct service the individual practitioner is able to provide. Collaboration occurs within the school system and also involves working with others outside the school system on behalf of school-age children and adolescents.

School-Linked Services

Most social services for children and adolescents are tied to the school. Whereas some social services are based in the school, many other community services are linked to the school. School-linked programs represent the collaboration of social workers with educators, community and civic organizations, and religious institutions in creating school-linked programs (Scannapieco, 1994). Formal links include explicit agreements, such as Memoranda of Understanding and contracts, as well as joint training and supervision of practitioners. Informal links, including working relationships and communication, are also utilized.

To provide social services to pupils in need, school social workers often must turn to human service organizations outside the school. They refer young people for specialized diagnostic, assessment, preventive, interventive, and rehabilitative services.

It is incumbent on school social workers, as mandated reporters, to appraise the child welfare office of suspected child maltreatment. Communication between school and child welfare authorities is particularly important in regard to school-age children who are in foster care, children who are in the process of being adopted, and adolescents who have legal difficulties, including juveniles who are in need of supervision.

Adolescents from high-risk urban environments are prone to engage in delinquent behavior, become unmarried teen parents, and become dependent on social assistance programs for income (National Center for Children in Poverty, 1990). When young people engage in actions that threaten the life or well-being of others or are involved in activities that damage school property, school officials summon law enforcement officials to intervene. Police are routinely posted at many public high schools and are readily available to deal with problematic behaviors by groups or solitary individuals.

School social workers assist pupils who are in trouble with the law. Some youngsters commit crimes on school property that result in them being involved with the correctional system. For other pupils, involvement with the correctional system is ongoing and may predate their involvement with the school social worker. Youngsters who are involved with correctional systems, including adolescents who are in custody, continue to require schooling and social services. Many such youngsters have family difficulties, child welfare problems relating to placement (including foster care and adoptions and issues of abuse or neglect), substance abuse disorders, and mental disorders.

School health, which is an ecological concept, is a function of the physical and human environment of the school. It is influenced by the health of the families whose children attend the school, the communities to which the children belong, and the community in which the school is located. Schools vary in regard to the extent to which they are healthy environments for children and adolescents. School health concerns increase from elementary school, where they are often minimal, to middle school, where they are noticed, to high school, where they are often significant issues. School health reflects the well-being as well as the incidence and prevalence of physical and mental disorders of children and adolescents. Many pupils who are seen by school social workers have physical and mental disorders that comprise the focus of clinical attention or underlie the problems for which they are seen. Increasingly, school social workers and other staff take steps to promote the physical and mental health of children and adolescents.

School social workers play a key role in the gateway to mental health treatment. They witness troubled behavior within the school setting and are in contact with teachers and parents who also observe it. Disruptive behavior, including oppositional, defiant conduct problems and attention deficit hyperactivity, is noticed by the teacher and is frequently the cause of referral to school social workers. School social workers commonly refer youngsters in severe emotional distress who are in need of urgent care to mental health agencies. They frequently utilize the diagnostic and treatment services of mental health agencies for children and adolescents whom they recognize and assess as having a mental disorder. Mental health agencies are equipped to make definitive diagnoses and implement treatment plans.

Teenage pregnancy, crime and delinquency, violence, and automobile accidents occur more frequently when adolescents use alcohol and other drugs. For some older children and adolescents who experiment with alcohol and other drugs, substance abuse is temporary whereas for others it becomes a lifelong problem. Unfortunately, the possession, use, or distribution of illicit substances, along with the potential for violence, often occurs on and around school property. School social workers aim to prevent substance abuse, and they intervene when youngsters are apprehended for substance abuse. They refer adolescents to specialized substance abuse treatment facilities in the community. Families and Schools Together (FAST) is a substance abuse prevention program for elementary schoolchildren that serves whole families (McDonald, Bradish, Billingham, Dibble, & Rice, 1991).

Some schoolchildren have infectious and contagious diseases. Currently, one of the greatest public health concerns is the development of HIV+ status and the transmission of the AIDS virus. Although recent developments in the treatment of HIV/AIDS have been promising, it remains a deadly disease. Therefore, prevention is essential. Prevention is based in part on health education of children and adolescents about the known methods of transmission of disease, including sexual activity, and how youngsters can avoid getting the disease.

Historically, teenage girls who became pregnant were stigmatized and shunned by their communities. Often, they lived in separate residential facilities and experienced disruptions in their schooling. Currently, greater accommodations are made for pregnant teenagers to continue their schooling. Arrangements are made to help take care of their infants. Nevertheless, teenage pregnancy remains a crucial turning point in the lives of young women, who are often faced with child-care burdens at an early age. The hazards to teenage mothers' educational, vocational, career, and social development are abundant. Opportunities for Parenting Teens is a school social work program that involves coordinated service utilization, support groups, and linkage to community services for pregnant and parenting teens (Weinman, Solomon, & Glass, 2000).

School Social Work Roles

School social workers' academic qualifications in social work range from a baccalaureate to a doctoral degree, with many holding a master's degree. Professional training provides a knowledge of interpersonal relationships; individual, family, and group functioning; interviewing and counseling skills; ethics; human diversity; community development; and community resources.

Social workers are expected to maintain clients' rights to confidentiality and informed consent. However, children do not always understand the complexity of the issues involved. Moreover, school social workers are often pressured by other school personnel to reveal confidential information (Berman-Rossi & Rossi, 1990; Kopels, 1992).

School social workers document their practice and utilize efficient and effective methods, such as a structured, goal-directed approach. Cognitive-behavioral approaches are especially effective methods of direct service for targeted problems. School social workers use single-system designs to determine their effectiveness with particular cases.

School social workers help pupils, families, and schools with problems related to emotions, including aggression and anger, depression, stress, and unhappiness. They also help them cope with family issues including child abuse and neglect, parenting, separation/divorce, and remarriage. Furthermore, they work with problems related to alcohol and drug abuse, attendance, behavior, classroom, communication, death and dying, peer relationships and social skills, self-esteem, and sexuality.

Parents, teachers, and children often contact social workers through the school at which the child is enrolled or through a school board office. The services that school social workers offer include advocacy, agency liaison, assessment, attendance, case conferences, classroom interventions, community development, community referrals, consultation, family counseling, group work, individual counseling, multicultural outreach, outreach to parents, parenting skills, policy development, practical aid, prevention of problems such as suicide, child abuse, aggression and violence, and staff development.

School social workers practice with four sets of constituencies. First, they work with pupils to receive the maximum possible benefit from their educational opportunities. They help pupils understand themselves as well as improve their social relationships with peers, teachers, family members, and the community. They aid them in improving their self-esteem, in coping with stress, and in developing their decision-making skills.

Second, they work with parents to encourage them to participate actively and effectively in their children's education. They help parents understand their children's social and emotional development and meet their children's social and emotional needs. They assist parents in understanding the programs in the school and community that are available to students with special needs. They enable parents to use school and community resources effectively.

Contact with parents and families is an essential aspect of school social work with children and adolescents. Many children and adolescents have family difficulties that are evidenced in school. School social workers can remediate some family issues. Some youngsters have academic difficulties at school because their home life is stressful and unsupportive or their parents are divorcing. School social workers can intervene by working with youngsters' families as well as offering support and group services at the school.

Third, they work with schools to promote their understanding of the many psychosocial, family, health, cultural, social, and economic factors that affect students' abilities to make the most of their school experience. They assist schools to use their resources more fully in meeting the educational, social, and emotional needs of their students. They help schools develop policies that address the social and emotional needs of students.

As a school-based profession, school social work is directly related to the teaching and pupil personnel professions. School social workers provide counseling and information to children and adolescents. They work with counselors, psychologists, teachers, nurses, and principals. They cooperate with health care and educational practitioners and school administrators. Diverse professional training within the field of school-based services contributes to differing perspectives on the problems of children and adolescents.

School social workers draw on their joint expertise in delivering services. Moreover, in working in schools with children and adolescents who are faced with a combination of health, mental health, education, and behavior problems, teamwork has the potential to deliver considerable knowledge and a broad range of perspectives about the nature and potential resolution of such difficulties. Many teams function well despite interdisciplinary rivalries and competition between team members for status and resources. They are often able to deliver a concerted, consistent, and powerful response to troubled children within school systems. Radin (1992) developed a 17-item instrument for the assessment of school social workers as team members. The instrument assesses the team as a whole as well as the individual school social worker on the team.

Fourth, school social workers help communities understand school policies, programs, and practices. They enable communities to minimize environmental factors that inhibit or interfere with pupil learning. They aid communities in the development of resources that adequately meet the needs of students and their families.

The roles of school social workers vary between communities. One role is primarily that of the diagnostician of social problems. A second role includes both assessment and intervention, including crisis intervention. A third role encompasses overseeing a large school system and promoting the prevention of social problems.

Constable, Kuzmickaite, Harrison, and Volkmann (1999) conducted a survey of the role expectations of school social workers in Indiana. They found that the school social worker's role is multifaceted. Four interrelated and frequently performed sets of tasks and skills included (1) consultation within the school system and teamwork relationships; (2) assessment in direct service and program development; (3) direct personal work with children and parents in individual, group, and family modalities; and (4) assistance with program development within schools.

An ecological model of social work practice in schools emphasizes the communication links between pupils, their schools, and their communities. Human diversity adds to the complexity of the model. An ecosystems perspective, which derives from the ecological approach and which also utilizes a social systems framework, is useful in current school social work practice.

Corbett and Farber (1990) proposed three models of providing social services in the schools. In the role expansion model, the teacher counsels, helps, and serves as a liaison with home and social agencies. In the organizational expansion model, school social workers and other professionals are hired as part of the school staff. In the system supplementation model, the school makes referrals to external agencies and practitioners. Tapper, Kleinman, and Nakashian (1997) proposed a system partnership model that provides a structure for a partnership, collaboration, and integrated service delivery among schools, social agencies, and criminal justice agencies.

Kapp (2000) developed a school social work program model consisting of resources, such as funding; staff activities, including direct services to students; program processes, for example, intake/referral; immediate outcomes, including ongoing physical, emotional, and social needs being met; intermediate outcomes, for example, troubled families introduced to and provided access to community resources; and long-range outcomes, such as students becoming productive members of society.

Future of School Social Work

The future of school social work depends in part on trends in society, education, and the professions. For instance, the Internet provides increasing educational, cultural, and communication opportunities for young people and their families, as well as the school social workers who serve them.

Some social problems, including school-based violence, intergroup conflicts, social class disparities, differences in academic achievements and abilities, and meeting the needs of children with behavioral, emotional, and learning disorders appear to persist. Furthermore, increasing recognition and development of knowledge of child and adolescent mental health and its relationship to physical health, child and adolescent development, and substance abuse also impact school social work.

Moreover, a movement toward and an availability of alternative, private, parochial, and home school education, with attendant opportunities for the development of school social work are increasing. Most alternative schools are directed toward students with attendance or discipline problems who are at risk for becoming dropouts. They include nonpublic schools, such as parochial and military schools, and preparatory schools for upper-class students. Alternative schools are small, have a supportive environment, provide individualized attention, give young people choices in their education, have an on-site governance and are egalitarian, provide for participation and sharing by family and community, clearly communicate well-defined standards and rules, are specialized, and are subject to accountability and evaluation (Franklin, 1992).

Changes in schooling will engender new patterns of social service delivery to children and adolescents. The conception of schooling and social services is changing such that some schools house health clinics. The nature, type, and amount of social services located within future schools is in the process of being determined. School-based health clinics must develop a broader base of support to bring appropriate and effective services to needy schoolchildren and adolescents who are at risk for developing serious health disorders. Clinics need to develop newer, innovative programs that meet emerging social and health problems and to find more effective ways of working with minorities and other cultural groupings.

Many schools, particularly urban schools in major metropolitan areas, have increasing diversity in the language and cultural characteristics of their student body. In the future, school social workers will need to understand youngsters from many world cultures. In the United States, projected demographic trends pose major challenges in delivering effective, culturally sensitive, preventive, interventive, and remedial school-based and school-linked social services. Social workers need to forge new alliances with members of other cultures to bridge gaps and provide translation services to youngsters and their families.

Conclusion

School social work is a distinctive field of practice with ties to both social work and education. The goals of school social work include the improvement of conditions in schools to further the social well-being and cognitive development of children and adolescents.

The social context of learning includes the numerous social problems prevalent in contemporary schools and communities. The social composition of the school encompasses the sociodemographic characteristics, including socioeconomic status, residence, gender, nationality, language, and culture of the pupils. Many public schools in the United States are very diverse in social composition. Some classrooms in metropolitan urban areas consist largely of many children who speak different languages.

Various social forces, including cooperation and competition, conflict, attraction and repulsion, and group and intergroup dynamics come into play in the school. School social workers attempt to promote a positive culture for children and adolescents that allows choice, is culturally relevant, and is constructive to youngsters' development. Many social services for children and adolescents are school based or school linked. Many social workers who assist school-age children and adolescents, including child welfare and mental health social workers, interface with the school system.

Schools provide a variety of counseling programs to pupils both within classrooms and as additional programs outside classrooms. Innovative problem-solving training approaches are offered to youngsters. Subjects such as health and social studies provide educational material that overlap with the information provided by counseling programs. Pupil personnel team members, including school social workers, counselors, and psychologists, provide counseling to children and adolescents.

School social workers assist children, families, schools, and communities to ensure that all pupils are able to take advantage of their educational and social opportunities. Moreover, by serving as a link between the school and the particular concerns of students and their parents, school social workers help parents increase their understanding of children, improve parenting skills, deal with family stress and crisis, learn more about school programs, and make better use of community resources.

School social workers deliver preventive and interventive social-emotional educational programs, at times in tandem with the classroom teacher. Assessment is useful in preventing difficulties of children and in determining the need for intervention. Traditionally, school-based services have focused on intervention in which a social problem is identified and assessed, and treatment is offered. Increasingly, such services are preventive in nature, as it is realized that social problems in the schools, including violence and school failure, have devastating consequences.

Some schoolchildren are victims, perpetrators, or observers of violence. The concern is to minimize the potential for future reoccurrence of violence. Children who suffered from physical maltreatment are more likely to use violence as a means of solving conflicts than are other children. School social workers provide postvention services to forestall the development of future difficulties by family members of children or adolescents who have committed suicide or who have been perpetrators or victims of violence. Many children and adolescents who have mental disorders can be helped by social workers, which is the focus of the following chapter.

CHAPTER

9 Methods and Practices in Mental Health Agencies

Child and adolescent mental health is a relatively new area of discovery and practice and encompasses emotional regulation, conflict resolution, the ability to love self and others, and adequate functioning in family, school, and community systems. The importance of mental health in the development of children and adolescents is paramount. It is becoming increasingly apparent that much child psychopathology is developmental in nature (Achenbach, 1982).

This chapter focuses on understanding young people with mental disorders and promoting their mental health; preventing developmental psychopathology; the emotional difficulties of children; and the major types of mental disorders experienced by children and adolescents, including stress and anxiety, mood disorders, disruptive behavior disorders, cognitive deficits and head injuries, eating disorders, schizophrenia and autism, and substance abuse. Child and adolescent mental health is considered in terms of service delivery systems and school, family, and community systems. Child sexual abuse is discussed as a mental health issue.

Promoting the Mental Health of Children and Adolescents

Mental health difficulties of children and adolescents are often difficult for adults to comprehend and accept (Dulmus & Wodarski, 1996). Five factors contribute to this situation. One, some evidence exists that children's behavioral and emotional problems have increased in the United States (Achenbach & Howell, 1993). Two, mental disorders of children and adolescents can vary from mild to severe. Three, some mental health problems threaten the lives of children and adolescents. Four, individual children often have more than one disorder. Five, stigma associated with many mental health disorders, confusion about their origin and nature, and concern about becoming mentally ill affect access, use, and effectiveness of mental health service delivery for children and adolescents (Rog, 1992).

Mental health services for children and adolescents include case management or service coordination; community-based inpatient psychiatric care; individual and group counseling; crisis residential care; crisis outreach teams; day treatment; education and special education services; family support; health services; independent living supports; intensive, in-home family-based counseling; legal services; protection and advocacy; psychiatric consultation; recreation therapy; residential treatment; respite care; self-help and support groups; small therapeutic group care; therapeutic foster care; transportation; tutoring; and vocational counseling.

The effects, including efficacy and effectiveness, of mental health care on children and adolescents, which are variable, are a function of the type of disorder, type of treatment, and treatment compliance. Many disorders persist for many years, even into adulthood.

Special categories for child and adolescent mental disorders, including speech, learning, and feeding disturbances and elimination disorders, first appeared in the DSM-II publication of the American Psychiatric Association (APA, 1968). Currently, in the DSM-IV-TR, disorders usually first diagnosed in infancy, childhood, or adolescence include mental retardation, characterized by low intellectual and adaptive functioning; learning disorders, characterized by lower than expected academic functioning; motor skills disorders, including difficulties in motor coordination; speech and language communication disorders; pervasive developmental disorders in several developmental domains; attention deficit and disruptive behavior disorders; persistent feeding and eating disorders of infancy or early childhood; vocal and/or motor tic disorders; disorders of elimination in inappropriate places; and other disorders of infancy, childhood, or adolescence, such as separation anxiety disorder (APA, 2000).

For diagnosis, prevention, intervention, and rehabilitation to be effective, it is helpful for young people to understand their mental health difficulties. They also need to be understood and to receive support from practitioners, relatives, teachers, classmates, friends, and neighbors. Social workers attempt to accomplish such ends by providing parallel services to family members, conducting interviews, implementing group work, and offering psychoeducation to schools and communities.

Prevention of Developmental Psychopathology

The prevention of mental disorders among infants, children, and adolescents occurs at three levels (Berlin, 1990). Primary prevention encompasses efforts to maintain mental health among youngsters who show no signs of mental disorder. It involves the recognition of potential developmental problems and intervention to prevent the emergence of such problems as disabling disorders. Primary prevention efforts include prenatal care, work on fetal alcohol syndrome, nutrition of pregnant women, attachment, early intervention programs, intervention in regard to temperament, reparenting programs, nurturing environments for children, public schools, early child stimulation programs, being attuned to learning and developmental problems, and education regarding sexuality. Consultation with mental health agencies and schools using individual and group interventions promotes primary prevention through education and training, program changes, and changes in the structure of the delivery system (Granello, 1995).

Secondary prevention involves work with children and adolescents who have some signs and symptoms of mental illness yet are functioning well. It encompasses very early recognition of disturbances or disorders and prompt and early intervention to prevent serious limitations of the capacities of young people to live, function, and adapt adequately. Secondary prevention is useful in helping parents who have children with disabilities, working with neglected and abused children who are withdrawn and violent, focusing on learning problems and hyperactivity among children, dealing with preschool children of depressed mothers, and helping children who have mental retardation and neurological problems. Childhood depression and suicide attempts, attention deficit hyperactivity disorder (ADHD), learning problems, and mental retardation among school-age children are also the focus of secondary prevention (Lamarine, 1995). For adolescents, secondary prevention encompasses issues of depression, anger, violent behavior, truancy, gangs involved in substance abuse, suicidal threats, auto accidents, homicides, and pregnancy.

A secondary prevention program with Native American adolescent females helped these young women from chaotic families, who are truant and failing in school, abusing drugs, and at high risk for becoming pregnant and alcoholic (Berlin, 1988). They received an education that encompasses child care, child development, parenting skills, sexuality, and substance abuse through a supportive group where they made friends.

Tertiary prevention is akin to rehabilitation in that it involves working with children and adolescents who have been severely impacted by mental disorders. It involves early treatment of mental disorders to enable functional adaptation in living. Problems that are dealt with include child and adolescent schizophrenia, depression, antisocial behavior caused by severe child abuse, multiple personality disorders in sexually abused young women, ADHD, eating disorders, and borderline and narcissistic personality disorders. Treatments include individual, marital, and group psychotherapy, and pharmacotherapy.

Dumka, Roosa, Michaels, and Suh (1995) developed a five-stage model for prevention program development that they used to create an intervention, the Raising Successful Children Program, designed to reduce child mental health problems among low-income, ethnically diverse families. The first stage of the model is problem analysis, consisting of defining the problem/goal, identifying risk and protective factors, and determining accessibility of the risk group. The second stage is program design, consisting of consulting the target group, selecting change objectives, choosing outcome evaluation instruments, picking change models, deciding on the extensiveness of the prevention program, planning a recruitment and retention strategy, and designing the procedural elements of the program. The third stage, pilot testing, consists of recruitment and retention evaluation, process evaluation, formative evaluation, and program revision. The fourth stage is advanced testing. The fifth stage is dissemination.

Emotional Problems of
Children and Adolescents

In the course of their development, young children normatively learn to display their emotions. Positive emotions include love, joy, contentment, and happiness. Negative emotions include guilt, sadness, frustration, anger, fear, shame, and embarrassment. The expression of negative emotions by children is often uncomfortable for family members.

Many children and adolescents have emotional difficulties, including a restricted range of expression of emotions; flat affect; the preponderance, prevalence, or persistence of negative emotions; vicissitudes or swings in emotions; and the furtherance of behavioral problems and social dysfunction. Some of these difficulties stem from child welfare issues and problems related to attachment, separation, and loss of important figures or persons in their lives, as well as associated grief. Children who feel very sad for a limited period of time are reacting to a loss in a normative, acceptable manner. However, children who continue to grieve a loss for a very long period of time may develop a mood disorder. Cultural factors associated with bereavement influence the presentation of negative feelings, the duration of loss, the acceptability and manner of grieving, and the willingness to seek and receive mental health diagnosis and treatment.

Psychological tasks for bereaved children occur at three stages (Baker & Sedney, 1996). Early tasks associated with grieving encompass the child understanding that someone has died and its implications, and protection of themselves, their physical bodies, and their families. Middle-phase tasks are associated with mourning a loss. The tasks include emotional acceptance of the loss, reevaluating the relationship to the deceased, and bearing the emotional pain that accompanies the loss. Late tasks, which sequentially follow the middle-phase tasks, include forming a new sense of personal identity that incorporates the loss and the identification with the deceased person; investing in new emotional relationships; consolidating and maintaining a durable internal relationship to the dead person; fully returning to age-appropriate developmental tasks and activities; and coping with the periodic resurgence of emotional pain, particularly on anniversaries.

Several persons may recognize and assess emotional problems of children and adolescents. Youngsters may recognize that they are having difficulty and, in turn, speak with family members, friends, or others about their problems. Parents and family members may recognize a change in the emotional state of a child. For instance, Aunt Pauline notices that her niece Juliette is grieving. However, because Juliette is usually depressed, it is difficult for Pauline to identify the problem.

The young person's emotional state may be noted by perceptive school teachers and officials. If difficulties emerge either in the youngster's academic performance or conduct, they may alert parents or guardians about them. Mental health professionals may be called on to formally diagnose an emotional problem as a mental disorder. Goals for the treatment of the emotional problems of children and adolescents include the furtherance of (a) the experience and expression of positive emotions, (b) the reduction of the experience and expression of negative emotions, (c) the experience and expression of emotions to fall within a normal range, and (d) the situational appropriateness of the experience and expression of emotions. Moreover, the acceptability of expressing and verbalizing various emotions exists within a cultural context.

Serious emotional disturbances (SED) refer to mental disorders that severely disrupt the daily functioning of children and adolescents in home, school, or community settings. Systems of care provide a full range of educational, health, mental health, operational, recreational, social, and vocational services to children and adolescents with SED so as to improve youngsters' functioning in those settings (Stroul & Friedman, 1986). These include residential services, outpatient services, day treatment services, family preservation and reunification services, therapeutic foster care, crisis and emergency services, case management and individualized care, and family support services and groups (Kutash & Rivera, 1995).

The aims of family support programs are to promote attentive, responsive, and nurturing parenting; personal development and well-being of parents; and sound child development. The programs are designed to empower parents to help themselves and their children (Zigler & Black, 1989). Social workers in such programs provide ongoing support to families from pregnancy through early childhood (Weissberg, Caplan, & Harwood, 1991).

Sometimes the life of the youngster with SED is placed in jeopardy. In most, but not all instances such disturbances last at least one year. It is estimated that about 12 to 20 percent of children and adolescents have a mental health problem and that about 5 percent of children and adolescents are affected by SED (National Institute of Mental Health, 1990). The most common diagnoses are anxiety disorders, enuresis, conduct disorder (CD), and ADHD (Hoagwood & Koretz, 1996).

Global impairments reportedly occur in about 12 percent of children, and specific impairments, such as school failure or trouble with the law, occur in about 2 percent of children (Costello & Tweed, 1994). It is estimated that only about 20 to 33 percent of children and adolescents with mental health problems receive help (Saxe, Cross, & Silverman, 1988; Tuma, 1989; U.S. Congress, Office of Technology Assessment, 1986). Community surveys have found that 6 to 17 percent of children and adolescents with a diagnosable mental disorder received a mental health service in the past year (Bird et al., 1990). A study of the use of services by children with SED indicated that about 37 percent received mental health services (Burns et al., 1995).

Types of Mental Disorders

Stress and Anxiety

Children and adolescents are subject to a variety of stressors in their daily lives, which vary in seriousness, intensity, impact on their lives, and association with life circumstances and social problems. For most children and adolescents, daily stressors such as forgetting homework or being ignored by a peer in middle school are minor, with little impact on the youngster. However, being involved in a life-threatening accident can have a major impact on the child. Social workers help young people to acquire cognitive coping skills. Children and adolescents learn to develop their confidence in and ability to make reassuring self-statements about coping with anxiety, imagery, progressive relaxation exercises, and social skills.

Children and adolescents can be helped to develop and engage in relaxing natural activities. First, the social worker helps the youngster identify favorite relaxing activities from a larger set of activities, such as sports, reading, music, arts, and crafts. The social and activity dimensions of sports, camping, and dancing promote relaxation. Then they help ensure that the young person has access to and resources to engage in relaxing activities. Friendships and social relationships also are an important aspect of promoting relaxation. The social worker facilitates youngsters' social learning of social skills in small groups, through naturalistic processes, as in sports, and through role playing and problem-solving discussion.

For many young people, anxiety or nervousness is normatively associated with developmental transitions. Children experience anxiety when separating from their parents or when entering school for the first time. Adolescents experience anxiety when changing schools or when beginning to date. Anxiety is usually related to youngsters' difficulty in coping with stress. The anxiety experienced by children and adolescents is a potentially serious problem that ought to be assessed when the young person feels that their anxiety is overwhelming; when family members, school personnel, or community residents report that they are exhibiting a high degree of nervous behavior; or when their anxiety significantly interferes with their daily functioning.

Many children experience and manifest nervousness, particularly in stressful situations, such as taking a test at school. Some anxiety is beneficial in keeping children and adolescents attentive to potential threats in their environment. However, some young people develop one or more of five anxiety disorders that represent an exaggeration of normative, functional anxiety.

One, some youngsters develop obsessive-compulsive disorder (OCD), which is characterized by repetitive intrusive thoughts or behaviors that are meant to control anxiety but are disruptive, dysfunctional, and ineffective in controlling anxiety. Although many children and adolescents go through a period in which they engage in compulsive behaviors, such as repeatedly washing their hands, counting, arranging and rearranging objects, or avoiding stepping on the cracks on the sidewalk; most leave such actions behind them as they develop. However, youngsters who develop OCD spend a great deal of time and energy attending to obsessions or participating in compulsive activities, thereby restricting the amount of time available to them for studying, socializing, and relaxing. Even though youngsters with OCD sometimes are aware that their thoughts or actions seem to be devoid of meaning and are indeed distressing, they have a hard time stopping their repetition.

Two, children and adolescents who have generalized anxiety disorder (GAD) tend to worry about both improbable and probable events on a fairly regular basis. Their worries appear to be extreme and unrelated to any recent event. Youngsters who have GAD tend not to be in control of their worries, which may prevent them from having new experiences to promote their social and emotional development. Children and adolescents with GAD are usually tense and self-conscious. They complain about physical discomforts that do not appear to have a physical basis. They have a marked need for reassurance.

Three, some youngsters develop phobias, or specific fears that come about as a result of conditioning or association. Children and adolescents with phobias have unrealistic or excessive fears about situations, such as being in an enclosed area, or fear of objects, such as water, that they consequently tend to avoid. Youngsters with social phobias are afraid of being criticized by others. Phobias are detrimental to children and adolescents, because they restrict their activities, but are eminently treatable by behavior therapy.

Four, some children develop panic disorder, which consists of repeated panic attacks with no readily identifiable cause. The attacks consist of dizziness, intense fear, a pounding heartbeat, nausea, and sweating. These attacks are so terrifying that children and adolescents with panic disorder avoid anxiety-producing places or situations. Some children with panic disorder do not want to go to school; and some do not want to be separated from their parents. Such difficulties may be hard for afflicted youngsters to explain to adults.

Five, children and adolescents who experience traumatic stressors, such as physical or sexual abuse or being subject to a disaster sometimes develop post-traumatic stress disorder (PTSD). Youngsters who live in families and neighborhoods or who attend schools where violent events occur are at risk for developing PTSD. Youngsters with PTSD repeatedly experience the traumatic event through memories, flashbacks, and distressing thoughts. They avoid people, places, and situations they associate with the trauma and often have difficulty sleeping.

Anxiety disorders are relatively common; at least 10 percent of children and adolescents have them, and about half the youngsters with anxiety disorders have another mental disorder too (Kashani & Orvaschel, 1990). Young people who are very shy, as well as those whose parents have an anxiety disorder, are at risk for developing an anxiety disorder. Untreated anxiety disorders can lead to the child missing school days or leaving school early; having unsatisfactory peer relations; low self-esteem; substance abuse; subsequent problems in work situations; and adult anxiety disorder. Treatments for anxiety disorders include cognitive-behavioral treatment; individual psychotherapy; family therapy; parent training; and medication.

Major Depression, Suicidal Behavior, and Manic-Depressive Disorder

Children and adolescents are prone to experience major depression. Their developmental level, insight, knowledge of mental health, and ability to understand, label, and verbalize their emotional state are factors in the assessment and treatment of depression. Estimates are that 3 to 6 percent of children and as many as 12 percent of adolescents experience depression. The National Institute of Mental Health and the American Academy of Child and Adolescent Psychiatry, respectively, estimate that 1.5 to 3 million U.S. children are seriously depressed (Brody, 1997). A family history of depression increases the risk that a child or adolescent will develop depression. Youngsters who have experienced a major depression are at risk for developing another depression and other mental health problems.

Children and adolescents with major depression make cognitive errors, endorse negative attributions, and have low self-esteem (Tems, Stewart, Skinner, Hughes, & Emslie, 1993). They feel sad and worthless, and cry, and look tearful. They believe that they are unattractive, are unable to do anything right, and that their life is hopeless. Their school performance declines. They appear more lethargic and less interested in participating in activities, such as play, that they had previously enjoyed. Their appetite and sleep patterns change. They express vague physical complaints. Their drawings express sad themes.

It is difficult to recognize depression in adolescents because mood swings are a normative aspect of adolescence. Unfortunately, school staff and parents often perceive and label depressed children who show learning problems or social incompetence as apathetic, immature, rebellious, slothful, and unmotivated (Lamarine, 1995). Nevertheless, previously sociable adolescents who stop spending time with their peers and verbalize feelings of hopelessness and lack of enjoyment are likely to be experiencing depression.

Children who feel very sad are unable to function in their usual manner. They are unable to attend school or if they go to school, they are unable to participate satisfactorily in academic and social activities. They have difficulty participating in family activities and outings, as well as in community events. They are turned inward.

Children and adolescents who experience major depression and do not value their current lives are at risk for attempting suicide. However, some youth who experience severe depression do not attempt suicide, and some youth who attempt suicide do not experience severe depression. Osman and colleagues (1998) created the Reasons for Living Inventory for Adolescents, a measure that is useful in assessing adolescent suicidal behavior. Five correlated factors were identified, namely (1) future optimism, (2) suicide-related concerns, (3) family alliance, (4) peer acceptance and support, and (5) self-acceptance.

The spectrum of suicide consists of thoughts, gestures, attempts, and "successes." Young people who contemplate committing suicide are at risk for attempting suicide. Gestures, which represent calls for help, indicate that a child has unacknowledged and unmet needs. Gestures increase the probability that in the future they will attempt or commit an act of suicide. Social workers conduct wide-ranging assessments and diagnoses to determine what needed help is to be delivered.

A suicide by a child or adolescent signals or indicates failure to the parents. Following a suicide by a child or adolescent, family members and friends wonder why they did not know that the youngster was suicidal; they blame themselves for not having prevented the suicide. The loss of a child is very difficult for parents. Self-help group resources include Compassionate Friends and Mended Hearts. Furthermore, a concern arises that family members and classmates will model their behavior on that of the youngster who committed suicide and commit "copycat suicides."

Some children and adolescents who are at risk for suicide experience manic-depressive disorder. Bipolar disorder or manic-depressive illness is marked by exaggerated mood swings between extreme lows or depression and extreme highs, namely excitedness or manic phases, with moderate mood periods interspersed. In the manic phase children or adolescents talk incessantly, sleep little, and show poor judgment. Many adolescents who experience bipolar disorder continue to experience it throughout their lives. Clinicians usually have a more difficult time diagnosing manic-depressive disorder than depression. It is still rarely expected that a child or adolescent actually is experiencing a manic-depressive disorder. More typically, depression is suspected. To recognize and diagnose manic-depressive disorder, clinicians are aware of or observe the child in a manic phase as well as in a depressive phase. Thus, they must observe the child or have access to observational material on multiple occasions. Furthermore, clinicians may have a difficult time differentiating between the enthusiasms of childhood and a manic phase, or between a high of adolescence, which may be confused with or confounded with substance abuse, and a manic phase.

Major depression in children and adolescents is often treated by antidepressant medication, such as fluoxetine, in consultation with a medical and psychiatric evaluation. Individual, family, and group therapies, and cognitive-behavioral treatment programs are useful. Manic-depressive disorder is treated with medication provided in consultation with medical and psychiatric evaluations. Cognitive-behavioral treatment programs supplement such treatments. Psychoeducational interventions help improve the understanding and acceptance of the disorder by the youngster and his or her family.

Aggression and Conduct Disorder

Social workers in mental health settings often receive reports from parents and teachers about children and adolescents who "act out." Such children have externalizing behavior problems characterized by aggression, attention problems, delinquency, destructiveness, hyperactivity, impulsivity, and noncompliance (Achenbach & Edelbrock, 1978).

Social workers assess what is normal behavior and what appears to be a mental disorder. They determine how much aggression is normative for an individual youngster who lives in a family, resides in a neighborhood, and attends a school. Virtually all young children occasionally engage in behavior that is the opposite of what is requested or expected of them. However, when such behavior becomes extreme or frequent, it may turn into oppositional defiant disorder (ODD), which is diagnosed when the youngster behaves in a hostile and defiant manner for at least 6 months. If CD is present, ODD, which can start in preschoolers, is not diagnosed.

Moreover, most adolescents engage in some behavior that is unacceptable, antisocial, or illegal. If such behavior becomes part of the youngster's character or personality structure and is a dominant force in their lives, they may ultimately develop a criminal career and antisocial personality disorder in adulthood.

School-age youngsters who act out their feelings or impulses toward others in extensive destructive activity for a period of 6 months or longer manifest CD, which is a disruptive behavior disorder. Children with CD violate both the basic rights of others and society's rules and expectations. As they move into adolescence, their infractions usually become more serious and include aggression, fire setting, lying, theft, truancy, and vandalism. For most children with CD, patterns of conduct problems and antisocial behavior do not persist throughout life. Risk factors for the development of CD include a fussy temperament; inconsistent rules and harsh discipline; lack of guidance and supervision; frequent change of caregivers; poverty; maltreatment; and a delinquent peer group. Up to 10 percent of children and adolescents are estimated to have CD.

Two pathways exist to CD (Hinshaw, Lahey, & Hart, 1993). The least prevalent pathway, which has the most unfavorable long-term prognosis, is characterized by the onset of conduct problems in early childhood, for example, in preschool. Children in the early-starter pathway commit more serious offenses, for example, violent offenses. Boys are more likely than girls to enter the early-starter pathway.

The more prevalent pathway, which has a more favorable long-term prognosis, is characterized by the onset of conduct problems in adolescence. Children in the late-starter pathway commit less serious offenses, for example, property offenses. Girls with conduct problems, who are more likely to enter the late-starter pathway (McGee, Feehan, Williams, & Anderson, 1992), are at risk for teen parenthood. As parents they are at risk of having an unresponsive parenting style with their own children, who in turn are more at risk for having early developmental lags and developing significant externalizing behavior problems (Serbin, Peters, McAffer, & Schwartzman, 1991).

Treatments for CD include parent training in handling the behavior of the child or adolescent; family therapy; problem solving, anger control, and social skills training for children or adolescents; community residential programs for adolescents and community-based services that treat the child as a member of family and community systems; and school treatments (McMahon & Wells, 1989). Social workers help youngsters develop constructive, intermediate, and assertive forms of social behavior and help them avoid the destructive extremes of aggression and violence, and passive and nonassertive social behavior. Some social workers use nondirective play therapy with persistently aggressive and defiant young children (Carroll, 1995). They encourage parents of adolescents with CD to attend support groups for mutual exchange of information, advice, and ideas.

Treating CD successfully is very difficult. Family treatment is marked by a high rate of sporadic participation and premature dropout (Prinz & Miller, 1994). Those children and families who leave treatment early are likely to experience severe CD and delinquent behaviors, high levels of stress in a mother's life, and poverty (Kazdin, 1990).

Attention Deficit Hyperactivity Disorder

Children vary in regard to their activity level and degree of organization. School-age children are expected to sit quietly and attend to their surroundings. However, some children are unable to sit still, focus attention, take turns, and keep quiet; they are impulsive, easily distracted, bother others, interfere with learning, and disrupt attentional processes in the classroom. In the past, children with such difficulties have been labeled as having hyperactivity, hyperkinesis, minimal brain dysfunction, and attention deficit disorder, and currently are labeled as having ADHD.

Current views suggest the existence of three types of ADHD. Children with the inattentive type of ADHD have short attention spans; are easily distracted; do not pay attention to details; make many mistakes; fail to finish things; are forgetful; do not seem to listen; and are disorganized. Children with the hyperactive-impulsive type of ADHD fidget and squirm, do not stay seated or play quietly, run or climb a great deal or do so when they are not supposed to, talk excessively or inappropriately, blurt out answers before questions are completed, do not take turns, and interrupt others. The most common type of ADHD—combined ADHD—is a combination of the inattentive and hyperactive-impulsive types. Diagnosis of one of the three types is made when symptoms began before the age of 7 and lasted 6 or more months.

Such a typology of ADHD is consistent with the work of Halperin, Newcorn, Sharma, Healey, Wolf, Pascualvaca, and Schwartz (1990), who distinguished between those ADHD children characterized by inattention and learning problems and those characterized by conduct problems. Indeed, attention consists of one dimension of arousal or alertness and another dimension of impulsivity (Mesalum, 1990).

ADHD is fairly common; up to about 5 percent of children have it (Barkley, 1990). About three times as many boys have ADHD as do girls. Being active is insufficient for children to be considered truly to have ADHD. Children with such disorders also tend to act in a relatively disorganized manner. Furthermore, the characteristic patterns must be present in more than one setting to be considered to have ADHD. Children and adolescents with ADHD are at risk for ODD or CD, anxiety disorder, depression, difficulties in speech and language development, learning disabilities, and adult personality and substance abuse disorders (Shelton & Barkley, 1994).

According to Barkley (1989), six approaches have proven efficacy with children with ADHD: (1) medication (stimulants and antidepressants), (2) behavior therapy in the clinic or laboratory, (3) parent training, (4) training teachers in classroom behavior management, (5) cognitive-behavior therapy, and (6) combined treatments. Many children are assessed by physicians and receive medication for ADHD. Indications for the use of medication are persistent and severe inattention, impulsivity, and hyperactivity, which cause functional impairment at school and usually also at home and with peers (Dulcan, 1986). Stimulants increase activity in the parts of the brain that are underactive in children and adolescents with ADHD. Antidepressants and tranquillizers are also sometimes helpful. Side effects of medications include weight loss, decrease in appetite, and temporary slowing in growth among some children.

Behavioral methods are implemented at home by family members or at school in special classrooms. Such methods include teaching parents and teachers how to manage and change the behavior of children or adolescents with ADHD, such as rewarding good behavior; a daily report card to link home and school, along with parental rewards for good school performance and behavior; summer and Saturday programs; special classrooms that use intensive behavior modification; and classroom aides who are specially trained in working with youngsters with ADHD.

Cognitive Deficits and Head Injuries

The physical causes of cognitive deficits of children and adolescents include illness, disease, and accident. Cognitive and language development are dependent, in part, on brain development. Head injuries affect the brain and impede the cognitive and language development and functioning of the child or adolescent. Accidents among children and adolescents who participate in athletics, including bicycle riding and horseback riding, are a prime source of head injuries.

The psychosocial causes of cognitive deficits of children and adolescents include poverty, inadequate housing, and nonaccidental injury. Nonaccidental injuries refer to intentional injuries inflicted on children and adolescents. Medical experts examine the nature and cause of the injury. Child welfare authorities are mandated to protect the child from further maltreatment.

Global cognitive deficits, which include mild, moderate, severe, and profound levels of mental retardation, influence many aspects of functioning. Specific cognitive deficits occur in particular aspects of learning, for example, mathematics. Cognitive deficits of children and adolescents, including behavior problems, substance abuse, and other mental disorders, may be accompanied by other problems. Social workers reduce risk factors for cognitive deficits in children and help family members acquire the resources needed for improving the cognitive functioning of their children. Furthermore, they inaugurate or promote means of improving cognitive skill acquisition through instruction and the creation and maintenance of a stimulating and safe environment.

Cognitive skills are enhanced and cognitive deficits are remediated by social workers using a team approach with participation from school, health, and child welfare practitioners. Neurodevelopmental social workers provide clinical social services to children and adolescents with acute and chronic illnesses and their families. They promote culturally appropriate family-centered care of patients by identifying, interpreting, and reducing psychosocial factors contributing to physical and mental illness. They use skills in assessment, crisis intervention, children's protection, and bereavement support (Bacon, 1996). Other team members have specific expertise in the neuropsychological assessment of children and adolescents, and in psychopharmacology of children with cognitive deficits. For instance, pediatric neuropsychological evaluations encompass the cognitive areas of general intellect; visual, perceptual, and motor; language; attention; memory; executive functions; academic achievement; and behavior.

Eating Disorders

Given the relationship of eating to physical growth and development, eating disorders have the potential to have a major impact on the health and well-being of youngsters. Young people with eating disorders are afraid of gaining weight.

Children and adolescents who have eating disorders such as anorexia nervosa eat too little and are put at risk for starvation and even death. About 1 percent of adolescent girls and a small number of adolescent boys have anorexia nervosa (Barbosa-Saldivar & Van Itallie, 1979). Other youngsters with bulimia nervosa eat too much food at one time, putting their health at risk with becoming overweight. To prevent gaining weight, they get rid of the food they have eaten by taking enemas or laxatives, exercising incessantly, and vomiting. Estimates are that about 2 percent of youngsters have bulimia nervosa.

Disturbances and distortions in perceptions of body image underlie the development of eating disorders among children and adolescents. Often, they do not see themselves as others do and therefore do not necessarily recognize how thin they have become. Some young people with eating disorders have no bounds to their desire to be thin and believe they cannot be too thin. They are unable to tolerate the smallest amount of body fat, which they equate with "being fat."

Eating disorders develop within a family context and represent the youngster's desire to maintain a degree of control about eating and food intake. A cultural component to eating disorders exists as well, as seen in the prevalence of such disorders in Western countries where an abundant food supply exists and where the cultural ideal of beauty is thinness. Many persons with eating disorders are adolescent females who are concerned about their appearance and body image. Adolescents often attempt to hide eating disorders from family and friends by wearing baggy clothing, which makes it difficult to detect their weight loss.

Eating disorders are related to depression in children and adolescents. A common symptom of depression is reflected in eating much less or much more than is usual for the individual. Nevertheless, eating disorders, although they may appear as a symptom of depression, also represent a particular class of disorders in their own right.

Schizophrenia and Autism in Children

Childhood-onset schizophrenia is a severe version of one of the most serious mental disorders. Unfortunately, children with schizophrenia usually have a poor premorbid adjustment, high rates of insidious onset, and poor outcomes (Asarnow, 1994). Symptoms exhibited by very young children with schizophrenia include lethargy (newborns), perseveration (3 to 12 months), and hypotonia and phobias (2 years) (Bryan, 1993).

The ability of children with schizophrenia to experience pleasure is less than that of other children. Youngsters who have schizophrenia have difficulties in contact with reality as observed by their delusions or disordered thoughts and hallucinations; they sense things that objectively do not exist. Social workers distinguish between healthy children who have imaginary playmates and youngsters with schizophrenia and related disorders who hear and see things or people. While schizophrenia is rare in childhood, about 3 out of every 1,000 adolescents has it. Many children with schizophrenia also have other mental disorders, including CD, ODD, depression, or dysthymic disorder (Russell, Bott, & Sammons, 1989). Psychotropic medication is prescribed for children and adolescents with schizophrenia.

Autism or autism spectrum disorder appears during infancy. Such children show little awareness of others and have major problems in interpersonal interaction and communication. Their behavior appears strange, inappropriate, and repetitive, including head banging, rocking, and spinning things. Estimates are that 1 out of 1,000 children have autism spectrum disorder. Autism is treated by behavior therapy.

Substance Abuse

Adolescent substance abuse is a major social problem. Moreover, many adolescents with substance abuse disorders also have other mental disorders. Adolescent substance abuse is associated with pregnancy, sexually transmitted diseases, school difficulties, automobile accidents, CD, violence, and juvenile delinquency. Substance abuse during adolescence is sometimes a precursor to adult substance abuse with attendant health, mental health, occupational, and social difficulties.

Environmental factors play an important role in adolescent substance abuse. The greater is the presence of substance abuse in adolescents' school, family, and community, the greater is the likelihood that they will become involved in substance abuse. However, at times family members do not realize that their child is abusing drugs.

Adolescents with substance abuse disorders participate in the purchase and sale of a wide range of licit and illicit substances, including alcohol, nicotine, caffeine, marijuana, cocaine, and heroin. Many adolescent substance abusers are polydrug abusers. Use of licit substances, including alcohol and nicotine, require attaining the age of majority before adolescents are allowed to purchase and use them legally. Illicit substances, by definition, carry criminal penalties associated with their production, sale, purchase, and use.

Substance abuse is a socially learned phenomenon. Youngsters who are exposed to models who participate in substance abuse are tempted to engage in such activity. Adolescents frequently perceive a subset of drugs, namely hardcore drugs such as heroin, as comprising substance abuse. Many may underestimate the risks associated with drug abuse and may overestimate their ability to stop taking drugs once they have begun to use or abuse them.

Motivational factors also play a role in substance abuse and recovery. Youngsters abuse drugs as an escape from personal and social problems, as a novel experience, or at the urging of friends. Recovery from substance abuse requires motivation to return to a drug-free state.

Social class and culture play significant roles in substance abuse. Norms about the use of various substances, such as alcohol, vary widely among ethnic groups. Differential rates of alcoholism among various ethnic groups may have a genetic component.

Drug abuse prevention programs, which have had varying rates of success, focus on education about the nature and effects of harmful substances. An interaction exists between the developmental and personality characteristics of adolescents, including thrill seeking and risk taking, with the prevention program itself. Prevention programs that emphasize antidrug messages have been criticized for providing information and temptation to those youngsters who seek to break society's rules. Adolescents respond differentially to prevention programs. Some youth respond to such programs by refraining from substance abuse whereas others become involved with substance abuse. Prevention efforts begun in middle school potentially avert involvement with drugs during adolescence. Effective programs should be constructive in nature and give young people hope. Youngsters whose values are that drug abuse is unacceptable tend to be more resilient in coping with an environment which promotes drug use.

Adolescent substance abuse is treated in mental health and substance abuse inpatient hospitals and outpatient clinics. Youngsters who are addicted to drugs take many years to overcome their addictions as they spiral through treatment programs. Treatment of adolescent substance abuse encompasses social skills training. Assertiveness skills are useful in resisting drug use. Peer groups influence substance abuse such that in high school society one adolescent peer group that is least involved in school activities and most negatively labeled has the most favorable attitudes toward alcohol and drug use, the lowest levels of perceived harm from substance use, and the highest levels of substance abuse (Downs & Rose, 1991). Youngsters who abuse drugs in such a peer group are faced with a culture that supports substance abuse. Social workers help many youngsters in such peer groups.

Mental Health Services

Children and adolescents with mental health problems are present in schools, foster homes, group homes, juvenile detention facilities, and substance abuse treatment agencies (Hoagwood & Koretz, 1996). The child mental health services system consists of mental health and substance abuse, general health, education, child welfare, and juvenile justice sectors, which have inpatient, residential, partial, outpatient, emergency, and preventive components (Burns, Angold, & Costello, 1992). The mental health and substance abuse sector includes psychiatric hospital, residential treatment center, group home, day treatment, case management, mobile crisis team, and drug abuse and suicide prevention programs. The general health sector includes general hospital, day treatment, psychotropic medication, hospital emergency room, anticipatory guidance programs, and health promotion curriculum. The education sector encompasses residential treatment centers, partial hospitalization, counseling, special classes, social skills development, health curriculum, conflict–resolution programs, and problem-solving programs. The child welfare sector provides therapeutic foster care, respite care, in-home treatment, case management, family preservation, family support programs, and in-home aides. The juvenile justice sector includes detention centers, group homes, probation counseling, conflict–resolution programs, peer group mediation, and gang prevention. A team approach is used to provide individualized and culturally sensitive care to children and adolescents and their family in or near their home.

School Mental Health

Many mental health problems have their roots in or are exacerbated by children's school experiences (Maughan, 1988). Poor achievement motivation, low aspirations and expectations for educational accomplishment, inadequate school performance, and dropping out of school are risk factors for conduct problems, depression, substance abuse, teenage pregnancy, and suicide (Elliott, Huizinga, & Menard, 1989). School systems provide the most efficient and systematic means of promoting the health and well-being of children and adolescents (Weissberg, Caplan, & Harwood, 1991).

Children and adolescents with mental health problems generally attend school. Youngsters with mental health problems who do not attend school include children who demonstrate school refusal, are truant, and drop out of school. Children and adolescents with mental health problems, including psychosis, ADHD, ODD, and CD, often experience school problems, including social difficulties pertaining to getting along with others and academic difficulties referring to difficulties in learning material.

Learning disorders affect the ability of young people to receive or express information. Problems with attention, coordination, spoken and written language, and self-control interfere with learning to read, write, and do math. About 5 percent of public schoolchildren are identified as having a learning disorder. Most youngsters with mental health problems attend the same schools as other youngsters. However, some young people attend special schools that are part of a residential treatment facility or a hospital setting for children with emotional disturbances or other mental health problems.

Youngsters in special education programs include those with mental retardation and other developmental disabilities that require major instructional accommodations, and those with severe emotional and behavioral problems that make it difficult for them to get along with others in a regular classroom setting. Children and adolescents who are placed in special education classrooms consisting entirely of youngsters with difficulties have less opportunities for social interaction with nondisabled youngsters.

More children receive mental health services in schools than in mental health settings (Zahner, Pawelkiewicz, DeFrancesco, & Adnopoz, 1992). The West Australian Child Health Survey noted a relationship among parental disciplinary style, school staffing resources, and school environment with child mental health problems (Zubrick et al., 1995). Recommendations of the survey included finding ways to raise the level of parental involvement and support of the schools; increasing support of students, parents, and teachers; and alleviating extreme poverty in the community.

Family Mental Health

The mental health of children and adolescents occurs within a family context. Many mental health problems, such as anxiety, depression, and CD, occur within families (Kazdin, 1991). Social workers assess to what extent mental disorders are prevalent within a family, to what extent they are inherited genetically or transmitted psychosocially from one generation to another, and to what extent the family dynamics are conducive to mental health.

Family difficulties, including violence, separation and divorce, and child maltreatment influence the social and emotional development of young people and are related to their mental health (Goodyear, 1990). Attachment theory is a component of a developmental perspective furthering the understanding of mental disorders of children and adolescents (del Carmen & Huffman, 1996). Children of parents who are unresponsive, violent, unpredictable, neglectful, or punitively rejective are at risk of developing psychopathology (Crittenden, 1995). Experiences of father violence during childhood predict the development of psychiatric symptomatology in women (Downs & Miller, 1998). Moreover, mental health problems also contribute to family difficulties because families have a difficult time coping with mental health problems of children (Edwards, Schulz, & Long, 1995).

Social workers involve family members in enhancing the mental health of children and adolescents. The parents of only children with mental health problems are usually more willing to seek help than parents of two children (Richards & Goodman, 1996). Treatment of children of divorce should include both the custodial and noncustodial parent (Campbell, 1992). Receiving mental health services requires a parent or guardian who is willing and able to recognize a mental health problem and seek services for the youngster. Families vary in their knowledge of mental disorders, as well as their use of mental health care and services. They also vary in their ability to access services, including transportation and the financial means to pay for services, such as insurance.

Racial minority children and adolescents, including African Americans and Native Americans, have greater difficulty attaining adequate mental health care than do majority children and adolescents. A telephone engagement intervention has demonstrated efficacy for increasing initial attendance for child mental health treatment by inner-city families (McKay, McCadam, & Gonzales, 1996). Strategic Structural Systems Engagement, a planned and purposeful way of joining and diagnosing a family from the initial contact to the first therapy interview, has been shown to be effective in bringing hard-to-reach Hispanic families into treatment (Santisteban, Szapocznik, Perez-Vidal, Kurtines, Murray, & LaPerriere, 1996).

Sexual Abuse

Mental health problems within families are assessed and treated within child and family service agencies. The child protective and juvenile service units of child and family welfare agencies, which are concerned with child maltreatment and with the special difficulties of adolescents in need of supervision or shelter, also deal with child and adolescent mental health issues. Sexual abuse is sometimes accompanied by other forms of child maltreatment, including physical or emotional abuse or neglect, which makes treatment more complex. Indeed, the most difficult cases of child abuse include those in which a combination of physical, emotional, and sexual abuse are repeated over many years by members of several generations of the child's family (McFarland & Lockerbie, 1994).

Sexual abuse is a serious child and family welfare problem that often has serious mental health consequences. Many cases of dissociative identity disorder appear to follow sexual abuse. Sexual abuse, which often appears as overt, inappropriate sexual behavior in young children, is treated in mental health agencies. Sexual abuse puts adolescents at risk of sexually acting out and makes them vulnerable to pregnancy and sexually transmitted diseases, which are the main risks of teenage sexual behavior. One out of four sexually active adolescents are infected with a sexually transmitted disease prior to high school graduation (Pruitt,

1999). About 1 million teenagers become pregnant each year, with almost half giving birth. Furthermore, many adolescents report a high prevalence of engaging in HIV-related risk behaviors (DiClemente, Stewart, Johnson, & Pack, 1996). Long-term consequences of sexual abuse include difficulty in forming constructive adult sexual relationships.

Moreover, many juvenile sex offenders are victims of sexual abuse. Treatment of adolescent sex offenders is usually confrontational and punitive. A survey of practitioners by Muster (1992) suggested that treatment ought to be flexible and not limited to a confrontational style.

Children who are sexually abused, like other children, form ideas about the reasons for entering treatment such as that therapy is an indication of illness, is punishment, is an accusation, and is another form of abuse (Haugaard, 1992).

Community Mental Health

Community and public health factors, such as crime and stress, are related to the development and manifestation of mental disorders. Children and adolescents live in communities that vary in regard to their levels of anger, hostility, and violence. Children who are exposed to high levels of community violence are susceptible to develop a variety of mental disorders, including anxiety disorders.

In conducting assessments of children and adolescents, social workers consider five broad questions pertaining to mental health in their communities. One, to what extent are mental health disorders of children and adolescents manifested within the community? Two, how do community services and agencies prevent and treat mental disorders of children and adolescents? Three, how does community functioning affect the mental well-being of young people? Four, how do community mental health agencies affect or interact with the functioning of other community agencies with which the youngster is involved? Five, how successfully are mental disorders treated within the community?

Most mental disorders of children and adolescents can be treated or managed within supportive communities. Community treatment of mental disorders is ideal for most youngsters because it allows them access to community institutions, family living, schooling, and recreation. Children and adolescents are involved in community recreational settings, including YWCA, YMCA, YWHA, YMHA, scouting, and Boys and Girls Clubs. They participate in sports teams, which allows them to develop their social competence. For some young persons, community participation encompasses being involved with law enforcement officials and child welfare authorities.

Many settings, including hospitals, clinics, employee assistance centers, family service agencies, and child guidance and evaluation clinics, promote the mental health of children and adolescents. Behavioral health centers provide mental health assessments, referrals, and admission 24 hours a day. They also provide child and adolescent services. In providing specialized, age-appropriate care, they have separate inpatient acute units, including a child acute unit and an inpatient acute adolescent unit. They also provide the following services: partial hospital programs; child residential programs; adolescent residential programs; adolescent intensive outpatient programs treating substance abuse; aftercare programs; support groups; and occupational therapy. Behavioral health centers offer a continuum of care emphasizing mental health and substance abuse issues for children and adolescents.

Conclusion

Mental disorders of children and adolescents either appear early in life or represent a childhood version of disorders that usually appear in adulthood. Psychopathology has a developmental context. Emotional development begins in infancy. Young children normatively experience and have little control over the vicissitudes of their emotions. Sadness, which is a normal emotion, is a matter of concern when it becomes the predominant emotion experienced by children or adolescents. Social workers realize that children and adolescents experience depression and know that it is treatable. Furthermore, some youngsters experience bipolar disorder involving manic and depressive states. Children with disruptive behavior disorders are likely to experience difficulties concerning learning, anxiety, depression, hyperactivity, and peer relationships.

Biological and environmental factors place children and adolescents at risk for developing mental disorders. Biological factors include damage, such as a head injury, to the central nervous system. Environmental factors include exposure to toxins such as lead; violence; stress; and loss of significant others.

Cognitive functioning has taken on increased significance in understanding and treating children and adolescents with mental disorders. Cognitive deficits are discovered in and have an important influence on the social functioning of young people in school, family, and community settings.

Community factors influence the mental health of children and adolescents. Young people display varying levels and types of mental disorders within community settings. To help youngsters with mental disorders function in community settings, social workers engage in assessment, prevention, and treatment activities. Interviewing children and their family members is an important professional activity for promoting mental health. A psychosocial approach is useful in providing an allied and supportive intervention for the treatment of mental disorders experienced by young persons.

Some serious difficulties, such as sexual abuse, which are not mental disorders per se, are detected by social workers. The focus of the following chapter is on child welfare.

10 Methods and Practices in Child Welfare Agencies

Child welfare is a complex area of social work intended to protect children and adolescents and provide social services for them. It has gradually evolved from nineteenth-century practices, including placing poor children in almshouses and attempting to solve the problems of children and communities by means such as sending children west on orphan trains.

Over the years, beliefs, values, and practices about child welfare have changed. Debate about the appropriate degree of governmental involvement in the lives of families is ongoing. Values have swung between an emphasis on the importance of families to a primary concern about the safety of the child. Current services, which are based on the Adoption and Safe Family Act of 1997 (P.L. 105-89), are child-centered and family focused.

This chapter begins by clarifying the primary child welfare system and some of the broad issues related to service delivery and the court system decision-making process. Essential theories are identified and discussed. Then a case is used to illustrate the procedures and practices. Options for continued care of children are considered, including returning the child to the parents, adoption, and long-term foster care. Child welfare services are usually provided under the auspices of a social welfare agency, often referred to as the child welfare agency, the Office of Community Services, or the Department of Children and Families.

In the past, child welfare agencies provided a broad range of services, which were primarily aimed at prevention, through supportive services to families. As needs grew, agencies were forced to reduce preventive services and add more protective activities. Presently, entry to these services is basically by way of reports of abuse or neglect of children.

Currently, the services of child welfare agencies can generally be classified as supportive, supplemental, or as a substitute for caregiving by parents (Costin et al., 1991). Services are designed to support and reinforce the parents' ability to meet the needs of the child by providing casework in the home, protective services, and services to unmarried parents. Supplemental services for parents, which vary among communities, have often included homemaker services and day-care services. Services to substitute for parental care are fostering care, group care services, and adoption services. In most communities, the largest number of children served are in foster care programs.

Social workers in child welfare agencies provide a myriad of programmatic services. They serve on the crisis intervention hot line, investigate reports of neglect and abuse, work with families and children, arrange for foster care and adoptions, and serve in training units or other special services.

Risk Assessments

The definition of child abuse has been, and continues to be, debated. For instance, many people do not consider hitting or spanking to be abuse of the child. They believe abuse occurs only when visible signs or marks have been left on the child's body. Others argue that any type of physical or emotional punishment administered by an adult is abuse. Definitions of abuse are also based on differing cultures and segments of society. Mather and Lager (2000, p. 124) define abuse as follows:

> *Physical Abuse:* Physical acts by parents or caretakers that caused physical injury to the child or might have created this scenario.
>
> *Emotional Maltreatment:* Acts such as berating, ignoring, abandoning or isolating a child which creates a situation of impairment for the child.

These definitions impact services, programs, and practices in a given community. Some agreement about the parameters of the definitions must be determined at the local level, at which subtle shifts in definition and practices may occur. A tragic event in a specific case may tip the balance, either in the favor of the unity of the family or the protection of the child. For example, a child who has been reported to the child protection unit, but not yet investigated, is seriously injured or killed by a parent. The view for many in the community shifts rapidly from one that supports family unity to one of concern for child protection. "The origins of such a community judgment lie in a mix of professional expertise and scientific knowledge, on the one hand, and culture and local standards, on the other" (Garbarino, Stott, & faculty of the Erickson Institute, 1992, p. 110).

Abuse does not occur only in the home; it may also happen in the community. Examples of abuse are mistreatment in a residential setting, sexual assault by a teacher in school, and neglect of an infant in a nursery school. Society has a responsibility to protect children from abuse in all situations.

Neglect, which is another form of maltreatment, is seen as an act of omission rather than commission. Often children who are being neglected may not be visible to the public and are more likely to be reported by other institutions, such as hospitals, schools, and health clinics. For example, if a child has accidently been burned and requires contact with a physician on some regular basis, and appointments are consistently not kept, child protection is notified. This is identified as medical neglect and requires intervention of a social worker.

Several types of neglect are identified in society (Child Welfare League of America, 1991). Physical neglect involves failure to protect children from physical risk. Problems in hygiene, housing conditions, lack of health care or treatment of illness may be viewed as neglect and require intervention. Environmental risks may be identified either in the home or in the area where the child is allowed to play. Another form of neglect is emotional neglect. A common example of this is the failure to thrive (FTT) infant. In these cases, neglect may involve the child not being fed or stimulated by the environment in which he or she lives. FTT is usually identified by physical, emotional, and developmental signs. The FTT baby may not gain weight but rather lose weight. The infant or young child may not be interested in the world around him or her and may not want contact with others. Other forms of neglect identified are educational, child care, and lack of supervision.

Helping professionals are required by law to report suspected abuse and neglect cases to the child welfare office. Physicians, teachers, social workers, psychiatrists, psychologists, and others are mandated to report if they even suspect that abuse may be occurring. It is not required that they provide proof, only that abuse or neglect is suspected.

After a report of neglect or abuse, a decision about the need and type of service required is based on a risk assessment. An investigation is done to substantiate the validity of the report and the need for service. An essential concern of the protective service worker is child safety. To determine the degree of danger, a risk assessment is performed as thoroughly and quickly as possible to protect the well-being of the child and family. Many instruments for assessment have been developed, but none of them are perfect (Cohn, 2000). A major criticism is that they often do not take into account the multicultural, gender, or age issues as they relate to the child and family (Mather & Lager, 2000). Visual assessment is helpful in quickly gathering data, but is only a beginning for a much more thorough investigation. Children, parents, teachers, neighbors, and friends may be contacted in this process. Material is gathered about the family of origin that is especially relevant in abuse situations. Repetitive patterns of abusive behavior may be discovered. This material is important to help the worker determine details about interventions that would be helpful in working with this family.

Many areas of critical decision making must be used in risk assessment. A decision must be made regarding the immediate risk of danger to the child or adolescent. Services or actions may be necessary to protect the child during the investigation. The social worker considers whether it is necessary to remove the child from the home for his or her safety. Finally, the social worker determines whether a case plan can be developed to address the fact that the child is at risk (Pecora, Whittaker, Maluccio, Barth, & Plotnick, 1992).

Decision Making

Making decisions about the safety of the child is a tremendous responsibility for the protective service worker and is hampered and complicated by the vagueness and variety of definitions of the concepts applied to these situations. Concepts such as the best interest of the child, reasonable effort, and child well-being are identified as criteria for making decisions. To provide meaning to such terms and determine their existence, child well-being scales have been developed but often are not used because of the lack of definition or of a model to guide their development (Seaberg, 1988).

Development and use of a scale would assist practitioners in making the weighty decisions required in protective services regarding the need for protection and the best means of accomplishing this. A number of reasons explain why this type of scale could not be successfully used across the United States. First, parents will ultimately be held accountable for the well-being of their children. Second, the current standards are intuitive and differ in many communities, neighborhoods, regions, religions, cultures, and ethnic groups. Third, standards of child well-being change over time. Fourth, standards are escalating because of the recognition of children's rights. Finally, because society is based on a governmental standard of the family's right to privacy, the criteria can only be set at a minimal level of expectations.

Seaberg (1988) suggests that the development of criteria of child well-being to be used across the United States is very remote. Some regional offices of child welfare develop their own checklist and use it as one of the tools in decision making regarding the well-being of the child. Intuition continues to play a major role in the determination of well-being.

After a determination has been made about the safety of the child, several possible consequences can occur. The report may be unsubstantiated, and it is decided that no services are needed. Or it may be concluded that no immediate risk to the child is evident, but the family needs help and is willing to accept services. The nature of the help provided at this time could be family services or family preservation services. Family service involves direct work with the family, attempting to help members learn new skills and new ways of resolving problems. Generally these services are short term, 6 to 12 weeks, and involve weekly visits to the home. The help given by the social worker may be a referral to other services in the community. This is a voluntary relationship and the client or worker can terminate the relationship at any time.

A case involving family services was the Miller family, who had been reported to the Child Welfare Agency because the 10-year-old boy, Melvin, was out of control. He stayed out late or sneaked out after the parents were asleep. He had run away from home on several occasions and was frequently absent from school. Mr. Miller worked 10 to 12 hours a day and was often not at home to discipline him. When Mr. Miller was at home he attempted to correct Melvin's behavior with physical punishment. Mrs. Miller suggested that sometimes he "got too rough" with Melvin and hurt him. She stated that she did not know what to do. Sometimes Mrs. Miller felt she was "too easy" on Melvin, "but he didn't do what she said anyhow."

She stated that they had two girls younger than Melvin, but she did not have any trouble with them. Mrs. Miller said that she really needed help and it would be "all right" if the worker could help. A time was set to meet with Mrs. Miller once a week. The major focus for these sessions was to teach Mrs. Miller some techniques for disciplining Melvin. These sessions continued for 13 weeks and were terminated when Mrs. Miller was feeling more competent in disciplining Melvin and when things were going better. Mrs. Miller said she did not think they needed any further help at this time.

Family preservation is a short-term intensive service to children at risk and their families. Originally, the service was to be provided for 4 to 6 weeks. Often, the worker was in the home or with the family for 4 to 8 hours a day. This method provided opportunities for teaching, modeling, and intervening in potentially destructive and explosive interactions in the family. Later, experimentation was done about the length of service and level of intensity. Reported research outcomes have been mixed about the success of these programs. Families receiving these services and social workers providing these services, however, have attested to the positive support that is available (Mather & Lager, 2000).

The White family had been referred many times because neighbors suspected that the children were being abused. The family consisted of Mrs. White, a 17-year-old son, Jon, an

11-year-old girl, Maria, and 5-year-old George. Mr. White was not in contact with any of the family except the oldest boy. The children all had different fathers and the location of Maria's and George's fathers were unknown. The family had been reported to the Child Welfare Agency numerous times. These reports of abuse had been unsubstantiated. However, it had been clear that the family was in need of service. Mrs. White had refused help from family service workers.

This time, a call from the police department required child welfare to become involved, again. Maria had been caught leaving the grocery store with a package of meat that had not been paid for. In exploring this matter, it was found that Mrs. White had told Maria that there was nothing in the house to eat; they did not have any meat for dinner. Maria was attempting to supply the meat that Mrs. White had said was needed.

This incident precipitated family preservation services for this family. Mrs. White needed help arriving at a technique for disciplining George that did not involve using a belt or a coat hanger. Maria appeared to be used as the delinquent to carry out Mrs. White's delinquent thoughts and ideas. Mrs. White had a history of disappearing for several days at a time, drinking, using marijuana, and fighting with the neighbors.

The plan was for the social worker to be in the home in the afternoon when George and Maria returned from school, which seemed to be the time when many problems began. The older boy did not seem to be a part of these difficulties. He was in and out of the house, sometimes living with his father. This plan would allow the social worker's presence to model behavior for the family as well as directly intervening in the interaction among the family members. She also could teach Mrs. White and the children new, more positive ways to communicate and interact. This plan was expected to make changes in this family to create a more peaceful environment both for the family and for the neighborhood in which they lived.

Another possible decision is to remove the child from the home to provide protection. Children who are at great risk may be removed immediately with the permission of the court or a petition for removal may be made to the court to remove them as soon as possible. If it is decided that immediate removal of one or more children is necessary, a court process is required. If a child is removed, a court hearing is held, and if it is determined that he or she is in need of care, the child becomes a ward of the court. Reports are made and hearings are held by a judge to monitor progress on a regular basis. Specific services may be ordered, and determination of the ongoing disposition of the case is made by the court.

An exception to the identified court process occurs if the child of concern is Native American. The purpose of the Indian Child Welfare Act of 1978 was to protect the rights of Native American children from disproportional numbers being placed in foster or adoptive homes. If the child is living on the reservation, the case is handled through the tribal system of authority. If not living on the reservation, children of Native American descent may request to have their case heard by tribal council through their parents, guardians, or the court.

Working with Involuntary Clients

Families of children who are being investigated and possibly removed are involuntary clients who usually are angry, hostile, and often uncooperative. Involuntary clients feel forced or pressured to seek and accept contact with helping professionals (Rooney, 1992). Often both the involuntary client and social worker are reluctant to begin work together; this is a relationship that may be very difficult to form and to use in a productive manner. Special skills and techniques are required to develop a working relationship with many of these families.

To begin contact with a mother whose child has just been removed requires the social worker to make advance preparations. The social worker can expect that the mother will be very upset, sad, and hostile toward a representative of an agency who has taken her child from the home. Rooney (1992) describes several steps to be taken in this process of "getting ready." First, reviewing all available case information is necessary. The family may have been in long-term contact with the agency, perhaps in another program, and a great deal of information may be available before contact is made by the current worker.

The social worker needs to be able to identify the legal requirements for service. For instance, certain conditions must be changed or improved for the child to be returned to the birth family. It is important that the social worker is very clear about these requirements, so that he or she can communicate these requirements to the family. If the child has been taken into custody because of neglect, the parent(s) need to know what must be done to be reunified with the child. For example, the teacher had reported that June had rashes all over her arms and legs and was continually scratching. As a result, sores had developed in some areas. Some conditions for the child to be returned home might be that the parents dispose of trash that has accumulated in the house, fix broken windows, and cut the weeds surrounding the house. These requirements must be viewed by the worker as nonnegotiable for the child's return.

Agency and institutional policies also may not be negotiable. On contact with the family, the social worker must clearly have in mind applicable policies. The job description for the social worker may identify how frequently contacts must be made with the family or what priorities may be assigned to specific requirements or roles.

The rights of the involuntary client must be explained to him or her. Although clients have been required to meet certain standards, they still have the right not to comply. This area needs to be thoroughly discussed with the parent(s) so that informed decisions can be made. After discussing both sides of the issues and looking at other possible options, the client can still choose to accept legal consequences if service is refused. The parents need to be aware of this as a choice.

This is an important step in letting the parents know that they are in charge of their lives and have power and control of what happens to them and their children. It may also be helpful in overcoming resistance. A client may at first choose not to comply and after experiencing the legal consequences may make a choice to use the services provided. Not only is it important for the parents to know their rights, but free choices also need to be identified. Mandated clients can also choose their attitude about accepting services. They may decide to make the best of the situation and simultaneously address some of their own concerns, or they may choose to comply passively or not at all.

Another step that is helpful in working with involuntary clients is to identify negotiable options. The social worker needs to be aware of discretion available in the interpretation of mandates and policies. They consider how a condition can be met in a variety of ways that would be acceptable in meeting legal requirements.

Often, examining one's own attitudes, some of which may interfere with providing services, is important for the social worker. This may occur with practitioners who have had a great deal of experience and an inclination to prejudge the client and the situation. "Avoiding prejudgment is important to make a legitimate offer of service that is not sabotaged from the outset" (Rooney, 1992, p. 153). Skepticism about the expected outcome is not helpful. The law requires that the social worker make a reasonable effort for the family to stay together. This can only be done when the practitioner approaches his or her task with hope and optimism about outcomes.

A final step in preparation for the initial session may be arranging for the contact. It must be noted that this option is often not available to the worker doing the investigative work in a case where danger of harm to the child is imminent. In this case, not allowing the family to prepare may be more helpful in gaining information.

Often, the setting for the initial contact is not ideal. The television may be on, and neighbors and children may be coming in and out of the home, creating a distraction from the content of the session. The client may be intimidated if the session is held in the social worker's office. Generally, the practitioner is unable to modify the environment and needs to be aware of the significance of the arrangements and what they communicate to the client. This allows the worker to be prepared to deal with these issues in the most sensitive and helpful manner.

Letting the mother know of her possible choices is important in the first sessions. The choices need to be constrained, that is, boundaries need to be placed around the possible choices, allowing her to choose within these limits. For example, the mother of June, the neglected child described previously, may decide that instead of cleaning up the weeds and replacing windows in the house, she will find a new place to live that is in better condition. This is a choice that would be acceptable to the worker as a first step. In contrast, a decision to pick up June from her foster home and move to another state would not be an acceptable option.

The social worker needs to emphasize that the choice of participation with the agency and court is the best way to reunite the family. A discussion of the benefits and costs related to any option selected by the client is useful in making a decision about the course of action. Rooney (1992) suggests that confrontation is most appropriate in working with involuntary clients as they decide about the potential consequences of their decisions.

The use of these suggested practices in working with involuntary clients is influenced by time, resources, and the discretionary powers available to the social worker in negotiating with the client. In child welfare, time is a primary concern because an assessment must be completed before the court hearing, which is expected to occur within a few days.

As the social worker continues to work with the parents, he or she must continue to act as a negotiator, mediator, advocate, and coach. However, authority may be used to reward and coerce the client into desired behaviors. Legitimate power is useful in giving help and enforcing and inducing compliance.

After work with the parents has been completed and the court has decided that the child can be reunited with the family, ending usually is approached with relief rather than the sometimes expected sadness and ambivalence that may occur in other settings. Important components of preparation for ending are reviewing problem reduction, task completion, steps in problem solving, and considering additional possible needs and potential future problems.

Another possible outcome at the time of ending is terminating parental rights and placing the child for adoption. A third possible ending is planning for the child to remain in foster care or kinship care, which reflects a change of the fundamental service goal for the child rather than an end of service provision per se. The primary goal is to provide a permanent home for the child. Long-term foster care developed because foster care drift had been a major problem in providing services for children. In earlier times, children in foster homes often were moved from home to home with many placements in a short period of time, creating a lack of permanence and continuity in their lives. Long-term foster care requires that the foster parents agree to keep the child until he or she reaches majority.

Some potential deficits of the foster child can be expected. Most of them have never experienced a continuity in relationships and have never learned psychologically healthy ways of connecting with others. Many have not resolved the grief of being separated from their birth parents. All this interferes with forming new attachments. Knowledge regarding these areas is important for the social worker to understand the behavior and specific needs of the child, to determine the need for referral for services, and to assist the foster parents or guardians with procedures and techniques for dealing with problem behaviors.

Attachment Theory

Child welfare practice requires a broad and diverse body of essential knowledge, including child development, family therapy, crisis theory, and methods of working with involuntary clients. In-depth information is required to assess child development at the time of the abuse or neglect report and in following the child's progression during the time that services are provided. The social worker must understand the dynamics of the relationships between family members, how these influence the functioning of the child, and means of intervention to help change the situation.

Crisis theory is required as suspected abuse or neglect is reported and investigations are completed. Usually, families and children are very upset, and many view intervention as a crisis in their lives. If children need to be removed, in almost every case this is perceived as a crisis both by the family and the children.

Theories and areas of knowledge that are critical to providing sound child welfare practice include working with involuntary clients, attachment theories, and the processes of loss and separation for children who are removed from their homes. The child welfare worker is not always required to provide therapy for the children but does need to know when the services of a specialist are required. This judgment can be most appropriately made when the worker is knowledgeable about the dynamics of the child's behavior.

Attachment issues are central to child development, especially for understanding and helping children who have been neglected or abused. Klaus and Kennell (1976) identify attachment as an affective tie that develops between the child and the caring, nurturing person(s) and binds them together in space and over time. For clarity, distinguishing between attachment and bonding is important. Bonding is a complex physiological and psychological tie between mother and child, which begins at conception and culminates at birth and continues onward (Reitz & Watson, 1992). Bonding is a function of the relationship that endures in the uterus and continues during the birth experience, which mother and child share. During pregnancy, two adaptive tasks need to be accomplished. First, the mother needs to identify the fetus as a part of herself. Later, as the fetus begins to move, the mother must become aware of the fetus as a separate individual (Klaus & Kennell, 1976). It is at this time that parents' fantasies about the child begin to emerge. Individuation of the child begins to occur.

During pregnancy, the mother's self-care impacts the development of the child. Sometimes prenatal abuse and neglect may occur. It can be expected that these and other events that occur during pregnancy affect the type and extent of the developing parent–child relationship (Fahlberg, 1991).

In contrast, attachment is a learned process. Through interaction between the infant and nurturing caregiver (usually the mother) over the first few years of life, attachment is expected to develop. "By definition, then, children are 'bonded' to their birth mothers and learn how to become 'attached' as a result of their earlier childhood experiences with nurturing caregivers" (Reitz & Watson, 1992, p. 133).

Development of Attachment

This process of attachment occurs as both the caregiver and the infant reach out to each other. If either rejects the response of the other over a period of time, a secure attachment may not develop. The infant's urge for closeness and attachment is so strong that if the caregiver does not respond, the infant tries to draw that person to itself. If the infant still does not receive a positive response, she or he may begin to cling and whine, which results in anxious attachment (Ainsworth, 1978). The infant who receives positive responses is more likely to develop a secure attachment.

The uninformed observer may mistakenly assess the anxious, insecure child as one who is securely attached. The insecure child is more involved with the parent than the truly securely attached infant, who can explore the environment because of the strength of the relationship with the caregiver. Specific behaviors of parents and other caretakers expressed in reciprocal interaction, the arousal–relaxation cycle, and the claiming process all help promote secure attachment.

Reciprocal interaction occurs between the caregivers and child as he or she grows and develops. As the infant fusses and cries, the parents respond. Bowlby (1970) suggested that two characteristics of the caregiver's responses affect the degree and kind of attachment that results. One characteristic is the speed and strength of response; the other is the extent to which the parent initiates interactions. As stimulus occurs from one partner to the other, that person is encouraged to continue the interaction. These interchanges are pleasurable for both, and each stimulates the other to continue. The more interactions the infant has with the parent, the more attached he or she becomes (Ainsworth, 1978; Howe, 1996).

When the infant experiences tension and displeasure either externally or internally, she begins to move her arms and legs, her face becomes red, and she begins to cry. This is the beginning of the arousal–relaxation cycle, which involves a *need* felt by the child, followed by feelings of his or her *displeasure*. It is expected that the displeasure will encourage a response from the caregiver and provide a *satisfaction* of the need and finally *quiescence* for the child. As the child discharges tension, the parents' role is helping the child return to quiescence.

Problems in the attachment cycle may occur either if the parents fail to respond to the infant's displeasure or if the parents meet the child's need even before it is expressed by the child. If the child is not yet aware of a need and the resulting displeasure before needs are met, he or she will not make the connection with the parent as a helping person who can give comfort.

Not all infants are positively responsive to touching and closeness with the caregiver (Sroufe, 1985). Some babies do not display behaviors that promote attachment. Sometimes, the infant's discomfort is not signaled to parents, therefore the need goes unmet. Some infants appear to have perceptual thresholds that are higher or lower than normal (Delacato, 1974; Simpson & Rhole, 1998). These children would not experience consistency in the relief of displeasure, which is essential for attachment to develop.

Claiming behaviors are also required for the development of attachment. Usually during the parents' initial contact with the infant, claiming behaviors begin. The parents look at the size and shape of the infant's head and count the toes and other body parts to assure themselves that their child is normal physiologically. A little later, parents may begin to explore the body of the child more carefully, looking for family resemblances. Finally, the examination is likely to focus on the uniqueness of this little person.

When the child is claimed, parents experience a feeling of entitlement. However, if the child is disclaimed, it is important that the parents be allowed to grieve for the child that they did not get and later, hopefully, claim and cherish the infant they have. Even after the child is older, these needs for reciprocal interaction, the arousal–relaxation cycle, and claiming can be met to begin to develop the attachment of the child to their current caretaker.

Attachment as a Prerequisite for Healthy Development

A secure attachment is crucial to the development of trust and the capacity for intimacy (Levy, 1998; Tizard & Rees, 1974). It plays a critical role in the process of socialization and the development of conscience. Children are able to give up behaviors to safeguard their major attachments (Bowlby, 1970).

Sroufe, Fox, and Pancake (1983) found that children who are securely attached as infants have greater self-esteem and express more positive affect and less negative affect later in life than do children who are anxiously attached. It is hypothesized that when secure infant–caregiver attachments are not established, developmental consequences in social, emotional, and cognitive processes arise (Fahlberg, 1991; Garmezy & Rutter, 1983; Pasick & Pasick, 1985; Zeanah & Emde, 1994). The child's relationship with the primary caregiver influences how they interact with others and how they approach problem solving (Cox & Lambrenos, 1992; Isabella & Belsky, 1991). After having developed a primary attachment with the caregiver, the child extends the relationship to include other family members.

Once an attachment develops, it persists, even in the absence of the caregiver. Throughout a lifetime, attachments provide connections to others and help children develop their sense of self. These early attachment relationships aid children in their quest for identity and provide a prototype for future interpersonal relationships. Fahlberg (1991) concluded that securely attached children are more resilient, independent, compliant, empathic, and socially competent.

Effects of Family Dysfunctions on the Development of Attachment

If the child is securely attached, even though he or she was reared by substitute caregivers or in day care, the strongest ties remain with the parents (Cummings, 1980; Farran & Ramey, 1977). Insecure attachment has been identified as the basis for the development of psychopathology in children (Rutter, 1995). In the DSM-IV, attachment disorders are clearly distinguished from pervasive developmental disorders, such as autistic disorder, Rett's disorder, childhood disintegrative disorder, and Asperger's disorder (American Psychiatric Association, 2000). "DSM-IV nosology also ties these disorders etiologically to parental abuse/neglect or to extremes of caregiving, such as children raised in institutions" (Lyons-Ruth, Zeanah, Benoit 1996, p. 458).

The relationship between interrelated family and child factors appears to produce predictable, identifiable developmental directions (Egeland, Pianta, O'Brien, 1993: Lyons-Ruth, Alpern, & Repacholi, 1993). Crack cocaine–exposed infants are likely to be fragile, hyperexcitable, fussy, and unable to be consoled (Combrinck-Graham, 1995). These behaviors can be expected to contribute to an unsatisfactory infant–caregiver relationship. Children who are exposed to drugs are more impulsive, deficient in play skills, less goal directed, and less securely attached than non-drug-exposed toddlers.

It has been found that the parents' use of drugs and the ensuing guilt also produce conditions not conducive for the development of healthy attachment relationships. These conditions may result in the child's exposure to extremes of sudden, harsh punishment, perhaps child abuse, along with guilt-ridden overindulgence and gentle kindness. Such parental behaviors may lead to inappropriate or anxious attachments for the child. Both prenatal and postnatal situations resulting from parenting behaviors and child-care environments are closely related to the lack of development of attachment. Intrauterine care, including lack of medical care and proper diet, resulting in low birth weight and substance abuse affect the mother–child relationship and the ability to develop healthy, strong attachments (Wolfe, 1987).

The family and society further affect attachment relationships for children. In the United States, one in four infants is born to unwed mothers. These mothers, many of whom are immature and lack adequate medical care, are at risk for having premature infants. Parents of newborns may respond by withdrawal, overcompensation, or with levels of stimulation that are beyond the infants' tolerance. According to Garbarino and Benn (1992), "The stresses of premature parenthood, together with confusing and poorly organized behaviors presented by the preterm infant, often undermine the synchrony of the early parent–infant relationship" (p. 139). Apparently, lower socioeconomic-status mothers are under significant stress and tend to have babies who are less securely attached. Pressure related to providing food, shelter, and other demands of daily living detract from the mother's time and ability to relate adequately to her infant.

Studies have shown that regardless of the cause of the disruption of attachment, the separation of the child and caregiver has been linked to physical abuse (Kennel, Voos, &

Klaus, 1976), failure to thrive, and to many competence deficits (Bronfenbrenner, 1970). Ciccketti, Toth, and Bush (1988) report that the connections among abuse, neglect, and attachment difficulties point to the preponderance of inadequate relationship ties expected in working with children and adolescents in family preservation programs, foster care, and adoption programs in child welfare services. This interruption, deficiency, or lack of attachment becomes a primary area of focus for the social worker and foster caregiver.

Using Attachment Theory

A significant factor in conducting a risk assessment and determining whether the neglected or abused child should be placed is an assessment of the degree of attachment of the child with the caregivers. If attachment to the parents exists, it can be expected that placement outside the home will initially be very difficult for the child. However, after this has been worked through, the child will be able to relate to the new setting well because of his ability to expand the parameter of his attachment to other persons. If the child has been insecurely attached at the time of out-of-home placement, the initial separation from parents may not be difficult, but the new caretakers can be expected to have more difficulty in relating to the child. Because the child has not securely attached previously, attaching to the new caregivers will be more difficult. The social worker helps the new caregiver arrive at strategies for developing attachment.

Fahlberg's (1991) checklist for assessing attachment, which has been modified, encompasses multiple factors, including behaviors of the child and those of parents. Observations for the grade school years of the child encompass self-esteem, relationships with others, authority relationship, initiative and competence, and emotional responses. The factors for the parent include response to the child, accepting the child's feelings and emotions, and setting appropriate limits and expectations.

Strategies for Developing Attachment for Children in Care

If the child is determined to be insecurely attached, planning strategies are important to promote the child attaching more securely in his new setting. As noted by Frieberg (1977), the 3- or 4-year-old child cannot easily attach, so time is important in attempting to correct this deficit. The three ways of attaching previously mentioned—the arousal–relaxation cycle, the positive interaction cycle, and positive claiming—can be used to promote attachment even at a later time.

The arousal–relaxation cycle for older children may be used to meet either physical or psychological needs. When the child or adolescent feels discomfort, which may be expressed as fear, anxiety, rage, sadness, or extreme joy or excitement, the caregivers, who may not be able to meet the specific needs, can allow the child to express them. The caregiver role is one of being empathic and supportive until the intense feelings subside. "The barriers to attachment are lowered and a child is, for a brief period, open to developing trust for the available adult" (Fahlberg, 1991, p. 57).

Positive interaction cycles are also useful in promoting attachment of older children and adolescents. The cycles involve either initiating or responding to positive interactions, which vary in their complexity, for example, giving a compliment, playing games, or giving a hug.

In positive claiming, the focus needs to be on similarities rather than on differences. Many ways of claiming can be demonstrated to older children. A picture of the child can be prominently displayed along with other children in the family. Also, the child can be included in family rituals, especially birthday celebrations and holidays.

The degree of claiming is a key issue. Some children placed in foster care expect to be later adopted by that family whereas others expect to be in foster care on a temporary basis. Being aware of the expected outcome for each child in placement is important. The social worker can help the caretaker develop specific individualized strategies for the appropriate degree of claiming for an individual child.

Separation, Loss, and Mourning

Stress is created for children by actual or threatened separation from the family. In addition to leaving the family, separation entails departing from all the surroundings and routines to which the child has become accustomed. Separation and loss universally carry a measure of harm. In addition to the child being affected in the immediate situation, attachment impairment may result from and contribute to subsequent placements and disruptions (Barth & Berry, 1988). The destination of the child after separation is an important factor to consider in assessment. Separation to a family rather than an institution has been found to produce the least acute distress (Robertson & Robertson, 1971).

Factors affecting the intensity of a particular child's response to separation include the child's age at separation, mother–child relationship, previous separation experiences, duration of separations, the child's predisposition, the effects of a strange environment, and the nature of the child's situation after separation (Steinhauer, 1991). The age of the child is of special importance. Quinton and Rutter (1976) found that the intensity of separation is likely to be great between the ages of 6 months and 4 years. This period is especially significant in the physical and mental development of the child; an interruption in this process could be expected to be traumatic.

The prior mother–child relationship has been found to be a significant factor. The child with a secure attachment, on being separated, shows less short-term distress than does the child with less secure relationship ties. In contrast, long-term separation may be especially stressful for the securely attached child.

Another intensifying factor is the temperament or genetic predisposition of the child. If the child is predisposed to withdraw rather than approach in a new situation and has a low threshold and high intensity of response to stimuli, separation will be more traumatic (Steinhauer, 1991). If the child has experienced other separations in the past with unfortunate consequences, his or her expectation for this separation will also be negative. If trust was reinforced as the child experienced previous separations, he or she would be expected to experience less distress.

Whatever the reason, interruptions in parenting caused by separation and loss universally carry a measure of harm (Fahlberg, 1991). Placement away from parents and a familiar environment is a crisis for any child because it involves movement from the known to the unknown. Remembering that a crisis has positive aspects is important. During a crisis a foster child's feelings about separation become much more accessible, and an adopted child may be able to bond with his or her new adoptive parents more easily. According to Fahlberg (1991), "One of the most serious challenges of child welfare work is helping children cope with these traumatic separations" (p. 141). Separation refers to the physical loss of a particular mother but not necessarily the simultaneous loss of mothering. Separation from a meaningful relationship precipitates an acute sense of loss. To recover from this loss entails a period of grieving.

The stages of the child's reactions to separation are preprotest, protest, despair, detachment, and adjustment (Bowlby, 1951; Rutter, 1978). In the preprotest stage the threat for the child is the threat of separation, rather than actual separation. As the child begins to express this fear no matter how subtly, the worker needs to explore the concerns. Some more elusive reactions displayed during this process are manifested in changes in moods, behaviors, and attitudes. At school, children are likely to become quiet and withdrawn, or may act out and experience a drop in grades (Combrinck-Graham, 1995). The social worker helps the child acknowledge the fear that is being experienced and discusses the fear and the associated anxieties.

After a decision has been made to move the child into a foster home or other new setting, the protest stage comes into full play. If possible, the child is prepared for this move while still in her own home, which allows the child a certain sense of security while this issue begins to be worked through. During this stage, the child needs to be encouraged to express all the anger and belligerence that is felt. Only after feelings are expressed, and at least partially dealt with, can the child begin to clearly comprehend the situation. It is at this point that the child can develop a readiness to accept the reality of the situation. During this period a move to foster care or an adoptive home is less traumatic for the child (Fahlberg, 1991).

This begins the period of despair and mourning in which grief and sadness appear. Successful mourning is achieved by gradually withdrawing interest, caring, and feelings invested in the lost attachment figure. The mourning process must be completed before the child can accept the finality of the loss and can freely transfer his feelings to a parent substitute. Studies have found that the more insecure the attachment is, the more intensely the child is likely to resist separation. They may also be expected to have more difficulty mourning successfully (Klyhylo, Kay, & Rube, 1998; Parkes & Stevenson-Hinde, 1982; Stayton & Ainsworth, 1973). According to Steinhauer (1991), children mourn best with adult assistance. Indeed, without such aid, the child is likely to experience long-term effects, such as permanent detachment, chronic depression, persistent and diffuse rage, chronic dependency on others, antisocial behavior, and poor self-esteem (Siu & Hogan, 1989).

After the child has been placed, despair may be the most predominant stage of mourning. The child is likely to be listless, apathetic, lethargic, and withdrawn, and may have no hope of returning home. Even after this stage has partially been worked through, the child may remain in limbo, feeling detached from others. If these feelings are present over a long period, feelings of abandonment may result in a permanent detachment. Attempting to help the child develop a substitute attachment during this time is essential (Goldstein, Freud, & Solnit, 1979).

Recently, the child's need to detach from his or her parents to move successfully into placement has been questioned. Current beliefs and practices in foster care support the idea that a child who is well attached to parents can easily attach to others. Children have the capacity to maintain several attachments at the same time, which allows them to maintain close connections with their parents while in foster care. This continuing connection is important if the case plan is to unify the family.

Additional behavioral problems may become evident as the child or adolescent is placed away from their family of origin. The child who has attachment problems further complicated by trauma, such as abuse, is susceptible to develop a response model that may require treatment by specialists. Indeed, James (1994) reports that provocative behaviors are often seen in children who have attachment problems. These children are likely to seek out dangerous situations and respond to positive and neutral events with provocative, destructive behavior. "These behaviors in turn provide relief from unbearable, escalating anxiety associated with trauma that the child cannot otherwise attain because the child has *no available, viable attachment relationship*" (James, 1994, p. 17). Because children may not have learned to self-soothe and protect themselves by experiencing and learning from primary attachment figures, they are likely to be limited in managing their own emotional and physical arousal.

Provocation is seen in the child who has had an enjoyable time on an outing, and whose behavior at the end of the outing calls for punishment. Other destructive behaviors often seen are self-mutilation, hurting animals, physically assaulting others, eating disorders, provoking abuse, damaging new clothing or a gift, and destroying other property. James (1994) explains that children involved in such behaviors are often affected by distorted alarm systems. Their feelings of terror and helplessness are stimulated by cues, such as sights, sounds, and smells, that are identified with traumatizing events. Lacking the cognitive labels to identify the emotions, they have difficulty distinguishing between emotions such as excitement, fear, and terror. A child experiencing these problems may be stimulated and become excited by play. Because the child cannot distinguish excitement from terror, he is caught in a cycle of escalating alarm.

According to James (1994), the numbing response breaks the cycle of escalating alarm. Relief takes the form of numbing emotional and physiological feelings, dissociation, social withdrawal, emotional and kinetic constriction, and avoidance of tactile/emotional stimulation. The numbing response interrupts the alarm cycle; as the numbing ceases the child is again open to the alarm response.

The provocative behaviors just described are displayed by children who are unable to experience relief through protective numbing. The purpose of their behavior is to help trigger the numbing response and thus gain relief from unbearable anxiety. Their actions typically involve risk of severe punishment, self-harm, and harm to others. In the alarm-numbing response model, "an alarmed child consciously or unconsciously engages in provocative or otherwise dangerous behavior to increase his state of anxiety to the level where a numbing response is automatically invoked" (James, 1994, p. 22). The numbing response provides relief that cannot otherwise be attained.

Recognizing the maladaptive model for responding by the child should alert the social worker that intensive professional work with the child and primary attachment figures is of great importance. Special support and suggestions for responses to the child may be needed by the foster care parents to sustain the child while receiving specialized treatment.

The Case of Nancy

To understand child welfare procedures and practices, the case of Nancy and her family is presented. Most of the work focuses on Nancy's placement in foster care. Although the siblings, who need the social worker's attention and protection, were also removed, for clarity's sake, the work for and with them is not discussed. Because of their ages, most of the direct work involves their mother and the foster mother.

The Report

Most states maintain a 24-hour hot line for receiving anonymous reports of suspected abuse or neglect. Persons making the reports do not have the burden of proving abuse, only describing the factors they observed that lead them to suspect abuse. Often, the hot-line staff have special training for this job. They determine whether the situation is investigated and how quickly it is done. They are in the position of having to weigh the risks of one decision against the risk of another. Their decisions, which may have a lifelong impact, are designed to provide protection and essential services to children. They, alone or with the support of a supervisor, are responsible for determining the degree of risk involved in a reported situation. Usually, the reported cases are categorized according to the degree of suspected risk. Some cases need to be investigated within 24 hours; others can wait a bit longer, and others do not need to be investigated at all.

A report was called into the hot line one morning from a neighbor of the Stoke family. On interviewing the neighbor, it was reported that both neglect and abuse were suspected. The family consisted of the mother and three children. The neighbor reported that she did not know the exact ages of the children, but she estimated that the little boy and girl were probably less than 4 years of age and the older girl, Nancy, about 8 years old. Their mother worked in a bar at night and often had different men staying in the home, sometimes for a day or a few days. The neighbor thought the men staying there were probably customers from the bar.

The young children were often seen on the street at 11:00 P.M. and 12:00 A.M., running around and playing. No one knew where the 8-year-old girl was at these times, although it was presumed that she was probably in the house sleeping. The children were reported to be dirty and only partially dressed, even in cold weather. Sometimes, they knocked on the neighbors' doors asking for something to eat. It was unclear whether they were really hungry or whether this was just a way of getting attention. She noted that they looked "healthy enough."

Her major concern was the young children on the street at night, who appeared to be unsupervised and not cared for. It was also noted that the children, especially the boy, often had bumps, scrapes, and sometimes a black eye or bruise on their head. She also was concerned that the 8-year-old girl was in the house alone and even more concerned about her well-being when the different men were staying there. The neighbor had observed that the young children had been outside until late at night for the past week. She thought something needed to be done.

The Investigation

The hot-line worker decided that this family needed to be investigated and referred it to one of the child protection workers, who went out to the Stokes' home that afternoon. The child protection worker talked with the neighbors, Nancy, and school personnel. The worker directly observed that Nancy had several bruises on her head, arms, and legs. When asked about the bruises, Nancy answered by saying that she guessed that she just "bruised easily." When asked about her mother, Nancy shrugged her shoulders and indicated that she did not know where she was. That day, Nancy's younger siblings had been at home alone when Nancy returned from school, which did not seem to be unusual to Nancy. The worker attempted to contact Ms. Stoke but could not locate her. When she had not returned home at 8:00 P.M., the children were removed to emergency foster care. When Ms. Stoke was found, she indicated that one of her friends from the bar was supposed to look in on the children.

Ms. Stoke was confronted about her consistent lack of supervision of her children. She indicated that she did the best that she could and tried to have someone there to care for the children at night. She said that she did not have money for a baby-sitter and had to rely on some of her friends from the bar. Sometimes no one was available to stay with the children, and she thought that Nancy was old enough to care for her brother and sister. She also stated that she did not know how Nancy received so many bruises; she just thought that all kids did that.

As part of the investigation, the previous night the younger children were observed to be dirty, wearing only diapers that needed to be changed. Food was smeared on their faces and bodies. Dirty dishes were piled all over the kitchen, and cockroaches were on the table, sink, floor, and walls.

In talking with school personnel, it was discovered that Nancy had not been at school for a week and had many previous absences. Nancy was reportedly quiet at school and did not do her work. The teacher observed that Nancy seemed to daydream and to be preoccupied with things other than school. Nancy appeared to isolate herself from the other students and had no friends at school. In the teacher's words, "She stayed to herself."

A judge approved the removal of the children from the home, and the required court procedures were conducted. The court determined that the children would remain in foster care until proper supervision and child care could be put in place by Ms. Stoke.

Working with Birth Parents

The case is now being handled by a foster care worker who customarily practices simultaneously with the family of origin, the foster care family, and the child. A primary focus in the beginning is helping Ms. Stoke change the living situation and returning the children. Another major focus is working with the foster parents and children to help them adjust to the new home and deal with feelings and maladaptive behaviors.

After making an appointment with Ms. Stoke, the worker prepared himself for interviewing an involuntary client. He expected Ms. Stoke to be angry, hostile, and sad that the children were taken away from her. Indeed, on arrival at the home, Ms. Stoke vented many such feelings about the agency and the worker. Parents whose children have been placed are likely to feel alienated from society, antagonistic to authority figures, and experience an increased sense of inadequacy, powerlessness, and societal stigmatization (Steinhaur, 1991). Underlying the anger are feelings of failure, despondency, and guilt. Ms. Stoke was adamant that the children should not have been removed. She was anxious to find out what she needed to do to get the children returned. At the same time Ms. Stoke was worried that she might fail them again. These thoughts and underlying fears may create passive resistance. The social worker listened and indicated that he, too, wanted to see the children returned and that they needed to work together to accomplish this goal.

More information about the family and relationships as well as their strengths and deficits needed to be gathered. An assessment must be made of their history, current adjustment, and direct observations. This information is used continually in planning and working with the family and court system, with new facts and data added to this assessment as they are discovered. After gathering this information, a plan is made for the future of the children. Goals must be developed with Ms. Stoke to attempt to alleviate the conditions that had created the need for removal of the children. Ms. Stoke's involvement in assessing and decision making is important if possible.

Simultaneously, a permanency plan must also be made. Legislation for permanency planning was passed in the Child Welfare Act of 1980, which proposed to prevent placement of children out of their homes and to pursue adoption of those children who had to be removed. If the goals are not met and the family cannot be reunited in the future, a backup plan is made, and this was done for Nancy and her two siblings. This comprehensive plan, which is a part of the case plan, is agreed to by the birth parents and the worker and is approved by the court.

Just as the children deserve to be accepted as unique individuals, the birth parents too must be seen as individuals with differing backgrounds, cultures, interests, and values. By modeling good parenting skills, the social worker can help the parents identify choices, make use of logical consequences, and actively teach them ways to contend with difficult emotions.

Together, the birth parents and social worker must develop a reciprocal alliance focused on the goal of the return of the children. Parents have considerable knowledge about, and power over, their children, and their participation is essential. The social worker brings a responsibility for agency requirements and policies. In this relationship, Fahlberg (1991) reminds us that "appropriate modeling of flexibility, as opposed to rigidity, and conflict resolution, as opposed to using power-based maneuvers, are necessary components of successful work with families" (p. 238). Involvement of parents in the process of attempting to facilitate the return of their children helps them to experience how important they are in the lives of their children. Parents can be involved in identifying problems, information gathering, problem solving, placement processes, determining visiting schedules, participating in school and medical appointments, and accessing information about community resources.

Direct Practice with the Child

During the time that this work is being implemented, a focus is also on the child and the foster parents. The role of the social worker is to assist in the adjustment of the child and provide assistance as the child experiences separation, grief, and mourning. The degree of assistance needed is often determined by the caregiver's experience with other foster children and their specific knowledge and understanding of the processes impacting the child at this time.

When the foster parents are feeling inadequate in working with the foster child, the social worker's initial step is to support their efforts. If this is insufficient, the social worker often tries to teach and model behaviors and techniques that the foster parents can emulate in working with the child. A subsequent step is for the social worker to provide crisis intervention or brief direct services for the child. Next, the child may be referred to a specialist for further help.

Children placed with caregivers are likely to maintain an emotional distance from them. Often, they fear rejection, are conflicted in their loyalties and about their families, and project their anger on their caregivers. Children need to have expectations lowered for a period of time as they now attempt to relate to two families. Sometimes, professional helpers are reluctant to explore the child's feelings about their situation. The worker may be attempting to protect the child from a hostile discussion and may be hesitant to elicit painful feelings.

As a beginning step in understanding the needs of the child, awareness of resilience and factors related to adaptation are very useful in assisting the child to cope with dysfunctional situations. Resilience involves the child's successful adaptation despite risk and adversity. It is the capacity of those who are exposed to risk factors to overcome them and avoid negative outcomes (Masten, 1994; Rak & Patterson, 1996; Rigsby, 1994).

Risk factors are defined as "any influences that increase the probability of onset, digression to a more serious state, or maintenance of a problem condition" (Coie, et al., 1993, p. 10). Dozens of studies have explored both risk and resilience. It has been found that two factors, risk and protective dynamics, and their interactions are the significant areas for viewing resilience at different system levels.

Kirby and Fraser (1997) have developed a crosscut view of the findings from many of these studies. Within the broad environmental conditions, risk factors include few opportunities for education and employment, racial discrimination and injustice, and poverty. Protective factors at this level are many opportunities for education, employment, achievement, and growth. At the system level of family, school, and neighborhood conditions, child maltreatment, interparental conflict, parental psychopathology, and poor parenting are risk factors. Social support, the presence of caring adults, positive parent–child relationships, and effective parenting are protective factors. Gender and biomedical problems are risk factors at the individual psychosocial and biological characteristics level. Protective factors at this level are an easy temperament, self-esteem and self-efficacy, competence in normative roles, and high intelligence.

To promote the healthy adjustment of maltreated foster children, an assessment needs to be made of these risk and protective factors. Protective factors can be matched to the risk factors allowing the worker to determine resources that need to be available in the foster home for a particular child. If the foster family cannot assist the children experiencing maladaptive emotions and behaviors occurring at this time, working closely with the social worker is essential. Time is a scarce commodity to the child welfare worker, who traditionally has a large caseload. However, children who experience a crisis require special attention from the social worker. Sometimes, brief work with a child can resolve a barrier that may be preventing her from adapting and adjusting to her new home.

Helping a child or adolescent in a child welfare setting requires a blend of knowledge of child development, an understanding of special issues of children in this system, and a mastery of the procedures, techniques, and skills to deal with such issues. Saari (1986) suggests that the final outcome in a treatment endeavor is determined by the interactions between the social worker's use of techniques and the growth processes of the particular child.

Nancy and her siblings were removed from their home as an emergency measure; no time was available to help them prepare for loss. Ideally, the social worker would have worked with the children before they were removed and prepared them for moving to their foster home. A normal response to loss includes signs of anger, pining, sadness, preoccupation with memories, and fantasies of the lost persons. Despair may be the most predominant stage of mourning, which is essential to the acceptance of loss.

Because the overall case plan developed for the family was insufficient for resolving the child's current problems, it was critical that an additional plan be created for working with the children in foster care. Once again, the plan for Nancy must include the goals and the units for attention, procedures and techniques to be used, and the roles and tasks to be fulfilled. The plan identifies both the process and outcome by specifying intermediate objectives as well as end goals. Objectives and their attainment are sequenced so they lead to goals. A first step is for the child to understand the events and why they occurred. She begins to comprehend the problem that caused her placement in foster care. Nancy knows that sometimes she and her siblings were hungry and that she was often left alone to care for the younger children. Nancy agreed that her foster mother fed them and cared for them, but she still wanted to go home.

Mrs. Allen, Nancy's foster mother, said that Nancy cried every night because she missed her mother. Mrs. Allen indicated that she had tried various ways to help the girl, but none of them had worked, and she did not know what to do. Ms. Stoke was clearly unable to provide and care for her children. A permanent placement such as adoption or long-term foster care was probably going to be required for Nancy. Mrs. Allen indicated that she would like to adopt Nancy if she became available for placement.

Nancy continued to mourn the loss of her mother. Mrs. Allen requested the assistance of the social worker, Mr. Jay, who began to develop a plan to help Nancy in grieving her loss. Mr. Jay knew that although it was important that Nancy express her feelings, because of her developmental level she could not be expected to fully verbalize them. Children such as Nancy are likely to benefit from play in which they can discuss and reenact events and express their inner feelings in symbolic forms in the presence of a safe adult.

A sequence of intermediate goals was developed to assist Nancy with mourning. As Nancy works through the process, this plan may need to be altered. After allowing Nancy to express her feelings adequately, helping her gradually withdraw interest, caring, and feelings invested in her birth parents and simultaneously develop an attachment to current caretakers would be important. The plan and sequence of activities follow:

- Nancy would go to the child welfare office and play in the playroom. Materials available would be puppets, building blocks, paper, crayons, and a play telephone.
- Regardless of the material selected by Nancy, the worker would listen for feelings expressed about her mother and encourage further discussion.
- The playroom would be used for an indefinite period of time, allowing Nancy to express her feelings. (It could be expected that repetition of significant play could help her work out these feelings.)
- Additional techniques for helping Nancy with mourning include using face cards depicting a variety of emotions, drawing, and using puppets, rag dolls, and a paper bag to act out real feelings.
- Role playing (or pretend play) is also very helpful in furthering Nancy's understanding of the circumstances causing the separation.
- After Nancy used many of the materials in the playroom to express her loss, she could be expected to become less interested in the playroom. She would be encouraged to take walks with Mrs. Allen, her foster mother, in the new neighborhood to become better acquainted with her surroundings and to stimulate her interest in her new environment. (This also is a way for Nancy to spend time alone with her foster mother to encourage an attachment with her.)

The role of the foster parents concerning attachment has two components. The child needs to develop healthy attachments so that continued growth and development is facilitated. Once this has occurred, the child needs to be aided in extending attachments and behavior gains.

As indicated in this case, meeting the child's needs and helping her deal with her grief leads to gradual attachment to the new caregiver and bonding to other children living in the home. The arousal–relaxation cycle is crucial even with older children. This cycle may begin with either physical or psychological needs and may involve either behaviors or emotions. In helping the child, the primary role of the adult is to be supportive and empathic during the expression of these emotions.

The child's mourning is related to the loss of the parents and also reflects the insecurity related to the discordant nature of the natural family prior to coming into care. Points of entry into the child's mourning process may be accessible to the social worker even after the major work has been done. Often, after a visit with birth parents, the child is sad and again expresses anger and grief at having to return to the foster home. This is an opportune time for the worker to intervene and help the child or adolescent work through these feelings. Again, allowing the expression of emotions is most important in overcoming this transitional mourning.

Another entry point for the worker to continue to help the child mourn is through helping the child to make connections with persons in different roles in his life. For example, the child may be expressing anger at the foster mother because of his anger with his birth parents in the past. These feelings are then displaced onto another adult female, namely the foster mother.

A third point for the social worker to intervene may be when the child expresses recurrent themes in conversations, play, or behavior. The worker can explore with the child or adolescent the purpose of repetitive behavior and promote an understanding of the situation and the child's underlying feelings.

Reminiscing is a useful method for expressing feelings about the loss that has occurred in the new living situation. In game format reminiscing allows some degree of structure in which to guide the interactive process. The worker and child or adolescent can sit together and take turns at reminiscing with each other about the child's past or present circumstances. To encourage the child to express more underlying emotions about his or her situation, the rule in this game is that when a positive reminiscence is stated, it must be followed by a negative one.

With older children and adolescents, an effective way to bring out underlying emotions is the use of a "hot seat" or "empty chair." The child may pretend that mother is sitting in the chair, and the child can express feelings without reservation. This exercise may also be useful in helping the child or adolescent develop a better understanding of the circumstances causing separation from the birth parents. Awareness is likely to be gained as the child takes the role of the parent in this pretend activity.

Mourning must be completed before the child can accept the finality of the loss. The child is then free to transfer feelings to a parent substitute. Fahlberg (1991) suggests that if the child is to be adopted or to remain in long-term foster care, it is important to receive permission from the birth parents and to allow them to say good-bye to their child. Ideally conveyed in person or alternatively expressed by mail or telephone call, this action allows the child freedom to feel and to express more connections to the parent substitutes.

As Nancy moved through the steps of the plan, it was suggested that Mrs. Allen think of ways to begin to claim Nancy to further develop their new relationship. One way of her doing this might be to place a picture of Nancy on the shelf along with those of the other family members. To hug her or put an arm around her shoulder to indicate her belonging and her importance to the family would also promote attachment. To encourage attachment it is important to involve Nancy in family events and tell her of the family rituals that can be expected in the future. These events can increase communication, create feelings of connectedness, add to family stability, and provide a sense of belonging.

Although some foster children may be expected to remain in the home for long periods of time or to be adopted, others are only placed temporarily. Differing degrees of claiming are based on the specific conditions for the individual child. Consideration needs to be given to the composition of the foster family, the foster child's relationship and contact with birth parents, and the long-term plan for the child.

In addition to being involved in early crisis situations of placement and adjustment, the social worker is frequently called on to deal with other dilemmas during the placement of and long-term plans for the child. After the child has been placed in temporary foster care, the court along with the social worker and family determine the long-term outcome for the child.

Options for Continued Care

Options for care of the child include reunification of the family, kinship care, adoption, and long-term foster care. For Nancy, the plan was reunification of the family if Ms. Stoke successfully followed through with the case plan. Otherwise, Nancy could expect to stay in long-term foster care with Mrs. Allen until voluntary relinquishment of Ms. Stoke or termination of parental rights by the court. At that point, Nancy could be adopted by Mrs. Allen.

The first option for care of Nancy and her siblings was reunification with their mother, a process that begins at the same time that the children are removed from their family. Pecora, Whittaker, Maluccio, Barth, and Plotnick (1992) found that several principles prepared the family of origin and the child for reentry. On a continuum, some behaviors can move the family and child in the direction of reunification. The families studied began by writing and phoning their child, moving to visitation of the child, and finally to partial reentry of the child through longer visits in the home.

Warsh, Pine, and Maluccio (1996) identified several principles for family reunification. First, placing emphasis on continuity of care for children and the belief that children are best reared in their homes is important. The family and child must be guided by a competence-centered perspective that includes family empowerment, using advocacy and social action, promoting family strengths, including all those that the child considers to be family, and providing needed services and supports. Another requirement is teamwork among the many partners while respecting all forms of diversity.

Other principles are commitment to early and consistent child and family visiting. Often, parents are reluctant to visit their children in the foster home because these strangers may know a great deal about the birth family and the conditions that precipitated the placement. Involving foster parents and caseworkers as members of the service delivery team is required. Even after reunification, services may need to be continued for a period. Finally, the importance of empowerment of staff by training and supervision is recognized.

Ongoing communication is a major factor in maintaining connections for children expecting to be reunited with their birth parents. Visiting needs to be a planned part of the service plan for the family. The purpose of visiting is to affirm family relationships and to help family members cope with changing relationships (Pine, Warsh, & Maluccio, 1993). Visiting empowers and informs parents, and it enhances the well-being of the child. It also helps the family to confront reality and provides a time and place to practice new behaviors. Observing the visits between the birth parents and child helps the social worker determine the child's readiness to return home.

Some worker activities are required to aid the family and child in maintaining their connections. A visitation plan needs to be developed; visiting arrangements and preparations must be coordinated and modified as needed. Other worker responsibilities are evaluating, interpreting, and documenting visits, and assisting the child's return home (Pine, Warsh, & Maluccio, 1993). Along with ongoing communications, involvement of all family members, with an emphasis on empowerment, is important. Finally, from the very beginning of this process, plan must be made for interaction among the family, child, foster parents, and social worker. Bicknell-Hentges (1995) identified the following stages in the reunification process: (1) defining the family, (2) fear and distrust,

(3) idealism, (4) reality, (5) second phase of fear, and (6) return. The social worker, family, child, and foster family need to be aware that these stages are normal and can be expected.

A model of reattachment therapy was developed for ameliorating disturbances in the young maltreatment victim and for helping reestablish more healthy relationships with the primary caretaker (Frazier & LeVine, 1983). This process involves developing a substantial relationship with the worker and then helping the child learn ways to induce attachment behaviors from others. If Ms. Stoke cannot or will not meet the agreed-on goals in a timely manner, after receiving support from the social worker and direction from the court, an optional plan is put into place.

Another option for placement might have been extended family foster care or kinship care. If extended family had been available, Nancy could have been placed with relatives until it was safe for her and her siblings to return to their mother. Kinship care has been found to be less harmful to the child (Berrick, Barth, & Needle, 1993) and allows the family continuity to be better stabilized (Mills & Usher, 1996). Adoption also is a possible long-term plan for Nancy. Mrs. Allen has expressed her interest in adopting Nancy. If Ms. Stokes is unable or unwilling to make her home safe for her children, her parental rights could be terminated, allowing Mrs. Allen to adopt Nancy.

Issues in Adoptions

Children are adopted when they lose their parents, are relinquished for adoption, or become wards of the state because parental rights are severed. Most children in foster care are older ethnic or racial minorities and have special needs. Often, these children do not have the same opportunities to be adopted as healthy white infants.

The role of the social worker in adoptions is to secure the best family possible to meet the needs of the child. This requires that the potential adoptive family be carefully assessed and the child's needs clearly identified. The adoptive family must be made aware of the child's special needs before the adoption process is completed to help prepare them for any issues that might be expected to arise.

Children adopted because parental ties are severed are usually older and may have had a great deal of contact with their birth parents before adoption. Sometimes, even after adoption, some communication is continued with some members of the natural family. Therefore, the usual issue of the identity of the parents may be only a minor concern for some of these children. Others may know their parents' names but have no further knowledge about them as persons. Still others, who have been in the foster care system for many years, do not remember their birth parents and indeed are even more confused about them because of their many foster home placements. A special concern is that adopted children are always faced with the possibility of removal (disruption) from their new adoptive families. Older and disabled children are especially vulnerable to this outcome.

Often, major adjustments are required both by the adoptive parents and by the adoptee. For example, consider the confusion that occurred when Lisa first arrived within an adoptive home. The adoptive mother, Mrs. Nichols, was very upset and unsure how to handle a situation with her newly adopted daughter, Lisa. Lisa's adoptive father had told Lisa to get her sweater to take on a family outing. Instead of just picking up her sweater, Lisa went directly to her adoptive mother and questioned whether she should take her sweater. She indicated her adoptive father had told her to do so, but she didn't know whether she should. Mrs Nichols was very disturbed that Lisa had not done what her adoptive father had told her to do. She seemed almost hysterical about this incident as she talked with the worker.

After some exploration, the worker began to understand the significance of the interaction. Mrs. Nichols felt very ill at ease with her new role as adoptive mother to a 9-year-old and wanted to feel that she was sharing the responsibility of this new task with her husband. Because Lisa did not accept Mrs. Nichols's husband's directions, she felt she had all the responsibility for Lisa. Mrs. Nichols was very angry with Lisa because, rather than complying with her adoptive father's directive, she had come to verify it with her. Furthermore, a potential difference in values between Mrs. Nichols and Lisa was immediately evident because Mrs. Nichols was clear that questioning a parent's directive would never have been tolerated when she was growing up.

The worker reminded Mrs. Nichols of the sexual abuse that Lisa had endured, initially with her father and then with a stepfather. It could be expected that Lisa would be very distrustful of men and would want to be sure that it was appropriate to follow their directions. As Mrs. Nichols recognized some of her own values and Lisa's previous experiences with men, she was able to relax and begin to sort out changes that both she and Lisa needed to make in the future.

LeVine and Sallee (1990) have identified phases of adoption adjustment. In the *preawareness phase,* the child is overactive, withdrawn, or often acts out. The *dim awareness phase* is characterized by talk about the child feeling different and confusion about past and present homes. In the *cognitive integration of biological and social differences phase,* a tendency to increase questioning about the family of origin and to oppose the adoptive parents is displayed. During the phase of *identity crisis* of the adopted adolescent, the family of origin and biological roots are of great concern. Finally, in the *concomitant acceptance of the biological and adoptive families phase,* the adoptive issues are resolved.

Identity development is a major issue both for adoptees and for children in long-term foster care. Foster care that entails many moves for the child may lead to a confused, incomplete, or immature identity. Adoptive children too may have had multiple placements before they are finally adopted and may not be able to sort out their birth family and their foster homes.

Children in substitute care need help in connecting their current life with their experience in their birth family. The creation and use of life books is an innovative method for helping the child to trace her background to the present. Biological, foster, and adoptive families are all included in the scrapbook of the child's life. Through the use of pictures, legal documents, letters, and other personal material, a history of the child's life is constructed to help the young person discover who she is.

Identity is a major concern for children who have had discontinuity in care. Identity has been defined as "the integrative effects of feelings, needs and roles that give a person a sense of individuality, worth, and purpose that is recognized by oneself and others" (Dixon

& Sands, 1983, p. 230). Clearly, children in foster care and those that have been adopted have not had an opportunity for a sense of identity to emerge. Triseliolis (1983) identified three factors that contribute to identity formation. First, the child or adolescent must experience feelings of being wanted and loved in a secure environment. Second, he or she must have knowledge about his or her personal history. Finally, the child or adolescent must experience the feeling of being perceived by others as a worthwhile person.

In recent years the recognition of the child's need for continuity has promoted *open adoptions.* In contrast, *closed adoptions* has features of secrecy and a total severance from birth parents at the point of legal finalization of the adoption. Because children in this system are often adopted at an older age, the idea of severance from the birth family is not a workable expectation. Many children who have been adopted continue to communicate regularly with their siblings who are still living with their birth parents.

Interracial adoptions continue to be an area of conflict. A major concern is that proportionately more ethnic and racial minority children are available for adoption than are Caucasian children. A belief underlying adoptions is that children should be placed without prejudice. Although it is acknowledged that cultural and racial support are important factors in the development of children, it is recognized that the major consideration needs to be the best interest of the child, which has priority over the desires of the potential adoptive parent. To accommodate ethnic and racial factors in adoptions, persons often make special efforts to recruit more adoptive homes in communities that can fulfill this need. Often, churches have been a primary resource for recruiting and providing homes suitable for placement of these children.

A group of children who were especially difficult to place in the past are those children once described as unadoptable. With the passage of the 1980 Adoption Assistance and Child Welfare Act, it became clear that these are children with special needs, and they are certainly adoptable if appropriate resources are available. Indeed, the Act provided subsidies for parents to secure resources for children with special needs who may have physical or mental disabilities or who suffer severe behavioral or psychological problems.

Conclusion

Social work with children in the child welfare system is a challenging task. Providing services to families and resources for protection of children is a primary concern. Merely removing a child from a home where neglect or abuse has occurred is usually not sufficient. In addition to working with birth parents, therapeutic work with the child is often required to help the child deal with his or her trauma as a consequence of both maltreatment and separation from the birth parents. The child can be referred to a therapist who specializes in working with traumatized children. At other times, working with the child and foster parents may become a real challenge for the social worker who may observe a barrier that is preventing the child from adjusting to the new living situation. As a result, the social worker may need to spend considerable time working with this particular situation. Sometimes, the caseload is large and the social worker may be reluctant to spend extra time on one case.

In one instance, a child who had seen his father shoot and kill his mother had not been given an opportunity to describe this scene and ventilate his feelings. The social worker, who was aware of the child and the incident, could help him to tell his story. After a few sessions, the worker noticed that the foster mother was no longer calling him to deal with a crisis in her home. The child was able to begin to adjust to the new family.

Many opportunities exist for therapeutic work with children in the child welfare system by skilled social workers. Working with children is complex because of the many facets and dynamics of behavior that are immediately evident to the practitioner. It can be very challenging, yet it is possible to interweave the open, unguarded revelations of the child into a more complete and accurate picture of the situation and arrive at solutions.

REFERENCES

Abbott, E., & Breckinridge, S. P. (1917). *Truancy and non-attendance in the Chicago schools.* Chicago: University of Chicago Press.

Abell, N., McDonell, J. R., & Winters, J. (1992). Developing a measure of children's prosocial tendencies: An initial validation of a self-report instrument. *Journal of Social Service Research, 16,* 19–47.

Achenbach, T. M. (1982). *Developmental psychopathology* (2nd ed.). New York: Wiley.

Achenbach, T. M., & Edelbrock, C. S. (1978). The classification of child psychopathology: A review and analysis of empirical efforts. *Psychological Bulletin, 85,* 1275–1301.

Achenbach, T. M., & Edlebrock, C. S. (1983). *Manual for the Child Behavior Checklist and Revised Child Behavior Profile.* Burlington: University of Vermont, Department of Psychiatry.

Achenbach, T. M., & Howell, C. T. (1993). Are American children's problems getting worse? A 13-year comparison. *Journal of the American Academy of Child and Adolescent Psychiatry, 32,* 1145–1154.

Addams, J. (1961). Child labor and pauperism. In R. E. Pumphrey & M. W. Pumphrey (Eds.), *The heritage of American social work* (pp. 278–283). New York: Columbia University Press. (Original work published 1903)

Admunson-Beckmann, K., & Lucas, A. R. (1989). Gaining a foothold in the aftermath of divorce. *Social Work in Education, 12,* 5–15.

Agranoff, R. (1991). Human services integration: Past and present challenges in public administration. *Public Administration Review, 51,* 533–542.

Aiello, T. (1999). *Child and adolescent treatment for social work practice.* New York: Free Press.

Ainsworth, M. D. S. (1978). *Patterns of attachment.* Hillsdale, NJ: Lawrence Erlbaum.

Allen-Meares, P. (1995). *Social work with children and adolescents.* White Plains, NY: Longman.

Allen-Meares, P., Washington, R., & Welsh, B. (1986). *Social work services in schools.* Englewood Cliffs, NJ: Prentice-Hall.

Altstein, H., & McRoy, R. G. (2000). *Does family preservation serve a child's best interests?* Baltimore: Georgetown University Press.

Amatea, E. S. (1989). *Brief strategic interventions for school behavior problems.* San Francisco: Jossey-Bass.

American Psychiatric Association. (1968). *Diagnostic and statistical manual of mental disorders* (2nd ed.). Washington, DC: Author.

American Psychiatric Association. (1994). *Diagnostic and statistical manual of mental disorders* (4th ed.). Washington, DC: Author.

American Psychiatric Association. (2000). *Diagnostic and statistical manual of mental disorders* (4th ed., revised). Washington, DC: Author.

Andreae, D. (1996). Systems theory and social work treatment. In F. J. Turner (Ed.), *Social work treatment* (4th ed., pp. 601–616). New York: Free Press.

Angel, R. J., & Angel, J. L. (1993). *Painful inheritance.* Madison: University of Wisconsin Press.

Annie E. Casey Foundation. (1999). *Kids count data book: State profiles of child well-being.* Baltimore: Author.

Arnold, L. E. (1990). Stress in children and adolescents: Introduction and summary. In L. E. Arnold (Ed.), *Childhood stress* (pp. 1–22). New York: Wiley.

Arnold, L. E., & Carnahan, J. A. (1990). Child divorce stress. In L. E. Arnold (Ed.), *Childhood stress* (pp. 373–404). New York: Wiley.

Asarnow, J. R. (1994). Annotation: Childhood-onset schizophrenia. *Journal of Child Psychology and Psychiatry, 35,* 1345–1371.

Atkins-Burnett, S., & Allen-Meares, P. (2000). Infants and toddlers with disabilities: Relationship-based approaches. *Social Work, 4,* 371–379.

Aust, C. F. (1990). Using the client's religious values to aid progress in therapy. *Counseling and Values, 34,* 125–129.

Axline, V. M. (1947). *Play therapy.* Boston: Houghton Mifflin.

Axinn, J., & Levin, H. (1992). *Social welfare: A history of the American response to need* (3rd ed.). White Plains, NY: Longman.

Bacon, J. B. (1996). Support groups for bereaved children. In C. A. Corr & D. M. Corr (Eds.), *Handbook of childhood death and bereavement* (pp. 285–304). New York: Springer.

Baglow, L. J. (1990). A multidimensional model for treatment of child abuse: A framework for cooperation. *Child Abuse and Neglect, 14,* 387–395.

Baker, J. E., & Sedney, M. A. (1996). How bereaved children cope with loss: An overview. In C. A. Corr & D. M. Corr (Eds.), *Handbook of childhood death and bereavement* (pp. 109–129). New York: Springer.

Bandura, A. (1976). *Social learning theory.* Englewood Cliffs, NJ: Prentice-Hall.

Baptiste, Jr., D. A. (1993). Immigrant families, adolescents and acculturation: Insights for therapists. *Marriage and Family Review, 19,* 341–363.

Barbosa-Saldivar, J. L., & Van Itallie, T. B. (1979). Semistarvation: An overview of an old problem. *Bulletin of the New York Academy of Medicine, 55,* 744–797.

Barkley, R. A. (1989). Attention-deficit hyperactivity disorder. In E. J. Mash & R. A. Barkley (Eds.), *Treatment of childhood disorders* (pp. 39–72). New York: Guilford Press.

Barkley, R. A. (1990). *Attention deficit hyperactivity disorder.* New York: Guilford Press.

Barth, R. P., & Berry, M. (1988). *Adoption and disruption: Rates, risks, and responses.* New York: Aldine de Gruyter.

Baruth, L. G., & Burggraf, M. Z. (1983). Helping single-parent families. *Counseling and Human Development, 15,* 1–15.

Beardslee, W. (1990). Stress from parental depression: Child risk, self-understanding, and a preventive intervention. In L. E. Arnold (Ed.), *Childhood stress* (pp. 351–372). New York: Wiley.

Beck, A. (1976). *Cognitive therapy and the emotional disorders.* New York: International Universities Press.

Beck, A. T. (1964). Thinking and depression: II. Theory and therapy. *Archives of General Psychiatry, 10,* 561–571.

Beck, J. (1995). *Cognitive therapy: Basics and beyond.* New York: Guilford Press.

Becker, E. (1999, April). Juvenile justice system under scrutiny. *Monitor,* p. 49.

Becker, J. V., & Bonner, B. (1998). Sexual and other abuse of children. In R. J. Morris & T. R. Kratochwill (Eds.), *The practice of child therapy* (3rd ed., pp. 367–389). Boston: Allyn & Bacon.

Bedell, J. R., & Lennox, S. S. (1997). *Handbook for communication and problem-solving skills training.* New York: Wiley.

Behrman, R. E., & Quinn, L. S. (1994). Children and divorce: Overview and analysis. *Future of Children: Children and Divorce, 4,* 4–14.

Beitchman, J., Nair, R., Clegg, M., Ferguson, B., & Patel, P. (1986). Prevalence of psychiatry disorders in children with speech and language disorders. *Journal of the American Academy of Child Psychiatry, 25,* 528–553.

Ben-David, A. (1995). Family functioning and migration: Considerations for practice. *Journal of Sociology and Social Welfare, 22,* 121–137.

Ben-David, A., & Erickson, C. A. (1990). Ethnicity and the therapist's use of self. *Family Therapy, 17,* 211–216.

Benard, B. (1991). *Fostering resiliency in kids: Protective factors in the family, school and community.* Portland, OR: Northwest Regional Education Laboratory.

Benda, B. B. (1995). The effect of religion on adolescent delinquency revisited. *Journal of Research in Crime and Delinquency, 32,* 446–466.

Benda, B. B., & Corwyn, R. F. (1997). A test of a model with reciprocal effects between religiosity and various forms of delinquency using 2-stage least squares regression. *Journal of Social Service Research, 22,* 27–52.

Benedek, R. S., & Benedek, E. P. (1979). Children of divorce: Can we meet their needs? *Journal of Social Issues, 35,* 155–169.

Berger, R. (1997). Adolescent immigrants in search of identity: Clingers, eradicators, vacillators and integrators. *Child and Adolescent Social Work Journal, 14,* 263–275.

Berlin, I. N. (1988). Early intervention and prevention of alcoholism and pregnancy in high risk American Indian female adolescents. *Proceedings of conference protecting our children.* Norman, OK: American Indian Institute, University of Oklahoma.

Berlin, I. N. (1990). The role of the community mental health center in prevention of infant, child and adolescent disorders: Retrospect and prospect. *Community Mental Health Journal, 26,* 89–106.

Berman-Rossi, T., & Rossi, P. (1990). Confidentiality and informed consent in school social work. *Social Work in Education, 12,* 195–207.

Berrick, J., Barth, R., & Needel, B. (1993). A comparison of kinship foster homes. In R. P. Barth, J. D. Berrick, & N. Gilbert (Eds.), *Child welfare research review.* New York: Columbia University Press.

Bicknell-Hentges, L. (1995). The stages of reunification process and the tasks of the therapist. In L. Combrinck-Graham (Ed.), *Children in families at risk: Maintaining the connections.* New York: Guilford Press.

Biddle, B. J. (1979). *Role theory: Expectations, identities, and behaviors.* New York: Academic Press.

Bird, H., Yager, T. J., Staghezza, B., Gould, M., Canino, G., & Rubio-Stipec, M. (1990). Impairment in the epidemiologic measurement of childhood psychopathology in the community. *Journal of the American Academy of Child and Adolescent Psychiatry, 29,* 796–803.

Bishop, D. R. (1992). Religious values as cross-cultural issues in counseling. *Counseling and Values, 36,* 179–191.

Bishop, D. V. (1998). Development of the Children's Communication Checklist (CCC): A method for assessing qualitative aspects of communicative impairment in children. *Journal of Child Psychology and Psychiatry and Allied Disciplines, 39,* 879–891.

Bisman, C. (1994). *Child and adolescent treatment for social work practice.* New York: Free Press.

Bithoney, W. G., McJunkin, J., Michalek, J., Snyder, J., Egan, H., & Epstein, D. (1991). The effect of a multidisciplinary team approach on weight gain in nonorganic failure-to-thrive children. *Journal of Developmental and Behavioral Pediatrics, 12,* 254–258.

Bowlby, J. (1951). *Maternal care and mental health.* Geneva: World Health Organization.

Bowlby, J. (1970). *Attachment and loss: Volume I: Attachment.* New York: Basic Books.

Braden, J. P., & Hightower, A. D. (1998). Prevention. In R. J. Morris & T. A. Kratochwill (Eds.), *The practice of child therapy* (3rd ed., pp. 510–539). Boston: Allyn & Bacon.

Brandenberg, N. A., Friedman, R. M., & Silver, S. E. (1990). The epidemiology of childhood psychiatric disorders: Prevalence findings from recent studies. *Journal of the American Academy of Child and Adolescent Psychiatry, 29,* 76–83.

Bremner, R. H. (1970). *American philanthropy.* Chicago: University of Chicago Press.

Brier, N. (1994, March). *Alternatives: Project Description.* Paper presented at the Annual Conference of the Learning Disabilities Association of America, Washington, DC.

Briggs, H. E., & Koroloff, N. M. (1995). Enhancing family advocacy networks: An analysis of the roles of sponsoring organizations. *Community Mental Health Journal, 31,* 317–333.

Brody, J. E. (1997, December 2). Invisible world of the seriously depressed child. *The New York Times,* p. B15.

Bronfenbrenner, U. (1970). *Two worlds of childhood.* New York: Russell Sage Foundation.

Brook, J. S., Whiteman, M., Balka, E. B., & Cohen, P. (1997). Drug use and delinquency: Shared and unshared risk factors in African American and Puerto Rican adolescents. *Journal of Genetic Psychology, 158,* 25–39.

Brooks, R., & Goldstein, S. (2001). *Raising resilient children.* Lincolnwood, IL: NTC/Contemporary.

Brownlee, K. (1994). Responding to client–therapist relationships in rural areas: The suitability of constructivist family therapy. *Family Therapy, 21,* 11–23.

Bryan, B. (1993). *Overview of childhood schizophrenia.* (ERIC Document Reproduction Service No. ED359471)

Bryan, T. (1991, April). *Assessment of students with learning disabilities who appear to be socially incompetent.* Paper presented at the Annual Conference of the Council for Exceptional Children, Atlanta, GA.

Bryan, T. (1997). Assessing the personal and social status of students with learning disabilities. *Learning Disabilities Research and Practice, 12,* 63–76.

Bui, K. V., & Takeuchi, D. T. (1992). Ethnic minority adolescents and the use of the community mental health care system. *American Journal of Community Psychology, 20,* 403–417.

Bumpass, L. L., Martin, T. C., & Sweet, J. A. (1991). The impact of family background and early marital factors on marital disruption. *Journal of Family Issues, 12,* 22–42.

Burcky, W., Reuterman, N., & Kopsky, S. (1988). Dating violence among high school students. *School Counselor, 35,* 353–358.

Burnette, D. (1997). Grandparents raising grandchildren in the inner city. *Families in Society, 78,* 489–501.

Burns, B. J., Angold, A., & Costello, E. J. (1992). Measuring child, adolescent and family service use. In L. Bickman & D. Rogs (Eds.), *New directions for program evaluation.* San Francisco: Jossey-Bass.

Burns, B. J., Costello, E. J., Angold, A., Tweed, D., Stangl, D., Farmer, E. M. Z., & Erkanli, A. (1995). Children's mental health service use across service sectors. *Health Affairs, 14,* 147–159.

Butterfield, W. H., & Cobb, N. H. (1994). Cognitive-behavioral treatment of children and adolescents. In D. H. Granvold (Ed.), *Cognitive behavioral treatment: Methods and applications* (pp. 63–89). Pacific Grove, CA: Sage.

Cairns, R. B., Leung, M., Gest, S. D., & Cairns, B. D. (1995). A brief method for assessing social development: Structure, reliability, stability, and developmental validity of the interpersonal competence scale. *Behaviour Research and Therapy, 33,* 725–736.

Callahan, S. (1991). *In good conscience.* San Francisco: Harper.

Campbell, T. W. (1992). Psychotherapy with children of divorce: The pitfalls of triangulated relationships. *Psychotherapy, 29,* 646–652.

Carlile, C. (1991). Children of divorce. *Journal of Educational Psychology, 4,* 231–234.

Carmichael, A. (1990). Physical development and biological influences. In B. J. Tonge, G. D. Burrows, & J. S. Werry (Eds.), *Handbook of studies on child psychiatry* (pp. 3–12). New York: Elsevier.

Carroll, J. (1995). Reaching out to aggressive children. *British Journal of Social Work, 25,* 37–53.

Carson, D. K., Klee, T., Perry, C. K., Muskina, G., & Donaghy, T. (1998). Comparisons of children with delayed and normal language at 24 months of age on measures of behavioral difficulties, social and cognitive development. *Infant Mental Health Journal, 19,* 59–75.

Chess, S. (1989). Defying the voice of doom. In T. Dugan & R. Coles (Eds.), *The child in our times* (pp. 179–199). New York: Brunner/Mazel.

Chethik, M. (1989). *Techniques of child therapy.* New York: Guilford Press.

Child Welfare League of America. (1991). *Core training for child welfare caseworkers curriculum.* Washington, DC: Author.

Chin, J. L. (1983). Diagnostic considerations in working with Asian-Americans. *American Journal of Orthopsychiatry, 53,* 100–109.

Christie, P., Newson, E., Newson, J., & Prevezer, W. (1992). An interactive approach to language and communication for non-speaking children. In D. A. Lane & A. Miller (Eds.), *Child and adolescent therapy* (pp. 67–88). Bristol, PA: Open University Press.

Christie, D. J., & Toomey, B. G. (1990). The stress of violence: School, community, and world. In L. E. Arnold (Ed.), *Childhood stress* (pp. 297–324). New York: Wiley.

Ciccketti, D., Toth, S., & Bush, M. (1988). Developmental psychopathology and incompetence in childhood: Suggestions for intervention. In B. B. Lahey & A. E. Kazdin (Eds.), *Advances in clinical child psychology* (Vol. 2, pp. 1–77).

Clingempeel, G. W., & Brand, E. (1994). Family-of-origin experiences and interpersonal schema in stepfamilies: Clinical implications. In D. K. Huntley (Ed.), *Understanding stepfamilies: Implications for assessment and treatment* (pp. 127–144). Alexandria, VA: American Counseling Association.

Coddington, R. D., & Troxell, J. R. (1980). The effect of emotional factors on football injury rates—A pilot study. *Journal of Human Stress, 14,* 3–5.

Cohn, N. A. (Ed.). (2000). *Child welfare: A multicultural focus.* Boston: Allyn & Bacon.

Coie, J. D., Watt, N. F., West, S. G., Hawkins, J. D., Asarnow, J. R., Markman, H. J., et al. (1993). The science of prevention: A conceptual framework and some directions for a national research program. *American Psychologist, 48,* 1013–1022.

Cole, D., & Kammer, P. P. (1984). Support groups for children of divorced parents. *Elementary School Guidance and Counseling, 19,* 88–94.

Cole, E., & Donley, K. S. (1990). History, values and placement policies in adoptions. In D. M. Brodzinsky & M. C. Schechter (Eds.), *The psychology of adoption* (pp. 273–274). New York: Oxford University Press.

Cole, M. (1991). On putting Humpty Dumpty together again: A discussion of the papers on the socialization of children's cognition and emotion. *Merrill-Palmer Quarterly, 37,* 199–208.

Coleman, J. M., McHam, L. A., & Minnett, A. M. (1992). Similarities in the social competencies of learning disabled and low achieving elementary school children. *Journal of Learning Disabilities, 25,* 671–677.

Coles, R. (1990). *The spiritual life of children.* Boston: Houghton Mifflin.

Coll, B. D. (1970). *Perspectives in public welfare.* Washington, DC: U.S. Government Printing Office.

Combrinck-Graham, L. (1990). *Giant steps: Therapeutic innovations in child mental health.* New York: Basic Books.

Combrinck-Graham, L. (1995). (Ed.). *Children in families at risk.* New York: Guilford Press.

Compher, J. V. (1993). Parent–school–child systems: Triadic assessment and intervention. In J. B. Rauch (Ed.), *Assessment: A sourcebook for social work practice* (pp. 159–171). Milwaukee, WI: Families International.

Compton, G. R., & Galaway, B. (1994). *Social work processes* (5th ed.). Pacific Grove, CA: Brooks/Cole.

Congress, E. P., & Lynn, M. (1994). Group work programs in public schools: Ethical dilemmas and cultural diversity. *Social Work in Education, 16,* 107–114.

Constable, R., Kuzmickaite, D., Harrison, W. D., & Volkmann, L. (1999). The emergent role of the school social worker in Indiana. *School Social Work Journal, 24,* 1–14.

Contreras, J. M., & Kerns, K. A. (2000). Emotion regulation processes: Explaining links between parent–child attachment and peer relationships. In K. A. Kerns, J. M. Contreras, & A. M. Neal-Barnett (Eds.), *Family and peers: Linking two social worlds* (pp. 1–25). Westport, CT: Praeger.

Corbett, T., & Farber, N. (1990). *Schools, families, and social services: An exploration of the emerging relationship between the education and the welfare systems.* Madison: University of Wisconsin, Institute for Research on Poverty.

Cormier, L. S., & Hackney, H. (1987). *The professional counselor: A process guide to helping.* Englewood Cliffs, NJ: Prentice-Hall.

Corwyn, R. F., Benda, B. B., & Ballard, K. (1997). Do the same theoretical factors explain alcohol and other drug use among adolescents? *Alcoholism Treatment Quarterly, 15,* 47–62.

Costantino, G., & Malgady, R. G. (1996). Culturally sensitive treatment: Cuento and hero/heroine modeling therapies for Hispanic children and adolescents. In E. D. Hibbs & P. S. Jensen (Eds.), *Psychosocial treatments for child and adolescent disorders: Empirically based strategies for clinical practice* (pp. 639–670). Washington, DC: American Psychological Association.

Costello, E. J., & Tweed, D. L. (1994). *A review of recent empirical studies linking the prevalence of functional impairment with that of emotional and behavioral illness or disorder in children and adolescents.* Report to the Center for Mental Health Services. Washington, DC: U.S. Government Printing Office.

Costin, L. B., Bell, C. J., & Downs, S. W. (1991). *Child welfare: Policies and practice* (4th ed.). New York: Longman.

Cox, A., & Lambrenos, K. (1992). Childhood physical disability and attachment. *Developmental Medicine and Child Neurology, 34,* 1037–1046.

Cozens, W. R. (1997). Key elements of agency survival. *Residential Treatment for Children and Youth, 14,* 53–62.

Crittenden, P. M. (1995). Attachment and risk for psychopathology: The early years. *Developmental and Behavioral Pediatrics, 16,* S12–S16.

Crittenden, P. M., & Ainsworth, N. D. S. (1989). Child maltreatment and attachment theory. In D. Cicchetti & V. Carlson (Eds.), *Child maltreatment* (pp. 432–463). New York: Cambridge University Press.

Crosson-Tower, C. (1998). *Understanding child abuse and neglect.* Boston: Allyn & Bacon.

Cummings, E. M. (1980). Caretaker stability and day care. *Developmental Psychology, 16,* 31–37.

Cunningham, P. J., & Hahn, B. A. (1994). The changing American family: Implications for children's health insurance coverage and the use of ambulatory care service. *The Future of Children: Critical Health Issues for Children and Youth, 4,* 24–42.

Curtis, P. A. (1990). The consequences of acculturation to service delivery and research with Hispanic families. *Child and Adolescent Social Work, 7,* 147–159.

Daka-Mulwanda, V., Thornburg, K. R., Filbert, L., & Klein, T. (1995). Collaboration of services for children and families: A synthesis of recent research and recommendations. *Family Relations, 44,* 219–223.

Davies, S. P., & Ecob, K. (1959). *The mentally retarded in society.* New York: Columbia University Press.

Davis, L. V. (1996). Role theory and social work practice. In F. J. Turner (Ed.), *Social work treatment* (4th ed., pp. 581–600). New York: Free Press.

Delacato, C. H. (1974). *The ultimate stranger.* New York: Doubleday.

del Carmen, R., & Huffman, L. (1996). Epilogue: Bridging the gap between research on attachment and psychopathology. *Journal of Consulting and Clinical Psychology, 64,* 291–294.

Delva-Tauili'ili, J. (1995). Assessment and prevention of aggressive behavior among youths of color: Integrating cultural and social factors. *Social Work in Education, 17,* 83–91.

DeWeaver, K. L. (1983). Deinstitutionalization of the developmentally disabled. *Social Work, 28,* 435–439.

DeWeaver, K. L., & Kropf, N. P. (1992). Persons with mental retardation: A forgotten minority in education. *Journal of Social Work Education, 28,* 36–46.

DiClemente, R. J., Stewart, K. E., Johnson, M. O., & Pack, R. P. (1996). Adolescents and AIDS: Epidemiology, prevention, and psychological responses. In C. A. Corr & D. E. Balk (Eds.), *Handbook of adolescent death and bereavement* (pp. 85–106). New York: Springer.

DiGirolamo, A. M., Quittner, A. L., Ackerman, V., & Stevens, J. (1997). Identification and assessment of ongoing stressors in adolescents with a chronic illness: An application of the behavior-analytic model. *Journal of Clinical Child Psychology, 26,* 53–66.

Dilulio, J. J. (1996). Saving the children: Crime and social policy. In I. Garfinkel, J. L. Hochschild, & S. S. McLanahan (Eds.), *Social policies for children.* Washington, DC: The Brookings Institution.

Dixon, S. L., & Sands, R. G. (1983). Identity and the experience of crisis. *Social Casework, 64,* 222–230.

Doel, M., & Marsh, P. (1992). *Task-centered social work.* London: Ashgate.

Doll, E. (1962). A historical survey of research and management of mental retardation in the United States. In E. P. Trapp & P. Himelstein (Eds.), *Readings on Exceptional Children* (pp. 21–67). Englewood Cliffs, NJ: Appleton, Century, Crofts.

Donahue, M. J., & Benson, P. L. (1995). Religion and the well-being of adolescents. *Journal of Social Issues, 51,* 145–160.

Donohue, B., Hersen, M., & Ammerman, R. T. (1995). Historic overview. In M. Hersen & R. T. Ammerman (Eds.), *Advanced abnormal child psychology* (pp. 3–19). Hillsdale, NJ: Lawrence Erlbaum.

Downs, S. W., & Nahan, N. (1990). Mixing clients and other neighborhood families. *Public Welfare, 48,* 26–33.

Downs, W. R., & Miller, B. A. (1998). Relationships between experiences of parental violence during childhood and women's psychiatric symptomatology. *Journal of Interpersonal Violence, 13,* 438–455.

Downs, W. R., & Rose, S. R. (1991). The relationship of adolescent peer groups to the incidence of psychosocial problems. *Adolescence, 26,* 473–492.

Dubois, B., & Miley, K. K. (1996). *Social work: An empowering profession* (2nd ed.). Boston: Allyn & Bacon.

Dubow, E. F., Schmidt, D., McBride, J., Edwards, S., & Merk, F. L. (1993). Teaching children to cope with stressful experiences: Initial implementation and evaluation of a primary prevention program. *Journal of Clinical Child Psychology, 22,* 428–440.

Dulcan, M. K. (1986). Comprehensive treatment of children and adolescents with attention deficit disorders: The state of the art. *Clinical Psychology Review, 6,* 539–569.

Dulmus, C. N., & Wodarski, J. S. (1996). Assessment and effective treatments of childhood psychopathology: Responsibilities and implications for practice. *Journal of Child and Adolescent Group Therapy, 6,* 75–99.

Dumka, L. E., Roosa, M. W., Michaels, M. L., & Suh, K. W. (1995). Using research and theory to develop prevention programs for high risk families. *Family Relations, 44,* 78–86.

Dupont, H. (1994). *Emotional development, theory and applications: A neo-Piagetian perspective.* Westport, CT: Praeger.

Duran-Aydintug, C. (1993). Relationships with former in-laws: Normative guidelines and actual behavior. *Journal of Divorce and Remarriage, 19,* 69–82.

Durant, W., & Durant, A. (1965). *The age of Voltaire.* New York: Simon & Schuster.

Duttweiler, P. C. (1995). *Effective strategies for educating students in at-risk situations.* Bloomington, IN: National Educational Service.

Earls, F. J. (1994). Violence and today's youth. *The Future of Children: Critical Health Issues for Children and Youth, 4,* 4–23.

Early, B. P. (1992). An ecological-exchange model of social work consultation within the work group of the school. *Social Work in Education, 14,* 207–214.

Eber, L., & Nelson, M. (1997). School-based wraparound planning: Integrating services for students with emotional and behavioral needs. *American Journal of Orthopsychiatry, 67,* 385–395.

Edwards, M. C., Schulz, E. G., & Long, N. (1995). The role of the family in the assessment of attention deficit hyperactivity disorder. *Clinical Psychology Review, 15,* 375–394.

Effron, A. K. (1980). Children and divorce: Help from an elementary school. *Social Casework, 61,* 305–312.

Egeland, B., Pianta, R., & O'Brien, M. A. (1993). Maternal intrusiveness in infancy and child maltreatment in early school years. *Development and Psychopathology, 5,* 359–370.

Eisenberg, W., Guthrie, L., Fabes, R. A., Reiser, M., Murphy, B. C., Holgren, R., et al. (1997). The relations of regulation and emotionality to resilience and competent social functioning in elementary school children. *Child Development, 8,* 295–311.

Ell, K. (1996). Crisis theory. In F. J. Turner (Ed.), *Social work treatment* (pp. 168–190). New York: Free Press.

Elliott, D. S., Huizinga, D., & Menard, S. (1989). *Multiple problem youth: Delinquency, substance use, and mental health problems.* New York: Springer-Verlag.

Elliott, S. N., & Gresham, F. M. (1992). *Social skills intervention guide.* Circle Pines, MN: American Guidance Service.

Ellis, A. (1977). The basic theory of rational-emotive therapy. In A. Ellis & R., Grieger (Eds.), *RET handbook of rational-emotive therapy* (pp. 3–34). New York: Springer.

Emery, R. E., & Forehand, R. (1994). Parental divorce and children's well-being: A focus on resilience. In R. J. Haggerty, L. R. Sherrod, N. Garmezy, & M. Rutter (Eds.), *Stress, risk and resilience in children and adolescents: Process, mechanisms and interventions* (pp. 64–99). New York: Cambridge University Press.

Epstein, L. (1980). *Helping people: The task-centered approach.* St. Louis: C. V. Mosby.

Epstein, L. (1992). *Brief treatment and a new look at the task-centered approach.* New York: Macmillan.

Evans, C., & Eder, D. (1993). "No exit": Processes of social isolation in the middle school. *Journal of Contemporary Ethnography, 22,* 139–170.

Everett, F., Proctor, N., & Cartmell, B. (1983). Providing psychological services to American Indian children and families. *Professional Psychology: Research and Practice, 14,* 588–603.

Ewalt, P. L. (1977). A psychoanalytically oriented child guidance setting. In W. J. Reid & L. Epstein (Eds.), *Task-centered practice* (pp. 27–49). New York: Columbia University Press.

Fahlberg, V. I. (1991). *A child's journey through placement.* Indianapolis, IN: Perspectives Press.

Fantuzzo, J. W. (1990). Behavioral treatment of the victims of child abuse and neglect. *Behavior Modification, 14,* 316–339.

Fargason, Jr., C. A., Barnes, D., Schneider, D., & Galloway, B. W. (1994). Enhancing multi-agency collaboration in the management of child sexual abuse. *Child Abuse and Neglect, 18,* 859–869.

Farran, D., & Ramey, C. (1977). Infant daycare and attachment behavior towards mothers and teachers. *Child Development, 48,* 1112–1117.

Farrington, D. P. (1991). Childhood aggression and adult violence: Early precursors and life outcomes. In D. J. Pepler & K. H. Rubin (Eds.),

Development and treatment of childhood aggression (pp. 5–29). Hillsdale, NJ: Lawrence Erlbaum.

Fatout, M. F. (1990a). Aggression: A characteristic of physically abused latency children. *Child and Adolescent Social Work Journal, 5,* 365–376.

Fatout, M. F. (1990b). Consequences of abuse on the relationships of children. *Families in Society, 2,* 76–81.

Fatout, M. F. (1996). *Children in groups: A social work perspective.* Westport, CT: Auburn House.

Fatout, M., & Rose, S. R. (1995). *Task groups in the social services.* Thousand Oaks, CA: Sage.

Finkelhor, D., & Berliner, L. (1995). Research on the treatment of sexually abused children: A review and recommendations. *Journal of the American Academy of Child and Adolescent Psychiatry, 34,* 1408–1423.

Forehand, R., & Kotchick, B. A. (1996). Cultural diversity: A wake-up call for parent training. *Behavior Therapy, 27,* 187–206.

Foxhall, K. (2000). A whole new book for complying with federal rules. *Monitor on Psychology, 31,* 68–69.

Frankel, F., & Myatt, R. (1994). A dimensional approach to the assessment of social competence in boys. *Psychological Assessment, 6,* 249–254.

Franklin, C. (1992). Alternative school programs for at-risk youths. *Social Work in Education, 14,* 239–251.

Frazier, D., & LeVine, E. (1983). Reattachment therapy: Intervention with the very young physically abused child. *Psychotherapy, Research and Practice, 29,* 90–100.

Frieberg, S. (1977). *Every child's birthright: In defense of mothering.* New York: Basic Books.

Furstenberg, F., Nord, C., Peterson, J., & Zill, N. (1983). The life course of children of divorce: Marital disruption and parental contact. *American Sociological Review, 48,* 656–668.

Gallagher, T. M. (1993). Language skill and the development of social competence in school-age children. *Language, Speech, and Hearing Services in Schools, 24,* 199–205.

Gallus, J. A., & Stinski, C. L. (1994, October). *The collaborative community/school conflict resolution model.* Paper presented at the conference for Safe Schools, Safe Students: A Collaborative Approach to Achieving Safe, Disciplined and Drug-Free Schools Conducive to Learning, Washington, DC.

Garbarino, J. (1992). *Children and families in the social environment* (2nd ed.). New York: Aldine de Gruyter.

Garbarino, J., & Benn, J. L. (1992). The ecology of childbearing and child rearing. In J. Garbarino (Ed.), *Children and families in the social environment* (2nd ed., pp. 133–177). New York: Aldine de Gruyter.

Garbarino, J., Stott, F. M., and the faculty of the Erikson Institute. (1992). *What children can tell us.* San Francisco: Jossey-Bass.

Gardner, R. A. (1993). *Child psychotherapy: The initial screening and the intensive diagnostic evaluation.* Northvale, NJ: Jason Aronson.

Garfield, S. L. (1994). Research on client variables in psychotherapy. In S. L. Garfield & A. E. Bergin (Eds.), *Handbook of psychotherapy and behavior change* (4th ed., pp. 190–228). New York: Wiley.

Garfinkel, I., Hochschild, J. L., & McLanahan, S. S. (Eds.). (1996). *Social policies for children.* Washington, DC: The Brookings Institution.

Garmezy, N., & Rutter, M. (Eds.). (1983). *Stress, coping and development in children.* New York: McGraw-Hill.

Garvey, C. (1977). *Play.* Cambridge, MA: Harvard University Press.

Geldard, K., & Geldard, D. (1997). *Counselling children: A practice introduction.* Thousand Oaks, CA: Sage.

Gelfand, B. (1988). *The creative practitioner: Creative theory and method for the helping services.* New York: Haworth Press.

Germain, C. B. (1991). *Human behavior in the social enviornment: An ecological view.* New York: Columbia University Press.

Germain, C. B., & Gitterman, A. (1980). *The life model of social work practice.* New York: Columbia University Press.

Ghuman, P. A. S. (1997). Assimilation or integration? A study of Asian adolescents. *Educational Research, 39,* 23–35.

Gibson, M., & Ogbu, J. (Eds.). (1991). *Minority status and schooling: A comparative study of immigrant and involuntary minorities.* New York: Garland Press.

Gilliland, B. E., & James, R. K. (1997). *Crisis intervention strategies* (3rd ed.). Pacific Grove, CA: Brooks/Cole.

Ginnott, H. (1961). *Group psychotherapy with children: The theory and practice of play therapy.* New York: McGraw-Hill.

Glasser, W. (1965). *Reality therapy.* New York: Harper and Row.

Glen, S. (1993). Testing the reliability of a new measure of life events and experiences in childhood: The Psychosocial Assessment of Childhood Experiences (PACE). *European Child and Adolescent Psychiatry, 2,* 98–110.

Glisson, C., & James, L. (1992). The interorganizational coordination of services to children in state custody. *Administration in Social Work, 16,* 65–80.

Golden, O. (1992). *Poor children and welfare reform.* Westport, CT: Auburn House.

Golden, R. (1997). *Disposable children: America's welfare system.* Belmont, CA: Wadsworth.

Goldstein, E. G., & Noonan, M. (1999). *Short-term treatment and social work practice.* New York: Free Press.

Goldstein, J. A., Freud, A., & Solnit, A. (1979). *Before the best interest of the child.* New York: Free Press.

Goodyear, I. M. (1990). Family relationships, life events and child psychopathology. *Journal of Child Psychology and Psychiatry, 31,* 191–192.

Granello, D. H. (1995). The use of primary prevention in mental health consultation. (ERIC Document Reproduction Service No. ED382905)

Granvold, D. K. (Ed.). (1994). *Cognitive and behavioral treatment: Methods and application.* Pacific Grove, CA: Brooks/Cole.

Greenberg, M. T., & Kusche, C. A. (1993). *Promoting social and emotional development in deaf children: The PATHS project.* Seattle: University of Washington Press.

Greene, G. J. (1996). Communication theory and social work treatment. In F. J. Turner (Ed.), *Social work treatment* (pp. 116–145). New York: Free Press.

Gregory, J. F. (1997). Three strikes and they're out: African American boys and American schools' responses to misbehavior. *International Journal of Adolescence and Youth, 7,* 25–34.

Greif, G. L., & DeMaris, A. (1990). Single fathers with custody. *Families in Society, 71,* 259–266.

Gresham, F. M., & Elliott, S. N. (1990). *Social skills rating system.* Circle Pines, MN: American Guidance Service.

Grimm, D. W. (1994). Therapist spiritual and religious values in psychotherapy. *Counseling and Values, 38,* 154–164.

Group for the Advancement of Psychiatry. (1982). *The process of child therapy.* New York: Brunner/Mazel.

Guerney, L. F. (1983). Client-centered (nondirective) play therapy. In C. E. Schaefer & K. J. O'Connor (Eds.), *Handbook of play therapy.* New York: Wiley.

Gunn, S. W. (1998). The quality imperative: An answer to the chaos of the behavioral healthcare environment. *Residential Treatment for Children and Youth, 16,* 35–65.

Guralnick, M. J. (1990). Social competence and early intervention. *Journal of Early Intervention, 14,* 3–14.

Guralnick, M. M. (1992). A hierarchical model for understanding children's peer-related social competence. In S. L. Odom, S. R. McConnell, & M. A. McEvoy (Eds.), *Social competence of young children with disabilities: Issues and strategies for intervention* (pp. 37–64). Baltimore: Brookes.

Gustafson, L., & Allen, D. (1994). A new management model for child welfare. *Public Welfare, 52,* 31–40.

Haley, J. (1984). *Ordeal therapy.* San Francisco: Jossey-Bass.

Haley, J. (1987). *Problem-solving therapy* (2nd ed.). San Francisco: Jossey-Bass.

Halperin, J. M., Newcorn, J. H., Sharma, V., Healey, J. M., Wolf, L. E., Pascualvaca, D. M., et al. (1990). Inattentive and noninattentive ADHD children: Do they constitute a unitary group? *Journal of Abnormal Child Psychology, 18,* 437–449.

Hamilton, B. (1996). Ethnicity and the family life cycle: The Chinese-American family. *Family Therapy, 23,* 199–211.

Handen, B. L., (1997). Mental retardation. In E. J. Mash & L. G. Terdal (Eds.), *Assessment of childhood disorders* (3rd ed.). New York: Guilford Press.

Harold, N. B., & Harold, R. D. (1991). School-based health clinics: A vehicle for social work intervention. *Social Work in Education, 13,* 185–194.

Hart, B., & Risley, T. R. (1995). *Meaning differences in the everyday experience of young American children.* Baltimore: Paul H. Brookes.

Hartup, W. W. (1992). *Having friends, making friends, and keeping friends: Relationships as educational contexts.* Urbana, IL: ERIC Clearinghouse on Elementary and Early Childhood Education. (ERIC Document Reproduction Service No. ED345854)

Haugaard, J. J. (1992). Sexually abused children's opposition to psychotherapy. *Journal of Child Sexual Abuse, 1,* 1–16.

Haynes, K. S., & Holmes, K. A. (1994). *Invitation to social work.* White Plains, NY: Longman.

Heffer, R. W., & Kelley, M. L. (1994). Nonorganic failure to thrive: Developmental outcomes and psychosocial assessment and intervention issues. *Research in Developmental Disabilities, 15,* 247–268.

Heflinger, C. A., & Northrup, D. A. (2000). Community-level changes in behavioral health care following capitated contracting. *Children and Youth Services Review, 22,* 175–193.

Hegar, R. L., & Scannapieco, R. L. (1999). *Kinship foster care: Policy, practice, and research.* New York: Oxford University Press.

Henderson, S. E., & Sugden, D. (1992). *Movement assessment battery for children.* London: The Psychological Corporation.

Herrenkohl, E. C., Herrenkohl, L. R. C., & Egolf, B. (1994). Resilient early school-age children from maltreating homes: Outcomes in late adolescence. *American Journal of Orthopschiatry, 64,* 921–932.

Herring, R. D. (1989). American Native families: Dissolution by coercion. *Journal of Multiculural Counseling and Development, 17,* 4–13.

Herring, R. D. (1990). Understanding Native-American values: Process and content concerns for counselors. *Counseling and Values, 34,* 134–137.

Hetherington, E. M., Cox, M., & Cox, R. (1979). Play and social interaction in children following divorce. *Journal of Social Issues, 35,* 27–48.

Hewett, F. M., & Forness, S. R. (1984). *Education of exceptional learners* (3rd ed.). Boston: Allyn & Bacon.

Hinshaw, S. P., Lahey, B. B., & Hart, E. L. (1993). Issues of taxonomy and comorbidity in the development of conduct disorder. *Development and Psychopathology, 5,* 31–49.

Hoagwood, K., & Koretz, D. (1996). Embedding prevention services within systems of care: Strengthening the nexus for children. *Applied and Preventive Psychology, 5,* 225–234.

Hodge-Williams, J., Doub, N. H., & Busky, R. (1995). Total quality management (TQM) in the nonprofit setting: The Woodbourne experience. *Residential Treatment for Children and Youth, 12,* 19–30.

Hodges, W. F., Buchsbaum, H. K., & Tierney, C. W. (1983). Parent child relationships and adjustment in pre-school children in divorced and intact families. *Journal of Divorce, 7,* 43–57.

Hoffman-Plotkin, D., & Twentyman, C. T. (1984). A multi-model assessment of behavior and cognitive deficits in abused and neglected preschoolers. *Child Development, 55,* 794–802.

Holaday, M., Leach, M. M., & Davidson, M. (1994). Multicultural counseling and intrapersonal value conflict: A case study. *Counseling and Values, 38,* 136–151.

Hollinger, J. H. (1991). Introduction to adoption law and practice. In J. H. Hollinger (Ed.), *Adoption law and practice* (pp. 1–19). New York: Matthew Bender.

Hollingsworth, L. D. (2000). Adoption policy in the United States: A word of caution. *Social Work, 45,* 183–186.

Homonoff, E. E., & Maltz, P. F. (1991). Developing and maintaining a coordinated system of community-based services to children. *Community Mental Health Journal, 27,* 347–358.

Hooper-Briar, K., Broussard, C. A., Ronnau, J., & Sallee, A. L. (1995). Family preservation and support: Past, present and future. *Family Preservation Journal, 1,* 5–24.

Howe, D. (1996). *Attachment and loss in child and family social work.* Brookfield, VT: Avebury.

Hughes, D. C., & Luft, H. S. (1998). Managed care and children: An overview. *The Future of Children, 8,* 25–38.

Hughes, J. N., & Baker, D. B. (1990). *The clinical child interview.* New York: Guilford Press.

Hurlock, E. B. (1942). *Child development.* New York: McGraw-Hill.

Isabella, R., & Belsky, J. (1991). International synchrony and the origins of infant–mother attachment: A replication study. *Child Development,* *62,* 373–384.

Jacobs, T. J., & Charles, E. (1980). Life events and the occurrence of cancer in children. *Psychosomatic Medicine, 1,* 11–24.

Jacobson, D. S. (1994). Critical interactive events and child adjustment in the stepfamily: A linked family system. In D. K. Huntley (Ed.), *Understanding stepfamilies: Implications for assessment and treatment* (pp. 73–86). Alexandria, VA: American Counseling Association.

James, B. (1994). *Handbook for treatment of attachment–trauma problems in children.* New York: Free Press.

Janis, I. L. (1982). *Groupthink: Psychological studies of policy decisions and fiascoes.* Boston: Houghton Mifflin.

Janssen, J., DeHart, J., & Gerardts, M. (1994). Images of God in adolescence. *International Journal for the Psychology of Religion, 4,* 105–121.

Jarrett, R. L. (1995). Growing up poor: The family experiences of socially mobile youth in low-income African-American neighborhoods. *Journal of Adolescent Research, 10,* 111–135.

Johnson, C. F., & Cohn, D. S. (1990). The stress of child abuse and other family violence. In L. E. Arnold (Ed.), *Childhood stress* (pp. 267–296). New York: Wiley.

Johnson, D. H., & Gelso, C. J. (1982). The effectiveness of time limits in counseling and psychotherapy: A critical review. *Counseling Psychologist, 9,* 70–83.

Johnson, L. C. (1992). *Social work practice: A generalist approach* (4th ed.). Boston: Allyn & Bacon.

Jordan, W. J., Lara, J., & McPartland, J. M. (1996). Exploring the causes of early dropout among race-ethnic and gender groups. *Youth and Society, 28,* 62–94.

Kadushin, A. (1980). *Child welfare services: An introduction.* (3rd ed.). New York: Macmillan.

Kagan, S. L. (1991). *United we stand: Collaboration for child care and early education services.* New York: Teachers College Press.

Kahn, A., & Kamerman, S. B. (1992). *Integrating services integration: An overview of initiatives, issues, and possibilities.* New York: Columbia University, The National Center for Children in Poverty.

Kalter, N. (1977). Children of divorce in an outpatient psychiatric population. *American Journal of Orthopsychiatry, 47,* 40–51.

Kalter, N. (1987). Long-term effects of divorce on children: A developmental vulnerability model. *American Journal of Orthopsychiatry, 57,* 587–600.

Kalter, N., Schaefer, M., Lesowitz, M., Alpern, D., & Pickar, J. (1988). School-based support groups for children of divorce. In B. H. Gottlieb (Ed.), *Marshaling social support: Formats, processes, and effects* (pp. 165–185). Newbury Park, CA: Sage.

Kalter, N., & Schreier, S. (1994). Developmental facilitation groups for children of divorce: The elementary school model. In C. W. LeCroy (Ed.), *Handbook of child and adolescent treatment manuals* (pp. 307–342). New York: Lexington Books.

Kaminsky, H. (1986). The divorce adjustment education and support group for children. *Conciliation Courts Review, 24,* 45–49.

Kanner, L. (1962a). *Child psychiatry* (3rd ed.). Springfield, IL: Charles C. Thomas.

Kanner, L. (1962b). Emotionally disturbed children: A historic review. *Child Development, 33,* 97–102.

Kanoy, K. W., & Cunningham, J. L. (1984). Consensus of confusion in research on children and divorce: Conceptual and methodological issues. *Journal of Divorce, 7,* 45–71.

Kapp, S. A. (2000). Defining, promoting, and improving a model of school social work: The development of a tool for collaboration. *School Social Work Journal, 24,* 20–41.

Kardon, S. D. (1995). Section 504: Developing a social work perspective in schools. *Social Work in Education, 17,* 48–54.

Karoly, J. C., & Franklin, C. (1996). Using portfolios to assess students' academic strengths: A case study. *Social Work in Education, 18,* 179–186.

Kashani, J. H., & Orvaschel, H. (1990). A community study of anxiety in children and adolescents. *American Journal of Psychiatry, 147,* 313–318.

Kaslow, F. W., & Schwartz, L. L. (1987). *The dynamics of divorce: A life cycle perspective.* New York: Brunner/Mazel.

Katz, M. S. (1976). *A history of compulsory educational laws.* Bloomington, IN: Phi Delta Kappa.

Kaufman, J., & Zigler, E. (1989). The intergenerational transmission of child abuse. In D. Cicchetti & B. Calson (Eds.), *Child maltreatment: Theory and research on the causes and consequences of child abuse and neglect* (pp. 129–150). Cambridge: Cambridge University Press.

Kazdin, A. E. (1990). Premature termination from treatment among children referred for antisocial behavior. *Journal of Child Psychology and Psychiatry, 31,* 415–425.

Kazdin, A. E. (1991). Effectiveness of psychotherapy with children and adolescents. *Journal of Consulting and Clinical Psychology, 59,* 785–798.

Kelly, E. W. (1990). Counselor responsiveness to client religiousness. *Counseling and Values, 35,* 69–72.

Kennell, J., Voos, D., & Klaus, M. (1976). Parent–infant bonding. In R. Helfer & C. H. Kempe (Eds.), *Child abuse and neglect: The family and community.* Cambridge, MA: Ballinger.

Key, E. (1909). *Century of the child.* New York: Putnam.

Kirby, L. D., & Fraser, M. W. (1997). Risk and resilience in childhood. In M. W. Fraser (Ed.), *Risk and resilience in childhood: An ecological perspective* (pp. 10–33). Washington, DC: NASW Press.

Klaus, M. H., & Kennell, J. H. (1976). *Maternal-infant bonding.* St. Louis, MO: Mosby.

Klyhylo, W. H., Kay, J., & Rube, D. (1998). (Ed.). *Clinical child psychiatry.* Philadelphia: Saunders.

Knitzer, J., & Yelton, S. (1990). Collaborations between child welfare and mental health. *Public Welfare, 48,* 24–33.

Kohlberg, L. (1978). Revisions in the theory and practice of moral development. *New Directions for Child Development, 2,* 83–87.

Kopels, S. (1992). Confidentiality and the school social worker. *Social Work in Education, 14,* 203–204.

Koroloff, N. M., & Briggs, H. E. (1996). The life cycle of family advocacy organizations. *Administration in Social Work, 20,* 23–42.

Kostoulas, K. H., Berkovitz, I. H., & Arima, H. (1991). School counseling groups and children of divorce: Loosening attachment to mother in adolescent groups. *Journal of Child and Adolescent Group Therapy, 1,* 177–192.

Kranzler, E. M. (1990). Parent death in childhood. In L. E. Arnold (Ed.), *Childhood stress* (pp. 405–422). New York: Wiley.

Krener, P. G., & Sabin, C. (1985). Indochinese immigrant children: Problems in psychiatric diagnosis. *Journal of the American Academy of Child Psychiatry, 24,* 453–458.

Krill, D. F. (1996). Existential social work. In F. L. Turner (Ed.), *Social work treatment* (4th ed., pp. 250–281). New York: Free Press.

Kuehl, B. P. (1993). Child and family therapy: A collaborative approach. *The American Journal of Family Therapy, 21,* 260–266.

Kurdek, L. A., & Siesky, A. E. (1980a). Children's perceptions of their parents' divorce. *Journal of Divorce, 3,* 339–378.

Kurdek, L. A., & Siesky, A. E. (1980b). The effects of divorce on children: The relationship between parent and child perspectives. *Journal of Divorce, 4,* 85–99.

Kurtines, W. M., & Szapocznik, J. (1996). Family interaction patterns: Structural family therapy in contexts of cultural diversity. In E. D. Hibbs & P. S. Jensen (Eds.), *Psychosocial treatments for child and adolescent disorders: Empirically based strategies for clinical practice* (pp. 671–700). Washington, DC: American Psychological Association.

Kutash, K., & Rivera, V. R. (1995). Effectiveness of children's mental health services: A review of the literature. *Education and Treatment of Children, 18,* 443–477.

Lachar, D. (1993). Symptom checklists and personality inventories. In T. R. Kratochwill & R. J. Morris (Eds.), *Handbook of psychotherapy with children and adolescents* (pp. 38–57). Boston: Allyn & Bacon.

LaGreca, A. M., & Vaughn, S. (1992). Social functioning of individuals with learning disabilities. *School Psychology Review, 21,* 340–347.

Lamarine, R. J. (1995). Child and adolescent depression. *Journal of School Health, 65,* 390–393.

Lambert, M. C., Weisz, J. R., & Knight, F. (1989). Over- and undercontrolled clinic referral problems of Jamaican and American children and adolescents: The culture general and the culture specific. *Journal of Consulting and Clinical Psychology, 57,* 467–472.

Lantz, J. (1996). Cognitive theory of social work treatment. In F. J. Turner (Ed.), *Social work treatment* (4th ed., pp. 94–115). New York: Free Press.

Lassonde, L. (1996). Learning and earning: Schooling, juvenile employment, and the early life course in late nineteenth century. *Journal of Social History, 29,* 839–863.

LeCroy, C., & Rose, S. R. (1986). Helping children cope with stress. *Social Work in Education, 9,* 5–15.

LeCroy, C. W., & Ryan, L. G. (1993). Children's mental health: Designing a model social work curriculum. *Journal of Social Work Education, 39,* 318–327.

Lee, J. W., Rice, G. T., & Gillespie, V. B. (1997). Family worship patterns and their correlation with adolescent behavior and beliefs. *Journal for the Scientific Study of Religion, 36,* 372–381.

Leffert, J. S., & Siperstein, G. N. (1996). Assessment of social-cognitive processes in children with mental retardation. *American Journal on Mental Retardation, 100,* 441–455.

Leon, A. M. (1999). Family support model: Integrating service delivery in the twenty-first century. *Families in Society: The Journal of Contemporary Human Services, 80,* 14–24.

Levine, E. S., & Sallee, A. L. (1999). *Child Welfare: Clinical Theory and Practice.* Dubuque, IA: Eddie Bowers.

Levine, M., & Levine, A. (1992). *Helping children: A social history.* New York: Oxford University Press.

Levy, T. H. (1998). *Attachment, trauma, and healing: Understanding and treating attachment disorders.* Washington, DC: Child Welfare League of America Press.

Lewit, E. M., & Baker, L. G. (1994). Race and ethnicity: Changes for children. *Future of Children: Critical Health Issues for Children and Youth, 4,* 134–144.

Lieberman, A. F. (1990). Culturally sensitive intervention with children and families. *Child and Adolescent Social Work, 7,* 101–120.

Lieh-Mak, F., Lee, P. W. H., & Luk, S. L. (1984). Problems encountered in teaching Chinese parents to be behavior therapists. *Psychologia, 27,* 56–64.

Lindsey, D. (1994). *The welfare of children.* New York: Oxford University Press.

Lindsey, D., & Henly, J. R. (1997). The future of child welfare. In M. Reisch & E. Gambrill (Eds.), *Social work in the 21st Century* (pp. 100–118). Thousand Oaks, CA: Sage.

Lochman, J. E., & Dodge, K. A. (1994). Social-cognitive processes of severely violent, moderately aggressive, and nonaggressive boys. *Journal of Consulting and Clinical Psychology, 62,* 366–374.

Long, K. (1983). The experience of repeated and traumatic loss among Crow Indian children: Response patterns and intervention strategies. *American Journal of Orthopsychiatry, 52,* 116–126.

Lourie, I. S., & Katz-Leavy, J. (1991). New directions for mental health services for families and children. *Families in Society: The Journal of Contemporary Human Services, 72,* 277–285.

Lucco, A. A. (1993). Assessment of the school-age child. In J. B. Rauch (Ed.), *Assessment: A sourcebook for social work practice* (pp. 71–89). Milwaukee, WI: Families International.

Luckasson, R., Coulter, D. L., Polloway, E. A., Reiss, S., Schalock, R. L., Snell, M. E., et al. (1992). *Mental retardation: Definition, classification, and systems of support* (9th ed.). Washington, DC: American Association on Mental Retardation.

Luthar, S. S., & Zigler, E. (1991). Vulnerability and competence: A review of research on resilience in childhood. *American Journal of Orthopsychiatry, 61,* 6–22.

Lyons-Ruth, K., Alpern, L., & Repacholi, B. (1993). Disorganized infant attachment classification and maternal psychosocial problems as predictors of hostile-aggressive behavior in the preschool classroom. *Child Development, 64,* 572–585.

Lyons-Ruth, K., Zeanah, C. H., & Benoit, D. (1996). Disorder and risk for disorder during infancy and toddlerhood. In E. J. Mash & R. A. Barkley (Eds.), *Child psychopathology* (pp. 457–492). New York: Guilford Press.

Madanes, C. (1991). *Strategic family therapy.* San Francisco: Jossey-Bass.

Maki, M. T. (1990). Countertransference with adolescent clients of the same ethnicity. *Child and Adolescent Social Work, 7,* 135–145.

Mandell, D., & Birenzweig, E. (1990). Stepfamilies: A model for group work with remarried couples and their children. *Journal of Divorce and Remarriage, 14,* 29–41.

Markstrom-Adams, C., Hofstra, G., & Dougher, K. (1994). The ego-virtue of fidelity: A case for the study of religion and identity formation in adolescence. *Journal of Youth and Adolescence, 23,* 453–469.

Marshall, H. M. (1996, June). *Enhancing young children's social competence: Enhance!/Social competence program (ESCP): A field developed program for children, teachers and parents.* Paper presented at the Head Start National Research Conference, Washington, DC.

Martin, E. W., Martin, R., & Terman, D. L. (1996). The legislative and litigation history of special education for students. *The Future of Children: Special Education for Students with Disabilities, 6,* 25–39.

Martin, T. F. (1993). The new American family service agency. *Families in Society: The Journal of Contemporary Human Services, 74,* 178–181.

Mash, E. J., Dozois, D. J., & Barkley, R. A. (1996). Child psychopathology: A developmental-systems perspective. In E. J. Mash & R. A. Barkley (Eds.), *Child psychopathology* (pp. 3–62). New York: Guilford Press.

Masten, A. S. (1994). Resilience in individual development: Successful adaptation despite risk and adversity. In M. C. Wang & E. W. Gordon (Eds.), *Educational resilience in inner-city America* (pp. 3–25). Hillsdale, NJ: Lawrence Erlbaum.

Masten, A. S., Best, K. M., & Garmezy, N. (1990). Resilience and development: Contributions from the study of children who overcome adversity. *Development and Psychopathology, 2,* 425–441.

Mather, J. H., & Lager, P. B. (2000). *Child welfare.* Belmont, CA: Brooks/Cole.

Maughan, B. (1988). School experiences as risk/protective factors. In M. Rutter (Ed.), *Studies of psychosocial risk: The power of longitudinal data* (pp. 200–220). New York: Cambridge University Press.

Maultsby, M. (1975). *Help yourself to happiness.* New York: Institution for Rational Living.

McAfee, O., & Leong, D. (1994). *Assessing and guiding young children's development and learning.* Boston: Allyn & Bacon.

McCord, J. (1983). A forty-year perspective on effects of child abuse and neglect. *Child Abuse and Neglect, 7,* 265–270.

McDonald, L., Bradish, D. C., Billingham, S., Dibble, N., & Rice, C. (1991). Families and schools together: An innovative substance abuse prevention program. *Social Work in Education, 13,* 118–128.

McFarland, R. B., & Lockerbie, G. (1994). Difficulties in treating ritually abused children. *The Journal of Psychohistory, 21,* 429–434.

McGee, R., Feehan, M., Williams, S., & Anderson, J. (1992). DSM-III disorders from age 11 to age 15 years. *Journal of the American Academy of Child and Adolescent Psychiatry, 31,* 50–59.

McKay, M. M., McCadam, K., & Gonzales, J. J. (1996). Addressing the barriers to mental health services for inner city children and their caretakers. *Community Mental Health Journal, 32,* 353–361.

McKinzie, J. K. (1993). Adoption of children with special needs. *The Future of Children: Adoptions, 3,* 62–72.

McLanahan, S., & Booth, K. (1989). Mother only families: Problems, prospects and politics. *Journal of Marriage and the Family, 51,* 557–580.

McMahon, R. J., & Wells, K. C. (1989). Conduct disorders. In E. J. Mash & R. A. Barkley (Eds.), *Treatment of childhood disorders* (pp. 73–134). New York: Guilford Press.

Meichenbaum, D. (1977). *Cognitive behavior modification.* New York: Plenum Press.

Meltzer, M. (1967). *Bread and roses: The struggle of American labor.* New York: Knopf.

Memon, A., Cronin, O., Eaves, R., & Bull, R. (1993). The cognitive interview and child witnesses. *Issues in Criminological and Legal Psychology, 20,* 3–9.

Mental health needs of children in foster care: A case of benign neglect? (1996). Summary of a forum, University of Minnesota.

Mervis, B. A. (1989). Shaggy dog stories: A video project for children of divorce. *Social Work in Education, 12,* 16–26.

Mesalum, M. M. (1990). Large-scale neurocognitive networks and distributed processing for attention, language, and memory. *Annals of Neurology, 28,* 597–613.

Meyer, L. H., Cole, D. A., McQuarter, R., Reichle, J. (1990). Validation of the Assessment of Social Competence (ASC) for children and young adults with developmental disabilities. *JASH, 15,* 57–68.

Meyers, M. K. (1993). Organizational factors in the integration of services for children. *Social Service Review, 67,* 547–575.

Michelson, L., & Wood, R. (1980). A group assertive training program for elementary school children. *Child Behavior Therapy, 2,* 1–9.

Miller, L. C. (1972). School behavior checklist: An inventory of deviant behavior for elementary school children. *Journal of Consulting and Clinical Psychology, 38,* 134–144.

Mills, C., & Usher, D. (1996). A kinship care case management approach. *Child Welfare, 75,* 600–618.

Mohsin, M., Nath, S. R., & Chowdhury, A. M. R. (1996). Influence of socioeconomic factors on basic competencies of children in Bangladesh. *Journal of Biosocial Sciences, 28,* 15–24.

Monkman, M., & Allen-Meares, P. (1985). The TIE framework: A conceptual map for social work assessment. *Arete, 10,* 41–49.

Moritsugu, J., & Sue, S. (1983). Minority status as a stressor. In R. D. Felner, L. A. Jason, J. N. Moritsugu, & S. S. Farber (Eds.), *Preventive psychology: Theory, research and practice* (pp. 162–174). Elmsford, NY: Pergamon Press.

Morris, R. J., & Kratochwill, T. R. (1998). *The practice of child therapy.* Boston: Allyn & Bacon.

Morrison, K., & Stollman, W. (1995). Stepfamily assessment: An integrated model. *Journal of Divorce & Remarriage, 24,* 163–182.

Morrissey, J. P., Johnsen, M. C., & Calloway, M. O. (1997). Evaluating performance and change in mental health systems serving children and youth: An interorganizational network approach. *The Journal of Mental Health Administration, 24,* 4–22.

Mosher, J. P., & Handal, P. J. (1998). The relationship between religion and psychological distress in adolescents. *Journal of Psychology and Theology, 25,* 449–457.

Muster, N. J. (1992). Treating the adolescent victim-turned-offender. *Adolescence, 27,* 441–450.

National Center for Children in Poverty. (1990). *Five million children: A statistical profile of our poorest young children.* Columbia University, New York: School of Public Health.

National Commission on Children. (1991). *Beyond rhetoric: A new American agenda for children and families* (Publication No. 91-22834).

Washington, DC: U.S. Government Printing Office.

National Institute of Mental Health. (1990). *Research on children and adolescents with mental, behavioral and developmental disorder.* Rockville, MD: National Institute of Mental Health.

Nelsen, J. C. (1980). *Communication theory and social work practice.* Chicago: University of Chicago Press.

Nettles, S. M., & Pleck, J. H. (1994). Risk, resilience, and development: The multiple ecologies of black adolescents. In R. J. Haggerty, L. R. Sherrod, N. Garmezy, & M. Rutter (Eds.), *Stress risk and resilience in children and adolescents: Processes, mechanisms, and interventions* (pp. 147–181). New York: Cambridge University Press.

Newacheck, P. (1992). Characteristics of children with high and low usage of physician services. *Medical Care, 30,* 30–42.

Newton-Logstron, G., & Armstrong, M. I. (1993). School based mental health services. *Social Work in Education, 15,* 187–191.

Ninness, H. A. C., Glenn, S. S., & Ellis, J. (1993). *Assessment and treatment of emotional or behavioral disorders.* Westport, CT: Praeger.

Norris-Shortle, C., Young, P. A., & Williams, M. A. (1993). Understanding death and grief for children three and younger. *Social Work, 38,* 736–741.

Northen, H. (1982). *Clinical social work.* New York: Columbia University Press.

Norton, A. J., & Miller, L. F. (1992). *Marriage, divorce and remarriage in the 1990s* (U.S. Bureau of the Census, Current Population Reports, Series P-23, No. 180). Washington, DC: U.S. Government Printing Office.

Nunez, R. (1995). Family values among homeless families. *Public Welfare, 53,* 24–32.

Nurcombe, B., & Partlett, D. F. (1994). *Child mental health and the law.* New York: Free Press.

O'Brien, J. D. (1981). Talking with and listening to children. *Bulletin of the New York Academy of Medicine, 57,* 382–386.

Oden, S., & Asher, S. R. (1977). Coaching children in social skills for friendship making. *Child Development, 48,* 495–506.

O'Donnell, J., Hawkins, J. D., & Abbott, R. D. (1995). Predicting serious delinquency and substance abuse among aggressive boys. *Journal of Consulting and Clinical Psychology, 63,* 529–537.

Office of Juvenile Justice and Delinquency Prevention. (1995, June). *Juvenile justice bulletin: OJJDP update on programs.* Washington, DC: U.S. Department of Justice, Office of Justice Programs.

Oosterhoff, A. (1994). *Classroom applications of educational measurement.* New York: Merrill.

O'Reilly, E., & Morrison, M. L. (1993). Grandparent-headed families: New therapeutic challenges. *Child Psychiatry and Human Development, 23,* 147–159.

Orton, J. L. (1996). *Strategies for counseling children and their parents.* Pacific Grove, CA: Brooks/Cole.

Osman, A., Downs, W. R., Kopper, B. A., Barrios, F. X., Baker, M. T., Osman, J. R., et al. (1998). The Reasons for Living Inventory for Adolescents (RFL-A): Development and psychometric properties. *Journal of Clinical Psychology, 54,* 1063–1078.

Parad, H. J., & Parad, L. G. (1990). *Crisis intervention.* Milwaukee, WI: Family Service of America.

Parish, T. S., & Wigle, S. E. (1985). A longitudinal study of the impact of parental divorce on adolescents' evaluation of self and parents. *Adolescence, 20,* 239–245.

Park, I. H., & Cho, L. (1995). Confucianism and the Korean family. *Journal of Comparative Family Studies, 26,* 117–134.

Parkes, C. M., & Stevenson-Hinde, L. (Eds.). (1982). *The place of attachment in human behavior.* New York: Basic Books.

Parson, E. R. (1993a). Ethnotherapeutic empathy (EthE)—Part I: Definition, theory, and process. *Journal of Contemporary Psychotherapy, 23,* 5–18.

Parson, E. R. (1993b). Ethnotherapeutic empathy (EthE)—Part II: Techniques in interpersonal cognition and vicarious experiencing across cultures. *Journal of Contemporary Psychotherapy, 23,* 171–182.

Pasick, P. L., & Pasick, R. S. (1985). The developing child. In J. Laird & A. Hartmann (Eds.), *A handbook of child welfare: Context, knowledge, and practice* (pp. 178–192). New York: Free Press.

Pasley, K., Rhoden, L., Visher, E. B., & Visher, J. S. (1996). Successful stepfamily therapy: Clients' perspectives. *Journal of Marital and Family Therapy, 22,* 343–357.

Paster, V. S. (1985). Adapting psychotherapy for the depressed, unacculturated, acting-out, black male adolescent. *Psychotherapy, 22,* 408–417.

Pasternack, R., & Peres, Y. (1990). To what extent can the school reduce the gaps between children raised by divorced and intact families? *Journal of Divorce and Remarriage, 15,* 143–157.

Patel, N., Power, T. G., & Bhavnagri, N. P. (1996). Socialization values and practices of Indian immigrant parents: Correlates of modernity and acculturation. *Child Development, 67,* 302–313.

Pawliuk, N., Grizenko, N., Chan, Y. A., Gantous, P., Mathew, J., & Nguyen, D. (1996). Acculturation style and psychological functioning in children of immigrants. *American Journal of Orthopsychiatry, 66,* 111–121.

Pecora, P., Whittaker, J., Maluccio, A., Barth, R., & Plotnick, R. (1992). *The child welfare challenge: Policy, practice and research.* New York: Aldine de Gruyter.

Peretti, P. O., & Wilson, T. T. (1995). Unfavorable outcomes of the identity crisis among African-American adolescents influenced by enforced acculturation. *Social Behavior and Personality, 23,* 171–175.

Perlman, H. H. (1957). *Social casework: A problem-solving process.* Chicago: University of Chicago Press.

Pinderhughes, E. (1995). Empowering diverse populations: Family practice in the 21st century. *Families in Society, 76,* 131–140.

Pine, B. A., Warsh, R., & Maluccio, A. N. (1993). *Together again: Family reunification in foster care.* Washington, DC: Child Welfare League of America.

Plenk, A. M. (1993). *Helping young children at risk: A psycho-educational approach.* Westport, CT: Praeger.

Popple, P. R., & Leighninger, L. (1996). *Social work, social welfare and American society* (3rd ed.). Boston: Allyn & Bacon.

Popple, P. R., & Leighninger, L. (1999). *Social work and social welfare in American society* (4th ed.). Boston, MA: Allyn & Bacon.

Porro, B. (1996). *Talk it out: Conflict resolution in the elementary classroom.* Alexandria, VA: Association for Supervision and Curriculum Development.

Prinz, R. J., & Miller, G. E. (1994). Family-based treatment for childhood antisocial behavior: Experimental influences on dropout and engagement. *Journal of Consulting and Clinical Psychology, 62,* 645–650.

Pruitt, D. B. (1999). *Your adolescent: Emotional, behavioral, and cognitive development from early adolescence through the teen years.* New York: HarperCollins.

Pryor, C. B. (1992). Integrating immigrants into American schools. *Social Work in Education, 14,* 153–159.

Pryor, C. B., Kent, C., McGunn, C., & LeRoy, B. (1996). Redesigning social work in inclusive schools. *Social Work, 41,* 668–676.

Pumphrey, R. E., & Pumphrey, M. W. (Eds.). (1961). *The heritage of American social work.* New York: Columbia University Press.

Quinton, D., & Rutter, M. (1976). Early hospital admissions and later disturbance of behavior: An attempted replication of Douglas' findings. *Development of Medical Child Neurology, 18,* 447–459.

Radin, N. (1990). A new arena for school social work practice: At-risk infants and toddlers. *Social Work in Education, 12,* 275–281.

Radin, N. (1992). A peer feedback approach to assessing school social workers as team members. *Social Work in Education, 14,* 57–62.

Radke-Yarrow, M., & Sherman, T. (1990). Hard growing: Children do survive. In J. Rolf, A. Masten, D. Ciccketti, K. H. Nuerchterlein, & S. Wintraub (Eds.), *Risk and protective factors in the development of psychotherapy* (pp. 97–119). New York: Cambridge University Press.

Rak, C. F., & Patterson, L. E. (1996). Promoting resilience in at-risk children. *Journal of Counseling & Development, 74,* 368–373.

Rauch, J. B. (Ed.). (1993). *Assessment: A sourcebook for social work practice.* Milwaukee, WI: Families International.

Reder, P., & Eve, B. (1981). Some considerations on the clinic treatment of children of divorce. *British Journal of Medical Psychology, 54,* 167–173.

Reid, W. (1979). *The task-centered system.* New York: Columbia University Press.

Reid, W. J. (1996). Task-centered social work. In F. J. Turner (Ed.), *Social work treatment* (pp. 617–640). New York: Free Press.

Reid, W. J., & Bailey-Dempsey, C. (1995). The effects of monetary incentives on school performance. *Families in Society: The Journal of Contemporary Human Services, 76,* 331–340.

Reid, W. J., & Shyne, A. (1969). *Brief and extended casework.* New York: Columbia University Press.

Reinecke, M. A., Dattilio, F. M., & Freeman, A. (1996). General issues. In M. A. Reinecke, F. M. Dattilio, & A. Freeman (Eds.), *Cognitive therapy with children and adolescents: A caseload for clinical practice* (pp. 1–9). New York: Guilford Press.

Reitz, M., & Watson, K. W. (1992). *Adoption and the family system.* New York: Guilford Press.

Richards, H., & Goodman, R. (1996). Are only children different? A study of child psychiatric referrals, A research note. *Journal of Child Psychology and Psychiatry, 37,* 753–757.

Rigsby, L. C. (1994). The Americanization of resilience: Deconstructing research practice. In M. C. Wang & E. W. Gordon (Eds.), *Educational resilience in inner city America* (pp. 45–76). Hillsdale, NJ: Lawrence Erlbaum.

Roberts, A. R. (1991). Conceptualizing crisis theory and crisis intervention model. In A. R. Roberts (Ed.), *Contemporary perspectives in crisis intervention and prevention* (pp. 3–17). Englewood Cliffs, NJ: Prentice-Hall.

Robertson, J., & Robertson, J. (1971). Young children in brief separation: A fresh look. *Psychoanalytic Study of the Child, 26,* 264–315.

Robison, S., & Binder, H. (1993). Building bridges for families. *Public Welfare, 51,* 14–20.

Rog, D. J. (1992). Child and adolescent mental health services: Evaluation challenges. *New Directions for Program Evaluation, 54,* 5–16.

Rogers, C. R. (1986). Client-centered therapy. In L. L. Kutash & A. Wolf (Ed.), *Psychotherapist's casebook* (pp. 197–208). San Francisco: Jossey-Bass.

Roizblatt, A., & Pilowsky, D. (1996). Forced migration and resettlement: Its impact on families and individuals. *Contemporary Family Therapy, 18,* 513–521.

Rooney, R. H. (1992). *Strategies for work with involuntary clients.* New York: Columbia University Press.

Rose, S. R. (1989a). Members leaving groups: Theoretical and practical considerations. *Small Group Behavior, 20,* 524–535.

Rose, S. R. (1989b). Teaching single parents to cope with stress through small group intervention. *Small Group Behavior, 20,* 259–269.

Rose, S. R. (1998). *Group work with children and adolescents: Prevention and intervention in school and community systems.* Thousand Oaks, CA: Sage.

Rose, S. R. (1999). Towards the development of an internalized conscience: Theoretical perspectives on socialization. *Journal of Human Behavior in the Social Environment, 2,* 15–18.

Rost, D. H., & Czeschlik, T. (1994). Popular and intelligent? Rejected and dumb? A sociometric study with 6,500 primary school children. *Zeitschrift-fur-Sozialpsychologie, 25*(2), 170–176.

Rowe, W. (1996). Client-centered theory: A person-centered approach. In F. J. Turner (Ed.), *Social work treatment: Interlocking theoretical approaches* (pp. 69–93). New York: Free Press.

Rozendal, F. G. (1983). Halos vs. stigmas: Long term effects of parent's death or divorce on college students' concepts of the family. *Adolescence, 18,* 947–955.

Ruggles, S. (1994). The origins of African-American family structure. *American Sociological Review, 59,* 136–151.

Russell, A. T., Bott, I., & Sammons, C. (1989). The phenomenology of schizophrenia occurring in childhood. *Journal of the American Academy of Child and Adolescent Psychiatry, 28,* 399–407.

Rutter, B. (1978). *The parent's guide to foster family care.* New York: Child Welfare League of America.

Rutter, M. (1985). Psychological therapies in child psychiary: Issues and prospects. In M. Rutter & L. Hersov (Eds.), *Child and adolescent: Modern approaches* (2nd ed., pp. 9–20). Oxford: Blackwell Scientific Press.

Rutter, M. (1988). The role of cognition in child development and disorder. *Annual Progress in Child Psychiatry and Child Development,* 77–101.

Rutter, M. (1990). Psychosocial resilience and protective mechanisms. In J. Rolf, A. S. Masten, D. Cicchetti, K. H. Nuechterlein, & S. Weintraub (Eds.), *Risk and protective factors in the development of psychotherapy* (pp. 181–214). New York: Cambridge University Press.

Rutter, M. (1995). Clinical implications of attachment concepts: Retrospect and prospect. *Journal of Child Psychology and Psychiatry, 36,* 549–571.

Rycus, J. S., & Hughes, R. C. (1998). Adoptions. In J. S. Rycus & R. C. Hughes (Eds.), *Field guide to child welfare: Placement and permanence.* Washington, DC: Child Welfare League of America.

Saayman, G., & Saayman, R. (1989). The adversarial legal process and divorce. *Journal of Divorce, 11,* 329–337.

Saccuzzo, D. P., Johnson, N. E., & Guertin, T. L. (1994). Information processing in gifted versus nongifted African American, Latino, and white children: Speeded versus nonspeeded paradigms. *Intelligence, 19*(2), 219–243.

Sam, D. L. (1992). Psychological acculturation of young visible immigrants. *Migration World, 20,* 21–24.

Sandberg, S., Rutter, M., Giles, S., Owen, A., Champion, L., Nicholls, J., et al. (1993). Assessment of psychosocial experiences in childhood: Methodological issues and some illustrative findings. *Journal of Child Psychology and Psychiatry, 34,* 879–897.

Santisteban, D. A., Szapocznik, J., Perez-Vidal, A., Kurtines, W. M., Murray, E. J., & LaPerriere, A. (1996). Efficacy of intervention for engaging youth and families into treatment and some variables that may contribute to differential effectiveness. *Journal of Family Psychology, 10,* 35–44.

Sarbin, T. R. (1954). Role theory. In G. Lindzey (Ed.), *Handbook of social psychology, Vol. 1* (pp. 223–258). Cambridge, MA: Addison-Wesley.

Sarri, C. (1986). *Clinical social work treatment: How does it work?* New York: Gardner Press.

Saxe, L., Cross, T., & Silverman, N. (1988). Children's mental health: The gap between what we know and what we do. *American Psychologist, 43,* 800–807.

Scannapieco, M. (1994). School-linked programs for adolescents from high-risk, urban environments: A review of research and practice. *School Social Work Journal, 18,* 16–27.

Schatz, M. S., & Horejsi, C. (1996). The importance of religious tolerance: A module for educating foster parents. *Child Welfare, 75,* 73–86.

Schreier, S., & Kalter, N. (1990). School-based developmental facilitation groups for children of divorce. *Social Work in Education, 13,* 58–67.

Schuerman, J. R., Rzepnicki, T. L., & Littell, J. H. (1994). *Putting families first.* New York: Aldine de Gruyter.

Schwartz, I. M., Barton, W. H., & Orlando, F. (1991). Keeping kids out of secure detention. *Public Welfare, 49,* 20–26.

Seaberg, J. R. (1988). Child well-being scales: A critique. *Social Work Research and Abstracts, 24,* 9–15.

Sears, S. J., & Milburn, J. (1990). School-age stress. In L. E. Arnold (Ed.), *Childhood stress* (pp. 223–246). New York: Wiley.

Segal, J., & Segal, Z. (1989). Dealing with parents. *Journal of Divorce and Remarriage, 7,* 201–204.

Segal, L. (1991). Brief family therapy. In A. M. Horne & L. Passmore (Eds.), *Family counseling and therapy* (2nd ed., pp. 179–206). Itasca, IL: F. E. Peacock.

Segal, U. A. (1991). Cultural variables in Asian Indian families. *Families in Society, 72,* 233–242.

Selman, R. L., & Schultz, L. (1990). *Making a friend in youth: Developmental theory and pair therapy.* Chicago: University of Chicago Press.

Semrud-Clikeman, M. (1995). *Child and adolescent therapy.* Boston: Allyn & Bacon.

Serbin, L. A., Peters, P. L., McAffer, V. J., & Schwartzman, A. E. (1991). Childhood aggression and withdrawal as predictors of adolescent pregnancy, early parenthood, and environmental risk for the next generation. *Canadian Journal of Behavioural Science, 23,* 318–331.

Shelton, T. L., & Barkley, R. A. (1994). Attention deficit disorders in children. *Topics in Language Disorders, 14,* 26–41.

Sheppard, D. I., & Zangrillo, P. A. (1996). Coordinating investigations of child abuse. *Public Welfare, 54,* 21–31.

Shneidman, E. S. (1985). *Definition of suicide.* New York: Wiley.

Shor, R. (1998). The significance of religion in advancing a culturally sensitive approach towards child maltreatment. *Families in Society, 79,* 400–409.

Shure, M. B. (1994). *Raising a thinking child.* New York: Simon & Schuster.

Simeon, J. G., & Ferguson, H. B. (Eds.). (1990). *Treatment strategies in child and adolescent psychiatry.* New York: Plenum.

Simon, J. (1990). The single parent: Power and the integrity of parenting. *The American Journal of Psychoanalysis, 50,* 187–198.

Simpson, J. A., & Rhole, W. S. (Eds.). (1998). *Attachment theory and close relationships.* New York: Guilford Press.

Siperstein, G. N. (1992). Social competence: An important construct in mental retardation. *American Journal on Mental Retardation, 96,* iii–vi.

Siporin, M. (1975). *Introduction to social work practice.* New York: Macmillan.

Siu, S., & Hogan, P. T. (1989). Common clinical themes in child welfare. *Social Work, 34,* 339–344.

Sleeuwenhoek, H. C., Boter, R. D., & Vermeer, A. (1995). Perceptual-motor performance and the social development of visually impaired children. *Journal of Visual Impairment and Blindness, 89,* 359–367.

Smith, E. P., & Merkel-Holguin, L. A. (Eds.). (1996). *A history of child welfare.* New York: Child Welfare League of America.

Sokoloff, B. Z. (1993). Antecedents of American adoptions. *The Future of Children: Adoptions, 3,* 17–25.

Somers, M. L. (1976). Problem-solving in small groups. In R. W. Roberts & H. Northen (Eds.), *Theories of social work with groups* (pp. 368–394). New York: Columbia University Press.

Sroufe, L. A. (1985). Attachment classification from the perspective of infant–caregiver relationship and infant temperament. *Child Development, 56,* 1–14.

Sroufe, L. A., Fox, N. E., & Pancake, V. R. (1983). Attachment and dependency in development perspective. *Child Development, 54,* 1615–1627.

Stark, R. (1996). Religion as context: Hellfire and delinquency one more time. *Sociology of Religion, 57,* 163–173.

Stayton, D. J., & Ainsworth, M. D. S. (1973). Individual differences in infant responses to brief, everyday separation as related to other infant and maternal behaviors. *Developmental Psychology, 9,* 226–235.

Steiner, G. Y. (1981). *The futility of family policy.* Washington, DC: Brookings Institute.

Steinhauer, P. D. (1991). *The least detrimental alternative.* Toronto, Ontario, Canada: University of Toronto Press.

Sternberg, R. J. (1997). The concept of intelligence and its role in lifelong learning and success. *American Psychologist, 52,* 1030–1037.

Stilwell, B., Galvin, M., & Kopta, S. M. (1991). Conceptualization of conscience in normal children and adolescents, ages 5 to 17. *Journal of the American Academy of Child and Adolescent Psychiatry, 30,* 16–21.

Stilwell, B. M., Galvin, M., Kopta, S. M., & Norton, J. A. (1994). Moral-emotional responsiveness: A two-factor domain of conscience functioning. *Journal of the American Academy of Child and Adolescent Psychiatry, 33,* 130–139.

Stolberg, A. L., & Mahler, J. L. (1989). Protecting children from the consequences of divorce: An empirically derived approach. *Prevention in Human Services, 7,* 161–176.

Strahan, B. J. (1994). *Parents, adolescents, and religion.* Corranbong, New South Wales: Avondale Academic Press.

Strauss, J. B., & McGann, J. (1987). Building a network for children of divorce. *Social Work in Education, 9,* 96–105.

Stroul, B. A., & Friedman, R. M. (1986). *A system of care for severely emotionally disturbed children and youth* (revised). Washington, DC: Georgetown University Child Development Center, Child and Adolescent Service System Program (CASSP) Technical Assistance Center.

Sugarman, D. B., & Hotaling, G. T. (1989). Dating violence: Prevalence, context, and risk markers. In M. A. Pirog-Good & J. E. Stets (Eds.), *Violence in dating relationships* (pp. 3–32). New York: Praeger.

Sundel, S., & Sundel, M. (1993). *Behavior modification in human services* (3rd ed.). Newbury Park, CA: Sage.

Szepkouski, G. M., Gauvain, M., & Carberry, M. (1994). The development of planning skills in children with and without mental retardation. *Journal of Applied Developmental Psychology, 15*(2), 187–206.

Taft, J. (1937). The relation of function to process in social case work. *The Journal of Social Work Process, 1,* 1–18.

Takeuchi, D. T., Bui, K., & Kim, L. (1993). The referral of minority adolescents to community mental health centers. *Journal of Health and Social Behavior, 34,* 153–164.

Tallal, P., Townsend, J., Curtiss, S., & Wulfeck, P. (1991). Phenotypic profiles of language-impaired children based on genetic/family history. *Brain and Language, 41,* 81–95.

Tapper, D., Kleinman, P., & Nakashian, M. (1997). An interagency collaboration strategy for linking schools with social and criminal justice services. *Social Work in Education, 19,* 176–188.

Tems, C. L., Stewart, S. M., Skinner, J. R., Hughes, C. W., & Emslie, G. (1993). Cognitive distortions in depressed children and adolescents: Are they state dependent or traitlike? *Journal of Clinical Child Psychology, 22,* 316–326.

Terman, D. L., Larner, M. B., Stevenson, C. S., & Behrman, R. E. (1996). Special education for students with disabilities: Analysis and recommendations. *The Future of Children: Special Education for Students with Disabilities, 6,* 4–24.

Tharp, R. G. (1991). Cultural diversity and treatment of children. *Journal of Consulting and Clinical Psychology, 59,* 799–812.

Thomlison, B., & Thomlison, R. (1996). Behavior theory and social work treatment. In F. J. Turner (Ed.), *Social work treatment* (pp. 39–68). New York: Free Press.

Thompson, C. L., & Rudolph, L. B. (1988). *Counseling children* (2nd ed.). Pacific Grove, CA: Brooks/Cole.

Thompson, R. A. (1994). Emotion regulation: A theme in search of definition. In N. A. Fox (Ed.), The development of emotion regulation (pp. 25–52). *Monographs of the Society for Research in Child Development, 59* (Serial No. 240).

Tizard, B., & Rees, J. (1974). A comparison of the effects of adoption, restoration to the natural mother, and continued institutionalization on the cognitive development of four year old children. *Child Development, 45,* 92–99.

Toseland, R. W., & Rivas, R. F. (1995). *An introduction to group work practice* (2nd ed.). Boston: Allyn & Bacon.

Tremblay, R. E., Pagani-Kurtz, L., Masse, L. C., Vitaro, F., & Pihl, R. O. (1995). A bimodal preventive intervention for disruptive kindergarten boys: Its impact through mid-adolescence. *Journal of Consulting and Clinical Psychology, 63,* 560–568.

Triseliotis, J. (1983). Identity and security in adoption and long term fostering. *Adoption and Fostering, 7,* 22–31.

Tudor, K. (1996). *Mental health promotion: Paradigms and practice.* London: Routledge.

Tuma, J. (1989). Mental health services for children: The state of the art. *American Psychologist, 44,* 188–199.

Turner, F. J. (1996). An interlocking perspective for treatment. In F. J. Turner (Ed.), *Social work treatment: Interlocking theoretical approaches* (pp. 699–711). New York: Free Press.

Turner, J., & Jaco, R. M. (1996). Problem-solving theory and social work treatment. In F. J. Turner (Ed.), *Social work treatment: Interlocking theoretical approaches* (pp. 503–522). New York: Free Press.

U.S. Bureau of the Census. (1992). 1990 Census of population, 1990 CP-1-4, General population characteristics. Washington, DC: U.S. Government Printing Office.

U.S. Congress. (1994). *Catalogue of hope: Crime prevention programs for at-risk children.* Washington, DC: Senate Committee on the Judiciary.

U.S. Congress, Office of Technology Assessment, Delinquency Prevention Services. (1991). In *Adolescent Health, Vol. 2, Background and effectiveness of selected prevention and treatment services* (pp. 583–589). Washington, DC: U.S. Department of Justice.

U.S. Congress, Office of Technology Assessment. (1986). *Children's mental health: Problems and services.* Washington, DC: U.S. Government Printing Office.

U.S. Department of Education. (1994). *Sixteenth annual report to Congress on the implementation of the Individuals with Disabilities Education Act.* Washington, DC: U.S. Government Printing Office.

U.S. House of Representatives Select Committee on Children, Youth, and Families. (1989). *No place to call home: Discarded children in America.* Washington, DC: U.S. Government Printing Office.

Van Aken, M. A. G. (1992). The development of general competence and domain-specific competencies. *European Journal of Personality, 6,* 267–282.

Van Gorder, E., & Hashimoto, B. (1993). Hawaii reaches out to the multineeds child. *Public Welfare, 51,* 6–13.

Vigilante, F. W. (1990). Family and school responses to learning disabilities: An interactive perspective. *Social Work in Education, 12,* 151–165.

Voydanoff, P. (1995). A family perspective on services integration. *Family Relations, 44,* 63–68.

Wachtel, E. F. (1994). *Treating troubled children and their families.* New York: Guilford Press.

Wagner, M. M., & Blackorby, J. (1996). Transition from high school to college: How special education students fare. In *Future of children: Special education for students with disabilities: Analysis and recommendations* (Vol. 6, pp. 103–120).

Wagner, M., Blackorby, J., Cameto, R., & Newton, L. (1993). *What makes a difference? Influences on postschool outcomes of youth with disabilities.* Menlo Park, CA: SRI International.

Walker, H. M., Schwarz, I. E., Nippold, M. A., Irvin, L. K., & Noell, J. W. (1994). Social skills in school-age children and youth: Issues and best practices in assessment and intervention. *Topics in Language Disorders, 14,* 70–82.

Wallerstein, J. S., & Kelly, J. B. (1976). The effects of parental divorce: Experiences of the child in later latency. *American Journal of Orthopsychiatry, 46,* 256–269.

Wallerstein, J., & Kelly, J. B. (1979). Children of divorce: A review. *Social Work, 24,* 468–475.

Wallerstein, J., & Kelly, J. (1980). *Surviving the breakup: How children and parents cope with divorce.* New York: Basic Books.

Wang, M. C., Haertel, G. D., & Walberg, H. J. (1994). Educational resilience in inner cities. In M. C. Wang & E. W. Gordon (Eds.), *Educational resilience in inner-city America* (pp. 45–76). Hilldale, NJ: Lawrence Erlbaum.

Warsh, R., Pine, B. A., & Maluccio, A. N. (1996). *Reconnecting families: A guide to strengthening family reunification services.* Washington, DC: Child Welfare League of America.

Waterman, B. B. (1994). *Assessing children for the presence of a disability*. Washington, DC: National Information Center for Children and Youth with Disabilities.

Watkins, K. P., & Durant, L. (1996). *Working with children and families affected by substance abuse*. West Nyack, NY: Center for Applied Research in Education.

Watson, K. W. (1992). Providing services after adoption. *Public Welfare, 50,* 5–13.

Wattenberg, E. (1994). Neglected children: Killing them softly. In *Children in the shadows: The fate of children in neglecting families*. Proceedings of a conference, Minneapolis, University of Minnesota.

Watzlawick, P., Beavin, J. H., & Jackson, D. D. (1967). *Pragmatics of human communication: A study of interactional patterns, pathologies, and paradoxes*. New York: Norton.

Webb, N. B. (1996). *Social work practice with children*. New York: Guilford Press.

Weiner, M. L. (1985). *Cognitive experiential therapy: An integrative ego psychotherapy*. New York: Brunner/Mazel.

Weiner, N. (1989). Violent criminal careers and violent criminals: An overview of the literature. In N. Weiner & M. E. Wolfgang (Eds.), *Violent crimes, violent criminals* (pp. 35–138). Newbury Park, CA: Sage.

Weinman, M. L., Solomon, C., & Glass, M. B. (2000). The effect of a school-based program in increasing school performance, health, and behavioral outcomes among pregnant and parenting teens. *School Social Work Journal, 24,* 42–56.

Weissberg, R. P. (1990). Support for school-based social competence promotion. *American Psychologist, 45,* 986–988.

Weissberg, R. P., Caplan, M., & Harwood, R. L. (1991). Promoting competent young people in competence-enhancing environments: A systems-based perspective on primary prevention. *Journal of Consulting and Clinical Psychology, 59,* 830–841.

Weissberg, R. P., & Elias, M. J. (1993). Enhancing young people's social competence and health behavior: An important challenge for educators, scientists, policymakers, and funders. *Applied and Preventive Psychology, 2,* 179–190.

Weissbourd, R. (1996). *The vulnerable child: What really hurts America's children and what we can do about it*. Reading, MA: Addison-Wesley.

Weisz, J. R., Suwanlert, S., Chaiyasit, W., & Walter, B. R. (1987). Over- and undercontrolled referral problems among children and adolescents from Thailand and the United States: The *wat* and *wai* of cultural differences. *Journal of Consulting and Clinical Psychology, 55,* 719–726.

Wekerle, C., & Wolfe, D. A. (1996). Child maltreatment. In E. J. Mash & R. A. Barkley (Eds.), *Child psychopathology* (pp. 18–27). New York: Guilford Press.

Werner, E. E. (1984). Resilient children. *Young Children, 40,* 68–72.

Werner, E. E., & Smith, R. S. (1982). *Vulnerable but invincible: A longitudinal study of resilient children and youth*. New York: Cambridge University Press.

Werner, H. (1982). *Cognitive therapy: A humanistic approach*. New York: Free Press.

Westwood, M. J., & Ishiyama, F. I. (1990). The communication process as a critical intervention for client change in cross-cultural counseling. *Journal of Multicultural Counseling and Development, 18,* 163–171.

Whittington, R., Crites, L., Moran, G., Kreidman, N., & Beck, B. (1989). *Peace begins with me: A nonviolent values curriculum for K–6th grade studies*. Kailua, HI: Smith Somerset.

Widom, C. S. (1989). Does violence beget violence? A critical examination of the literature. *Psychological Bulletin, 106,* 3–28.

Williams, M. B. (1984). Family dissolution: An issue for the schools: An elementary school program. *Children Today, 13,* 25–26.

Wodarski, J. S., Kurtz, P. D., Gaudin, J. M., & Howing, P. (1990). Maltreatment and the school-aged child: Major academic, socioeconomic and adaptive outcomes. *Social Work, 35,* 506–513.

Wolf-Schein, E. G. (1998). Considerations in assessment of children with severe disabilities including deaf-blindness and autism. *International Journal of Disability, Development and Education, 45,* 35–55.

Wolfe, D. (1987). *Child abuse: Implications for child development and psychopathology*. Newbury Park, CA: Sage.

Woodard, K. L. (1994). Packaging effective community service delivery: The utility of mandates and contracts in obtaining administrative cooperation. *Administration in Social Work, 18,* 17–43.

Wright, H. C., Sugden, D. A., Ng, R., & Tan, J. (1994). Identification of children with movement problems in Singapore: Usefulness of the Movement ABC Checklist. *Adapted Physical Activity Quarterly, 11,* 150–157.

Youngstrom, N. (1991). Drug exposure in home elicits worst behavior. *American Psychological Association Monitor, 22,* p. 3.

Yu, P., & Berryman, D. L. (1996). The relationship among self-esteem, acculturation and recreation participation of recently arrived Chinese immigrant adolescents. *Journal of Leisure Research, 28,* 251–273.

Zahner, G., Pawelkiewicz, W., DeFrancesco, J. J., & Adnopoz, J. (1992). Children's mental health service needs and utilization patterns in an urban community: An epidemiological assessment. *Journal of the American Academy of Child and Adolescent Psychiatry, 31,* 951–960.

Zeanah, C. H., & Emde, R. N. (1994). Attachment disorders in infancy. In M. Rutter, L. Herov, & E. Taylor (Eds.), *Child and adolescent psychiatry: Modern approaches* (pp. 490–504). Oxford, England: Blackwell.

Zigler, E., & Black, K. B. (1989). America's family support movement: Strengths and limitation. *American Journal of Orthopsychiatry, 59,* 6–19.

Zimmerman, S. L. (1995). *Understanding family policy* (2nd ed.). Thousand Oaks, CA: Sage.

Zisewine, D., Schers, D., & Levy-Keren, M. (1996). Adolescents and Jewish identity: A research note. *Israel Social Science Research, 11,* 61–66.

Zubrick, S. R., Silburn, S. R., Garton, A., Burton, P., Dalby, R., Carlton, J., et al. (1995). *Western Australian child health survey: Developing health and well-being in the nineties.* Perth, Western Australia: Australian Bureau of Statistics and the Institute for Child Health Research.

INDEX